50:6

13

THE CENTURY PSYCHOLOGY SERIES

Kenneth MacCorquodale
Gardner Lindzey
Kenneth E. Clark

Editors

Human Memory

Benton J. Underwood

HUMAN MEMORY
Festschrift in Honor of
Benton J. Underwood

Edited by

Carl P. Duncan
Northwestern University

Lee Sechrest
Northwestern University

Arthur W. Melton
University of Michigan

New York
APPLETON-CENTURY-CROFTS
Educational Division
MEREDITH CORPORATION

Contributors

John C. Abra
University of Calgary, Calgary, Alberta, Canada

Bruce R. Ekstrand
University of Colorado, Boulder, Colorado

Geoffrey Keppel
University of California, Berkeley, California

Kenneth L. Leicht
Illinois State University, Normal, Illinois

Slater E. Newman
North Carolina State University, Raleigh, North Carolina

Leo Postman
University of California, Berkeley, California

Jack Richardson
State University of New York at Binghamton, New York

Willard N. Runquist
University of Alberta, Edmonton, Alberta, Canada

Rudolph W. Schulz
University of Iowa, Iowa City, Iowa

Barbara S. Uehling
Roger Williams College, Bristol, Rhode Island

William P. Wallace
University of Nevada, Reno, Nevada

Robert K. Young
University of Texas at Austin, Texas

Preface

This book is in honor of Professor Benton J. Underwood. By the spring of 1971 Underwood had completed 25 years in the Department of Psychology of Northwestern University. He had also received a number of honors. He was President of the Midwestern Psychological Association and President of both the Division of General Psychology and the Division of Experimental Psychology of the American Psychological Association. He has been a Vice-President of the American Association for the Advancement of Science and Chairman of its Section on Psychology. He is a member of the Society of Experimental Psychologists, and has been awarded the Society's Warren Medal. He is a member of the National Academy of Sciences.

To the editors of this volume, it seemed worthwhile to organize a conference on human memory, the area in which Underwood has achieved such an outstanding reputation, and to publish the proceedings of the conference in a *Festschrift* for him. One of the editors, Professor Arthur W. Melton of the University of Michigan, an early teacher of Underwood, served as chairman of the conference. Professor Leo Postman of the University of California, Berkeley, accepted the large task of summarizing Underwood's work in the keynote address. Eleven of Underwood's Ph.D. students, all currently active researchers themselves, wrote papers for the conference.

On March 19, 1971, the conference was held at Northwestern University. Following Postman's address, Melton conducted a discussion among the authors of the papers, all of whom were present. The discussion, although vigorous and appropriate to the occasion, was designed to air problems but avoid conclusions. It is, therefore, not reproduced in this volume.

The editors wish to thank, first, Postman and Underwood's students, who prepared papers for the conference and book. We also thank the National Science Foundation, which provided a grant to defray expenses of the conference.* Robert H. Strotz and Laurence M. Nobles, successive Deans of the College of Arts and Sciences of Northwestern University, graciously offered additional funds and facilities and provided a dinner for conference participants and friends. Donna Sistler was invaluable as the secretary through all stages of the conference and book. We thank the American Psychological Association for permission to reproduce Table 10 in chapter 3, and Tables 5, 7, and 8 in chapter 6; The University of Illinois Press for permission to reproduce Table 4 in chapter 6; and *Psychonomic Science* for permission to reproduce Figure 1 in chapter 9.

*National Science Foundation Grant No. GB–23683.

Preface

All royalties from sales of the book will go to the Northwestern University Department of Psychology Fund. The Fund was established by Underwood to provide scholarships for graduate students in psychology.

C. P. D.

L. S.

A. W. M.

October, 1971

Contents

Contents

Human Memory

1 | The Experimental Analysis of Verbal Learning and Memory: Evolution and Innovation

LEO POSTMAN
University of California, Berkeley

The quarter century since the end of the Second World War has been a period of ferment and change, but also of continuous steady progress, in the study of verbal learning and memory. I shall attempt to sketch in brief outline some of the conceptual developments and forward thrusts in empirical exploration. My picture of these trends will be selective as well as fragmentary. The perspective will be foreshortened because the evolution of the field will be viewed from the standpoint of what has been called American Functionalism. By its very nature, this approach defies a sharp and comprehensive definition. It combines a cluster of theoretical and philosophical predilections with a commitment to the experimental analysis of functional relations in learning and memory. The latter interest has, of course, been shared by investigators rooted in other theoretical positions, but there is a core of orienting attitudes that confers an intellectual identity on those working in the functionalist tradition.

THE FUNCTIONALIST APPROACH

What have been these orienting attitudes of the functionalists? First, there has been a continuing disposition to formulate the problems of learning and memory in associationistic terms. There are obvious historical reasons for this inclination toward association theory. The questions that Ebbinghaus asked and that were carried forward and elaborated by his successors concerned the conditions and characteristics of associative learning and memory. The principles of association were the bridge between the time-honored speculations of the philosophers and the empirical concerns of experimental psychologists. Perhaps most important, the acceptance of these principles led to the early development of a standard methodology: The procedures of serial and paired-associate learning, which became the conventional techniques of the verbal learning laboratory, were explicitly designed to chart the acquisition and retention of associative linkages. The availability of standardized methods favors the perpetuation of the theory to which these methods were originally anchored, and inevitably shapes the questions asked by new investigators.

1

For all that, the associationism of the functionalists has always been liberal and pragmatic, a descriptive framework rather than a dogma of mechanistic connectionism. The freedom from a priori theoretical constraints was well expressed in the comments on the concept of association that appeared in the introductory chapter of McGeoch's *Psychology of human learning* (1942): "Two or more psychological events will be said to be associated when, as a function of prior individual experience one elicits or stands for the other. The events in question may be of any kind whatever, as long as one calls for or stands for the other. They may be analytically small as a pin point of discriminated light and a single muscle twitch thereto; they may be as large as a total perceived field of objects and the most complex possible response which can be regarded as a single unit. The essential aspect of association is the relation between or among sequences of events" (p. 25). It is interesting to note McGeoch's further comment that the term "association" is not the only one that could be reasonably used to satisfy this definition. For example, it would be appropriate to speak of "organization" since the related events are organized into a sequence or a unit.

A second predilection of the functionalists, closely related to the first, has been for the use of stimulus-response language in the specification of associated events. This usage reflected a tempered acceptance of the behaviorist point of view, which was readily extended to the methodology of studies of verbal learning and memory. The preference for stimulus-response language was strongly reinforced by the systematic application to a wide range of empirical phenomena of the principles of classical conditioning, particularly the concepts of excitation, inhibition, and generalization. It was Clark Hull, of course, who took the lead in extending the laws of conditioning to complex phenomena of verbal as well as instrumental learning (e.g., 1935, 1940). Many of the empirical implications of this analysis were tested in a monumental series of experiments by Hovland (cf. McGeoch & Irion, 1952, ch. 5). These studies focused primarily on the interpretation of the effects of distributed practice in terms of temporal changes in the balance of excitatory and inhibitory tendencies. There was sufficient confirmation of the major deductions to lend face validity to the conditioning model. During the same period the formulation of Gibson's (1940) differentiation hypothesis and Osgood's (1946) complementary analysis of the role of response generalization served to ensure the continuing preeminence of conditioning principles in theoretical interpretations of verbal learning.

A third orienting attitude is as difficult to identify precisely as it has been important in shaping the directions of the research undertaken by functionalist experimenters: It can perhaps be described best as an insistence on a contrapuntal interplay of analysis and synthesis in the investigation of apparently simple as well as complex phenomena. Once a gross functional relation has been established, there is an attempt, through progressive experimental manipulations, first to isolate the subprocesses that contribute to the observed relation and then to determine their mode of interaction. The long-term search for the component subprocesses of transfer and the principles governing their joint operation is a familiar case in point. This general approach is not limited, of course, to any one group of investigators, but it has been pursued most consistently by those working in the functionalist tradition.

The achievements of functionalist research formed the core of McGeoch's classical summary of the field in *The psychology of human learning*, which appeared in 1942. In retrospect it is possible to say that this book came at the end of the first era of the "newest science" originated by Ebbinghaus. It had been an era of exploration and consolidation—exploration of a wide range of empirical phenomena and consolidation of a basic methodology and a heuristically useful conceptual framework. The pages of McGeoch's book reflect clearly the orienting attitudes of the functionalist mainstream: a pragmatic associationism, an open-minded alliance with behavior theory, and a commitment to experimental analysis directed toward the derivation of the complex from the simple.

If the time span covered by McGeoch's survey was one of exploration and consolidation, then the next quarter century on which we are looking back today may be viewed as a period of reassessment and innovation. While much of the work continued to be guided by the orienting attitudes defining the functionalist tradition, there has been a progressive reassessment of empirical generalizations, combined with major innovations in both methodology and conceptual orientation. In an attempt to capture, however incompletely, some of the sweep of these developments, we will touch on the changes that have been occurring in four domains of inquiry: the formation of verbal associations, discriminative processes in verbal learning, transfer of training, and interference and forgetting.

ASSOCIATIVE LEARNING

When we set out to trace the changes in the prevailing conceptions of associative learning, our natural point of departure is the S-R formula of behavior theory, which became a basic unit of analysis in the study of verbal learning as well. This usage has typically implied certain assumptions about the conditions of association: The effective stimuli are manipulated by the experimenter, the responses are emitted by the subject, and the S-R connection grows stronger as a function of practice. How deceptively simple this formula has turned out to be! Experimental analysis has progressively generated fundamental questions about the appropriate definition of the effective stimulus, the conditions of response availability, and the mechanisms responsible for the establishment of associative relations. Today the S-R formula has primarily a shorthand value in denoting a complex chain of events delimited by the presentation of an objective stimulus at one end and the occurrence of the prescribed response on the other.

Stimulus selection. Let us begin with the stimulus. It has been said that the definition of the stimulus is the most difficult task of perceptual theory. One would assume, and for a long time investigators of human learning did assume, that the analysis of verbal learning would be free of this difficulty because the stimuli of interest are presented under conditions ensuring their errorless perception. However, veridical perception does not *ipso facto* determine the effective stimulus in associative learning. The subject remains free to choose any component feature of the total stimulus as the associative cue, provided that feature is uniquely related to the prescribed response. Thus, there may be, and often is, a discrepancy between the nominal and the functional stimulus in associative learning (Underwood, 1963). Cue selection typically serves to facilitate acquisition; thus, the more meaningful element of a redundant compound is almost invariably chosen (Underwood, Ham, & Ekstrand, 1962). However, like other decision processes, stimulus selection is subject to biases and influenced by stereotypes. For example, even though responses may be equally easy to learn to colors and to words as stimuli, subjects show a clear preference for the latter. Furthermore, methods of stimulus selection are learning skills that are fixated and improved through practice. As a result of experience, the subject becomes increasingly adept at selecting a particular component of a complex stimulus (Richardson & Chisholm, 1969). Under conditions of transfer the advantages conferred by this skill may balance the interferences entailed by the persistent utilization of identical stimulus elements (Williams & Underwood, 1970).

Historically, the emphasis on cue selection represented an interesting shift away from a prior concern with the role of contextual stimuli. It was recognized early (e.g., Dulsky, 1935; Pan, 1926) that responses become associated not only to the nominal stimulus designated by the experimenter but also to the context in which these nominal stimuli were presented. Thus, the functional stimulus was seen as comprising contextual elements in addition to the nominal cue. The shift to a concept of selection was foreshadowed when it was found in one experiment (Weiss & Margolius, 1954) that greater associative strength accrued to a class of stimuli designated as contextual, viz., colors, than to the nonsense syllables which were the nominal cues. It took a decisive insight, however, to discern the full implications of these results and to reverse the conceptual field, as it were, away from contextual enrichment to the principle of selection (Underwood, 1963). This shift was in accord with the *Zeitgeist*. If there is any merit in the somewhat hackneyed distinction between a passive and an active learner, it may well be applicable here. The emphasis on contextual cues was in line with the classical continuity principle: any and all stimuli that impinge on the sensorium are associated to the response. Such a state of affairs is consistent with the picture of a passive subject. Selection implies an active learner who, consciously or not, decides on the features of the environment to which he will attend and which he will utilize in meeting the requirements of the experimental task.

The facts of cue selection made it clear that there is no necessary one-to-one correspondence between the event contingencies manipulated by an experimenter and the associations formed by the subject. Nevertheless it would have been a mistake to overinterpret such findings and to dismiss out of hand the possibility of "pure contiguity" learning. Under appropriate conditions the experimental facts proved otherwise. Even when there is clear evidence of stimulus selection, associations can be shown to develop between the preferred and the nonpreferred elements of the compound. A related finding is that in verbal discrimination learning, which is a nonassociative task, connections are formed between the correct and incorrect members of the pairs in the list. Such connections are, indeed, strong enough to become an effective source of interference when these items are rearranged in a subsequent paired-associate task (Spear, Ekstrand, & Underwood, 1964). One should not miss the heuristic implications of such findings. When there is evidence for the use of strategies and for rule-governed behavior, it is tempting to argue on that basis against the validity of such fundamental but apparently simple principles as contiguity. The facts do not, however, always compel a choice between mechanistic and cognitive principles of learning. The application of strategies and rules does not preclude the operation of the law of contiguity.

The reassessment of the paradigm of serial learning. The systematic importance of the distinction between nominal and functional stimuli has been highlighted by the recent vicissitudes of the theory of serial learning. Ever since the days of Ebbinghaus, the principle of associative chaining had been accepted without question in theoretical interpretations of serial learning: It was taken for granted that the mastery of a serial task reflected the development of an associative sequence, i.e., the functional as well as the nominal stimulus for a given response in a serial list was the immediately preceding item. In a major departure from established doctrine, this assumption was called into serious question when appropriate transfer tests failed to yield the expected evidence for the establishment of associative chains in the course of serial learning (cf. Underwood, 1963; Young, 1968). Subsequent experiments showed the empirical facts to be more complex and inconclusive than they had appeared to be at first. The hypothesis of associative chaining may ultimately not be discarded entirely, but it is clear that it cannot provide a comprehensive account of the process of serial learning. Alternative mechanisms, such as association to ordinal position, have already been identified, but the search for the functional stimuli in serial learning is far from over. From a historical point of view, one is tempted to say that the challenge to the principle of associative chaining severed one of the few remaining threads of direct continuity with the era of Ebbinghaus. There is no simple translation from the temporal order of nominal events to the structure of associations.

So much for the distinction between the nominal and the functional stimulus. In writing the propositions of his theoretical system, Hull used to put a dot on the S of the S-R formula to differentiate the effective stimulus being conditioned to a reaction from the physical energy impinging on the subject. In the context of the verbal learning experiment, the dot would have to signal not just a translation into afferent impulses but a series of complex transformations which must be gradually identified by experimental analysis.

Response learning.   When we turn to the R term of our formula, we find that the changes in our conception of the response component of associative learning have been at least as profound as in the case of the S term. Let us consider in very broad outline the evolution of these changes. It is important to remember to begin with that, historically, associations referred to sequences of ideas, and it was within this theoretical framework that the operations for the study of verbal learning were originally developed. In that context there was, of course, no distinction between stimuli and responses; consequently, interest focused on those properties of verbal units which determined the ease and stability of associative connections. Thus, when, contrary to Ebbinghaus's hopes, nonsense syllables turned out to vary widely in difficulty, they were scaled in terms of association value. The translation of the existing experimental operations into stimulus-response terms occurred later in conformance to behaviorist methodology, but in the specification of the terms of the S-R formula the emphasis remained on the dimension of associability.

It was only when the asymmetry of the effects of stimulus and of response meaningfulness became apparent that the distinction between cue utilization and response production came into clear focus. Once the importance of the availability of responses, as integrated units in the subject's repertoire, became recognized, two systematic questions came to the fore: What are the conditions determining response availability, and how do variations in availability influence the course of associative learning?

By its very nature, the question concerning the determinants of response availability called for a searching examination of the influence of preexperimental language habits. It had been a commonplace assumption that transfer from prior language habits was responsible for the obvious differences in the difficulty of verbal units. However, the sources of these differences and the underlying dimensions of variation remained to be fully identified. A first major step was to impose order on the multiplicity of indexes and scales which had been used over the years in classifying the wide range of possible verbal units—from rare trigrams to familiar words. The diversity of normative measures proved to be largely reducible to complementary manifestations of a single underlying dimension, viz., frequency of linguistic usage. (The discussion that follows is based for the most part on Underwood & Schulz, 1960).

To serve as a useful explanatory tool and as a predictor of performance, the concept of frequency had to be specified more precisely. Was it frequency of reading, hearing, or speaking a given sequence of elements that was critical for response availability? The evidence has converged on the conclusion that the emitted rather than the experienced frequency is the critical determinant of response availability. This conclusion accords well with a useful new formulation of the role of response availability in associative learning, viz., the principle of "spew" which holds that the order in which subjects emit verbal units in a test situation will be a direct function of the frequency of past emissions. Thus, the higher the frequency of its past usage, the more readily will a response become available to enter into new associations. The subject's verbal spew is, howeer, highly selective. From the beginning of practice, items from outside the list are imported very rarely, even though they may be of considerably higher frequency than the prescribed ones. A selector mechanism comes into play that allows the learner to discriminate accurately and consistently between the currently required responses and the rest of his verbal repertoire. The nature of this mechanism is still not clearly understood, although it appears likely that the necessary discriminations are based on such attributes as the recency and frequency of situational occurrence as well as on the semantic characteristics of the units.

Two-stage analysis.   It is now apparent that there are properties of the responses as such that exert a major influence on performance in a learning task. The availability of the prescribed response is of primary importance. It is worth emphasizing that the evidence points to response-related processes that are clearly nonassociative in nature, such as the differentiation between the classes of appropriate and inappropriate units. The most significant consequence of the experimental isolation of response-specific processes has been the firm establishment of the two-stage model of associative learning. The conception has proved to be a powerful one: It has served as a productive framework for the systematic exploration of the different subprocesses of acquisition. The model has gained validity time and again from the finding that task variables such as meaningfulness and intralist similiarity have reliably different effects when they are manipulated on the stimulus and on the response side. The operative principle is, of course, that response manipulations can influence both stages, and stimulus manipulations only the associative stage.

Meaningfulness and coding.   Of these asymmetries, there is one that has posed a continuing and elusive puzzle: Why do variations in stimulus meaningfulness typically have only quite limited effects on speed of acquisition? It can be seen that, contrary to what is true for responses, stimulus integration is not critical, but association value, in a broad sense of the term, should be. This problem continues to await resolution. It is useful to recall the existence of these particular puzzling facts because of the increasing reliance in many different explanatory context on processes of stimulus encoding (e.g., Martin, 1968). Appealing as it may be intuitively, the concept of stimulus encoding has had, apart from the phenomena of cue selection, only scant empirical support. For example, the possibility of transforming difficult nonsense stimulus into familiar words has relatively limited positive effects on acquisition. Moreover, such encoding occurs only when the transformations are obvious (Underwood & Erlebacher, 1965).

It should be noted here that a similar picture emerged when the process of response coding was brought under careful experimental scrutiny. On the assumption that such a process plays an important role in response learning, the speed of acquisition of a set of nonsense items should be related directly to the availability of transformational rules that permit an encoding of the nominal units in terms of familiar words. This expectation has received only limited confirmation. The availability of coding rules facilitates performance only when decoding is extremely simple, e.g., based on a single transformational rule. Even under these optimal circumstances the positive effects on acquisition are far from dramatic. Under some conditions the use of a coding system may actually inhibit learning (Underwood & Erlebacher, 1965). Such results may be limited to codes introduced by the experimenter, but they do sound a note of caution. Codes and strategies are undoubtedly important in many problem-solving and learning situations, but subjects have a way of being far more chary of them than theorists.

Mediation. In the classical S-R formula there is usually an arrow leading from the S to the R, signifying the associative connection. It has become a commonplace observation that such direct "rote" connections are rare and difficult to form, and that the association between S and R is likely to be established with the aid of mediators. This assumption has considerable face validity, but it has been easier to invoke implicit mediators after the fact than to force them into the open, as it were, by experimental procedures pointed directly at them. The implicit associative response, which ranks high among the mediators assumed to function in associative learning, is a case in point. To make the implicit associative response explicit it was necessary to make a detour and to go outside the confines of paired-associate learning, where it would remain, by definition, covert.

The most direct and convincing evidence for the actuality of implicit associative responses (IARs) has come from experiments on false recognition (Underwood, 1965). Here the procedure focuses directly on the effects of specified IARs: The question in these experiments has been whether normative associates assumed to be covertly elicited by presented stimulus words are later erroneously recognized as having themselves occurred in the list. The answer has been clearly in the affirmative.

It has also been possible to show that IARs, which carry the semantic classification of the successive verbal units in a list, may be largely responsible for the systematic effects of conceptual similarity on acquisition (Underwood, Ekstrand, & Keppel, 1965; Underwood & Freund, 1969; Wood & Underwood, 1967). The studies in which this analysis was developed cannot be considered in detail here. Suffice it to say that the logic of the experimental designs again generated detailed predictions about the observable characteristics of performance reflecting the occurrence of specified IARs. While there are undoubtedly many other mediating reactions, the actuality of IARs has by now been well documented. A one-step association may be the exception rather than the rule.

The changing view of associative learning. It is by now apparent that experimental analysis directed toward the component subprocesses of acquisition has carried us well beyond the traditional schema of a single-step S-R association as the basic unit of associative learning. It can no longer be taken for granted that the nominal and the functional stimulus are identical; response learning and associative learning have been shown to be analytically separable processes that bear different relations to task variables and to the conditions of practice; and the establishment of the prescribed associations is seen as the end product of a sequence of mediating events.

At the same time some of the key mechanisms borrowed from conditioning theory—excitatory potential, reactive and conditioned inhibition—have been falling into disuse as a consequence of cumulative experimental setbacks. The critical tests of the validity of these principles in verbal learning had been sought in studies of distributed practice and reminiscence. The tests had met with some success initially. As is well known, subsequent analyses of these phenomena, carried out in many years of painstaking experimentation, thoroughly reversed the picture. The influence of distributed practice on acquisition and retention, which at one time had appeared robust and dependable, turned out to be complexly determined and often small in magnitude. It remains possible that the favorable effects of distribution that are found reflect the dissipation of inhibition. If so, the effective inhibitory process probably retards the development of associative strength and thus is very different in character from that postulated by the neobehaviorists (cf. Underwood & Ekstrand, 1967). Today, Hull's valiant attempt to deduce in precise quantitative detail some of the basic phenomena of verbal learning from the principles of classical conditioning is a fascinating but closed chapter in the history of the discipline.

DISCRIMINATIVE PROCESSES

As the limitations of the S-R formula became apparent, the traditional methods of associative learning lost their exclusive status in the laboratory. Serial and paired-associate learning came to be regarded, as of course they should be, not as general models of acquisition but as analytic paradigms with a limited range of application. Thus, when interest focused on nonassociative mechanisms, other experimental paradigms assumed increasing importance. One of these has been verbal discrimination learning. The analysis of this task is not only of intrinsic interest but has far-reaching general implications: There are few, if any, verbal tasks that do not comprise a discriminative component.

The frequency principle in verbal discrimination. Investigations of the verbal discrimination task have given us a new purchase on the operation of frequency-dependent mechanisms in learning. There is by now a substantial body of support for the hypothesis that in the acquisition of a verbal discrimination list the subjective difference in situational frequency favoring the correct over the incorrect alternative in each pair is normally the basic cue determining the subject's choices (Ekstrand, Wallace, & Underwood, 1966). The power of the hypothesis has been brought home by its ability to generate a wide variety of testable predictions, some of which appeared at first glance to be counterintuitive. For example, prior familiarization with the correct alternatives, which raises their situational frequency, has been shown to facilitate subsequent discrimination learning; by contrast, and for the same reason, familiarization with the incorrect alternatives has a negative effect (Underwood & Freund, 1968). Taken together, the recent studies of verbal discrimination learning have established situational frequency as an attribute that subjects can discriminate reliably and use as a cue to responding. Situational frequency obviously is a potential discriminative cue in a wide variety of other learning situations as well. Whenever the to-be-remembered units are drawn from the subject's linguistic repertoire, correct performance is contingent in the first instance on the differentiation of the presented items, to which some situational frequency has accrued, from the rest of the learner's vocabulary. Thus, the range of application of the frequency rule soon came to be extended, in particular to the process of recognition.

The frequency principle in recognition. For those working within the framework of association theory, the problem of recognition had remained a perpetual item of unfinished business. Small wonder that such should have been the case since the defining requirement of the recognition task—the segregation of the old from the new, or the familiar from the unfamiliar—is nonassociative in nature. There are today various theoretical models describing mechanisms that could perform this function. However, such models usually leave unspecified the concrete cues that guide the subject's choices at the time of test. That is precisely where the hypothesis of frequency discrimination has come into its own: There is persuasive evidence that the recognition of an item as old reflects a discrimination of situational frequency: The judged frequency is higher (at least one) for old items than for new items (zero). In accord with the hypothesis, it is possible to change the accuracy of recognition by increasing the experienced frequency of either correct items or distractors, improving performance in the former case and degrading it in the latter (Underwood & Freund, 1970a). Whatever the subject judges to have occurred frequently in the experimental context, he recognizes as old.

The attributes of memory. Consider the general systematic implications of the correlation between the perceived situational frequency of a verbal item and the probability of its correct recognition. Frequency must be regarded not as just a physical count of event occurrences; it is registered as a discriminable attribute of memory. Now frequency is clearly only one of the attributes of events that can be registered as a result of experience or practice. Thus, it becomes reasonble to conceive of a memory as being composed of a multiplicty of attributes only one or a few of which are tapped by the performance requirements of a given test (Underwood, 1969). Some of the characteristics that are stored in memory are independent of the nature of the learning task, such as those related to the time of occurrence, spatial location, and frequency of the experienced events. Other characteristics are specific to a given task; in the case of verbal materials, these include orthographic and associative attributes.

During acquisition and retention some attributes, such as frequency, serve primarily a discriminative function, whereas others, notably the associative ones, are a source of retrieval cues. As we have seen, frequency discriminations enable the subject to decide whether an item is new or old, and hence whether it is an appropriate or an inappropriate response. When recall is required, however, it is the associative attributes which give the learner access to the prescribed response. It becomes reasonable to suppose that the probability of successful retrieval will increase directly with the number of different attributes that have been incorporated into the memory for a given item.

The view of memory as a complex of attributes foreshadows a basic revision of our conception of the effects of repetition on associative learning. The probability of recall may increase progressively as a function of repetition not so much because associative bonds are strengthened but because successive presentations provide an opportunity for the establishment of multiple retrieval attributes. Such an account of the effects of continued practice points away not only from the classical S-R formula but also from the conception of acquisition as a gradual change in associative strength. So the transformations and modifications of the classical model of association accumulate. In the end the only continuity that is left may be one of operational and linguistic conventions. Within the framework of the functionalist tradition these transformations will continue to be deliberate and gradual, and paced by the logic of the empirical evidence.

TRANSFER OF TRAINING

When we turn to developments in the analysis of transfer of training, we find, as expected, that they mirror in all essential respects the changing conceptions of the process of acquisition. It could not be otherwise because transfer measures the influence of prior practice on new learning.

Generalization and transfer. Historically, the experimental analysis of transfer was guided primarily by the application to the phenomena of verbal learning of the concept of generalization. In the context of classical conditioning, the principle of generalization referred, of course, to the spread of habits from a training stimulus to neighboring points along a sensory dimension. The possibility of extending the principle to verbal transfer has hinged on the validity of two assumptions: (a) that the critical relations between successive verbal tasks can be translated into continua of similarity, and (b) that transfer represents the spread of habits along these continua. Neither assumption has withstood the test of time unscathed.

To determine a gradient of generalization, it is necessary to order the test stimuli along a dimension of similarity. In the case of verbal stimuli, the generalization is mediated rather than primary. The similarity is that of the mediating reactions elicited by the given array of words. Such semantic similarity cannot be specified in physical terms, of course, but it can be scaled satisfactorily on the basis of subjects' ratings. With the aid of such operations, the concepts of stimulus and of response generalizations have proved heuristically useful. Although the expected gradients have often failed to materialize, generalization theory did on balance provide a productive framework for the exploration of similarity relations between successive verbal tasks. There have been increasing indications, however, that even when orderly effects of similarity are observed, generalization, in the sense of habit spread along a perceptual continuum, may not be the operative mechanism.

While the meaningful similarity of items and the strength of the associative connection between them are correlated, it is the latter relationship which appears to be critical in many transfer situations. On this assumption mediational chaining rather than generalization is implicated as the source of transfer, particularly when the similarity relation obtains between successive responses (A-B, A-B'). Once the initial association is formed, it serves to mediate the second response, i.e., the chain A-B-B' can be readily completed. In many situations it is difficult to decide between explanations in terms of generalization and of mediation. However, when transfer performance is virtually perfect, as it sometimes is under conditions of stimulus identity and response similarity, a mediational interpretation becomes more plausible than the assumption of a flat gradient of generalization (Barnes & Underwood, 1959). Although the mediation hypothesis has not been free of empirical difficulties, it appears to encompass a wider range of transfer phenomena than the principle of generalization, and with fewer ad hoc assumptions. It remains an open question whether it will be useful to postulate the operation of both these mechanisms. In any event, associative mediation is proving to be a viable alternative to the classical concept of generalization. Once more the link between verbal learning and conditioning is weakened if not severed.

Given the validity of the two-stage analysis of acquisition, it is clear that neither generalization nor mediation can account for all the potential components of transfer. The range of application of these mechanisms is inherently limited to the associative component of learning. This limitation was made explicit a long time ago by Osgood (1949) when he constructed his well-known surface: He predicted (incorrectly) zero transfer whenever the stimuli in successive lists are unrelated. It is now well established, however, that apart from any associative relations, prior response integration can be an important source of transfer. With responses of low meaningfulness, there is substantial facilitation under the C-B, and even the A-Br, paradigm.

It is now generally recognized that the transfer effects observed in any given situation originate from multiple sources, some of which are task-specific whereas others reflect the development of higher-order skills. Experimental investigations are, therefore, directed primarily toward the identification and assessment of the component subprocesses of facilitation and interference. One major approach has consisted of the comparison of key paradigms, with a view to determining the contribution of different components, singly and in combination (e.g., Twedt & Underwood, 1959). Another line of investigation has sought to isolate a particular component of interest by examining the interaction between task variables and paradigms of transfer. For example, if stimulus differentiaton is a source of facilitation, as traditional formulations would have it, an interaction is to be expected between the degree of intralist similarity and the amount of negative transfer under the A-D relative to the C-D paradigm: the less discriminable the stimuli, the greater should be the benefit conferred by prior differentiation. Rather surprisingly, this prediction was supported only weakly, if at all (Underwood & Ekstrand, 1968b). Thus, component analysis continues to bring under experimental scrutiny potentially important but as yet unverified assumptions about the subprocesses of transfer.

While substantial progress has been made in the experimental isolation of the components of transfer, the effective mechanisms of facilitation and interference are still far from being fully understood. It is one thing to demonstrate that conflicting forward associations are a source of negative transfer; to specify exactly how the associative interference is generated is quite another. Thus, consider the A-B, A-D paradigm. Why does the existence of the prior association, A-B, slow down the acquisition of A-D? The usual explanation is sought in the classical principles of habit interference: In the transfer phase A continues to elicit B, and the resulting competition of responses delays the acquisition of A-D. When all is said and done, however, there is little direct support for the effectiveness of the postulated mechanism of response competition in producing negative transfer. As has been known for a long time, interlist intrusions occur extremely rarely; thus, it has become conventional to keep the hypothesis intact by assuming that the competing responses remain largely covert. Being in that sense unobservable, the mechanism of response competition has been difficult to disprove. The classical hypothesis of response competition may provide a very incomplete account of the process of negative transfer because it rests on the implicit assumption that a fixed functional stimulus enters into association with successive responses. However, as we have seen, it is useful to think of the functional stimulus not as being fixed but rather as having multiple potential attributes that may vary in importance from one occasion to the next. Within this framework, a rather different view is suggested of the process of unlearning old responses to a given nominal stimulus and substituting new ones: "In unlearning, the attribute (or attributes) of one memory is displaced to another. During A-C learning in the A-B, A-C paradigm, C replaces B as the associative attribute of A so that A cannot directly serve as an attribute in the recall of B. That unlearning is seldom complete suggests that other attributes, specific to A-B pairs, do not become unlearned during acquistion" (Underwood, 1969, p. 570).

What may be critical, then, in the production of negative transfer is that the substitution of a second response for the first necessitates the establishment of a new set of attributes in lieu of the old. It takes time to discard some of the old attributes and to develop new ones, which may in addition be less effective as discrimination and retrieval cues. Consequently, the course of transfer learning is slowed down. The implications of this approach to negative transfer and unlearning remain to be explored. A shift is indicated, however, away from the mechanics of habit interference to an emphasis on discriminative and retrieval processes in transfer. These conceptual shifts have already influenced our approach to the problem of forgetting. It is to this problem that we turn in the next and final section of this paper.

INTERFERENCE AND FORGETTING

The processes of acquisition and retention, or of learning and memory, are intertwined inextricably; by the very definition of these terms, it cannot be otherwise. In the interest of experimental anlysis there has been a pragmatic accommodation to this state of affairs. The problems of method and interpretation that are at issue here were stated clearly by McGeoch (1942): "At the level of logical analysis this division [between learning and retention] is clear, because an act must be fixated before it can be retained. . . . For the sake of convenience, the distinction between learning and retention has been given a different meaning than the logically analytic one, *learning* being used to designate the acquisition of changes in behavior during a specified time or up to a certain level, and *retention* being used to mean any measured persistence of these changes after practice ceases. Any measured failure of such persistence is called *forgetting*" (p. 4).

The measurement of retention. In light of this problem of definition, it becomes understandable why in the study of retention, perhaps more than in the investigation of any other topic in our field of interest, methodological and theoretical developments have been so closely tied to each other. The measurement of retention must necessarily proceed in two stages: Acquisition must first be carried to a specified level, and subsequent changes in performance are then evaluated with respect to this baseline. The question always is how much has been lost of what was originally learned. The problem of measurement entailed by this question has proved to be beset with difficulties. Historically, the major source of error has been the general reliance on fixed criteria of performance in the assessment of the degree of original learning, with forgetting measured in terms of decline from the criterion. As is now well known, attainment of a common criterion does not necessarily imply equality of the degree of learning. The faster the rate of acquisition, the higher is the associative strength at criterion. To obtain an unbiased index of the terminal level of performance, it is necessary to determine the growth function for correct responses and to estimate the score to be expected on a test trial immediately after the end of practice. Successive probability analysis (Underwood, 1954, 1964) has provided one workable solution to this problem. The improved methods of measurement have led to the revision of some long-standing assumptions about the variables that influence the rate of forgetting. With degree of learning controlled, slow learners are not found to forget any more than fast ones; a high degree of intralist similarity does not enhance the amount of retention loss; and the expected inverse relation between meaningfulness and forgetting typically fails to materialize. Thus, there has come to the fore a near invariance that poses a major puzzle for theories of memory: Over a wide range of conditions and materials the amount of long-term retention appears to be fixed by the degree of original learning. With that factor held constant, the best prediction is that there will be no differences in retention.

The definition of retention in terms of a two-stage operation has continued to create analytic and theoretical difficulties as new methods of studying memory have come into prominence. Foremost among these has been the array of ingenious techniques used to chart the course of short-term memory. Here the distinction between learning and retention encounters intuitive doubts and is often difficult to translate into appropriate operations. Thus, consider the fact that a single trigram is recalled perfectly immediately after its presentation, regardless of whether it is of high or low meaningfulness. Is it safe to assume that these two items have been fixated equally well; if not, how are differences in forgetting after a few seconds to be interpreted? Is a divergence of the retention functions to be attributed to the factor of meaningfulness, or to inequality of fixation masked by the ceiling of perfect performance? Problems such as these (cf. Underwood, 1964) have contributed to persistent disagreements about the continuity of short-term and long-term processes, and about the interpretation of the principles governing the former.

Related issues have arisen in the analysis of free-recall learning (cf. Tulving, 1968). Again, any one word can surely be recalled with a probability of 1.0 immediately after it has been exposed; but does it follow that successive free-recall tests reflect entirely changes in retention, and not in fixation? Such issues still await resolution. They are mentioned here to emphasize the close tie between guiding assumptions about appropriate operations of measurement and theoretical inferences about memory processes. Such a tie exists, of course, in all fields of inquiry, but a consensus on defining operations has been more difficult to achieve in the measurement of memory than in many other areas. However, to the extent that apparent theoretical disagreements can be reduced to methodological ones, the prospect for their ultimate resolution is favorable.

Cumulative proactive inhibition and forgetting. It was a methodological insight that drastically changed the accepted answer to a question asked by investigators of forgetting from Ebbinhaus on. How rapidly does an individual forget a task he learned in the laboratory to a criterion of perfect recitation? Ebbinghaus' curve showed rapid and heavy losses, with the index of saving declining to 60 percent after 20 minutes, and about 34 percent after 24 hours. Many subsequent experimenters recorded losses of a comparable order of magnitude. Here, then, was a formidable problem of interpretation for any memory theorist, whatever his persuasion. If he was an inteference theorist, he was bound to appeal to retroactive effects, but what kind of uncontrolled interpolated activities would produce such massive losses in so short a period of time? Nor was it reasonable to assume that memory traces decayed at such a devastating speed. There was a disturbing discrepancy, moreover, between the experimental facts and common-sense observation, for in daily experience the retention of memorized facts did not appear to be as precarious as the laboratory findings implied.

The resolution of this problem is very well known, and the analysis on which it was based (Underwood, 1957) has by now found its way into our textbooks. It was, of course, the proactive interference from the many prior experimental tasks that caused Ebbinghaus to forget so much so fast; and so it was for the subjects in the laboratories of Ebbinghaus' successors who, according to prevailing custom, were tested many times over in carefully counterbalanced designs. A naive subject, free from these proactive effects, retains about 80 percent after 24 hours.

The reexamination of the facts of single-list forgetting had far-reaching methodological and theoretical implications. It became clear that naive subjects had to be used if interest centered on extraexperimental conditions of forgetting. This implication has been generally accepted, although the transfer of the principle to experiments on short-term memory has been slow (cf. Keppel & Underwood, 1962). Cumulative proactive inhibition was established as a major determinant of forgetting for materials learned in the laboratory; it was plausible to invoke a similar mechanism in accounting for the effects of extraexperimental sources of interference. In any event, the explanatory problem for memory theorists, and the exponents of the interference hypothesis in particular was reduced to apparently manageable proportions. In considering the problem of extraexperimental forgetting, they now had to account for no more than a 20 percent loss during a 24-hour interval. As we shall see presently, interference theorists did try to tackle this problem, but the 20 percent stubbornly refused to yield to their efforts. (Perhaps it is better to be baffled by 20 than by 70 percent!) That brings us to the changing scene in interference theory.

Two-factor theory. The last quarter century has been a period of ferment, marked both by significant advances and troublesome setbacks, for the interference theory of forgetting. At the beginning of this period stands the formulation of the two-factor theory (Melton & Irwin, 1940), which provided the basic framework for all the major developments that followed. These developments have been reviewed in detail too recently to warrant recounting here. Let me, therefore, touch only very briefly on some of the highlights, and particularly on items of unfinished business.

The turning point in the contemporary course of interference theory was a methodological innovation—the introduction of the MMFR test (Barnes & Underwood, 1959). As is often true for methodological breakthroughs, the MMFR test was an elegantly simple device, translating a fundamental theoretical question into sharp operational terms. The application of this test served to establish, in study after study, the actuality of the phenomenon of unlearning postulated by two-factor theory. But as the phenomenon became readily reproducible and manipulable, the explication of the underlying mechanism of unlearning acquired increasing urgency. Does the analogy to extinction give us best purchase on this mechanism? There is a growing array of facts which create difficulties for this conception: Why is unlearning never complete, no matter how extended and interferring the interpolated activity? Why does the loss of responses, or of contextual associations, progress so much more rapidly than the unlearning of specific associations? And spontaneous recovery, when it is found, appears to bear only a superficial resemblance to its counterpart in conditioning. It has become clear that in this area of inquiry, as in many others, the conceptualizations derived from conditioning theory are proving inadequate. In trying to understand unlearning, we will surely have to address ourselves, explicitly and systematically, to the role of discriminative and retrieval processes that are well outside the boundaries of classical extinction theory. The quotation given earlier, which speaks of unlearning in terms of the displacement of attributes from one memory to another, clearly points in this direction.

As the empirical facts of retroaction were clarified, the interpretative puzzles deepened, at least temporarily. The same is true for proactive inhibition. A major strength of two-factor theory has been its ability to derive the phenomena of retroactive and proactive inhibition from a common set of principles; both kinds of interference could be seen as complementary manifestations of the same mechanisms. The key to the disctintion between them was inherent in the definition of the two factors: Retroactive inhibition reflects both unlearning and response competition, proactive inhibition only the latter. It is rather intriguing to note that the very methodological innovation which validated the two-factor interpretation of retroactive inhibition served to create problems for that same theory when attention was focused on proactive inhibition. The theory implies that there should be no evidence of proactive losses when retention is measured by MMFR since this test is presumably immune to the effects of response competition and hence should reflect unlearning only. Contrary to this deduction, proactive decrements have been registered consistently on MMFR tests. Prior learning appears to produce a deficit in retention that is not readily attributable either to unlearning or to response competition. It is fair to say that the source of this deficit remains to be explained.

The phenomena of proactive inhibition observed under conventional conditions of testing have remained consistent with the hypothesis of response competition at recall. At the same time, however, the critical importance of discriminative processes in regulating the amount of interference has been brought to the fore. For example, proactive inhibition is reduced dramatically if not eliminated altogether when prior learning is widely distributed whereas the acquisition of the test list is massed (Underwood & Ekstrand, 1966). The difference in practice schedules is a source of powerful discriminative cues, perhaps "temporal tags," that permit the successful differentiation of the successive tasks. Discriminative cues based on differences in situational frequency are equally effective in maintaining differentiation and thus minimizing proactive inhibition (Underwood & Ekstrand, 1968a). Again the thrust of the evidence points beyond the classical mechanisms of habit interference and the principles of conditioning.

Extraexperimental sources of interference.   Under this heading (Underwood & Postman, 1960) an attempt was made to generalize to forgetting outside the laboratory the principles of retroactive and proactive inhibition established under controlled experimental conditions. The point of departure was a strong hypothesis of interference: The ultimate objective is to account for most if not all forgetting in terms of retroactive and proactive effects. This is the position traditionally espoused by interference theorists, at least implicitly. There were, however, some important differences between the most recent formulation and earlier approaches to this problem. First the sources of extraexperimental interference were now specified. Forgetting was expected to occur to the extent that prescribed associations were in conflict with the learner's preexperimental language habits, specifically his letter-sequence and unit-sequence habits. Second, emphasis was shifted from retroactive to proactive mechanisms of interference. Language habits are the products of a lifetime of preexperimental learning; hence their influence will be primarily proactive, although complementary retroactive effects cannot be ruled out. Thus, it became plausible to speculate that conflicting language habits were extinguished or suppressed during the acquisition of a laboratory task but recovered over time to become sources of interference at recall. Tests of the hypothesis call for the comparisons of retention functions for materials assumed to vary in their susceptibility to extraexperimental interference.

The outcome of such empirical tests can be summarized only too briefly. With a few scattered exceptions, the deductions from the theory failed to be supported. Neither the linguistic probability of letter sequences nor the meaningfulness of integrated units has been found to have a consistent influence on the rate of long-term forgetting. It is results such as these that have pointed to a principle of retention invariant with degree of learning. What is the reason for these empirical failures? The most obvious possibility is, of course, that the interference interpretation of extraexperimental forgetting is fundamentally wrong. There has been some reluctance, however, to accept this answer, primarily because it is difficult to envisage a basic discontinuity between the phenomena of forgetting studied in the laboratory and those that occur outside the laboratory, especially in the absence of better documented alternative explanations.

Persistent attempts have, therefore, been made to uncover shortcomings of existing formulations and experimental procedures that might account for the empirical failures without compelling a total rejection of the hypothesis. One important line of inquiry considered the question of whether the manipulated conditions of interference studied in formal experiments on retroactive and proactive inhibition are representative of those that obtain outside the laboratory. For example, in contrast to the usual arrangements in the laboratory, language habits are acquired under conditions of widely distributed practice. It was possible to show that even in the laboratory proactive inhibition is greatly reduced when the prior interfering task is learned under a spaced rather than a massed schedule (Underwood & Ekstrand, 1966). The implication is that the massive difference between practice schedules—widely distributed learning of the language habits and relatively massed learning of the laboratory tasks—permits an accurate differentiation between the experimental associations and the verbal sequences reflecting daily usage. If this conclusion is valid, it confronts us with a dilemma: We must either find a way of breaking down this differentiation between laboratory tasks and language habits or concede that the hypothesis of extraexperimental interference is not testable under controlled conditions. Even if we escape from this dilemma and do find ways of tapping the differential effects of language habits on the retention of experimental associations, we will still have the problem of explaining the losses that occur ordinarily, constant though they may be for many different kinds of materials.

Regardless of the validity of the interference hypothesis, it is probably fair to say that in our thinking about retention we have stressed task variables and conditions of learning at the expense of the fine-grain analysis of the process of remembering, i.e., recalling and recognizing. That brings us back to the conception of memory as a constellation of attributes. In interpreting measurements of retention, it is necessary to focus on both the attributes of the memory and the attributes that are critical with respect to the requirements of the retention test (Underwood, 1969, p. 569). That means asking specific experimental questions about temporal changes in the effectiveness of discriminative attributes and and retrieval attributes. Some important steps have already been taken in this direction in studies examining the retention of a verbal discrimination (Underwood & Freund, 1970b) and of frequency information (Underwood, Zimmerman, & Freund, 1971). Whether or not the forgetting of discriminative and retrieval attributes can be subsumed under principles of interference becomes a question of major theoretical significance. As we reformulate and revise the construct of memory, we may be entering upon an important new phase in the development of interference theory.

CONCLUDING REMARKS

We have ended the last section of our review, as well as earlier ones, with an emphasis on unresolved questions and unfinished business. That is well in keeping with the orienting attitudes of the functionalist tradition. The central value that has grown out of this tradition is the insistence on the identification, through experimental manipulation and analysis, of the component processes of learning and memory. One is never satisfied with just observing an orderly functional relation. The next questions always are: Are the mechanisms that we have postulated really at work? What other orderly relations should we be able to observe if our assumptions are correct? Are there alternative interpretations and how can we pit them fairly against the ones we favor? There is little chance for complacency or dogma to flourish in such a climate of inquiry.

Freedom from dogma has meant continuous evolution and innovation, in both methodology and theory. The changes have been slow and deliberate, but their cumulative impact has been to alter the complexion of the field. Many of the certainties of the 1940s have been questioned and become uncertainties—the mechanisms of serial learning, the effects of distribution of practice, the relation between meaningfulness and retention, the strong hypothesis of interference, to refer back to just a few. The links to classical associationism and the alliance with conditioning theory are today more of a historical than of functional importance. But the attitudes that originally made these influences dominant— the commitment to objectivity of language and precision of measurement— remain even though the questions may be about the attributes of memory rather than the elicitation of responses by stimuli.

It is customary today to speak of a revolution in our field and in support of this view to point to the upsurge of enthusiastic activity in such areas as the study of short-term memory and of organization in recall. These endeavors have, indeed, been highly productive and have given us a wealth of new facts (and of models!). But if we disregard the fashions of language and of model building in this era of information processing and computer analogies, it seems fair to say that the hard core of facts added under these new auspices flows into, and does not supersede, the mainstream that had its source in the classical studies of rote learning.

I have tried to touch upon some of the major landmarks in the continuous evolution of our field during the last quarter century. It has been a period of methodological advances, productive self-criticism, and theoretical growth. Before concluding, let me make explicit what you have undoubtedly known all along. In developing this account I have drawn, with a few scattered exceptions, on the work of only one man. So great is the debt of gratitude that we owe to Benton J. Underwood.

REFERENCES

Barnes, J. M., & Underwood, B. J. "Fate" of first-line associations in transfer theory. *Journal of Experimental Psychology*, 1959, 58, 97–105.

Dulsky, S. G. The effect of change of background on recall and relearning. *Journal of Experimental Psychology*, 1935, 18, 725–740.

Ekstrand, B. R., Wallace, W. P., & Underwood, B. J. A frequency theory of verbal discrimination learning. *Psychological Review*, 1966, 73, 566–578.

Gibson, E. J. A systematic application of the concepts of generalization and differentiation to verbal learning. *Psychological Review*, 1940, 47, 196–229.

Hull, C. L. The conflicting psychologies of learning—a way out. *Psychological Review*, 1935, 42, 491–516.

Hull, C. L., Hovland, C. I., Ross, R. T., Hall, M., Perkins, D. T., & Fitch, F. B. *Mathematico-deductive theory of rote learning.* New Haven: Yale University Press, 1940.

Keppel, G., & Underwood, B. J. Proactive inhibition in short-term retention of single items. *Journal of Verbal Learning and Verbal Behavior*, 1962, 1, 153–161.

Martin, E. Stimulus meaningfulness and paired-associate transfer: an encoding variability hypothesis. *Psychological Review*, 1968, 75, 421–441.

McGeoch, J. A. *The psychology of human learning.* New York: Longmans, Green, 1942.

McGeoch, J. A., & Irion, A. L. *The psychology of human learning.* New York: Longmans, Green, 1952.

Melton, A. W., & Irwin, J. M. The influence of degree of interpolated learning on retroactive inhibition and the overt transfer of specific responses. *American Journal of Psychology*, 1940, 53, 173–203.

Osgood, C. E. Meaningful similarity and interference in learning. *Journal of Experimental Psychology*, 1946, 36, 277–301.

Osgood, C. E. The similarity paradox in human learning: a resolution. *Psychological Review*, 1949, 56, 132–143.

Pan, S. The influence on context upon learning and recall. *Journal of Experimental Psychology*, 1926, 9, 468–491.

Richardson, J., & Chisholm, D. C. Transfer of cue selection based on letter position. *Journal of Experimental Psychology*, 1969, 80, 299–303.

Spear, N. E., Ekstrand, B. R., & Underwood, B. J. Association by contiguity. *Journal of Experimental Psychology*, 1964, 67, 151–161.

Tulving, E. Theoretical issues in free recall. In T. R. Dixon & D. L. Horton (eds.), *Verbal behavior and general behavior theory*. Englewood Cliffs, N. J.: Prentice-Hall, 1968.

Twedt, H. M., & Underwood, B. J. Mixed vs. unmixed lists in transfer studies. *Journal of Experimental Psychology*, 1959, 48, 111–116.

Underwood, B. J. Speed of learning and amount retained: a consideration of methodology. *Psychological Bulletin*, 1954, 51, 276–282.

Underwood, B. J. Interference and forgetting. *Psychological Review*, 1957, 64, 49–60.

Underwood, B. J. Stimulus selection in verbal learning. In C. N. Cofer & B. S. Musgrave (eds.), *Verbal behavior and learning*. New York: McGraw-Hill, 1963.

Underwood, B. J. Degree of learning and the measurement of forgetting. *Journal of Verbal Learning and Verbal Behavior*, 1964, 3, 112–129.

Underwood, B. J. False recognition produced by implicit verbal responses. *Journal of Experimental Psychology*, 1965, 70, 122–129.

Underwood, B. J. Attributes of memory. *Psychological Review*, 1969, 76, 559–573.

Underwood, B. J., Ekstrand, B. R., & Keppel, G. An analysis of intralist similarity with experiments on conceptual similarity. *Journal of Verbal Learning and Verbal Behavior*, 1965, 4, 447–462.

Underwood, B. J., & Ekstrand, B. R. An analysis of some shortcomings in the interference theory of forgetting. *Psychological Review*, 1966, 73, 540–549.

Underwood, B. J., & Ekstrand, B. R. Effect of distributed practice on paired-associate learning. *Journal of Experimental Psychology Monograph Supplements*, 1967, 73, No. 4, Part 2.

Underwood, B. J., & Ekstrand, B. R. Linguistic associations and retention. *Journal of Verbal Learning and Verbal Behavior*, 1968, 7, 162–171. (a)

Underwood, B. J., & Ekstrand, B. R. Differentiation among stimuli as a factor in transfer performance. *Journal of Verbal Learning and Verbal Behavior*, 1968, 7, 172–175. (b)

Underwood, B. J., & Erlebacher, A. H. Studies of coding in verbal learning. *Psychological Monographs*, 1965, 79, No. 13.

Underwood, B. J., & Freund, J. S. Two tests of a theory of verbal-discrimination learning. *Canadian Journal of Psychology*, 1968, 22, 96–104.

Underwood, B. J., & Freund, J. S. Further studies on conceptual similarity in free-recall learning. *Journal of Verbal Learning and Verbal Behavior*, 1969, 8, 30–35.

Underwood, B. J., & Freund, J. S. Testing effects in the recognition of words. *Journal of Verbal Learning and Verbal Behavior*, 1970, 9, 117–125. (a)

Underwood, B. J., & Freund, J. S. Retention of a verbal discrimination. *Journal of Experimental Psychology*, 1970, 84, 1–14. (b)

Underwood, B. J., Ham, M., & Ekstrand, B. R. Cue selection in paired-associate learning. *Journal of Experimental Psychology*, 1962, 64, 405–409.

Underwood, B. J., & Postman, L. Extraexperimental sources of interference in forgetting. *Psychological Review*, 1960, 67, 73–95.

Underwood, B. J., & Schulz, R. W. *Meaningfulness and verbal learning.* Philadelphia: Lippincott, 1960.

Underwood, B. J., Zimmerman, J., & Freund, J. S. Retention of frequency information with observations on recognition and recall. *Journal of Experimental Psychology*, 1971, 87, 149–162.

Weiss, W., & Margolius, G. The effect of context stimuli on learning and retention. *Journal of Experimental Psychology*, 1954, 48, 318–322.

Williams, R. F., & Underwood, B. J. Encoding variability: tests of the Martin hypothesis. *Journal of Experimental Psychology*, 1970, 86, 317–324.

Wood, G., & Underwood, B. J. Implicit responses and conceptual similarity. *Journal of Verbal Learning and Verbal Behavior*, 1967, 6, 1–10.

Young, R. K. Serial learning. In T. R. Dixon & D. L. Horton (eds.), *Verbal behavior and general behavior theory.* Englewood Cliffs, N. J.: Prentice-Hall, 1968.

2 | List Differentiation and Forgetting

JOHN C. ABRA
University of Calgary, Calgary, Alberta, Canada

Current versions of interference theory (Keppel, 1968) suggest that recall of a learned habit depends in part on list differentiation (LD), which will be defined as the ability to discriminate between competing habits and assign each to its appropriate list. While the present paper is ostensibly concerned with the relationship between LD and forgetting, a moral will also become apparent; specifically, recently initiated research programs should never be suggested as topics for papers. In the early stages of investigation a problem usually seems to be surrounded by an almost Descartian clarity. A few crucial experiments, reaching to its very heart, should solve it. At this stage the report, already crystal-clear mentally, would seem to demand only a few leisurely hours at the typewriter. As these idyllic daydreams gallop totally out of control, the most manic stage envisages Nobel Prizes for Verbal Learning or the like. The small difficulty that no such award is presently available is conveniently repressed.

That this pleasant sequence of events is entirely utopian became painfully apparent to the present writer as data accumulated and neat theoretical preconceptions slowly disappeared beneath a sodden weight of contradictions, unanticipated methodological problems, etc. A more realistic assessment, with the benefit of hindsight, is that the serpent in the Garden is a harbinger of innocence compared to data, and the experimental method a product of the same sadistic mind that gave us the rack and music in elevators. Now given this state of affairs, to save the day one could resort to a concise theoretical paper of rapierlike insight and telling rationale, which conveniently ignores the available data. Unfortunately for one's peace of mind, Northwestern training eliminates even this comfortable avenue of escape. Several years of subtle conditioning have internalized a complete commitment to the precedence of data over theory. Thus, an advance warning is probably politic. This paper is consistent mainly in its inconsistency, since no explanatory framework currently on the market seems applicable to all the LD data. A nagging suspicion remains that a more indicative title would be "List Differentiation as a Precursor of Schizophrenia."

We began to study LD for two rather different reasons. Several of our previous studies of forgetting had manipulated some seemingly unrelated

25

variables; yet, in retrospect, intuition suggested that all these variables might have affected LD and the data were so explained. Consequently, direct studies were conducted to verify these notions. A second and perhaps less obvious impetus was the mid-January weather in Western Canada and the quaint parking regulations at the University of Calgary. Within an assigned lot one parks wherever space is open. Later, when one attempts to retrieve one's car, the spot occupied on the day in question must be identified and discriminated from other places used previously. In this daily game of "Alberta roulette" a correct identification, thereby avoiding a walk to the wrong end of the lot, obviously has more than academic interest when the temperature is $-20°F$. We hope to improve these discriminations by uncovering the major determinants of LD.

The central portion of this paper will discuss some situations in which LD may be implicated. However, a brief examination of contemporary interference theory and the development of LD as an explanatory and empirical phenomenon will first be presented. This far from exhaustive historical survey seeks only to elucidate early hypotheses which have affected the direction of subsequent studies. Many of these initial studies have been rendered obsolete by later methodological developments. Consequently, the advance of ideas, rather than data and design, will be stressed. Also, since the division between history and current events is always arbitrary, many studies will be considered later along with the situations to which they are particularly related.

INTERFERENCE THEORY—TERMINOLOGY AND FACTORS

This theory, which attributes forgetting of a learned habit to interference from other learning, has been well summarized at several stages of its development (Postman, 1961; Keppel, 1968). The purpose here is to present some common terms and abbreviations which will be used throughout the paper, as well as some pertinent problems facing current versions of the theory. The association whose retention is under study is usually called original learning (OL). Interference can then originate from two sources: (a) interpolated learning (IL), which occurs between the learning and recall of OL, and (b) prior learning (PL), which occurs before OL is acquired. In laboratory studies of these sources a control group, having learned only OL, is compared in retention to experimental groups which, in addition to OL, have learned either IL or PL. The inferiorities of the IL and PL groups to the control are referred to as retroactive inhibition (RI) and proactive inhibition (PI) respectively.

The facts of interference as produced by RI and PI are not in question, although there is some doubt that all forgetting is due to interference. But the theory also· professes to explain the functional relationships uncovered between manipulated variables and interference. To this end, various determining factors have been enumerated. At present, these include unlearning, spontaneous recovery, response competition, generalized response competition, and LD (Keppel, 1968). (It is amusing to remember, as we contemplate this impressive array of concepts, that Melton and Irwin's (1940) two-factor theory was once thought in some circles to be unparsimonious.) As these factors are usually understood, they may be separated into two categories. Unlearning and recovery reflect, respectively, decrements in OL strength during IL, and reinstatement of some of this lost strength over an extended retention interval following IL. Since these factors are due to modifications in OL strength prior to the recall test, they may be called strength factors. Obviously unlearning would serve to increase RI and decrease PI while recovery would have the opposite effects.

The second category of factors includes those operative at the time of recall; thus, unlike strength factors, these should depend on the type of retention test employed. Response competition arises when incompatible responses are attached to identical or similar stimuli. In such situations the stronger response should be elicited; equivalent strength would produce mutual blockage. In contrast, generalized response competition (GRC) refers to competition from List 2 as a whole, regardless of the degree of interlist stimulus similarity, because of a supposed bias to emit responses from a list just learned. Thus specific response competition should contribute to both RI and PI, while GRC would tend to increase RI and decrease PI. Moreover these properties of GRC should reverse as the retention interval lengthens, since the set for List 2 would probably diminish over time.

The last factor, LD, which is of major concern here, is a second-order interference factor in that it is usually thought to be an inverse constituent of response competition (Postman, 1961; Keppel, 1968). This notion that one factor affects another raises a more general problem. While factors often seem to be regarded as independent, in fact their values conceivably could affect one another. This point will be discussed along with the related problem of measurement.

In early studies of interference S attempted to recall the OL response during a short period; a response from the interfering list was an intrusion. Initially, interference observed in this specific recall was attributed entirely to specific response competition (McGeoch, 1932). Beginning with Melton and Irwin's (1940) unlearning proposal, however, additional factors were invoked as interference phenomena became more complex.

It is generally agreed that all these factors affect specific recall. Their individual study requires measurement techniques holding all other factors constant. In this way the factor under review can be operationally defined and gain the status of an intervening variable rather than a hypothetical construct (Marx, 1951). Also, since still more factors having face validity can doubtlessly be invented, those that are sufficient to explain the variance in interference can be isolated. In other words, if manipulated variables fail to affect the operational measure in any manner that gives better understanding of interference phenomena, perhaps the factor so measured is unnecessary.

Much work of late has sought purer measures. Typical is the painful trial and error (see Postman, 1961) preceding Barnes and Underwood's (1959) development of the MMFR measure of unlearning. This technique required S, at an unpaced rate, to attempt to recall all the responses associated to a particular stimulus. Even more frustrating is that such measures, once obtained, often prove inadequate later. Thus, recent evidence (Postman, Stark, & Fraser, 1968) indicates that MMFR, which seemed ideal for eliminating the variability of recall factors, may be affected by GRC. As will become apparent, the same "search and destroy" sequence has arisen with a technique (Winograd, 1968a) that we used to measure LD.

In fact, while each interference factor has its accepted operational referent, none of these is convincingly free from contamination. When such confoundings are indicated, the obvious course is to discover a new measure which controls the extraneous factor. But if the factors are closely related, this search may be an exercise in futility; furthermore, these interrelationships are a valid theoretical concern. How one proceeds when such a correlation seems impossible to "break" is, I suppose, a matter of taste. One possibility is to take the bull by the horns and infer cause from correlation by suggesting directionality for the relationship, choosing the alternative that can best explain the available data. Thus, Postman et al.'s (1968) findings indicate that unlearning and recovery depend on changes in GRC, while some of our work (Abra, 1969) suggests that recovery may be determined by the amount of unlearning. Yet this avenue of attack can easily get out of hand and produce collective nonsense. Some of my Discussion sections of late have not been entirely blameless in this respect. In various places in the literature it has been suggested that unlearning may determine LD, LD determine GRC, and GRC unlearning. Some of these hypothesized relationships may of course be quite valid, but such intellectual ring-around-a-rosy, while possessing certain aesthetic virtues, hardly increases theoretical understanding.

A second line of attack when two factors prove difficult to measure independently is to eliminate one factor as unnecessary. For example, if both unlearning and recovery are explicable entirely in terms of changes in GRC, are they not redundant concepts? A persistent application of this approach might reverse the recent and exasperating tendency for factors and their hypothesized interrelationships to come forth and multiply in abundance. The question is obviously one of parsimony; the increased complexity of interference theory is only defensible if it is necessary. In fact, the situation is becoming so confusing that some, in their despair, may be tempted to commit the ultimate heresy and turn to decay theory.

Historical Development of LD

As an explanatory device, LD originated in two initially related yet increasingly divergent lines of development. Gibson (1940) was probably responsible for introducing the concept into common usage. In her influential theory, she maintained that stimulus generalization tendencies among items either in the same list or (in certain circumstances) in successive lists would retard learning. Therefore differentiation, i.e., extinction of these tendencies, would be necessary. Spontaneous recovery of generalization, leading to losses in differentiation, caused forgetting over time. Thus, as Underwood (1961) has indicated, differentiation and generalization were opposing processes, with assignment of priority apparently unsettled. Studies emanating from the Gibson tradition have of course been legion in the succeeding years, and some of these will be relevant to matters considered here. In fact, the Gibsonian construct could possess identical, or at any rate similar, properties to differentiation in the sense that it is used here.

The term LD as an interference constituent arose during the debate concerning Melton and Irwin's (1940) Factor X (see Postman, 1961). At issue was the reason for overt interlist intrusions at recall, which Melton and Irwin attributed to response competition. Since RI continued to increase at higher levels of IL while intrusions declined, this unexplained interference was laid at the door of the mysterious Factor X, tentatively identified as the unlearning of List 1 during List-2 learning. But Thune and Underwood (1943), while accepting the usefulness of unlearning, showed that attributing Factor X interference entirely to this construct gave it some unlikely properties, e.g., it would have to decrease at very high levels of List-2 learning.

We shall concentrate on the expanded and formalized version of their argument presented by Underwood (1945). He tried to account for all interference within essentially a two-factor theory of response competition, while also bringing PI into the framework of interference theory. Thus, ostensibly he attributed all measured RI to "the interference of the interpolated responses at the time of the attempted recall of thy original responses" (p. 24), i.e., to response competition. (In fact, unlearning slipped in the back door as an additional albeit minor, determinant of interference. That RI produced more interference than PI necessitated this addition. Moreover, since this difference was constant beyond low degrees of interfering learning, unlearning was regarded as complete after "a few" trials of IL.)

According to Underwood both the associative strength of IL and LD determined response competition. Failures to respond depended on the first factor; thus Factor X interference was largely due to implicit IL intrusions which were rejected by S as incorrect, yet which prevented emission of the correct response within the limited recall time. Overt intrusions, on the other hand, were, in the main, thought to be inversely related to LD except when practice on the two competing lists was precisely equal. At this point both LD and intrusions would be minimized by mutual "blocking." Underwood's analysis of LD, anticipating much later work, will now receive our attention.

Two major postulates concerning LD were advanced; that (a) it increases in a positively accelerated manner with IL trials and (b) it decreases with the interval between the end of IL and the recall test. The relation in the first postulate, incapable of explaining the initial *increase* in intrusions with IL, was later changed to curvilinearity (Underwood, 1949). More important, this postulate, together with the paper's general tone, implicates input frequency as a determinant of LD, anticipating Winograd's (1968a) position. Moreover, the idea that relative frequency, i.e., the frequency differential between competing responses, is the primary precursor anticipates the frequency theory of verbal-discrimination learning (Ekstrand, Wallace, & Underwood, 1966). In this situation, seemingly analogous to the requirements of LD, the development of a frequency differential is again emphasized, although in this case frequency refers to responses made by *S* rather than to input.

The second postulate was initially an extension of the first. A constant retention interval, i.e., time between OL and the recall test, meant that more IL trials would inevitably reduce the interval between the end of IL and recall. In other words, IL trials and the IL-recall interval were confounded. However, Underwood attempted to study the effect of the IL-recall interval by comparing items across IL conditions which had been correctly anticipated equally often. For example, an item emitted 8 times correctly in 8 trials was compared to an item correct 8 times in 16 trials. In this way the difference in strength as the interval changed was hopefully controlled; any differences in LD for these items across conditions were then attributed to the time per se.

For such items more intrusions occurred in the 8 than in the 16 IL-trials condition, indicating better LD in the latter condition which also had the shorter interval between the end of IL and recall. Thus was initiated the universal dictum that LD decreases over time, a notion that is more important than the second postulate as stated, and that has often been alluded to over the years, e.g., as a possible precursor of the increase in PI over time (Dallett, 1964). Ironically from an historical point of view, this conclusion is probably not warranted by the data giving rise to it. Even assuming that conditions comparable in strength were compared (are 7 reinforcements over 8 trials really equivalent to 7 over 16?), the conditions were not, and could not be, comparable in input frequency, already indicated as of primary importance. However, this early demonstration of the difficulty in controlling both frequency and strength has much contemporary relevance. As we shall see, this problem arises continually in studies of LD.

Two other findings from Underwood's (1945) paper are notable. First, intrusions were unaffected by the number of intefering lists when each was learned for a constant number of trials. Since these conditions probably differed in relative strength due to differential unlearning (Postman, 1965), frequency is again implicated as a constituent of LD. Secondly, with multiple interfering lists, the greatest frequency of intrusions came from the list contiguous to OL, especially with the PI situation. The resulting suggestion that temporal separation of tasks might affect LD anticipates recent thinking (Abra, 1969; Underwood & Freund, 1968a).

Subsequently Underwood (1949) introduced another major determinant of LD besides frequency. In studying PI he noted that interlist intrusions increased when PL was slightly stronger than OL. He suggested, therefore, that LD increased with the difference in strength between competing responses at the time of recall. Evidently strength, assessed as it was by degree of OL, was used interchangeably with frequency. Certainly no modification in the earlier thinking is mentioned. The change in terminology proably reflects the use of a performance rather than a trials criterion in this study. Nor was the inference of relative strength from learning data unreasonably so long as the strength of one list was thought to be unaffected by the learning of another. But the contructs of unlearning and recovery have superseded this independence hypothesis (Postman, 1961). Therefore, a distinction must be observed between frequency, in the sense of number of inputs, and strength, as assessed by some measure after all learning tasks are completed.

The study is also notable for two suggestions emanating from Gibson's theory, namely, that LD should increase with the absolute strength of each list and that the loss of LD over time, indicated by an increase in intrusions, could be due to recovery of extinguished generalization tendencies. More recently, generalization has been scarcely mentioned in LD studies as the divergence from the Gibsonian fountainhead increases. This trend may be unfortunate if generalization proves to be the antecedent process.

The relative strength notion received stronger support from Briggs (1957), who varied both OL and IL trials independently, and administered an MFR test, before OL relearning. In MFR, S saw the stimulus common to the two lists and produced the response which came to mind first; thus, relative strength is revealed since the stronger response should be given. These MFR data, when related to intrusions during relearning allowed relative strength and LD to be compared. With a few exceptions intrusions diminished as the relative strength differential increased. While this prior MFR test was a distinct methodological advance, it is still somewhat unsatisfactory for studying LD since absolute list strengths are not revealed.

In recent years virtually no new determinants of LD have been uncovered. An exception is the suggestion in Postman's (1961) survey of interference theory circa 1960 that LD should be inferior in the PI as opposed to the RI design. With a constant retention interval, a longer interval between the completion of learning and the recall test necessarily occurs in the PI situation. This interesting analysis has yet to be tested in a situation where the strength differential is equal.

Also, LD has occupied a relatively minor place in the growing arsenal of explanatory weapons possessed by interference theory, for which several reasons may be mentioned. The widespread relation of LD to response competition has led to its emphasis only under the relatively restricted conditions of specific recall. In contrast, most studies of the past decade have employed some variation of the MMFR measure, which supposedly eliminates recall factors. The bias toward MMFR was initiated by the need to study Melton and Irwin's hypothesized unlearning factor; later, the increase in PI over time motivated a rash of studies (e.g., Koppenaal, 1963; Birnbaum, 1965; Abra, 1967, 1968) searching, usually fruitlessly, for the Holy Grail of absolute spontaneous recovery over time.

But the continued use of MMFR undoubtedly stems from the observation of comparable interference in MMFR and specific recall (Postman, 1962b; Houston, 1966a); thereafter, strength factors were assumed to be the primary constituents of interference. This prevailing *zeitgeist* seems to be reversing. The accumulating evidence that other factors besides strength may be operating in MMFR has led to a renewed interest in recall factors, particularly GRC. Moreover Howe (1967) has shown that the expectation of increased interference in specific recall as opposed to MMFR can be fulfilled when a bias in measurement is eliminated (see also Keppel, 1968).

Additional cogent reasons for ignoring LD in particular have been voiced by Melton (1961). Initially he noted the terminological problem already raised here. Gibson's construct has acquired unanticipated connotations, requiring one to fathom the precise usage of the term. In other words, differentiation of "differentiation" is often difficult. The factors underlying Melton's remaining objections have probably impeded progress more profoundly. First, since LD is something *S* "does," stimulus control is lacking; the unanswered question, discomforting when LD is used as an explanatory device, is how he does it. Overcoming this problem really requires prior solution of another difficulty raised; no satisfactory measure of LD, uncontaminated by other factors, has been extant. Were this measure available, then potentially effective independent variables could be studied directly, suggesting answers to the first problem by providing clues as to conditions under which LD changes.

Some recent developments, having as yet unknown impacts, have constituted attacks on these difficulties. A major advance has been Winograd's (1968a) presentation of an attractive measurement technique, to be described shortly. A second development is a stimulating theoretical paper by Underwood (1969) discussing attributes of memory. A quotation from the abstract will perhaps capture its essence. "A memory is conceptualized as a collection of attributes which serve to discriminate one memory from another and to act as retrieval mechanisms for a target memory. The attributes identified are temporal, spatial, frequency, modality, orthographic, associative nonverbal, and associative verbal" (p. 559). Presumably material is internalized during exposure (in some sense, physiological or otherwise), along with the various extra- and intrasubject conditions present at the time. Obviously these attributes are potential differentiating cues. That is, as competing lists possess increasingly different attributes, LD should improve. Or, to use Underwood's words again, "The greater the number of different attributes making up a memory, and the less these attributes are parts of other memories, the less the interference (at recall)" (p. 570).

As it happened, when Underwood's article was published we were using Winograd's technique to study the effect of some of these attributes on LD. Both Underwood's thinking and our findings will be presented as each attribute is considered separately. But perhaps some personal observations may be made now. That attributes always function in the inferred causal manner contradicts some entirely introspective evidence. As I understand Underwood, a memory consists of a group of associated attributes; the target memory within this group is often not defined until the time of recall. (One exception occurs when S chooses attributes as memory aids for something he knows he will have to remember later.) Now the availability of the target memory depends, apparently, on the *prior* availability of its associated attributes.

But what of the case where one virtually reinstates an entire set of attributes in the imagination? How do the eliciting attributes become available, and why before the target? In this respect Underwood has referred to new and critical attributes evoked by a changed stimulus situation. Apart from the ugly path of infinite regress thereby opened, his notion still seems to me incapable of encompassing all the gaudy circumstances under which memories "pop into mind," e.g., lying in bed at night. But this minor objection aside, I have no doubts that the notion of attributes can be fruitfully applied to many memory phenomena.

Measures of LD

As mentioned, a recent advance has been our acquisition of a reasonable measurement technique. Intrusions, the measure employed in early studies, are notoriously infrequent and therefore subject to basement effects; thus these studies have limited applicability. Furthermore, since LD was introduced to explain intrusions (Underwood, 1945), their use as a means of assessment is uncomfortably circular. In MMFR studies identification of list membership for each response recalled has also been used; generally, scores with this technique have been quite high, even at longer retention intervals (Koppenaal, 1963). Unfortunately, this measure, limited to recalled items, is subject to the whims of availability.

However Winograd (1968a) has presented a technique which seems to avoid these difficulties. After several competing lists have been learned, all the items from all the lists are shown in a mixed order. As each item appear, S indicates the list to which he thinks it belongs. In addition, he indicates on a rating scale how sure he is that his judgement is correct. Typically, ratings of one to three reflect decreasing confidence that an item came from List 1, while ratings of four to six show increasing confidence of List-2 membership. Thus, the technique is probably more sensitive than a dichotomous measure.

The total number of correct identifications for items in both lists is then the simplest measure of LD, but probably more indicative is a rating-difference score, which considers S's confidence. The mean rating given to all the items in

List 1, correct or otherwise, is determined; a similar mean is obtained for List-2 items. The rating-difference score is then the difference between these means. Since more extreme ratings reflect greater confidence, larger difference scores indicate better LD. Usually the technique is used following free-recall learning, but adaptation to other methods, e.g., paired-associate learning (McCrystal, 1970), is simple. One limitation is that application of the rating-difference score measure to situations involving more than two learned lists seems difficult.

Other problems with the technique will now be considered. Some of these were evident through armchair speculation but most have been revealed through painful experience. The first problem concerns the presentation rate for the LD test. Keppel (1968) has objected to slow rates on the grounds that LD is supposed to be operative on paced tests and will likely be overestimated with slower testing. While this point is well taken, a somewhat leisurely 8-second rate is generally used; otherwise S may fail to meet the physical demands of the rating-scale test. We would rather err a little on the long side than have Ss miss slides, skip pages, etc.

While the technique probably eliminates availability as a factor, strength, unfortunately, still seems effective (unless strength is also viewed as dichotomous). As we have discovered to our sorrow, when a variable affects strength, e.g., by producing differential unlearning or recovery, an LD test of the variable will be affected by this strength difference across conditions. When such a difference has either been indicated, or suspected in advance, we have tried several tactics. Probably most satisfactory is to match Ss in absolute and relative strength, based on an MMFR test administered before LD. Contamination of the LD measure by practice effects from MMFR seems negligible, at least with paired-associate learning (McCrystal, 1970). However, this approach only works if strength differences are not large and if OL performance is equivalent; otherwise a speed-of-learning confound is introduced. Another possibility is to search, via pilot studies, for degrees of learning where the variable in question does *not* affect strength, and conduct the study at that point. While generalization from such a study is difficult, at least the variable's capability of affecting LD can be demonstrated. Unfortunately, these pilot studies border on stabbing in the dark; often the desired information is long in coming, by which time the population used has evaporated, giving one the opportunity to start all over again.

An additional problem with these approaches is that, as Winograd (1968a) has maintained, equating conditions on any one measure of strength does not insure their comparability on all such measures (Bahrick, 1964). While this point is valid, is it not better to control one measure of strength than none, especially when the controlled measure apparently affects LD? Anyone with a spare eon or two on his hands might want to try controlling all conceivable strength indicants.

Still another method, determining different numbers of presentation trials to administer across conditions such that strength is equivalent, seems unsatisfactory in retrospect. The conditions will inevitably differ in input frequency, which also affects LD (Winograd, 1968a). Thus, it is conceivable that the effect of some variables on LD cannot be determined conclusively, unless meditation becomes acceptable scientific methodology.

We shall now consider the variables individually that we have related to LD; Underwood's (1969) presentation would render our examination of other possible precursors redundant. We shall discuss our studies in the order that they were conducted, since methodological problems faced in earlier efforts dictated refinements introduced subsequently.

THE POINT OF INTERPOLATED LEARNING

During a constant OL-recall interval IL may occur at different points, producing a variation in the OL-IL (and inevitably the IL-recall) interval. With specific recall this point of interpolated learning (PIL) has, rather surprisingly, not affected RI (Archer & Underwood, 1951; Newton & Wickens, 1956). If, as seems intuitively reasonable, separation of OL and IL improves LD, then inverse variation of another factor with PIL could produce equivalent overall interference. This proposed balancing effect seems testable with MMFR, where LD is not effective.

Several such studies have been conducted recently. Houston (1967) found no difference between conditions having PIL immediately after OL and just before MMFR. However, two subsequent studies (Howe, 1969; Abra, 1969) both showed that the latter condition lessened recall. Evidence from these "successful" studies ascribed Houston's negative results to a basement effect. Specifically, in his immediate PIL condition a long retention interval combined with a relatively low degree of OL and high degree of IL produced a low level of recall, making any further loss unlikely.

Thus, it appears that PIL can affect MMFR in such a manner as to offset improved LD with increased separation of tasks. However, other findings from our study indicated that this analysis may be incomplete. More specifically, three groups had an OL-MMFR interval of 48 hours, with PIL either immediately after OL (48–0), 24 hours later (48–24) or prior to MMFR (48–48). A fourth group had PIL followed by MMFR 24 hours after OL (24–24). Conditions 24–c and 48–c were single-list controls which recalled after 24 and 48 hours, respectively.

In List-1 recall 48–48 was inferior to both 48–24 and 48–0, which did not differ. The superiorities of the latter groups could have been due eithe; to differential initial unlearning or to spontaneous recovery over time. The difference between 48–24 and 48–48 was clearly due to recovery. Initial unlearning in the empirical sense of an experimental-control difference on MMFR immediately after IL was closely comparable between 24- and 48-hour PIL, and absolute recovery in 48–24 was shown by its superiority to 24–24. On the other hand, while the conclusion is not clear-cut, we thought that less initial unlearning likely produced the superiority of 48–0. Unfortunately, absence of the appropriate groups for comparison meant that absolute and/or relative recovery could not be ruled out. Yet several studies (Koppenaal, 1963; Birnbaum, 1965; Abra, 1967) have shown absolute recovery over long intervals to be unlikely when OL and IL are learned successively, except with overlearning of List 1 (Adams, 1962; Silverstein, 1967).

But the important point is that the relation between MMFR and PIL was not linear. If, as intuition suggested, LD improves continuously with increasing task separation, then the proposed balancing effect would not work. Therefore we conducted a study of LD in conditions 48–0, 48–24, and 48–48. (Abra, 1970). Four alternate study and test trials of free-recall learning were used for both OL and IL. Unfortunately, this being our first LD study, we did not include a prior MMFR test; we shall suffer anon. Conditions 48–0 and 48–24 were again comparable, but this time both were inferior to 48–48; in other words, LD improved in a positively accelerated manner as the OL–IL interval lengthened. The intuitive approach suffers another setback.

A more complex balancing effect is therefore proposed for the absence of PIL effects in specific recall. This analysis admittedly includes some rather awesome inductive leaps, but it appears reasonable on the basis of the above data and generates some testable hypotheses. Possibly, as PIL is varied, unlearning, recovery, and LD are in balance, producing comparable overall interference. In addition, for any pair of the three groups examined, we suggest that one factor is equivalent, while the other two vary inversely. Groups 48–0 and 48–24 have comparable LD; more unlearning in the latter is offset by its recovery over time. In 48–0 and 48–48 recovery is constant, but 48–0 has both less unlearning and inferior LD. Unlearning is constant between 48–24 and 48–48 but recovery in the former group offsets inferior LD.

Several unverified assumptions, all of which can be tested empirically, should be recognized. Most notably, the positively-accelerated LD function, inferred from free-recall learning data, must be validated for paired-associate learning. Again, postulating less initial unlearning for 48–0 assumes recovery to be unlikely. Lastly the omission of other factors, notably GRC, may be serious. Recent experiments by Postman, Stark, & Henschel (1969) indicate that GRC can be an important determinant of PIL effects. Delayed PIL depressed MMFR not only with the A-B, A-C paradigm but also with A-B, C-D; the latter finding implicates GRC. Furthermore, delayed PIL generally increased the tendency to emit the response from the last list first when all the responses to a stimulus were produced in MMFR. This tendency, presumably reflecting the set for that list, is a commonly used measure of GRC.

Yet GRC may be present in our analysis under "unlearning" which, as used here in its empirical sense, may include two constituent *factors* of unlearning and GRC. If our MMFR measure was affected by GRC (Postman, Stark, & Fraser, 1968), our analysis would be incomplete but not necessarily wrong. Also, the methodology of Postman et al. differs rather drastically from the specific recall studies, having both shorter retention intervals and more infering lists. Possibly GRC is only important under these conditions.

In a second study reported in the same paper (Abra, 1970), LD followed IL immediately, with an OL-IL interval of either 1 minute or 48 hours. Four alternate study-test trials constituted OL, with IL presented for either 2, 4 or 6 trials. The rationale for the study is unimportant but the data were puzzling. While LD was generally superior when OL and IL were separated, the relationship reversed at the low degree of IL; here separation of tasks reliably *impeded* LD. I see no other way to account for this phenomenon than to assume, once again, that the MMFR relationship between 48—0 and 48—48 in free-recall learning is comparable to that obtained in paired-associate learning, and that it is due to differential unlearning rather than to recovery. (Recovery could not produce these effects since in this study the IL-LD interval was minimal.) It is then proposed that temporal separation of tasks mainly affects LD, not directly, but by way of its effect on relative strength. It is not maintained that time per se is ineffective; rather, that strength seems the more powerful of the two determinants.

Following this argument, when IL strength equals or exceeds OL, task separation would increase the strength difference by increasing unlearning and thus improve LD. However with IL weaker than OL, more unlearning would lessen the differential. In other words, we suggested that LD is affected by unlearning and recovery. This argument also accounts for the unexpected positively-accelerated relationship obtained in the first study between PIL and LD. With 48—0 and 48—24 comparable in both List-1 and List-2 availability, LD should be equivalent.

Other recent PIL findings will be examined from this point of view. That PI is reduced by task separation (Underwood & Freund, 1968a; Alin, 1968) seems to implicate LD. This effect may be due partly to relative strength differences across conditions (as Alin has in fact argued, although his analysis differs substantially from that presented here). Specifically, both our findings and the results of an MMFR test which Underwood & Freund administered after relearning indicate that at the time of OL recall, PL was probably weaker in the groups having separation of tasks. Therefore, the strength differential might be larger for this group. Yet this argument only applies if OL was stronger than PL. Since PL was greatly overlearned, this may not have been the case. With PL stronger, the relative strength position expects task separation to lessen LD; clearly no final conclusions are possible on this point.

Underwood and Freund also found that repeating some PL items in the OL list lessened, but did not eliminate, the superiority of the separated group. Such repetition could, it was argued, weaken the temporal discrimination which ordinarily helped the separated group. Again relative strength may also be involved. Paul and Silverstein (1968) have shown that nonrepeated items in List 2 produce less unlearning if the remaining List-2 items are repeated than if they are also new. Given that item repetition affects unlearning, it could have modified the strength differential so as to reduce LD.

Underwood (1969), in discussing the temporal attribute, considered, and largely rejected, strength as a cue to placement of memories along a temporal dimension. For example, he maintained that the use of strength would produce disorientation in time; some old memories are stronger than new, yet are easily identified as old. From the present standpoint such decisions are quite possible as long as a strength difference exists in either direction. Disorientation would only occur when ancient and new memories are of *equal* strength. For example, a label "stronger, therefore older" could be remembered. Extending this notion, the ubiquitous elderly person who "lives in the past," i.e., thinks of ancient events as contemporary, could reflect a loss of these rather complex labels. But we would argue that an equating over time of a vast store of memories, as happens for OL and IL in the laboratory (Koppenaal, 1963) is a more likely culprit; placement of memories in time then would be extremely difficult.

Certainly Underwood's evidence from single-task studies is difficult to refute, e.g., for a series of words varing in strength, judgments of position correlate with true position but not with strength. Yet the purpose here is not to dismiss time per se as a cue, which would not be warranted at present, but to show that strength may also function in a situation in which time is the more obvious source of discrimination. In short, our position is that both temporal and relative strength attributes may affect temporal dimensions.

RELEARNING

In an earlier study (Abra & Roberts, 1969) we examined the forgetting of, and the forgetting produced by, a relearned (RL) habit as compared to a corresponding OL habit. In both cases these habits were the third task S encountered. Somewhat surprisingly, RL and OL habits proved almost equally susceptible to unlearning, but they affected other tasks differently. Specifically, RL lessened unlearning of a prior task (Task 2) and retarded acquisition of a subsequent fourth task. In addition, the number of interlist intrusions increased notably following RL. We maintained that exposure to an RL task would demonstrate to S his forgetting of a task he once knew; in other words, he would learn about unlearning. Consequently, we suggested that he might increase implicit rehearsal, possibly in anticipation of future RL tasks. Supposedly the intrusions were simply overt manifestations of this rehearsal.

It was suggested, in turn, that such rehearsal might reduce LD by lessening the discrete temporal separation of tasks. (This reasoning could be extended to any situation that increases intrusion rate, e.g., Keppel & Rauch, 1966; Paul & Silverstein, 1968.) The study duly conducted to test this notion has some problems, notably the failure to control relative strength, which limit its interest.

However, one incidental finding seems worthy of discussion; for this purpose only the two groups which learned four tasks need be described. Three lists, labeled A, B, and C, were used. Both groups learned List B as Task 2, List A as TAsk 3, and List C as Task 4. However group RL–4 also learned List A as Task 1, so that Task 3 was RL for this group. On the other hand, group OL–4 learned a list of different materials (List X) for Task 1; thus Task 3 was their first encounter with List A.

While a pilot study had indicated the number of Task–3 trials necessary to control degree of learning, group differences were still apparent. Therefore ten Ss from each group were matched on degree of learning for all tasks. These groups were quite comparable in overall LD, but the results are virtually uninterpretable because of an obvious, and puzzling, difference in guessing bias. Both the percentage of incorrect items that were misplaced to each of the two incorrect lists, and the sheer number of guesses of each list, correct or otherwise, showed that RL–4 had a stronger bias to guess List B and to avoid List A. In both groups the number of List-C guesses conformed closely to the actual number of List-C items.

None of the methodological deficiencies in the study appear to account for this bias *against* guessing the RL list (the opposite tendency would seem more reasonable.) That the Ss were Canadian servicemen, suffering the trauma of unification of the Canadian armed services might indicate something. Interference factors, notably GRC, could be affected appreciably by this differential bias, but an easy extension to the results of our earlier study is not apparent. In short, we must leave this topic on an inconclusive note.

CHANGE OF CONTEXT

With specific recall, administering IL in a different physical environment to List-1 learning and recall reduces RI (Bilodeau & Schlosberg, 1951; Greenspoon & Ranyard, 1957). At least two interpretations of this change-of-context (CoC) effect are possible. Associations may be formed between list responses and the experimental context to achieve response availability (Underwood, 1964). These List-1 context associations should then ordinarily be unlearned during List-2 response learning. But learning List 2 under changed conditions would alter the relationship between List-1 and List-2 context associations to A-B, C-D from A-B, A-C. Unlearning would therefore be reduced (McGovern, 1964), producing the CoC effect.

Alternatively, a CoC might improve LD, again yielding the effect. Of course, in specific recall both unlearning and LD are not mutually exclusive, so that both could contribute to the effect. The portion not due to LD, which for convenience we shall attribute to unlearning can be assessed by studying CoC with MMFR. In such a study the effect was completely absent in both paired-associate (Abra & Kolb, 1970) and free-recall learning tasks (Abra &

Belton, 1969). List-1 recall was virtually identical for groups having changed and unchanged contexts for List-2 learning.

Our negative results probably reflect the fact that our unchanged as well as changed conditions involved being forced to leave the room between OL and IL. Strand (1970) showed that, at least in free-recall learning, the Coc effect only appeared when unchanged conditions did not have this disruption. Since Strand's study as well as our own included a change in posture for CoC, both environmental and kinesthetic changes during IL seem unimportant. Rather, the effect depends on different activities introduced during the intertask interval. Postural changes at this time are probably particularly important, since the early successful studies always included such changes (Rand & Wapner, 1967).

A study showing that a CoC reduces PI (Dallett & Wilcox, 1968) seems to implicate LD, but a concomitant change in presentation modality, which also affects LD (see below) makes this conclusion tenuous. Consequently, in a recent experiment we studied LD directly. Having learned something from our first efforts, we sought to control relative strength by recreating the conditions of the Abra & Belton (1969) study, in which a CoC had left availability for both lists unaffected. Although the particular population used was no longer available, the same lists, degrees of learning, etc., were employed with IL followed by MMFR and then the LD test. Counterbalancing the list used for List-1 learnin,g, and the particular contexts used for List 1 and List 2 produced eight groups, of which four had a Coc.

The effect of a CoC on MMFR was minor; nevertheless, in each CoC condition each of six Ss was matched with an S in the corresponding unchanged condition having the closest absolute and relative MMFR performance. Collapsing the counterblancing, therefore, produced changed and unchanged conditions of 24 matched Ss each, with absolute and relative strength, as well as OL and IL performance, virtually identical. The LD results can only be called frustrating. A consistent superiority of the CoC group in both rating-difference scores and total correct identifications failed to achieve even borderline significance. In addition, List-1 and List-2 items were separated into categories of strong, medium, and weak on the basis of number of correct recalls during learning. While LD performance declined with strength for both lists (contrary to the PIL study, in which List-1, but not List-2 strength was correlated with LD), an interaction between item strength and the CoC effect was not indicated.

Is anything more dissatisfying than a small but nonsignificant effect? Yet post hoc reevaluation suggests that under altered circumstances a CoC might affect LD to a greater extent. To be discriminating features, environmental attributes must be associated to the task items (Underwood, 1969). We used auditory presentation, which would lessen S's attention to the environment. To cite an extreme case, one could learn with one's eyes closed. But visual presentation, which demands some degree of attention, might enhance the effect of a CoC. The opposite extreme, maximizing attention to the context, might involve exposing items at different points around the room in a sort of verbal lightshow. Indeed Dallett & Wilcox's context-box, with its flashing lights, etc., has introduced elements of the discotéque into the verbal-learning laboratory. Pursuing this line of endeavor, if nothing else, might increase the number of students volunteering to be Ss.

CHANGE OF MODALITY

Although the effect of a change of modality (CM) from OL to IL has seldom been studied, some evidence (Inoue, 1968) indicates that RI is thereby reduced. However recent experiments in our laboratory suggest that a CM modifies both unlearning and LD. The effect on unlearning is complicated. Consistently, when OL is learned by visual presentation (VP) a change to auditory presentation (AP) has reduced unlearning appreciably, while a change from AP to VP has had no effect. At first, transfer differences produced by a CM seemed responsible but the effect has remained when varying the number of List-2 trials across conditions eliminated such differences in degree of IL. Furthermore, it has been manifest with both paired-associate and free-recall learning and regardless of differences in List-1 learning between VP and AP or the level of IL employed.

Our post hoc analysis of this result required some uproarious brainstorming sessions. It seems reasonable to follow Underwood (1969) and assert that the auditory component of a visual task (due to implicit rehearsal) is greater than the visual component of an auditory task. If such auditory activity during VP were augmented by a previous AP task, by a priming mechanism, then learning OL and IL by AP and VP, respectively, would be a less effective CM than the direction VP-AP. In the latter case, learning by VP has occurred before auditory rehearsal has been primed. We then grasped the straw that MMFR is seemingly affected by GRC, and suggested that overcoming GRC should be easier for VP-AP than for AP-VP, because of this larger interlist difference in response characteristics. The major point, of course, is that such predictions are amazingly precise when the data are already available.

As previous discussion has shown, that a CM affects unlearning complicates the determination of its effect on LD. In our free-recall learning studies an LD test followed MMFR, with analysis confined to situations in which a CM exerted no influence on the recall results. Specifically, pairs of conditions were selected, one of which had a CM for IL, such that pairs were closely comparable in degree of OL and IL, as well as List-1 and List-2 MMFR. For these groups a CM improved LD appreciably, an effect consistent across varying numbers of IL trials. In addition, apparently strength was again an authoritative factor. A CM from VP to AP only improved LD slightly. The reduction in unlearning, and the resultant diminishing of the relative-strength differential, seemingly offset the effect of a CM.

FREQUENCY

Frequency undoubtedly stands unchallenged as the preponderant deity on the Olympus occupied by discriminating attributes, if amount of discussion is acceptable as a primary criterion of divinity. Much of this has had its impetus from the aforesaid frequency theory of verbal-discrimination (VD) learning (Ekstrand, Wallace, & Underwood, 1966). In the two-choice VD task S must learn to anticipate the arbitrarily-chosen "right" member of a pair. Frequency theory attributes learning to the development of a difference in the total number of responses made to each item. Usually, more frequency accrues to the "right" member, because it is implicitly rehearsed more often. No attempt will be made here to review the many recent tests of this theory. Obviously the VD and LD tasks make many similar requirements of S. Yet once this is said, some considerations suggest that evidence should not be hastily extended from one situation to the other.

The VD and LD tasks typically involve simultaneous and successive discriminations, respectively; these two techniques may produce quite different results (Kimble, 1961). This problem is not unavoidable on either side; for example, a simultaneous test of LD, at least with paired-associate tasks, would be quite feasible (although its applicability to specific recall might then be questioned). But since this difference in techniques has thus far been manifest, comparability of presently available findings is doubtful.

A second, and seemingly more nearly insurmountable difference is that the VD task involves intentional learning. In tests of LD, in contrast, to conform to most interference studies, S is not told during learning that discrimination is required. Its necessity is certainly not apparent before the transfer task and, since LD variables have typically not affected transfer performance notably, seemingly becomes obvious only at the time of recall. The incidental-learning nature of the LD situation likely produces differences in S's method of attack.

In view of these differences, we shall say only that the VD theory has been successfully applied to many situations (e.g., Underwood & Freund, 1968b; Raskin, Boice, Rubel, & Clark, 1968), although some limitations have recently become evident (Underwood & Freund, 1970a, 1970b, 1970c). Instead we shall confine our attention to frequency insofar as it bears directly on LD. A central difficulty should be considered at the outset. As both Winograd (1968a) and Underwood (1969) have noted, strength, as assessed by a subsequent recall test often covaries with frequency. In earlier sections we tried to show that strength probably affects LD; if this is accepted, then the effect of strength independent of frequency seems demonstrated, frequency having been controlled in these studies. The purpose now is to ascertain whether frequency can also be effective.

It might also be mentioned that in the last analysis frequency may determine memory phenomena entirely by way of its effect on strength, in the sense of a property possessed by a presumed physiological substrate (memory trace, engram, or whatever). But again, various indices of this supposed trace strength are possible, and variables may affect these measures differentially (e.g., Costello, Belton, Abra, & Dunn, 1970). Holding to the position that frequency influences memory by way of strength does not exclude the possibility that frequency and a particular strength measure may vary somewhat independently.

Both Winograd (1968a) and Underwood (1969) have presented evidence that frequency can modify LD when strength, in the sense of availability, is controlled. In Winograd's studies, which we shall examine in some detail, frequency referred to the sheer number of presentation trials. To examine relative frequency, independent groups had trials of OL and either 1, 3, or 6 trials of IL; likewise, other groups had IL for 3 trials and OL for either 1, 3, or 6 trials. The 3–3 group (the first and second numbers in the designation represent the number of OL and IL trials, respectively) had both the smallest frequency differential and the worst LD.

The data also suggest that frequency is a more powerful determinant than strength. Comparisons for which relative strength and frequency make opposite predictions (e.g., frequency would expect group 3–1 to be superior to 3–3, while strength would predict the opposite) conformed to frequency expectations. In addition, it is puzzling that in comparisons of groups 3–1 versus 1–3 and 6–3 versus 3–6 (not presented statistically) the first group in each case performed somewhat better than the second (see Fig. 1, p. 6, Winograd, 1968a). It is likely, although recall was not measured, that unlearning would produce a larger strength differential in the second group mentioned for each comparison. Furthermore, since apparent recency (see below) would also benefit these same conditions, some unknown factor, seemingly of some magnitude, may be working in opposition here.

Absolute frequency, with relative frequency controlled, also seemed influential. With both lists presented for either 1, 3, or 6 trials each, LD improved with trials. This latter conclusion is not unambiguous, as Winograd himself admitted. If S discriminates between the lists on a temporal dimension, i.e., early versus late, then more List-2 trials could enhance the apparent recency of this list and improve LD. It is known that an item presented more frequently will be judged to have occurred more recently (Fozard & Yntema, 1966).

However Hintzman and Waters (1970) eliminated this problem by varying the frequency with which items occurred within a single presentation of List 1; the mean position of presentation remained constant across the levels of frequency. Since differential frequency was produced in List 1, judgements based on apparent recency should in this case lessen performance. Nevertheless, increased List-1 presentation frequency improved LD even when List 2 was presented for several trials; thus increased absolute frequency was helpful in situations where it actually decreased relative frequency. Unfortunately, Hintzman and Waters used an LD test in which all items were presented at once; both the simultaneous nature of this test, and the lack of control over presentation time per item may limit extension of their findings to specific recall. But at any rate they seem to have demonstrated the effectiveness of absolute frequency. In addition, they showed that a single item was more readily identified when presented early rather than late in List 1; again, temporal separation is implicated as a possible precursor of LD.

To the present writer the apparent increase in LD with absolute frequency seems to fly in the face of Weber's Law. With relative frequency held constant, differences in frequency should become less noticeable as absolute frequency increases. One explanation for this contradiction, that the relative strength differential increases concomitantly with absolute strength, does not seem to be the case. Some evidence from our laboratory indicates that groups 3–3 and 6–6 are quite comparable in this respect. However, that LD is poorer when words of high rather than low Thorndike-Lorge (1944) frequency must be discriminated (Winograd, 1968c) may suggest a resolution to this quandry. Perhaps a distinction needs to be drawn, as Underwood and Freund (1970b) have done for VD situations, between situational frequency (produced by laboratory input) and background frequency (from extraexperimental usage). It could then be maintained that Weber's Law does not hold for situational frequency, for which supposition there is some evidence (Underwood & Freund, 1970a).

Unfortunately, this analysis would apparently expect more forgetting for discriminations between words of high background frequency, as situational frequency is assimilated into background over time (Underwood & Freund, 1970b); such is not the case, at least over a 24-hour interval (Winograd, 1970c). At this point, application of Weber's Law seems more than a little confusing.

At any rate, the safest course, in the light of available data, is to accept absolute and relative frequency, as well as absolute and relative strength, as probable determinants of LD. That they are closely intertwined probably means that determination of priorities will be difficult. This suspicion is substantiated by the preliminary results from a study currently underway in which both OL and IL trials are varied independently (à la Winograd), with LD preceded by MMFR. It is virtually impossible, at this writing, to assign effects conclusively to any one of these variables, because of covariation of the others.

These supposed determinants can be applied to an understanding of other phenomena. Brown and Battig (1966) have shown that the addition of List-1 (old) pairs to List 2 can either facilitate or inhibit the acquisition of new pairs, depending on the strength and/or frequency of the old pairs. Possibly S's method of accomplishing within-list differentiation is modified by specific discriminating cues thereby being "primed." An increased tendency to use a particular cue could, in different circumstances, either augment or lessen interpair interference due to generalization.

We may also consider the effect of retention interval here. There is much support for the virtual cliché that LD declines over time (Winograd, 1968a; McCrystal, 1970), although Howe's (1967) failure to observe an increase in response competition over time stands in opposition. In turn, LD could possibly be applied to some well-documented time effects in forgetting, such as the increase in PI.

In contrast, the present position could regard this PI effect as at least partially a cause rather than a consequence of changes in LD. That PI also increases over time in MMFR (Koppenaal, 1963) suggests that LD is not entirely responsible for the effect. Perhaps some other factor, e.g., rehearsal of PL during the retention interval (Houston, 1969), changes the strength differential. Therefore LD and in turn PI in specific recall would be affected, leading to the rather novel assertion that PI produces PI. According to this analysis, if any PI is to be laid at the door of LD, clearly a more profound increase in PI over time must occur with specific recall as opposed to MMFR. In the absence of data contrary to this prediction, we conclude that changes in LD may still reasonably be held responsible for part of the PI effect in specific recall.

At any rate we are hoping to unravel the correlation between time changes in strength and LD somewhat with a study currently underway. As a first step, we have isolated degrees of OL and IL which will produce comparable List-1 and List-2 MMFR immediately. We would hope, then, that for such groups the relative strength differential would increase over time. Given this state of affairs, we hope to demonstrate an improvement in LD over time. However, in view of previous events in our laboratory, holding one's breath in anticipation of this finding would be distinctly unadvisable.

OTHER DETERMINANTS

This section will consider several attributes which could modify LD, although their effects have not been directly investigated. Rather than belabor a persistent point *ad nauseum*, we will simply assert at the outset that examination of these variables obviously requires the control of those already shown to be effective. This obstacle could prove difficult to surmount, particularly if the variable affects relative strength.

Intertrial interval.   When several prior lists are learned by massed practice (MP), distributed practice (DP) for the critical list reduces PI (Keppel, 1964). One possibility is that a lengthened intertrial interval allows PL to recover between OL trials, therefore increasing the number of extinction-recovery cycles. Recovery of PL during the retention interval would then be lessened and PI decreased. An alternative explanation is that when competing lists possess different intertrial intervals, LD is facilitated.

The evidence to date does not support either explanation conclusively. The factorial variation of intertrial interval for PL as well as OL would seem to allow a relatively clear test of the two positions. The extinction-recovery analysis would expect reduced PI whenever DP was used for OL, while according to the LD explanation PI should decrease whenever the lists differed in intertrial interval. The results have corresponded to LD expectations with one prior list (Houston & Reynolds, 1965) but to extinction-recovery with three prior lists (Houston, 1966b). The latter hypothesis also seems to predict reduced availability of PL as the OL intertrial interval lengthens; generally, this has not occurred (Keppel & Schwartz, 1965; Keppel, 1967). Finally, Forrester (1969), using an admittedly atypical situation, has presented some data not easily explicable by either position.

That differences in intertrial interval may facilitate LD has implications for possible interference stemming from language associations. Specifically, it has been suggested that if previously-acquired language habits are incompatible with laboratory learning, they should be unlearned but recover over time and interfere with the laboratory habit (Underwood & Postman, 1960). Among other things, this analysis predicts that the amount of language interference and therefore forgetting should change as the meaningfulness of the laboratory items is manipulated; this expectation has usually not been confirmed (e.g., Postman, 1962a; Underwood & Keppel, 1963).

The failure of language habits to produce interference in the anticipated manner may reflect extremely high differentiation between the two types of habits, due in part to intertrial interval (language, as opposed to laboratory learning would typically occur under DP conditions). In support, Underwood and Ekstrand (1966) demonstrated that laboratory PL produces little PI when it is learned by DP; further, this PI can be increased when some items from List 1 are repeated in List 2 to hinder differentiation (Underwood & Ekstrand, 1967).

Other discriminating cues may also facilitate differentiation between the two types of habits. Different learning contexts could be one such cue, although our previously-cited evidence suggests that it may be relatively ineffective. Another possibility is that differences in strength/frequency could be important (language habits would typically be much stronger). In fact it is remotely possible that intertrial interval improves language-laboratory differentiation because it affects the strength differential between the two habits. Underwood and Ekstrand (1966) also found that PL was not unlearned when it was acquired by DP. Thus, as Slamecka (1966) has also shown, language habits are apparently not unlearned in the laboratory.

Yet several considerations suggest that strength is not responsible for the effects of intertrial interval. First, variations in degree of PL, which would undoubtedly affect the strength differential, did not influence PI. Furthermore, when strong language associates are used for laboratory PL, PI is reduced compared to groups having unassociated pairs (Underwood & Ekstrand, 1968a). However, the language associates are less unlearned, therefore the strength differential would be smaller. If strength were the critical variable here, the language associates should have produced more PI.

To introduce an additional complexity, in contrast to the effect with unassociated pairs, more PL trials with language associates did increase PI. In other words, reducing the difference in situational frequency between PL and OL apparently diminished LD. The puzzle is that this reduction seems trivial when set against the large difference in background frequency between the two tasks which would still be present to serve as a discriminating cue. Why a few trials of situational frequency should overcome such a large difference in background frequency, especially after an extended retention interval, is unclear. At any rate, one wonders whether the effect of PL intertrial interval might also change if language associates were used for PL. In other words while intertrial interval may be the important discriminating cue between two associations learned in the laboratory, frequency may be more critical in distinguishing between language and laboratory habits.

Similarity. Gibson (1940) implicated similarity of items within a list as a central determinant of interitem generalization tendencies. With increased similarity, learning would suffer because of resultant difficulties in differentiation. In addition, recovery of generalization should produce a direct relationship between similarity and forgetting. More recently, losses in differentiation among response terms have also been indicted as possible causes of forgetting (Saltz & Youssef, 1964; Weiss, 1966). While stimulus similarity has often affected learning in the manner predicted by Gibson, forgetting has usually remained impervious to change (see Underwood, 1961). And when forgetting differences have been found, low similarity has sometimes produced the more profound loss (Joinson & Runquist, 1968).

In view of the importance attached to similarity in determining intralist differentiation, surprisingly little attention has been directed to the effect of interlist similarity on LD. One exception is Winograd's (1968b) study of interlist conceptual similarity, using free-recall learning of two lists followed by an LD test. Repeated categories were common to both lists in that some instances of the category were present in List 1 and others in List 2; nonrepeated categories were represented in only one of the lists.

Instances from repeated categories (which represented high similarity) had poorer LD; moreover, the size of the effect may have been underestimated. The nonrepeated items may have suffered from the mixed-list design, since repetition of some List-1 items in List 2 has been thought to affect LD for the remaining items in the list (Underwood & Freund, 1968a). Nor do these effects seem to reflect a difference in relative strength as a function of similarity. A subsequent experiment using MMFR showed that instances from repeated and nonrepeated categories had equivalent List-1 and List-2 availability.

Other suggestions of possible interlist similarity effects appear in the literature. In the A-B, A-B' paradigm (identical stimuli, similar responses) positive transfer is initially high but often declines over List-2 trials (Postman,

1964). The implicit use of the List-1 response as a mediator for the List-2 association is generally held responsible for the positive transfer (e.g., Barnes & Underwood, 1959). But it is quite likely that, as List-2 learning proceeds and the List-1 and List-2 associations become more comparable in strength, discrimination between the two associations would grow progressively more difficult. Therefore, the initial benefit gained from mediation would diminish. It follows, then, that LD should decline at somewhat higher levels of List-2 learning, compared to other transfer paradigms also having identical stimuli in the two lists. Furthermore, a marked increase in PI over time might be expected; there is some support for this supposition (Postman & Stark, 1964; Dallett, 1964).

Inferior LD during List−2 learning may also be responsible in part for the negative transfer usually observed in the A-B, A-C, and A-B, A-Br (same stimuli and responses in both lists, with items re-paired in List 2) paradigms, compared to a control group learning two unrelated lists. In other words, interlist stimulus similarity probably affects LD. Also, that negative transfer is particularly large in A-B, A-Br (Postman, 1964) could reflect especially great difficulty in determining list membership when both lists have the same items.

A further uninvestigated possibility is that intralist similarity could affect interlist differentiation. Thus a high-similarity list could produce a *gestalt*, rendering discrimination within the list difficult, but facilitating its differentiation from other lists. Such a process would in a sense be analogous to an S-R limitation effect observed in single lists of high similarity. For example, in a list containing several instances from each of several categories, responses are often misplaced to stimuli belonging to the same category as the correct stimulus, while misplacements to stimuli from other categories are rare (Underwood, Ekstrand, & Keppel, 1964). Thus, differentiation is poor within a category but very high between one category and another.

The predicted LD effect for high intralist similarity would be unlikely with identical stimuli or responses in the two lists; in such a case, changing the relationship of one item in the list to another could not facilitate between-list differentiation. Nor should the effect appear with two *completely* unrelated lists where LD would be maximal. It would seem most readily demonstrable at intermediate levels of interlist similarity; thus, it seems reasonable to expect the predicted effect of intralist similarity to interact with interlist similarity.

Relevant here is the unexpected failure of increased intralist stimulus similarity to reduce negative transfer in A-B, A-C (Underwood & Ekstrand, 1968b). Compared to a control, this paradigm should be favored at high similarity, where having accomplished stimulus differentiation during List-1 learning should be greatly advantageous. Possibily LD improved from low to high similarity more profoundly in the control group to offset this factor.

Number of interfering lists. Postman (1965) found that unlearning increased when IL involved learning four interpolated lists for 4 trials each, as opposed to one list for 16 trials. A corresponding result is evident in short-term memory (Lounsbury, 1970). Investigation of the effect of the number of PL or IL lists on LD would thus seem worthwhile, although negative results might well be anticipated. As noted earlier, while the number of interfering lists increases RI and PI, intrusions are unaffected (Underwood, 1945). In addition, Howe (1967) has shown that the amount of response competition remains constant as the number of lists increases, even though more unlearning should enlarge the strength differential.

Variations on this theme can be imagined. As Goggin (1968) has pointed out, a change in the number of IL lists actually involves two variables. A decrease in IL dominance relative to OL accompanies an increase in the number of interfering responses. Moreover, she has shown how the effects of these two factors may be separated. When more than one list constitutes IL, these lists may be alternated with one another during learning. By increasing the number of such alternations, transfer performance, and thus IL-dominance, can be decreased while holding the number of interfering lists constant. Goggin found that unlearning decreased directly with IL dominance. On the other hand, when IL is related to OL in an A-B, C-D manner dominance should not be influential because of the low degree of interlist stimulus similarity. As the number of interfering responses was increased in this situation, unlearning increased (Goggin, 1969). Both number of IL alternations as well as the number of interfering responses could affect LD.

Along the same lines, the number of different response terms in a list of constant length can be manipulated if in some cases the same response is used for more than one pair. When two lists differ in the total number of response terms used, a possible differentiating cue is present. Yet again indirect evidence does not suggest that this variable would affect LD to any major extent. Underwood, Freund, and Jurca (1969) found that, while List-1 unlearning generally increased with fewer List−2 responses, PI was unaffected by any difference between the two lists in the number of responses.

Backward associations. Acquisition of an association between two items A and B also produces a backward association B-A, as shown by S's capability of emitting the corresponding stimulus term when a response term is presented (Ekstrand, 1966). If, as Asch and Ebenholtz (1962) have asserted, backward and forward associations are simply two manifestations of the same underlying association, then equal amounts of unlearning should occur for both associations. In fact, some transfer paradigms show unlearning of one of these associations but not the other (e.g., Johnston, 1969). It follows that in such situations the relative-strength differential should differ in the two directions. Thus the rather novel prediction is generated that the degree of LD between two lists should depend on which association is tested. In practice, this prediction might be rather difficult to evaluate. It is possible that S may implicitly "turn around" associations to the direction most beneficial to discrimination. To counteract this tendency, a rapid presentation rate would be required for the LD test, which could introduce methodological problems.

Miscellaneous. Conceivably, any difference between two competing tasks, either in the nature of the tasks themselves or in the method of attack adopted by S, could serve as a discriminating attribute. For example, LD could improve if S adopts different coding devices (Zavortink & Keppel, 1968). Other possibilities suggest themselves. A change in the requirements of the task (e.g., Shuell & Keppel, 1967), or in the task itself (Goggin, 1967), in S's arousal level (Walker & Tarte, 1963), in presentation rate (Keppel & Mallory, 1969), and in the percentage of trials on which items are actually presented (Keppel, Zavortink, & Schiff, 1967) could all function as cues. Also, the set that S adopts during IL, e.g., to unlearn or to mediate (Dallett & D'Andrea, 1965), could affect the temporal separation of tasks by modifying the implicit occurrence of OL during IL. This latter argument is, of course, similar to that presented for relearning.

Finally, Ekstrand (1967) has shown that spending a retention interval asleep rather than awake reduces forgetting of OL in single-list as well as in RI and PI groups; in addition, it seemingly increases absolute recovery. These strength changes aside, intuition suggests that sleeping over a constant retention interval might diminish LD. Ekstrand's data give scant support to this supposition, although the single-list group improved slightly more with sleep than did the PI group, suggesting an increase in PI. It is also possible that sleep during an intertask interval would lessen any benefits accruing to LD from task separation. Distinctive events during such an interval, which might underly the facilitation produced by separation (Underwood, 1969), could be less tangible during sleep. However, in Prospero's words, "We are such stuff as dreams are made of. . . ." Perhaps dream occurrences could serve as discriminating cues.

A FINAL EVALUATION

We will begin this section by considering the utility of Winograd's (1968a) LD measure. In retrospect it seems that, while this technique is undoubtedly a useful tool, its limitations must be recognized. Clearly its apparent sensitivity to strength differences across conditions is a major problem. However it is difficult to imagine a measure which would not be so affected, given that strength factors are established before a retention test. The central problem, then, is to eliminate any such strength differences while avoiding a variation in total input frequency. Although there are few data on this point, possibily cycles of unlearning followed by relearning could meet this requirement. A variable could then be studied after such cycles to at least demonstrate its capability of affecting LD.

The next question involves the place of LD in interference theory. At present, it seems a useful construct in that it is modified by at least two variables, modality change and frequency, over and above their effects on other factors. The limited importance assigned to recall factors such as LD has, as we noted earlier, stemmed largely from the comparable interference observed in MMFR and specific recall (Postman, 1962b; Houston, 1966a). In these studies, wide differences between OL and IL strength at recall could have rendered LD impotent. Under different circumstances, with a smaller strength differential present, its influence might be more profound and inteference from recall factors be more impressive.

Given its usefulness, we should then consider the relation of LD to other interference factors. We have thus far avoided a discussion of the historically emphasized relationship between LD and specific response competition (Underwood, 1945). To the present writer, the latter seems the most dispensable of all the presumed factors. Its hypothesized properties can quite reasonably be incorporated between LD and GRC. In this age of ecology, perhaps a start can be made at clearing up the factor pollution by, ironically, dismissing the first factor to be introduced.

We have emphasized the supposed dependency of LD on strength factors. In contrast, others (Postman, Keppel, & Stark, 1965; Slamecka, 1966) have regarded differentiation during the transfer task as an antecedent determinant of unlearning. Neither standpoint seems completely vindicated at this stage. Our position does not account for changes in unlearning produced by likely discriminating cues, e.g., intertrial interval, while the alternative notion is weakened by the general failure of such cues to affect transfer performance. Also, there are indications that, in the case of PIL at least, LD during List-2 learning may vary directly rather than inversely with unlearning. It is noteworthy, however, that the two analyses are not necessarily incompatible. Conceivably, LD could operate during both transfer and retention and therefore, in a sense, determine itself. The question would then arise whether the two forms of LD possessed similar properties.

Perhaps we may end this paper on a personal note. We have lived rather intensively with LD for several years. Yet from a utilitarian angle this effort has been a complete waste of time. I am still unable to remember where I parked my car!

REFERENCES

Abra, J. C. Time changes in the strength of forward and backward associations. *Journal of Verbal Learning and Verbal Behavior*, 1967, 6, 640–645.

Abra, J. C. Time changes in the strength of extinguished context and specific associations. *Journal of Experimental Psychology*, 1968, 77, 684–686.

Abra, J. C. List-1 unlearning and recovery as a function of the point of interpolated learning. *Journal of Verbal Learning and Verbal Behavior*, 1969, 8, 494–500.

Abra, J. C. List differentiation and the point of interpolation in free-recall learning. *Journal of Verbal Learning and Verbal Behavior*, 1970, 9.

Abra, J. C., & Belton, P. S. Unlearning in free learning as a function of context change and retention interval. *Psychological Reports*, 1969, 24, 943—946.

Abra, J. C., & Kolb, B. The effect of changed List-2 learning conditions on List-1 unlearning. Paper presented at the meeting of the Canadian Psychological Association, Winnipeg, Man., May, 1970.

Abra, J. C., & Roberts, D. Unlearning and relearning. *Journal of Experimental Psychology*, 1969, 81, 334—339.

Adams, S. Temporal changes in the strength of competing verbal associations. Unpublished doctoral dissertation, University of California, Berkeley, 1962.

Alin, L. H. Proactive inhibition as a function of the time interval between the learning of the two tasks and the number of prior lists. *Journal of Verbal Learning and Verbal Behavior*, 1968, 7, 1024—1029.

Archer, E. J., & Underwood, B. J. Retroactive inhibition of verbal associations as a multiple function of temporal point of interpolation and degree of interpolated learning. *Journal of Experimental Psychology*, 1951, 42, 283—290.

Asch, S. E., & Ebenholtz, S. M. The principle of associative symmetry. *Proceedings of the American Philosophical Society*, 1962, 106, 135—163.

Bahrick, H. P. Retention curves: facts or artifacts? *Psychological Bulletin*, 1964, 61, 188—194.

Barnes, J. M., & Underwood, B. J. "Fate" of first-list associations in transfer theory. *Journal of Experimental Psychology*, 1959, 58, 97—105.

Bilodeau, I. McD., & Schlosberg, H. Similarity in stimulating conditions as a variable in retroactive inhibition. *Journal of Experimental Psychology*, 1951, 41, 199—204.

Birnbaum, I. M. Long-term retention of first-list associations in the A-B, A-C paradigm. *Journal of Verbal Learning and Verbal Behavior*, 1965, 4, 515—520.

Briggs, G. E. Retroactive inhibition as a function of degree of original and interpolated learning. *Journal of Experimental Psychology*, 1957, 53, 60—67.

Brown, S. C., & Battig, W. F. Supplementary report: second-list paired-associate facilitation produced by addition of previously learned first-list pairs. *Journal of Verbal Learning and Verbal Behavior*, 1966, 5, 320—321.

Costello, C. G., Belton, G. P., Abra, J. C., & Dunn, B. E. The amnesic and therapeutic effects of bilateral and unilateral ECT. *British Journal of Psychiatry*, 1970, 116, 69—78.

Dallett, K. M. Proactive and retroactive inhibition in the A-B, A-B' paradigm. *Journal of Experimental Psychology*, 1964, 68, 190—200.

Dallett, K. M., & D'Andrea, L. Mediation instructions versus unlearning instructions in the A-B, A-C paradigm. *Journal of Experimental Psychology*, 1965, 69, 460—466.

Dallett, K. M., & Wilcox, S. G. Contextual stimuli and proactive inhibition. *Journal of Experimental Psychology*, 1968, 78, 475—480.

Ekstrand, B. R. Backward associations. *Psychological Bulletin*, 1966, 65, 50—64.

Ekstrand, B. R. Effect of sleep on memory. *Journal of Experimental Psychology*, 1967, 75, 64–72.

Ekstrand, B. R., Wallace, W. P., & Underwood, B. J. A frequency theory of verbal-discrimination learning. *Psychological Review*, 1966, 73, 566–578.

Forrester, W. E. Distributed practice and retroactive inhibition in a minimal paired-associates task. *Journal of Verbal Learning and Verbal Behavior*, 1969, 8, 713–718.

Fozard, J. L., & Yntema, D. B. The effect of repetition on the apparent recency of pictures. Paper presented at the meeting of the Eastern Psychological Association, New York City, 1966. Cited by E. Winograd, List differentiation as a function of frequency and retention interval. *Journal of Experimental Psychology*, 1968, 76 (2, Pt. 2).

Gibson, E. J. A systematic application of the concepts of generalization and differentiation to verbal learning. *Psychological Review*, 1940, 47, 196–229.

Goggin, J. First-list recall as a function of second-list learning method. *Journal of Verbal Learning and Verbal Behavior*, 1967, 6, 423–427.

Goggin, J. Retroactive inhibition with different patterns of interpolated lists. *Journal of Experimental Psychology*, 1968, 76, 102–108.

Goggin, J. Retroactive interference with multiple interpolated lists. *Journal of Experimental Psychology*, 1969, 80, 483–488.

Greenspoon, J., & Ranyard, R. Stimulus conditions and retroactive inhibition. *Journal of Experimental Psychology*, 1957, 53, 55–59.

Hintzman, D. L., & Waters, R. M. Recency and frequency as factors in list discrimination. *Journal of Verbal Learning and Verbal Behavior*, 1970, 9, 218–221.

Houston, J. P. First-list retention and time and method of recall. *Journal of Experimental Psychology*, 1966, 71, 839–843. (a)

Houston, J. P. List differentiation and distributed practice. *Journal of Experimental Psychology*, 1966, 72, 477–478. (b)

Houston, J. P. Retroactive inhibition and point of interpolation. *Journal of Verbal Learning and Verbal Behavior*, 1967, 6, 84–88.

Houston, J. P. Proactive inhibition and undetected retention interval rehearsal. *Journal of Experimental Psychology*, 1969, 82, 511–514.

Houston, J. P., & Reynolds, J. H. First-list retention as a function of list differentiation and second-list massed and distributed practice. *Journal of Experimental Psychology*, 1965, 69, 387–392.

Howe, T. S. Unlearning and competition in List-1 recall. *Journal of Experimental Psychology*, 1967, 75, 559–565.

Howe, T. S. Effects of delayed interference on List-1 recall. *Journal of Experimental Psychology*, 1969, 80, 120–124.

Inoue, K. A study on interaction among sense modalities in memory. *Journal of Child Development*, 1968, 4, 28–37.

Johnston, W. A. The directionality of transfer and unlearning. *Journal of Verbal Learning and Verbal Behavior*, 1969, 8, 581–590.

Joinson, P. A., & Runquist, W. N. Effects of intralist stimulus similarity and degree of learning on forgetting. *Journal of Verbal Learning and Verbal Behavior*, 1968, 7, 554–559.

Keppel, G. Facilitation in short- and long-term retention of paired-associates following distributed practice in learning. *Journal of Verbal Learning and Verbal Behavior*, 1964, 3, 91–111.

Keppel, G. A reconsideration of the extinction-recovery theory. *Journal of Verbal Learning and Verbal Behavior*, 1967, 6, 476–486.

Keppel, G. Retroactive and proactive inhibition. In T. R. Dixon & D. L. Horton (eds.), *Verbal behavior and general behavior theory*. Englewood Cliffs, N. J.: Prentice-Hall, 1968.

Keppel, G., & Mallory, W. A. Presentation rate and instructions to guess in free recall. *Journal of Experimental Psychology*, 1969, 79, 269–275.

Keppel, G., & Rauch, D. S. Unlearning as a function of second-list error instructions. *Journal of Verbal Learning and Verbal Behavior*, 1966, 5, 50–58.

Keppel, G., & Schwartz, B. Response availability and conditions of interpolated practice. *Journal of Verbal Learning and Verbal Behavior*, 1965, 4, 489–493.

Keppel, G., Zavortink, B., & Schiff, B. B. Unlearning in the A-B, A-C paradigm as a function of percentage occurrence of response members. *Journal of Experimental Psychology*, 1967, 74, 172–177.

Kimble, G. A. *Hilgard & Marquis' conditioning and learning* (rev. ed.). New York: Appleton-Century-Crofts, Inc., 1961.

Koppenaal, R. J. Time changes in the strengths of A-B, A-C lists; spontaneous recovery? *Journal of Verbal Learning and Verbal Behavior*, 1963, 2, 310–319.

Lounsbury, J. W. Short-term retention of individual items. Unpublished M.A. thesis, University of Calgary, 1970.

Marx, M. H. Intervening variable or hypothetical construct? *Psychological Review*, 1951, 58, 235–247.

McCrystal, T. J. List differentiation as a function of time and test order. *Journal of Experimental Psychology*, 1970, 83, 220–223.

McGeoch, J. A. Forgetting and the law of disuse. *Psychological Review*, 1932, 39, 352–370.

McGovern, J. B. Extinction of associations in four transfer paradigms. *Psychological Monographs*, 1964, 78 (16, Whole No. 593).

Melton, A. W. Comments on Professor Postman's paper. In C. N. Cofer (ed.), *Verbal Learning and Verbal Behavior*. New York: McGraw-Hill, 1961.

Melton, A. W., & Irwin, J. McQ. The influence of degree of interpolated learning upon retroactive inhibition and the overt transfer of specific responses. *American Journal of Psychology*, 1940, 53, 173–203.

Newton, J. M., & Wickens, D. D. Retroactive inhibition as a function of the temporal position of interpolated learning. *Journal of Experimental Psychology*, 1956, 51, 149–154.

Paul, C., & Silverstein, A. Relation of experimentally produced interlist intrusions to unlearning and retroactive inhibition. *Journal of Experimental Psychology*, 1968, 76, 480–485.

Postman, L. The present status of interference theory. In C. N. Cofer (ed.), *Verbal Learning and Verbal Behavior*. New York: McGraw-Hill, 1961.

Postman, L. The effects of language habits on the acquisition and retention of verbal associations. *Journal of Experimental Psychology*, 1962, 64, 7–19. (a)

Postman, L. Retention of first-list associations as a function of the conditions of transfer. *Journal of Experimental Psychology*, 1962, 64, 380–387. (b)

Postman, L. Studies of learning to learn. II. Changes in transfer as a function of practice. *Journal of Verbal Learning and Verbal Behavior*, 1964, 3, 437–447.

Postman, L. Unlearning under conditions of successive interpolation. *Journal of Experimental Psychology*, 1965, 70, 237–245.

Postman, L., Keppel, G., & Stark, K. Unlearning as a function of the relationship between successive response classes. *Journal of Experimental Psychology*, 1965, 69, 111–118.

Postman, L., & Stark, K. Proactive inhibition as a function of the conditions of transfer. *Journal of Verbal Learning and Verbal Behavior*, 1964, 3, 249–259.

Postman, L., Stark, K., & Fraser, J. Temporal changes in interference. *Journal of Verbal Learning and Verbal Behavior*, 1968, 7, 672–694.

Postman, L., Stark, K., & Henschel, D. Conditions of recovery after unlearning. *Journal of Experimental Psychology*, 1969, 82, (1, Pt. 2).

Rand, G., & Wapner, S. Postural status as a factor in memory. *Journal of Verbal Learning and Verbal Behavior*, 1967, 6, 268–271.

Raskin, D. C., Boice, C., Rubel, E. W., & Clark, D. Transfer tests of the frequency theory of verbal-discrimination learning. *Journal of Experimental Psychology*, 1968, 76, 521–529.

Saltz, E., & Youseff, Z. I. Role of response differentiation in forgetting. *Journal of Experimental Psychology*, 1964, 68, 307–311.

Shuell, T. J., & Keppel, G. Retroactive inhibition as a function of learning method. *Journal of Experimental Psychology*, 1967, 75, 457–463.

Silverstein, A. Unlearning, spontaneous recovery and the partial-reinforcement effect in paired-associate learning. *Journal of Experimental Psychology*, 1967, 73, 15–21.

Slamecka, N. J. Differentiation versus unlearning of verbal associations. *Journal of Experimental Psychology*, 1966, 71, 822–828.

Strand, B. Z. Change of context and retroactive inhibition. *Journal of Verbal Learning and Verbal Behavior*, 1970, 9, 202–206.

Thorndike, E. L., & Lorge, I. *The teacher's word book of 30,000 words.* New York: Teachers College, Columbia University, 1944.

Thune, L. E., & Underwood, B. J. Retroactive inhibition as a function of degree of interpolated learning. *Journal of Experimental Psychology*, 1943, 32, 185–200.

Underwood, B. J. The effect of successive interpolations on retroactive and proactive inhibition. *Psychological Monographs*, 1945, 59 (3, Whole No. 273).

Underwood, B. J. Proactive inhibition as a function of time and degree of prior learning. *Journal of Experimental Psychology*, 1949, 39, 24–34.

Underwood, B. J. An evaluation of the Gibson theory of verbal learning. In C. N. Cofer (ed.), *Verbal Learning and Verbal Behavior*. New York: McGraw-Hill, 1961.

Underwood, B. J. The representativeness of rote verbal learning. In A. W. Melton (ed.), *Categories of human learning*. New York: Academic Press, 1964. Pp. 47–78.

Underwood, B. J. Attributes of memory. *Psychological Review*, 1969, 76, 559–573.

Underwood, B. J., & Ekstrand, B. R. An analysis of some shortcomings in the interference theory of forgetting. *Psychological Review*, 1966, 73, 540–549.

Underwood, B. J., & Ekstrand, B. R. Studies of distributed practice: XXIV. Differentiation and proactive inhibition. *Journal of Experimental Psychology*, 1967, 74, 574–580.

Underwood, B. J., & Ekstrand, B. R. Linguistic associations and retention. *Journal of Verbal Learning and Verbal Behavior*, 1968, 7, 162–171. (a)

Underwood, B. J., & Ekstrand, B. R. Differentiation among stimuli as a factor in transfer performance. *Journal of Verbal Learning and Verbal Behavior*, 1968, 7, 172–175. (b)

Underwood, B. J., Ekstrand, B. R., & Keppel, G. An analysis of intralist similarity in verbal learning, with experiments on conceptual similarity. *Journal of Verbal Learning and Verbal Behavior*, 1965, 4, 447–462.

Underwood, B. J., & Freund, J. S. Effect of temporal separation of two tasks on proactive inhibition. *Journal of Experimental Psychology*, 1968, 78, 50–54. (a)

Underwood, B. J., & Freund, J. S. Two tests of a theory of verbal-discrimination learning. *Canadian Journal of Psychology*, 1968, 22, 96–104. (b)

Underwood, B. J., & Freund, J. S. Relative frequency judgments and verbal discrimination learning. *Journal of Experimental Psychology*, 1970, 83, 279–285. (a)

Underwood, B. J., & Freund, J. S. Retention of a verbal discrimination. *Journal of Experimental Psychology*, 1970, 84, 1–14. (b)

Underwood, B. J., & Freund, J. S. Testing effects in the recognition of words. *Journal of Verbal Learning and Verbal Behavior*, 1970, 9, 117–125. (c)

Underwood, B. J., Freund, J. S., & Jurca, N. H. The influence of number of response terms on paired-associate learning, transfer, and proactive inhibition. *Journal of Verbal Learning and Verbal Behavior*, 1969, 8, 369–377.

Underwood, B. J., & Keppel, G. Retention as a function of degree of learning and letter sequence interference. *Psychological Monographs*, 1963, 77, No. 4 (Whole No. 567).

Underwood, B. J., & Postman, L. Extraexperimental sources of interference in forgetting. *Psychological Review*, 1960, 67, 73–95.

Walker, E. L., & Tarte, R. D. Memory storage as a function of arousal and time with homogeneous and heterogeneous lists. *Journal of Verbal Learning and Verbal Behavior*, 1963, 2, 113–119.

Weiss, E. Role of response availability in forgetting: a re-appraisal. *Psychonomic Science*, 1966, 5, 379–380.

Winograd, E. List differentiation as a function of frequency and retention interval. *Journal of Experimental Psychology*, 1968, 76 (2, Pt. 2). (a)

Winograd, E. List differentiation, recall, and category similarity. *Journal of Experimental Psychology*, 1968, 78, 510–515. (b)

Winograd, E. Retention of list differentiation and word frequency. *Journal of Verbal Learning and Verbal Behavior*, 1968, 7, 859–863. (c)

Zavortink, B., & Keppel, G. Retroactive inhibition in free-recall learning with alphabetical cues. *Journal of Experimental Psychology*, 1968, 78, 617–624.

3 | To Sleep, Perchance to Dream (About Why We Forget)

BRUCE R. EKSTRAND
University of Colorado, Boulder

One of the most challenging tasks confronting the modern verbal-learning theorist is to understand the process of forgetting. For the past few years we have been studying the effects of sleep during the retention interval on long-term memory in the hope that out of this work would emerge a synthesis or rapproachment of three major theories of memory: interference, decay or disuse, and consolidation. Unfortunately, I cannot as yet present such a synthesis. However, I would like to review our efforts and make some suggestions as to what such a synthesis might look like.

The basic phenomenon is known as forgetting and is operationally defined by demonstrating a decrease in recall performance as a function of the length of the retention interval. Thus, the basic independent variable is time and the basic dependent variable is performance on some kind of recall test. As we all know, recall is a monotonically decreasing function of the length of the retention interval. In other words, psychologists have demonstrated a lawful relationship between time and forgetting. Alas, establishment of a relationship does not explain why the relationship obtains.

Typically, when experimental procedures are employed involving independent and dependent variables, carefully controlled and measured by an experimenter, we conclude that observed changes in the dependent variable are *caused* by the independent variable. Such a conclusion has led to what is known as the *decay* or *disuse* theory of forgetting, which stipulates that forgetting is a manifestation or result of disuse which "leads to" decay. The important point was that use of the memory (e.g., rehearsal) was the only thing that could reduce forgetting (given a constant degree of learning) and that disuse of the memory (and not of other memories) was the source of forgetting. Thus, forgetting was passively caused by an event which did not occur during the retention interval (use of the memory) and not actively caused by an event which did occur.

It is no wonder that such a conception of forgetting was not acceptable to

Preparation of this paper was faciliated by Grant Number MH15655 from the National Institute of Mental Health; the original experiments presented in the paper were supported by this grant. The paper was written at the Institute for the Study of Intellectual Behavior which is supported by the Graduate School of the University of Colorado. I wish to thank William F. Battig for his helpful comments on the manuscript.

most if not all scientists (since it is not clear that anybody ever really believed it). And it is no wonder that the major alternative to a decay theory postulated that forgetting was actively caused by events taking place during the retention interval. Of course, this alternative is the interference theory of forgetting. The interference theory specifies that forgetting is caused by interference from other learning which the subject has accomplished. In the early part of this century, interference theorists specified that this new learning, which could produce forgetting, took place during the retention interval and acted retroactively on the original learning (OL) in an interfering manner, producing what is known as retroactive inhibition (RI). Thus, forgetting was identified as merely an instance of RI and the interpolated learning (IL) between OL and recall was identified as the cause of this forgetting.

It then became obvious from an interference viewpoint that forgetting should be preventable by the elimination of IL. Since we are probably learning something just about every waking moment, it seemed obvious that the simplest way to prevent IL was to eliminate wakefulness during the retention interval. And, the simplest way to eliminate wakefulness was to have the subjects sleep. Thus it was, in 1924, that Jenkins and Dallenbach published their now classic study of the effects of sleep during the retention interval on memory. Since sleep would prevent, or at least drastically reduce IL, an interference theory would have to predict that sleep would facilitate memory compared to a condition where the retention interval was filled with wakefulness. Decay theory would have to predict no effect of sleep since time continued to pass at the same rate during sleep as during wakefulness or since memories would not be used during sleep, i.e., disuse would be equally likely in sleep and wakefulness. The results of the experiment dealt a severe blow to this version of decay theory, when it was clearly shown that recall after intervals of sleep was substantially superior to recall after intervals of wakefulness.

The final death blow to mystical decay or disuse theory was dealt by our common academic grandfather, J. A. McGeoch, in 1932, when he pointed out that processes which are correlated with time are nevertheless not caused by time. The classic analogy was that iron rusted with time but that rusting was caused by oxidation and not by time. The reasoning of McGeoch and the unequivocal data of Jenkins and Dallenbach resulted in the demise of decay theory; subsequently, interference theory has remained as essentially the only major theoretical analysis of the forgetting process. If ever an experiment has been treated as a crucial experiment, it was the sleep experiment. It was replicated in 1932 by van Ormer and is now perhaps the one single experiment most likely to be cited in an introductory textbook. The validity of the experiment and its interpretation were accepted without question, including the naive form of decay theory which the experiment was said to have proven wrong. And interference theory marched onward to supremacy.

It was not until 1957 that the interpretation was questioned. This was done by our mentor, B. J. Underwood, in his classic paper "Interference and Forgetting." In the meantime, proactive inhibition (PI) coming from learning

(PL) taking place prior to OL had been discovered, and interference theory was immediately modified to include both RI and PI. What Underwood did was to suggest that since the Jenkins and Dallenbach experiment had involved many repeated measurements on only two subjects (each learned and recalled about 50 lists), there must have been substantial PI operating in their experiment. It was then possible to suggest that sleep facilitated recall by reducing PI rather than RI as was originally proposed. Nevertheless, forgetting was still attributed to interfering learning, and decay theory was still confined to the grave.

In 1960, Underwood and Postman published their version of an interference theory, attempting to explain the forgetting of a single list learned in the laboratory by naive subjects. By 1964 or so it was obvious that something was wrong with this theory. The major problem was that the theory predicted that the meaningfulness of the materials being learned should influence the amount of forgetting, and this just was not borne out by numerous experiments designed to test the theory, including my own master's thesis (Ekstrand & Underwood, 1965). Later, Underwood and I were to publish a paper (1966) lamenting the fact that the rate of forgetting appeared to be constant despite substantial differences in tasks and materials. We said, "Until we are able to identify the source or sources of interference producing the constant forgetting in the naive S the decay theorist has some grounds for glee." Well, he wasn't too gleeful in his grave, but this certainly aroused him, at least the one lurking in my own version of the grave. After all, this was virtually the first time I had ever heard the word decay inside Kresge Hall. Oh, there were some graffiti in the men's room, "Decay theory is alive and well in England," but I personally never believed graffiti.

In any case, these events led me to the sleep experiments, since they alone seemed to be the gravestone of decay theory and the cornerstone of interference theory. Three things about the sleep experiments seemed important to me when I examined the literature. The first had already been detected by Underwood (1957) and has been mentioned. The sleep experiments involved enormous amounts of formal PL and so the facilitation at recall could have been due to reduced PI after sleep. This left open the possibility that with naïve subjects sleep might not improve memory. Second, it seemed obvious to me that naïve decay theory was untenable, but that if one could tie the decay process to some physiological process, a decay theory could become respectable. Thus, we could conceive of some process, comparable to oxidation of iron, which could be a respectable cause of forgetting. Obviously, we do not know what this process is, and we probably won't until the neural basis of learning itself is determined. However, it did not seem unreasonable to me to postulate that such a process existed independently of whether or not new learning was occurring in the organism. Furthermore, it seemed reasonable to suggest that the rate parameter of this process might be positively correlated with body metabolism. Then, I became aware of the data from sleep physiology showing that body metabolism is lower during sleep than wakefulness and I thought, "Decay theory is alive (but not well) in the mind of a student of Benton J. Underwood." The sleep experiments were not the crucial experiments everyone thought, unless you believed in the mystical variety of decay caused by time.

The third thing I noticed was the experiment by Heine (1914) discussed by Woodworth and Schlosberg (1954). Heine was apparently influenced by the consolidation theory of retroaction first proposed by Müller and Pilzecker (1900). She felt that sleep, when compared to wakefulness, might facilitate consolidation, just as Müller and Pilzecker had demonstrated better memory after rest than after mental activity. She had subjects learn lists of nonsense syllables either immediately before going to bed or 2–3 hours before bedtime with relearning taking place 24 hours later. Mean savings were 45 percent in the first group and only 35 percent in the second group. Thus, memory was better when sleep came immediately after learning than when it came 2–3 hours after learning. This finding seems incompatible with an interference theory since both groups were awake and asleep for the same amount of time during the 24-hour retention interval, i.e., the amount of IL and thus RI should have been equal for the two conditions and memory should have been equal. But the facts were in accord with a consolidation theory. Somehow, the Heine data were ignored, and consolidation theory went the way of decay theory. But Carl Duncan, one of our Festschrift cochairmen, saw to it that this did not last past 1949 when he made the first controlled demonstration of retrograde amnesia produced by electroconvulsive shock. Since this discovery, consolidation theory has become one of the major analyses of the process of memory storage. James L. McGaugh and his associates have championed this theory and presented a formidable case that some such process must be involved in memory storage.

It now seemed to me that there were at least three possible reasons why sleep might facilitate memory: (1) sleep reduced RI or PI or both—the interference interpretation; (2) sleep involved a slowing in the rate of the catabolic process which caused forgetting—the decay theory interpretation; and (3) sleep facilitated the consolidation of recently acquired memories. It also seemed terribly important to find out which of these interpretations was correct, for the answer might have some important implications for a general theory of memory. I have been looking for the answer ever since.

I tackled the first problem in my dissertation under Underwood (Ekstrand, 1966, 1967). First, we asked how sleep might improve memory by reducing PI instead of or in addition to reducing RI. The answer seemed obvious. If sleep reduced the rate of spontaneous recovery of habits extinguished during OL, PI would be reduced. Unfortunately, my results indicated the exact opposite—sleep appeared to increase spontaneous recovery or, more accurately, it appeared to produce spontaneous recovery when no one else could find it. The second finding of my dissertation was that sleep facilitated recall of naive subjects who had learned only one list in the laboratory. These two observations immediately caused us to dismiss PL and reduce PI as an explanation for what I now call *the* *sleep effect*—better recall if the retention interval is filled with sleep than if filled with wakefulness. From an interference view then, the sleep effect must be due to reduced RI. This paralleled the developments taking place in interference theory where a full circle was happening. Originally RI was seen as the basis of forgetting, then PI took over as a result of Underwood's 1957 paper, and now once again we were looking back to RI to solve our problems (Keppel, 1968).

THE REVOLUTION IN SLEEP RESEARCH

All this time, while we were anticipating the turning of Stowe memory drums, the sleep physiologists were anticipating the movements of pen motors on electroencephalographs (EEG). A true revolution had taken place in the world of sleep physiology research, dating back to 1953. At that time, Aserinsky and Kleitman published an astounding paper suggesting that we could tell when a subject was dreaming by observing his eye movements using a monitoring technique known as the electrooculogram (EOG) and by observing his EEG. They discovered that periodically throughout the night subjects showed episodes of rapid eye movements (REM) in conjunction with what has become known as Stage I sleep defined in terms of the EEG. And, most importantly, dreaming appears highly correlated with REM. Subsequent research (see Hartman, 1967, 1970 for excellent summaries of this research) in the general area of sleep and dreaming has proceeded at an unbelievable pace and has produced massive amounts of new information that is difficult to keep up with. Here I will summarize only the most basic facts that have been discovered.

There are two basic kinds of sleep distinguished by the presence or absence of REMs and known accordingly as REM sleep and non-REM sleep (NREM). There are numerous other names for the two basic types but they need not concern us. Physiologically, the two types of sleep seem quite different. REM sleep does not look like sleep at all, for almost all physiological indices take on values during REM sleep that are close to wakefulness, yet the subject is behaviorally most certainly asleep. In addition to the presence of REMs, there is one other interesting feature of REM sleep, namely the loss of muscle tone, particularly in the neck region, as measured by the electromyogram (EMG). NREM sleep is usually divided into four major stages, I, II, III, and IV, defined solely by EEG characteristics and the absence of REM. The progression from I through IV is one of increasing depth of sleep as defined either physiologically or psychologically. Physiological indices generally show a progressive decline from waking levels as the subject passes from wakefulness to Stage I, then II, III, and finally IV. Stages III and IV are sometimes referred to as deep sleep and some investigators feel that they represent times of maximal physiological restoration of the body. Physiologically indexed, Stage IV and Stage REM seem truly qualitatively different and so REM sleep has been heralded as a third state of consciousness.

A normal night's sleep consists of an amazingly constant sleep cycle, approximately 90–100 minutes in length repeated 4–6 times throughout the night. The subject passes from wakefulness into Stage I and then progresses on down through Stages II and III to Stage IV. This is followed after some time by a rapid ascent back to Stage I, but this episode of Stage I is accompanied by REM and decreased EMG levels, i.e., the subject has entered REM sleep. Following the REM period, the cycle repeats itself, again plunging the subject down to Stage IV and then back up again to REM.

Across a normal night of sleep, the cycle will occur 4–6 times. There is one very important trend throughout the night, however. In each succeeding cycle the amount of time spent in the REM portion of the cycle increases and the amount of time spent in the Stage-IV portion decreases. Thus, while a normal night of sleep in the adult human consists of about 17 percent Stage-IV sleep and 22 percent REM sleep (Agnew, Webb, & Williams, 1966), most of the Stage IV sleep takes place in the first half of the night and most of the REM sleep takes place in the second half. This particularly true on the first night a subject sleeps in the laboratory. There is a first night effect (Agnew, et al., 1966) which is the label for the finding that subjects very often miss the first REM period on their first night in the laboratory for unknown reasons, but presumably related to the subjects' anxiousness about the recording procedures involving electrodes, etc.

When we examined the modern research literature on sleep and dreaming, we were struck by the physiological differences between REM and NREM sleep. An obvious hypothesis was that the rate of forgetting during sleep might be different in the two types of sleep. Some sleep researchers were, already interested in memory and there was one experiment in particular that intrigued us. Portnoff, Baekeland, Goodenough, Karacan, and Shapiro (1966) presented evidence which they interpreted as showing that NREM sleep was capable of disrupting memory. Their subjects were awakened periodically throughout the night and shown a single word on a screen. The subjects had to awaken and perceive the word, saying it out loud, after which the word was removed. On half the awakenings, the subjects were allowed to return to sleep immediately after word perception. On the other half, the subjects were kept awake for a 5-minute period working on a two-hand coordination task which presumably prevented rehearsal. After the 5-minute waking period, the subjects were then allowed to return to sleep. The subjects did not know that their memory for the words seen during the night was to be tested in the morning. Instead they thought that they were to be awakened from different sleep stages in order to see if performance on perceptual and motor tasks would be influenced. Morning recall tests (and recognition) revealed that memory was superior for words followed by the 5-minute waking period than for words followed by "immediate" return to sleep. There also was a significant correlation between time to sleep onset after word perception and memory: the quicker the sleep onset, the poorer the memory. Now it is NREM sleep that always occurs first in normal sleep onset, and never REM sleep. Thus, Portnoff et al. (1966) interpreted their results as follows. Memory storage involves a period of consolidation which if disrupted will lead to deficient memory. NREM sleep coming shortly after a learning experience is capable of disrupting this consolidation process, but if a 5-minute period of wakefulness is interpolated between learning and sleep, the memory will have consolidated sufficiently during wakefulness so as to be less susceptible to disruption by the ensuing NREM sleep.

By now we were very interested in the hypothesis that memory during sleep was a function of the stage of sleep. We reasoned that if the Portnoff et al. interpretation was correct, namely that NREM sleep disrupts memory, and that if the overall effect of sleep versus wakefulness during the retention interval favored sleep, then there must be a facilitating factor during sleep which was counteracting the memory inhibition produced by NREM sleep. It seemed obvious that REM sleep was the candidate for the facilitating factor. We thus came to the hypothesis that the rate of forgetting during sleep of materials learned just before sleep onset was a function of the amount of time the subject spent in REM and NREM sleep. We guessed that REM sleep was capable of facilitating memory and NREM was capable of disrupting it.

We were extraordinarily excited by this hypothesis, for if we could prove that it was true, it would mean grave difficulties for an interference theory and probably for a decay theory. Since both REM and NREM sleep are in fact sleep, the subjects should not be accomplishing IL during either stage and the amount of RI should be equivalent. In other words, an interference theory of the sleep effect would have difficulty explaining differential rates of forgetting in the two stages using an RI-based interpretation. It might be possible with a PI-based interpretation by postulating that the rate of spontaneous recovery of habits extinguished by OL was faster in NREM than REM sleep, but by now we were not impressed with extraexperimental PL as a source of PI.

With respect to a decay theory, there is evidence to indicate that body metabolism increases during REM sleep toward waking levels. Moreover, just about all physiological indices show REM sleep to be more "activated" and nearer to wakefulness than NREM sleep. Our hypothetical decay process would almost have to be going on at a faster rate during REM sleep than during NREM sleep, meaning that a decay theory would predict more forgetting during REM than NREM sleep. Our hypothesis was, of course, the opposite.

For the last two and a half years we have been trying to show that the rate of forgetting is different in the different sleep stages. Next I would like to tell you about the progress we have made in that time.

SLEEP AND MEMORY: A PROGRESS REPORT[1]

Chemical manipulation of REM time. Since we had hypothesized that REM sleep could facilitate memory, our first major experiment attempted to

[1] The experiments described in this section were carried out at the Research Center for the Study of Sleep and Dreams at the University of Colorado. I want to express my deepest thanks to the staff of the Center and particularly to Michael J. Sullivan. Without the cooperation and dedication of a large staff of talented research assistants and associates, this research, by its very nature, would have been impossible.

manipulate the amount of REM sleep during the retention interval. By increasing the percentage of a night's sleep spent in REM sleep we hoped to show that memory improved, and by decreasing REM percentage we hoped that memory would be decreased. There is no simple way to increase or decrease the amount of REM sleep. As mentioned earlier the sleep cycle is amazingly well regulated by physiological processes. The only feasible way to manipulate REM time seemed to be to influence these processes with psychoactive drugs. Most such chemicals either have no effect on REM time or they produce a significant decrease in REM time. It has proven difficult to produce increases.

Our original design was a 3 X 2 factorial with three drug conditions and two retention-interval activities (sleep or wakefulness). The three drug conditions were: (a) a placebo treatment, (b) a drug that increases REM time, and (c) a drug that decreases REM time. For the decreasing drug, we chose a combination of amobarbital and dextroamphetamine sulphate in a time-release "spansule" capsule (Dexamyl #2, SKF). For the increasing drug, we chose diazepam (Valium, 10 mg., Roche). As it turned out, only our choice for a placebo was intelligent. Dexamyl did decrease REM time, but it replaced the REM with wakefulness so that the Dexamyl-sleep condition did not sleep very well. Valium just did not produce the expected increase in REM time. Two additional drug treatments were added when we discovered these findings. To increase REM we turned to reserpine (Serpasil, Abbott, .25 mg per 25 lbs. of body weight). Pilot studies showed that reserpine did not increase REM time when administered just before sleep nor when administered 36 hours before sleeping on the critical retention night. Both effects had been reported elsewhere in the sleep literature, but we could not replicate them. We finally combined reserpine with one prior night of REM-sleep deprivation, and found that this produced a REM increase on the subsequent, critical night. The final procedure involved administering the reserpine 36 hours before the OL night. On the night prior to OL, the Ss slept in the laboratory and were physiologically monitored. Each time they attempted to enter REM sleep, they were awakened. It is known that this procedure results in a REM rebound on subsequent nights of sleep; if the subjects are left alone, they show a rebound of REM sleep as compared to baseline nights not preceded by REM deprivation. Thus, by combining reserpine with a prior night of REM depriviation, we were able to produce an increase in the amount of REM time on the OL night. To decrease REM sleep without increasing wakefulness, we then chose amitriptyline (Elavil, Merck, Scharp, and Dohme, 10 mg).

Combining all these groups left us with a 5 X 2 factorial design with five drug conditions (Serpasil, Valium, placebo, Dexamyl, and Elavil) and two retention-interval activities (sleep or awake). There were 16 subjects in each of the 10 cells. All subjects first volunteered for an experiment involving the administration of prescription drugs and sleeping in the laboratory. They were then randomly assigned to the different conditions, except that the Serpasil and Elavil conditions were run after it became apparent that the Valium and Dexamyl conditions did not have the desired effects. All subjects were screened by a physician for participation in the experiments.

Each subject learned a 20-pair list of paired associates for six trials, and was tested for recall eight hours later. Half the subjects slept in the laboratory while we monitored EEG, EOG, and EMG, and the other half of the subjects were dismissed from the laboratory during the retention interval. The sleep subjects learned at night and were tested for recall in the morning, and the awake subjects learned early in the morning and were tested that afternoon.

The results of this experiment are shown in Tables 1 through 4. Table 1 shows mean performance on the last OL trial, Table 2 shows mean performance on the recall trial, Table 3 shows the absolute loss score means (last OL trial minus recall), and Table 4 shows percent loss score means. Statistically speaking, in the loss and percent loss scores, only the main effect of sleep versus wakefulness was significant. Neither the main effect of drug treatment nor the desired drug by sleep-awake interaction was present.

Table 1. Mean number correct on the last learning trial as a function of drug condition and sleep versus wakefulness during the retention interval.

	Drug condition					
	Serpasil	Valium	Placebo	Dexamyl	Elavil	Average
Sleep	16.00	13.37	15.06	14.00	14.69	14.50
Awake	15.94	15.25	14.56	15.31	15.75	15.36
Average	15.97	14.00	14.31	14.66	15.22	

Table 2. Mean number correct at recall as a function of drug condition and sleep versus wakefulness during the retention interval.

	Drug condition					
	Serpasil	Valium	Placebo	Dexamyl	Elavil	Average
Sleep	15.44	12.06	14.06	13.25	12.94	13.55
Awake	11.50	11.75	10.00	10.69	12.56	11.30
Average	13.47	11.91	12.03	11.97	12.75	

Table 3. Mean absolute loss (number correct on last trial of OL minus number correct at recall) as a function of drug condition and sleep versus wakefulness during the retention interval.

	Drug condition					
	Serpasil	Valium	Placebo	Dexamyl	Elavil	Average
Sleep	.56	1.31	1.00	.75	1.75	1.07
Awake	4.44	3.50	4.56	4.62	3.19	4.06
Average	2.50	2.41	2.78	2.69	2.47	

Table 4. Mean percent loss as a function of drug condition and sleep versus wakefulness during the retention interval.

	Drug condition					
	Serpasil	Valium	Placebo	Dexamyl	Elavil	Average
Sleep	3.40	7.26	6.28	4.99	11.73	6.73
Awake	28.94	24.45	35.25	32.58	20.77	28.40
Average	16.17	15.85	20.77	18.78	16.24	

Separate 2 X 2 analyses of variance were done comparing each drug with the placebo treatment, and in no case was the drug by sleep-awake interaction significant. Scoring the sleep records revealed the following mean percentages of time in REM sleep: Serpasil = 25.45, Valium = 15.72, placebo = 17.31, Dexamyl = 7.73, and Elavil = 6.15. The large difference in REM time between the Serpasil and Elavil treatments was not accompanied by a significant change in the magnitude of the sleep effect, although the results are clearly in the predicted direction. Sleep produced an advantage of nine percentage points over wakefulness in the Elavil condition, but a 25 percentage point improvement in memory in the Serpasil condition. Thus, the sleep effect was larger when REM time was increased than when it was decreased, but the interaction was never significant in any of our analyses. While the results are suggestive, they are not particularly encouraging except, of course, that we once again demonstrated a large facilitative effect of sleep on memory. Average loss in the awake conditions was over four times as much as in the sleep conditions. The sleep effect is alive and well in Colorado.

REM deprivation.   Our second experiment (Ekstrand, Sullivan, Parker, & West, 1971) got us away from the enormous difficulties of doing research with drugs and humans. Rather than attempt drug manipulation of REM time, we decided to deprive subjects of REM sleep by the method of awakenings—awakening the subject each time he enters the REM state. We decided to focus on the spontaneous recovery phenomenon reported by Ekstrand (1967). Ekstrand had reported that sleep facilitated spontaneous recovery, perhaps because sleep, by preventing continued IL which would continue extinction, provided an environment maximally conducive to recovery. On the other hand, it might have been the case that the recovery was correlated with REM or NREM sleep.

Therefore, we looked at MMFR of List 1 in an A-B, A-C paradigm after an eight-hour retention interval filled with sleep. For one group of subjects, we awakened them each time they entered the REM state as measured by EEG, EOG, and EMG. For another group, we deprived the subjects of the Stage-IV variety of NREM sleep by awakening them at the onset of each Stage-IV episode. A third group of subjects received what we called the pseudodeprivation treatment. They received the same *number* of awakenings (yoked control) as the other two groups but they never were awakened during Stage REM or Stage IV.

Each subject learned two lists (A-B, A-C), each to a one-perfect criterion. He then slept in the laboratory under one of the three deprivation conditions and was tested for recall of both lists (MMFR) in the morning. No immediate unlearning control condition was included since we were not concerned about demonstrating spontaneous recovery; we were interested in first-list recall as a function of the deprivation condition. However, during the course of this experiment, Postman, Stark, and Fraser (1968) unequivocally demonstrated spontaneous recovery over 20-minute retention intervals. My assistants then made a very interesting suggestion. Since the immediate unlearning control in my dissertation had been tested immediately after A-C learning, and since most subjects take at least 20 minutes to fall asleep, could it be that the recovery I had observed had actually taken place before anyone fell asleep, i.e., during that 20-minute period before sleep? Perhaps so, and perhaps sleep had just protected the already recovered habits from further forgetting. At this point, we added two control conditions: an immediate control (IC) was tested immediately after A-C learning and a delayed control (DC) was tested 20 minutes after A-C learning, the 20-minute interval being filled with resting on a bed.

The results of the experiment were quite disappointing. The five groups did not differ significantly on any measure of List 1 or List 2 recall. There was, however, a substantial numerical difference between the IC and DC groups, with condition DC averaging 1.1 items more than IC on MMFR of List 1. The DC and experimental deprivation groups were quite similar. Naturally we interpreted this to mean that spontaneous recovery did take place over the initial 20-minute interval and this, of course, cast serious doubt on my earlier finding that sleep per se "produced" the recovery. Chances are the recovery had already taken place before sleep occurred.

More discouraging was the lack of any differences among the three deprivation conditions. Setting the spontaneous recovery issue aside, there should have been differences in either first-, second-, or combined-list recall if REM sleep facilitates memory. In other words, REM deprivation did not decrease (or increase) retention.

The Portnoff phenomenon. In developing doubts about our hypothesis that REM sleep facilitates memory, we were led back to the findings of Portnoff et al. (1966), showing that immediate sleep onset after learning resulted in poorer recall than if sleep was delayed by a 5-minute interval of wakefulness. We decided that this finding needed replication and extension to the list-learning situation we were employing, since Portnoff et al. had a "learning" task that was actually incidental learning of a single word presented as a perception task. We have now completed three experiments with this paradigm and the results justify our doubts.

In the first experiment, subjects learned four free-recall lists across a single night of sleep and were tested for recall of all lists in the morning. According to a Latin square design, each subject learned one list under each of four conditions which conformed to a 2 X 2 design. The subject was awakened either from REM sleep or from NREM sleep and received one study and one test trial on a single list of words using a free-recall procedure. The second variable was return to sleep: subjects were allowed to return immediately or they were kept awake for a 5-minute period of mirror drawing (delayed return). The recall results showed neither main effect or the interaction to be significant, although there was a suggestion of better recall of lists followed by wakefulness, particularly if the subject had been awakened for learning from REM sleep.

We felt that the repeated measures design of the above experiment might have been obscuring the effects of the two variables and so we did a second experiment in which each subject served in only one condition of the 2 X 2 design described above. Each subject learned two lists during the night, but both lists were learned under the same condition, either immediate or delayed return to sleep and either awakened from REM or NREM sleep. First of all, the results (Tables 5 through 8) showed that more words were learned when the awakening was from REM sleep than from NREM. Recall (out of 15) on the immediate test trial was 8.80 for subjects awakened from REM and 7.63 for subjects awakened from NREM. Unfortunately, there were no significant differences in the morning. The retention results (Tables 6 through 8) show numerically better performance (less loss and percent loss and more recall) in the delayed return condition, but the difference was never significant.

We were beginning to get somewhat paranoid about the magnitude of the variability we were finding in our data, as well as discouraged.

Table 5. Mean number correct on the OL test trial as a function of awakening and condition of return of sleep.

	Awaken from		
	REM	NREM	Average
Return to Sleep:			
Immediate	8.60	7.35	7.98
Delayed	9.00	7.90	8.45
Average	8.80	7.63	

Table 6. Mean number correct at morning recall as a function of stage of awakening and condition of return of sleep.

	Awaken from		
	REM	NREM	Average
Return to Sleep:			
Immediate	5.70	4.15	4.93
Delayed	6.85	5.60	6.23
Average	6.28	4.88	

Table 7. Mean absolute loss (OL test minus morning recall) as a function of stage of awakening and condition of return of sleep.

	Awaken from		
	REM	NREM	Average
Return to Sleep:			
Immediate	2.90	3.20	3.05
Delayed	2.15	2.30	2.23
Average	2.53	2.75	

Table 8. Mean percent loss as a function of stage of awakening and condition of return of sleep.

	Awaken from		
	REM	NREM	Average
Return to Sleep:			
Immediate	37.44	43.86	40.65
Delayed	26.03	29.70	27.87
Average	31.74	36.78	

The third experiment on the Portnoff phenomenon has just been completed by James N. West as a part of a master's thesis project he is doing in my laboratory. West's design was a 2 X 2 X 2 factorial. The first variable was the familiar immediate or delayed return to sleep. The second variable was whether or not (test or no test) the subject was given an immediate test following one study trial on a 15-word list. The no-test subjects were just told to memorize the list because we wanted to observe the EEG during memorizing. The third variable was the location of the retention interval within the night. The retention interval was reduced to three hours and was located in either the first half of the night (where most of the Stage-IV sleep occurs) or in the second half (where most of the REM sleep occurs). First-half subjects were awakened shortly after sleep onset, learned the list and returned to sleep. Three hours later they were awakened and tested for recall. Second-half subjects were awakened four hours after sleep onset, completed the free-recall task, returned to sleep (immediate or delayed), and were tested for recall three hours later. The test/no test variable had no effects on recall. The other variables did not affect OL (as measured by the test groups). The results for these two variables at recall, in terms of mean number of words recalled are shown in Table 9. Neither main effect nor the interaction was significant. After three experiments, we concluded that immediate versus delayed return to sleep does not affect memory in the one-trial list-learning situation we have employed. I might also mention that D. R. Goodenough has personally communicated to me that they have had trouble replicating the Portnoff phenomenon when very slight changes are made in the procedure, although a replication did occur when the exact conditions of the original Portnoff et al. experiment were reinstated. The phenomenon is obviously not a robust one, nor one with wide generality.

Table 9. Mean recall as a function of immediate or delayed return to sleep and first versus second half of the night.

	Half of the Night		
	First	Second	Average
Return to sleep:			
Immediate	4.08	2.75	3.42
Delayed	4.17	3.92	4.04
Average	4.12	3.33	

First versus second half of the night. In the last experiment described above dealing with the Portnoff phenomenon, we used first versus second half of the night as a variable. This was done because of the result of an experiment we had already completed in the laboratory and which I would like to describe for you now.

Another way to manipulate the amount of REM time during a retention interval, and to do so without interfering with sleep by the use of drugs or repeated awakenings, is to define the retention interval over either the first or second half of the night. Since most of the REM sleep occurs in the second half and most of the Stage-IV sleep in the first half, comparison of recall over first and second halves should reveal a difference if either REM or Stage-IV is critically involved with memory. Our first experiment with this variable (Yaroush, Sullivan, & Ekstrand, 1971) did just that.

There were three conditions, first half, second half, and awake. In this experiment, the retention interval was four hours. First-half subjects came to the laboratory, learned a single list of paired associates to a 10/15 criterion and then went to sleep. Four hours later they were awakened and tested for recall. Second-half subjects came to the laboratory and went right to bed. Four hours later they were awakened and completed OL after which they went back to sleep for the second half of the night. In the morning, four hours later, they were tested for recall. The awake subjects learned in the daytime and were dismissed from the laboratory for the retention interval.

The results (Table 10) were quite exciting to a group of people who are up all night in search of elusive significant differences. Recall in the first-half condition was significantly superior to recall in the other two conditions, which did not differ. In terms of percent loss from the criterion trial, the first-half mean was 14.01, the second half was 31.82, and the awake mean was 38.26.

Sleep did not facilitate memory compared to wakefulness when it was the second four hours of a night's sleep that filled the retention interval. And yet this was the segment of the night that contained most of the REM sleep.

Table 10. Mean performance in learning and on various recall measures in the Yaroush et al. study.

	First Half	Second Half	Awake
Number Correct Last Learning Trial	10.69	11.00	10.95
Number Correct (Absolute Recall) Paced Test	9.19	7.50	6.76
Absolute Loss Paced Test	1.50	3.50	4.19
Percent Loss Unpaced Test	14.01%	31.82%	38.26%
Number Correct Unpaced Test	10.82	8.82	8.63
Number Correct Matching	13.44	11.32	12.07
Relearning First Paced Test	11.25	9.50	9.44

To us, these results seemed exceedingly important. They suggested that REM sleep does not facilitate memory. Instead it appeared as if Stage-IV NREM sleep might be facilitating memory and that REM sleep might even be inhibiting memory. Furthermore, these results seemed inconsistent with an interference theory of forgetting, since both first- and second-half groups were asleep during the retention interval and were accomplishing equally low amounts of IL. The experiment obviously had to be replicated.

Janet F. Gann has just completed this replication in our laboratory. In designing her replication, there were two features of the Yaroush et al. study which concerned us. First, we had not collected physiological data on the subjects. Thus, it is possible that the awakening in the middle of the night for the second-half subjects completely disrupted the sleep cycle and that there may have been no difference between the halves in REM time or Stage-IV time. This, of course, would make the memory results difficult to understand. Secondly, the subjects in the second-half condition had been awakened from sleep for OL whereas subjects in the first-half condition learned the list before any sleep occurred.

Again there were three conditions: first half, second half, and awake. The two sleep conditions included monitoring EEG, EOG, and EMG so that sleep stages could be assessed. The retention interval was reduced to 3.5 hours. First-half subjects appeared at the laboratory and were prepared for monitoring after which they went to sleep. As soon as they reached Stage II (unambiguous sleep) they were awakened for OL, after which they returned to sleep for 3.5 hours and were then awakened again for recall. Second-half subjects went to sleep for four hours and then were awakened for OL after which they returned to sleep for 3.5 hours and were then tested for recall. Awake subjects again learned during the daytime and were dismissed from the laboratory during the retention interval.

The OL part of the experiment involved learning a paired-associate list to 10/15 by the study-test method, and learning a list of 10 paired nonsense shapes to 8/10 using a recognition study-test procedure. Half the subjects learned the verbal task first and half learned the visual task first. The shapes were selected for difficulty in verbal labeling and this task was included because we felt that processing of verbal memory might be different than visual memory.

The results (mean number of pairs correctly recalled) are shown in Table 11.

Table 11. Mean number of correct pairs recalled as a function of type of task and retention-interval condition.

	First Half	Second Half	Awake
Verbal Task	8.38	6.94	5.44
Shape Task	6.19	6.56	5.75

On the visual task, the three conditions were not significantly different. On the verbal task, we see that this study replicated the Yaroush et al. finding of an advantage of the first-half condition over the second-half condition. In this study, however, the second-half condition was significantly superior to the awake condition, whereas these two conditions did not differ significantly in the Yaroush et al. experiment. Results of the EEG scoring in both this experiment and West's master's thesis show that despite the awakening in the middle of the night, there is a large difference between the two halves of the night on both REM and Stage-IV sleep in the predicted direction, more REM and less IV in the second half.

These two experiments suggest that the course of memory is different in the two halves of the night and that different processes are probably operating in the two halves. The Gann experiment also suggests that verbal and visual memory are different, although we are not pleased with the nonsense shape task we employed, for various reasons.

It is difficult to reconcile these results with an interference theory alone. An RI-based interpretation of the sleep effect would have to predict that the two halves would be equal and both superior to the awake condition. Instead, the results suggest that either Stage-IV sleep is facilitating memory (by facilitating consolidation?), with REM sleep and sleep in general having no effect; or that

REM sleep is interfering with memory (by disrupting consolidation?) while sleep in general is having a positive effect due to prevention of IL and RI. In the latter case, the first-half condition would be superior to the awake condition due to the reduction in IL. Performance in the second half and the awake conditions would depend on the combination of the inhibitory effect of REM sleep and the positive effect of reduced IL. If these two factors carried equal weight, the second-half and awake conditions would not differ, and both would be inferior to the first-half condition. If the reduced IL factor was more potent, then we would expect the second-half condition to be superior to the awake condition as was found in the Gann experiment. I suppose that one could account for an inhibitory effect of REM sleep by saying that dreaming is comparable to IL. Or one could account for a facilitatory effect of Stage-IV by suggesting that mental activity during Stage-IV was like rehearsal of recent experience, producing retroactive facilitation, but at the moment these alternatives seem so unlikely that I even hesitated to suggest them to such a behavioristically oriented group of psychologists.

More likely, an explanation of these findings will rely on a consolidation process which can be facilitated by interpolation of Stage-IV sleep shortly after learning or inhibited by interpolating REM sleep shortly after learning. Additional support for a consolidation-based theory comes from work on the effects of the point of interpolation during the retention interval of a sleep period.

Point of sleep interpolation.   I have already mentioned to you the results of the experiment by Heine (1914) suggesting that recall was better when sleep came immediately after learning than when it was delayed by 2–3 hours. This was true despite the fact that the total amount of sleep and wakefulness during the constant retention interval was identical in the two conditions. And I have already pointed out the difficulty of interpreting this finding with an interference theory. The finding is consistent with a consolidation theory that suggests that either (a) wakefulness after learning interferes with consolidation or (b) sleep after learning facilitates consolidation. Heine's basic finding was replicated in 1961 by James L. McGaugh, the outstanding proponent of consolidation theory. In the experiment (McGaugh & Hostetter, 1961, cited by Hilgard & Atkinson, 1967) a 16-hour retention interval was used for two of the groups. One group learned and then slept for eight hours followed by eight hours of wakefulness. The second group learned and then was awake for eight hours followed by eight hours of sleep. Both groups were then tested for percent savings during relearning. The group which slept immediately after learning showed 86 percent savings, while the group which slept immediately before recall showed only 59 percent savings.

In view of the unpublished nature of the McGaugh and Hostetter results and the age and sample size of the Heine (1914) results, we felt that a repetition of the experiment was in order. Carol Coleman, (in an unpublished study) has done this replication in our laboratory. She had subjects learn a paired-associate list of 15 pairs to a one-perfect criterion and then she tested recall after 24 hours. One group, immediate sleep, went to bed for eight hours immediately after learning. These subjects were then released from the laboratory and spent the remaining 16 hours of the retention interval awake. The delayed sleep group was released from the laboratory shortly after learning and returned 16 hours later to complete the last eight hours of the retention interval asleep in the laboratory. Mean recall was 12.11 in the immediate sleep condition and 9.89 in the delayed sleep condition. Thus, it seems safe to conclude, based on three experiments, that sleep during a retention interval is more beneficial to memory if it comes immediately after learning than if it comes immediately before recall.

An interference theory could account for this effect of point of sleep interpolation by postulating that extraexperimental interference coming just after learning produces more RI than extraexperimental interference coming just before recall. If this were true, then prevention of immediate interference by immediate sleep would result in better recall than prevention of the delayed interference by delayed sleep. However, as we all know, interference theory makes the opposite prediction, at least when the interference is formal in nature, i.e., not extraexperimental. In an A-B, A-C, RI design, with a constant retention interval, interference theory predicts that interpolation of A-C immediately after A-B learning should produce less RI than interpolation of A-C just before A-B recall. This is because immediate interpolation of A-C leaves a long IL-to-recall interval during which time the A-B habits are supposed to recover strength, thereby reducing RI. When A-C interpolation is just prior to A-B recall, the IL-recall interval is zero, leaving no time for recovery and resulting in maximal RI. It is true that direct tests of this deduction from interference theory have not worked (Newton & Wickens, 1956; Houston, 1967) unless the paradigm was A-B, C-D (Newton & Wickens, 1956) or unless the retention interval was very short (Postman, Stark, & Henschel, 1969). But nowhere has there been a suggestion that delayed interference is *less* effective than immediate interference in producing RI. An interference theory is hard put to explain the effects of the point of interpolation of the sleep period.

Summary comment. Our research program on the effects of sleep on memory has not been successful to date in showing an unequivocal relationship between memory and stage of sleep. We have demonstrated that the first four hours of a night's sleep constitute a retention interval that results in higher recall than the second four hours. Since the distribution of REM and Stage-IV sleep is different in the two halves, this is certainly suggestive of a relationship between memory and sleep stages. However, chemical manipulation of REM time and mechanical deprivation of Stage IV or REM have not affected memory. Nevertheless, the first- versus second-half difference, and the effect of point of interpolation of the sleep period do represent findings difficult to reconcile with an interference theory. A decay theory might be able to account for the first-half, second-half effect, if it can be shown that the average metabolic rate during the second half of the night is higher than during the first half. However, a decay theory accounting of the effect of the point of sleep interpolation is difficult, although probably not impossible, to imagine.

It appears to us that a theory based upon the notion of a consolidation process is best capable of explaining all the effects of sleep on memory. Such a theory would have to suggest that sleep is capable of facilitating consolidation, compared to wakefulness. Furthermore, it would probably require the assumption that NREM sleep (and perhaps particularly Stage IV) is a sleep state particularly conducive to consolidation, while REM sleep is no more conducive to consolidation than wakefulness. Naturally, such a theory would stipulate that for the facilitating effect of sleep to occur, the sleep would have to come shortly after learning. Delaying the sleep would allow the consolidation process to run its course during wakefulness, after which augmentation (or inhibition) by sleep would be impossible.

Expecting to account for all the effects of sleep on memory with a single theoretical construct may be inappropriate. It is possible that sleep operates to facilitate recall both by facilitating consolidation and by preventing IL. For example, suppose Stage-IV sleep facilitates consolidation and Stage REM inhibits it. Then the difference (or lack of a difference) between the second four hours of sleep and wakefulness could be explained by the particular combination of the inhibitory effect of REM sleep and the positive effect from reduction of IL. Or it could be that sleep involves all three processes, reducing decay rate, facilitating consolidation, and prevention of IL.

We are not expecting that a consolidation theory will be able to account single-handedly for all possible effects of sleep on memory, although this might turn out to be the case. Nor are we suggesting that it can account for all aspects of human or even animal memory. We are, however, proposing that the experiments on the effects of sleep on memory can no longer be used as the ultimate cornerstone of an interference theory nor the gravestone of decay theory.

SPECULATIONS ON A SYNTHESIS

We all know that there is very strong evidence for what Postman (1969) calls the weak law of interference. Interfering learning is sufficient to produce forgetting. The strong law, that interfering learning is both necessary and sufficient to produce forgetting, is what is in question. The fact that the weak law of interference seems undoubtedly true means that any synthesis will have to include interfering learning as a basic cause of forgetting.

We also know that, at least in the area of animal memory, there is strong evidence for the existence of a consolidation process. Memory can be severely impaired by CNS insult (usually ECS) coming shortly after a learning experience. On the other hand, memory can be significantly improved by posttrial injections of chemical agents which increase brain activity. Some of these activating chemicals undoubtedly *increase* brain metabolism, meaning that a neural decay theory, tied to metabolism as an independent variable and forgetting as a dependent variable, is hard pressed to explain the facilitation in memory. These facts, coupled with the indirect evidence we find for a consolidation process in our sleep research, suggest to us that a synthesis will have to include a consolidation process.

Lately, it has become enormously popular to speak about memory in storage-retrieval terms. And it seems true that such a distinction has contributed significantly to our understanding of memory phenomena. A consolidation theory is certainly speaking mainly about storage. It is storage that is disrupted by ECS and it is storage that is improved by CNS stimulants. Given "normal" consolidation or storage of an experience, a consolidation theory does not seem to help us to understand the subsequent forgetting which occurs. Most human-memory investigators are dealing with this kind of situation—they do not use ECS, drugs, or sleep in their experiments. And it is no wonder that they do not typically (but see Landauer, 1969) find a consolidation notion to be very helpful. Moreover, a consolidation process is basically physiological in character and is typically tied to independent variables that are difficult or impossible to employ with normal human subjects. So the expert in human memory really is not in a position to study memory from a consolidation position; and so a consolidation theory does not seem to explain the kinds of experiments he does—his experiments factor out or hold constant consolidation in most cases, or at least he assumes they do.

Is it then fair to say that memory, as studied by the traditional verbal-learning theorist is basically a function of retrieval? In some respects this seems a reasonable possibility. For example, we are typically very concerned about carefully controlling the degree of original learning in any long-term memory study. In some sense we can think of this as factoring out storage processes. Proactive inhibition is interpreted as being due to competition among responses, clearly a kind of retrieval-performance notion. The correct response is stored and is available at the time of recall, but there is difficulty in retrieving the one, and only one, correct response. We retrieve too many alternative responses and have difficulty determining which is the correct one.

Retroactive inhibition is not so clear a case. As embodied in the two-factor theory, both storage and retrieval effects were implicated. Unlearning seemed basically a destruction of the stored information while competition, as in the PI case, seemed like a retrieval problem. More recently, however, the role of competition in RI has been questioned since, at least on recall tests given immediately after IL, there is no difference to speak of between paced and MMFR measures of RI. Thus the focus has been on unlearning. Still more recently we have seen Postman et al. (1969) suggest an interpretation for unlearning that no longer sounds unequivocally like a storage deficit. Instead, unlearning is seen as a response suppression phenomenon. The implication is clearly that the responses are in storage but that there is a failure to retrieve them due to a set to continue with the most recent "rules" for response retrieval.

Perhaps then both competition and unlearning are basically retrieval effects. Spontaneous recovery, another key interference concept, would also be a retrieval phenomenon if it merely represents the dissipation of response-set, generalized interference. Finally, list differentiation, an on-again, off-again interference construct, also appears to be a retrieval concept.

What I am trying to suggest is that traditional interference theory may be dealing only with memory retrieval without considering memory storage. The apparent disregard for storage processes may only be because the principles of interference theory have no relevance at the storage stage. In an analogous fashion, the principles of a consolidation theory seem to have no relevance for the retrieval stage. Perhaps then one possible synthesis is to consider consolidation as the basic theory of storage and interference as the basic theory of retrieval. Certainly these two notions are not mutually exclusive unless one takes the difficult stance of trying to account for all aspects of memory with a single basic construct.

Where does this leave decay theory? It is difficult to tell at this point for we still have not found experimental paradigms that allow for the unequivocal demonstration of a decay process. Nevertheless, I feel that we must consider decay as a potential member of our synthesis. It probably will come in through the back door unless some astounding breakthroughs appear in the study of the physical basis of memory. The back door is, of course, comparable to entering by default—when new memory phenomena appear that seem inexplicable in terms of interference or consolidation. In the area of sensory memory and short-term memory, the back door has already been violated. Unfortunately, given the present state of physiological knowledge about memory, a decay theory really amounts to no theory at all—it merely restates the fact that forgetting has occurred. We can imagine the day when this will not be true, but until then we can also understand the experimental psychologist's dislike for the construct.

When the day of a respectable decay process arrives, comparable to the discovery of the process which results in the formation of iron oxide, we can envision a three-stage synthesis. Recall would require (a) storage of information, (b) retention of the information over the retention interval, and (c) retrieval of the retained information. It is possible that the three theories might pair off with the three stages, with storage being governed by consolidation, retention by decay, and retrieval by interference. I am not overly sanguine about finding such a neat synthesis.

A more likely synthesis would have one or more processes operating on each stage. Adequate storage might basically depend upon a consolidation process, but failure in consolidation might arise from either decay or interference from other learning. Perhaps long-term storage (consolidation) depends upon maintaining the integrity of a short-term trace until consolidation is complete, such that consolidation would be stopped when a decay process in the short-term system had run its course or by direct interference with the short-term trace coming from immediately interpolated learning events. What I am suggesting, of course, involves a distinction between short- and long-term memory. However, I am also suggesting that *both* interference and decay principles would influence both types of memory, and that a consolidation process is what is involved in the transfer of information from short- to long-term memory.

Given adequate storage in long-term memory, retention might be totally a function of the decay process. However, suppose that what is stored consists not only of the information to be recalled but also of rules for the retrieval of that information. Then retrieval information might decay over time such that a retrieval failure would occur because of a retention failure, i.e., decay processes might influence retrieval as well as retention. While interfering learning might produce recall deficits principally by affecting retrieval conditions and possibly by affecting the integrity of the short-term trace, it might not have any effect on the retention of information adequately stored. Instead, interference would affect recall by causing the subject to apply inappropriate retrieval rules, and this could produce results that look like unlearning, suppression, competition, or loss of differentiation. In each case, however, the learned information would be in storage, so that poor retention was not responsible for the recall failure.

In conclusion, it is obvious that I feel that a synthesis is possible, even inevitable. Eventually we may even find out that decay, interference, and consolidation disruption are just different names for what physiologically is the same event, e.g., a modification in the configuration of a cell assembly or in the arrangement of RNA bases. Such a possibility makes me wonder about the value of the kind of speculation I have been engaging in. After reviewing my speculations, I feel that they probably have no implications for most students of memory. We each have worked out our own paradigms for the study of memory and we each find certain theoretical constructs most useful in interpreting the kinds of experiments we do. And we each typically find the other guy's constructs of little value, and for very good reasons. Thus, we each will go on with our research unaffected by the eventual possibility of a synthesis, and perhaps rightly so. Undoubtedly, the adequacy of any synthesis will depend upon the availability of basic knowledge about the components of the synthesis. And, if in the meantime, you choose to ignore the other guy's data, it will only mean that you will not be responsible for the inevitable synthesis. Probably none of us will be around then anyway, but be prepared for rolling over in your grave.

The hope for a synthesis is alive and well in Colorado. And only time will tell what the synthesis will be. (If time can tell, why can't it also cause forgetting? Oh, because time qua time. . . .)

REFERENCES

Agnew, H. W., Jr., Webb, W. B., & Williams, R. L. The first night effect: an EEG study of sleep. *Psychophysiology*, 1966, 2, 263–266.

Aserinsky, E., & Kleitman, N. Regularly occurring periods of eye motility and concomitant phenomena during sleep. *Science*, 1953, 118, 273–274.

Duncan, C. P. The retroactive effect of electroshock on learning. *Journal of Comparative and Physiological Psychology*, 1949, 42, 33–44.

Ekstrand, B. R. The effect of sleep on retention. Ph.D. dissertation, Northwestern University, Evanston, Illinois, 1966.

Ekstrand, B. R. The effect of sleep on memory. *Journal of Experimental Psychology*, 1967, 75, 64–72.

Ekstrand, B. R., Sullivan, M. J., Parker, D. F., & West, J. N. Spontaneous recovery and sleep. *Journal of Experimental Psychology*, 1971, 88, 142–144.

Ekstrand, B. R., & Underwood, B. J. Free learning and recall as a function of unit-sequence and letter-sequence interference. *Journal of Verbal Learning and Verbal Behavior*, 1965, 4, 390–396.

Hartman, E. *The biology of dreaming.* Springfield, Ill.: Charles C Thomas, 1967.

Hartman, E. (ed.). *Sleep and dreaming.* Boston: Little, Brown, 1970.

Heine, R. Uber wiedererkennen und ruckwirkende hemmung. *Psychologie Forschung*, 1914, 17, 13–55. Cited by Woodworth and Schlosberg, 1954.

Hilgard, E. R., & Atkinson, R. C. *Introduction to psychology.* New York: Hartcourt, Brace, and World, 1967.

Houston, J. P. Retroactive inhibition and point of interpolation. *Journal of Verbal Learning and Verbal Behavior*, 1967, 6, 84–88.

Jenkins, J. B., & Dallenbach, K. M. Oblivescence during sleep and waking. *American Journal of Psychology*, 1924, 35, 605–612.

Keppel, G. Retroactive and proactive inhibition. In T. R. Dixon and D. L. Horton (eds.), *Verbal Behavior and General Behavior Theory.* Englewood Cliffs, N. J.: Prentice-Hall, 1968.

Landauer, T. K. Reinforcement as consolidation. *Psychological Review*, 1969, 76, 82–96.

McGaugh, J. L., & Hostetter, R. C. Retention as a function of the temporal position of sleep and activity following waking. Unpublished manuscript, cited by Hilgard and Atkinson (1967).

McGeoch, J. A. Forgetting and the law of disuse. *Psychological Review*, 1932, 39, 352–370.

Müller, G. E., & Pilzecker, A. Experimentelle Beitrage zur Lehre vom Gedachtniss. *Zeitschrift Psychologie Erganzungsband*, 1900, 1, 1–288.

Newton, J. M., & Wickens, D. D. Retroactive inhibition as a function of the temporal position of interpolated learning. *Journal of Experimental Psychology*, 1956, 51, 149–154.

Portnoff, G., Baekeland, F., Goodenough, D. R., Karacan, I., & Shapiro, A. Retention of verbal materials perceived immediately prior to onset of non-rem sleep. *Perceptual and Motor Skills*, 1966, 22, 751–758.

Postman, L. Mechanisms of interference in forgetting. In G. A. Talland and N. C. Waugh (eds.), *The pathology of memory*, New York: Academic Press, 1969.

Postman, L., Stark, K., & Fraser, J. Temporal changes in interference. *Journal of Verbal Learning and Verbal Behavior*, 1968, 7, 672–694.

Postman, L., Stark, K., & Henschel, D. Conditions of recovery after unlearning. *Journal of Experimental Psychology, Monograph Supplement*, 1969, 82, No. 1, 1–24.

Underwood, B. J. Interference and forgetting. *Psychological Review*, 1957, 64, 49–60.

Underwood, B. J., & Ekstrand, B. R. An analysis of some shortcomings in the interference theory of forgetting. *Psychological Review*, 1966, 73, 540–549.

Underwood, B. J., and Postman, L. Extraexperimental sources of interference in forgetting. *Psychological Review*, 1960, 67, 73–95.

van Ormer, E. B. Retention after intervals of sleep and waking. *Archives of Psychology*, New York, 1932, No. 137.

Woodworth, R. S., & Schlosberg, N. *Experimental psychology*. New York: Holt, Rinehart and Winston, 1954.

Yaroush, R., Sullivan, M. J., & Ekstrand, B. R. The effect of sleep on memory. II: Differential effect of the first and second half of the night. *Journal of Experimental Psychology*, 1971, 88, 361–366.

4 | Forgetting

GEOFFREY KEPPEL
University of California, Berkeley

Why do we forget? This question has occupied the attention of numerous investigators in our field and still no adequate answer can be given. We will examine in this paper the successes and failures of one of these theories, an interference theory of forgetting. Interference theory, at least as it has been developed at Northwestern University and at the University of California at Berkeley, starts with experiments in which sources of interference are introduced in the laboratory and studied carefully in this context. I am referring, of course, to experiments where interference is generated in multilist situations, i.e., studies of retroactive and proactive inhibition. Processes and mechanisms developed with these designs are then extended to a situation in which interlist interference is presumed to be minimal, namely, the forgetting of verbal material by subjects for whom this is the first and only learning task in the laboratory. It is with this latter experimental paradigm that we will be primarily concerned in this paper.

Underwood and Postman (1960) suggested that a major source of forgetting is extraexperimental in nature, stemming from linguistic habits. Two classes of habits were identified: those involving the individual letters making up the verbal material being learned and recalled (letter-sequence habits) and those involving integrated sequences of letters such as words (unit-sequence habits). As a general principle, Underwood and Postman proposed a direct relationship between forgetting and the degree to which the material being learned is in conflict with letter or unit sequences which form some portion of the associative repertoire of the subject. The primary locus of this interference was thought to be *proactive*, reflecting the recovery during the retention interval of the conflicting linguistic habits presumed to be "extinguished" or "suppressed" during learning. A secondary locus was *retroactive*, reflecting the damaging influence upon the learned material of the conflicting habits experienced during the interval.

Tests of this theory have generally taken the form of a comparison of the forgetting rates for materials varying in the degree (or amount) of assumed

Research reported in this paper was supported by research grant MH-10249 from the National Institutes of Health. The paper was written at the Applied Psychology Unit, Cambridge, England, during the author's sabbatical leave. Work at the Unit was supported in part by a Fellowship awarded by the National Institutes of Health (1 FO3 MH47830–01).

linguistic interference. Variation in letter-sequence interference is accomplished by selecting nonword letter combinations representing different levels of meaningfulness, e.g., association value or transitional probabilities of letter combinations taken from language counts or from free-association tests. Consider, for example, two letter combinations, b-x and b-t. An examination of language counts or association norms would indicate that x is an unlikely response to b and that t is much more likely. Suppose one subject is asked to learn sequences of the first sort and another to learn sequences of the second sort. The theory indicates that in comparison with the high-probability sequences the low-probability sequences will be subjected to more letter-sequence interference during learning, which must be overcome (extinguished or suppressed) for learning to occur, and more interference at recall, due to the recovery (and use) of stronger conflicting letter-sequence habits during the retention interval. Variations in unit-sequence interference were accomplished originally by choosing words of low and high frequency of occurrence. Low-frequency words, such as *bramble, abbess*, and *lorry*, were assumed to enter into very few associations with other words, while high-frequency words, such as *answer, country*, and *woman*, would enter a large number of interword associations. Suppose that subjects are asked to practice a list of either low-frequency or of high-frequency words in which arbitrary interword sequences are to be learned. Under these circumstances, high-frequency words would be subjected to greater unit-sequence interference than low-frequency words during learning and at recall.

By 1966, a respectable number of tests of the Underwood-Postman theory had appeared in the literature. It is generally agreed that these experiments by and large failed to support the theory (see Keppel, 1968, pp. 197–201). Since that time several additional tests have been conducted. One purpose of this paper is to consider the data obtained subsequent to the 1968 review to see whether or not the rather negative overall evaluation of the theory can be changed. The remainder of the paper will consist of the consideration of an alternative theory of forgetting, one based on the postulation of nonspecific linguistic interference, which will then be followed by some comments concerning the form that a general theoretical account of forgetting might take.

LETTER-SEQUENCE INTERFERENCE: SOME RECENT EVIDENCE

Previous tests of the letter-sequence side of the Underwood-Postman theory, averaged over the experiments cited in the earlier review, indicate slightly more forgetting of letter sequences of low than of high probability, i.e., 22.2 percent and 19.8 percent forgetting over a retention interval of 1 day and 48.6 percent and 41.5 percent forgetting over a retention interval of 1 week. At the level of the individual experiment, differences were nonsignificant and inconsistent. In spite of this weak support of the theory, however, we decided to subject the notion of letter-sequence to additional experimental test. The justification for this was the introduction of a methodological improvement, which we will consider first before discussing the results.

In the typical experiment, subjects receiving low- or high-probability sequences to learn must be brought to the same degree of learning before the start of the retention interval; otherwise, differences in forgetting may be confounded with differences in degree of learning (cf. Underwood, 1964). This equation is usually accomplished by adjusting the number of training trials, with more trials being given to the subjects in the difficult conditions—the low condition, in this case. Since most subjects even in the difficult conditions will learn one or two pairs at the outset and have difficulty with the remaining ones, it is possible for these "early" pairs to be overlearned relative to the "later" pairs. In addition, the degree of overlearning will be much greater in the low-probability condition where considerably more overlearning trials will be administered as a result of the degree-of-learning adjustment. Since overlearning can benefit retention (e.g., Underwood & Keppel, 1963), there is a bias in favor of the low condition. It is possible in the earlier experiments, therefore, that the reduction in forgetting due to differential overlearning may have counteracted any increased forgetting due to letter-sequence interference which is predicted by the theory. To reduce this confounding, we turned to a method whereby "early" pairs are actually removed from the list and additional exposures of the more difficult pairs are provided. It was expected, then, that with this confounding reduced or eliminated the influence of the letter-sequence interference would now be observed.

Originally, we tested children (Amster, Keppel, & Meyer, 1970, Experiments I and II), the thought being that children who are beginning to spell and to read might be more susceptible to letter-sequence interference than are adults. The children learned seven letter-letter pairs of either low or high probability to a criterion of 6/7 correct responses. (If subjects did not attain this criterion on the test trial following the presentation of all seven pairs, missed pairs were re-presented until each had been correctly anticipated once. At this point all 7 pairs were presented and tested again, and the possible attainment of the learning criterion was again assessed.) The results of the different conditions of these two experiments were favorable to the theory, i.e., percentage forgetting over the 1-week retention interval was 50.1 percent and 39.4 percent for the low- and high-probability pairs, respectively. The experiment was repeated with college students in a third experiment, with an increase in the number of pairs from 9 to 11, a necessary change in the performance criterion (9/11), and an increase in the study and testing rates. Contrary to earlier experiments with college students, this experiment strikingly supported the theory: 53.7 percent and 28.8 percent forgetting of the low- and high-probability pairs, respectively.

Experiment I: Retention as a Function of Method and Response-Term Meaningfulness

The success of these experiments was attributed to the use of the adjusted method of learning, although there was no unequivocal evidence to indicate that this was the case. In an attempt to demonstrate the critical nature of the method, Marcia Johnson and I designed an experiment in which the adjusted method and the study-test method would be compared directly. The basic design consisted of eight groups formed by completely crossing the two methods (study-test and adjusted), two levels of letter-sequence strength (low and high), and two retention intervals (immediate and 48-hour). Rather than repeating exactly the earlier experiments, we shifted the manipulation of letter sequence interference from the associative locus of the previous studies to a response locus. More specifically, the previous learning materials consisted of letter-letter pairs (e.g., *b-x* versus *b-t*), where letter-sequence interference would affect primarily associative processes, while the present materials consisted of word-bigram pairs (e.g., *egg-bx* versus *egg-bt*), where letter-sequence interference would affect primarily response-learning processes. That is, it was assumed that the sort of interference presumed to affect performance with letter-letter pairs would operate on the process of response integration involved with the word-bigram pairs and thus affect the reproduction of responses during learning as well as recall. The expectation, therefore, was for greater forgetting by the subjects receiving the material with low-probability responses. It was also predicted that this outcome would be observed with the adjusted method and not with the study-test method for the reason given above.

Method. The materials consisted of bigrams paired with single-syllable, high-frequency nouns. Four basic lists of nine pairs were constructed, two made up of low-probability bigram responses and two of high-probability bigram responses. The average probabilities, defined in terms of the Underwood and Schulz (1960) letter-association norms (Appendix D), were both .018 for the low lists and .139 and .143 for the high lists. The stimuli were the same for all lists. Each set of bigrams was randomly paired with the stimuli twice to yield a total of eight lists, four at each probability level.

The materials were presented on 3 X 5-inch cards, by hand, timed with a metronome. Presentation rate for both study and test trials was 2 seconds per pair. Under the study-test method, all nine pairs were presented successively on study trials and stimuli alone were presented on test trials (i.e., standard alternating study-test procedure). Under the adjusted method, all pairs were presented on a *main* study trial and tested on the immediately following *main* test trial. Any items given correctly were then dropped out and the remaining pairs presented again for study and subsequent test. Again, correct pairs were eliminated and the remaining presented for study and test. These subtrials were continued until the subject responded correctly to each stimulus once. A new main trial then began. The attainment of the criterion of 6/9 correct responses was evaluated on a main test trial.

Following the attainment of the learning criterion, subjects were given a paced-recall test either immediately or 48 hours later. The subjects, 16 in each condition, were students at the University of California, Berkeley, some of whom were paid for their services. Subjects were assigned randomly to the eight basic conditions in the order of their appearance in the laboratory. Specific lists and stimulus-response pairings were balanced over the conditions.

Results. In learning, the list containing low-probability bigrams was more difficult to learn than the high list ($p < .05$). Other comparisons were not significant. Of primary interest, of course, are the recall data which are presented in Table 1. A consideration of the four means obtained with the study-test method reveals the typical outcome, namely, virtually no difference in the forgetting of the two lists. The percentage forgotten for the low and high lists were 39.1 percent and 42.3 percent, respectively. An inspection of the set of means associated with the adjusted method indicates a sizeable difference in the forgetting of the two sets of material, but a difference exactly opposite to expectations! More specifically, forgetting was 26.8 percent and 45.7 percent for the low and high lists, respectively. The statistical outcome of the three-way factorial indicated significant forgetting ($p < .01$) overall, but generally superior recall of material learned by the adjusted method, $F(1, 120) = 5.68, p < .025$. (This latter finding can be attributed to a consistent overshooting of the learning criterion by the adjusted subjects.) No interactions were significant. Even an analysis of the data from the adjusted method alone failed to show a significant interaction between List and Retention Interval, $F(1, 120) = 3.09, p > .05$.

Discussion. While the results depicted in Table 1 do not resolve the question concerning the usefulness of the adjusted method for the study of forgetting, they do indicate that variations in response-term interference do not produce the expected differences in forgetting. On the other hand, the experiments reported by Amster et al. (1970) gave support to the Underwood-Postman theory when the interference involved the stimulus-response association. Several possible explanations of this discrepancy should be mentioned.

Table 1. Mean pairs correctly recalled.

Interval	Study-Test Method		Adjusted Method	
	Low	High	Low	High
Immediate	6.06	6.50	6.75	7.25
48 Hours	3.69	3.75	4.94	3.94
% Forgetting	39.1	42.3	26.8	45.7

First, since a different collection of letter combinations were used in the two experiments, it is not known whether the bigrams used in this experiment would show differential forgetting if they had been used in the experiment of Amster et al. By way of comment, however, the variations in normative strength (.018 and .141) in the present experiment are nearly identical to those represented in Experiment III of Amster et al. (.015 and .152). If there is something peculiar about the particular letter combinations in the two experiments, the generality of the findings from both experiments may be questioned. Second, it is possible that the two types of manipulations simply are not equally "responsive" to variations in assumed letter-sequence interference. Perhaps the neutral stimulus term isolates or in some sense "protects" the response term from letter-sequence interference. Unfortunately, we have no direct information concerning the reasonableness of this possibility.

In summary, then, we must conclude that it is possible to produce differences in forgetting which are consonant with the postulation of letter-sequence interference but that such demonstrations are still in the minority and appear to "work" when the interference is primarily associative. We will now consider how the other half of the Underwood-Postman theory has fared empirically.

UNIT-SEQUENCE INTERFERENCE: SOME RECENT EVIDENCE

In the original formulation of the theory, it was assumed that with tasks in which arbitrary unit sequences must be performed, e.g., serial or paired-associate learning, increases in word frequency would be accompanied by increases in unit-sequence interference and, consequently, by increases in forgetting. Evidence summarized in the 1968 review indicated that this expectation was not upheld.

Several additional experiments have been reported subsequent to the review and we will mention these briefly: (1) Johnson (1964), in an experiment not mentioned in the earlier review, compared the forgetting of a *single* paired associate, one consisting of a high-frequency word (e.g., *paper*) paired with a nonsense syllable and the other of a nonsense word (e.g., *gojey*) paired with the same nonsense syllable. He found equivalent amounts of forgetting over four retention intervals ranging from 25 seconds to 2 weeks. (2) Underwood and Ekstrand (1967b) found the same amount of forgetting over 24 hours of lists of paired associates made up of high- or low-frequency words. This same equivalence was maintained over four successive lists. (3) Using a task requiring backward serial recall, Turnage and McCullough (1968) failed to find differential forgetting over a one-week retention interval for lists chosen from six levels of word frequency representing a wide range of values on the frequency dimension. (4) Walen (1970), also with the backward serial task, reported equivalent forgetting over 1 week of lists of low- or high-frequency words for children as well as for adult subjects. Again, the results continue to be negative.

As originally proposed by Underwood and Postman, unit-sequence interference is *associative* in nature, affecting the performance of the specific associations prescribed by the learning task. For this reason, experiments involving single words tested for recall (Turnage, 1967) or for recognition (Young, Saegert, & Linsley, 1968) do not appear to provide completely relevant tests of the unit-sequence theory. We will now turn to two unpublished experiments from our laboratory in which the specific focus was on associative performance.

It has been suggested that the manipulation of word frequency can produce positive as well as negative effects. The negative component is unit-sequence interference. Facilitation may show itself either as an aid to associative learning, when linguistic habits and the prescribed associations correspond or generalize, or to response learning, when the greater frequency of occurrence makes high-frequency words more recallable than low-frequency words (e.g., Postman, 1962a). Our goal in the next two experiments was to neutralize the benefits of word frequency to response learning. The method used to accomplish this goal used retention tests in which correct responses were provided and subjects had to indicate the correct ordering of the words. We will consider first a serial-learning task.

Experiment II: Retention of Serial Order as a Function of Word Frequency

In an early test of the unit-sequence hypothesis, Postman (1961) compared the learning and retention of serial lists consisting of words of either high or low frequency. Equivalent amounts of forgetting were observed over a one-week period when retention was assessed both by serial recall (Experiment I) and by free recall (Experiment II). The present experiment[1] also provided a comparison between high and low serial lists, but the assessment of learning and retention was by means of a serial reordering test in which on test trials the subjects reconstructed the serial order from a list of words provided. In this way, a relatively pure determination of the effect of word frequency on associative recall was obtained.

Method. Subjects learned a single 12-item serial list constructed from words of either high or low frequency. The words were selected from those listed in the California Norms (Postman, 1970), which were also used in the earlier study mentioned above (Postman, 1961). Two sets of words (two-syllable nouns) were randomly chosen from each frequency level [high = 1000–3300 and low = 1–3 occurrences in 4.5 million in the "L" count of Thorndike and Lorge (1944)]. No repetitions of first letters were allowed within a list. Each list was arranged in four different serial orders each of which was used equally in the experiment. In these four arrangements, no word appeared in the same ordinal

[1] Dr. Bonnie Z. Strand provided valuable assistance in the conduct of this experiment and of Experiment IV.

position twice nor followed nor preceded another word more than once. A study-test procedure was used. On study trials the words were presented on a Stowe memory drum at a 1-second rate. On test trials, subjects were given an alphabetical listing of the 12 words and asked to write down the correct serial ordering of the words; 45 seconds were provided for this task. A 10-second interval then followed while the experimenter corrected the protocol handed to her by the subject. Study-test cycles were continued until subjects reached a criterion of one perfect ordering. Following the criterial trial, subjects were given an additional retention test either immediately or after a 1-week interval. Unlimited time was given on this terminal test. Subjects were students at the University of California, Berkeley. There were 8 subjects in the two immediate groups and 24 subjects in the two delay groups. Subjects were assigned to conditions randomly in blocks containing 3 delay and 1 immediate subjects from each of the two frequency conditions. The two sets of words and four serial orders of each set were balanced over the four frequency-interval conditions.

Results. The high list was learned more quickly than the low ($\overline{X}$ = 6.28 and 7.91 trials, respectively), but the difference was not significant ($p > .10$). None of the other comparisons was significant. The results of the retention test are presented in Table 2. The data have been scored in terms of the number of correct word-word sequences. An inspection of the percentage loss scores indicates slightly less forgetting of the high-frequency list, an outcome opposite to the theory, but this difference, which is reflected in the Frequency X Interval interaction, was not significant ($F < 1$). Other methods of scoring, e.g., correctness of serial placement and comparison of serial-position curves, failed to change the conclusion that equivalent amounts of forgetting were found with the two types of material.

Experiment III: Associative Forgetting of Pairs as a Function of Word Frequency

The second test of the unit-sequence theory focusing on associative recall contrasted two paired-associate lists, one consisting of low-frequency words and the other of high-frequency words. Previous experiments, e.g., Postman (1962a,

Table 2. Mean word-word sequences reproduced.

	Frequency	
Interval	Low	High
Immediate	9.50	10.25
1 week	6.00	5.96
% Forgetting	36.8	41.8

Experiment I) and Underwood and Ekstrand (1967b), measured retention by recall and represented variations in frequency within a relatively restricted frequency range. In the present experiment[2], performance was assessed with an associative-matching test during learning and recall; as in the previous experiment, it was thought that an associative task might be more sensitive to the operation of unit-sequence interference on retention. Moreover, an attempt was made to sample levels of word frequency which reflect the near extremes of word frequency, from extremely rare, but "recognizable" words, to the most common words in the language.

Method. The design was a 2 X 2 factorial formed by crossing two levels of word frequency (high and low) with two retention intervals (immediate and 24 hours). The learning materials consisted of 16 word pairs. The low-frequency words were selected randomly from words found within the frequency range of 1–4 per 9 million (Thorndike-Lorge, 1944, Part II), while high-frequency words were selected randomly from the 500 most frequent words (Thorndike-Lorge, 1944, Part V). No attempt was made to hold form class constant; instead, we wanted a representative sample of word pairs constructed from the literal extremes of the frequency dimension. The only restrictions were the deletion of proper nouns, foreign words, and hyphenated words. Three independent lists were formed at each frequency level. Two pairings of each list were constructed.

An alternating study-test procedure was followed. The pairs were presented at a 2-second rate on the study trials. The test trials consisted of an associative-matching test in which each stimulus word appeared together with the correct response and three alternatives chosen randomly from the other 15 responses in the list. The testing rate was set at 4 seconds and subjects were given strong encouragement to guess. The materials were arranged in four random orders on study trials and four independent orders on test trials. Response alternatives for any given pair were changed on each of these test trials. Subjects were taken to a learning criterion of 11/16 correct matches. Following the attainment of criterion, subjects were given recall instructions and an additional test trial either immediately or after 24 hours. A total of 18 subjects was run in each of the four conditions. Subjects were students at the University of California, Berkeley, all of whom were paid for their services. Assignment to conditions was random in blocks of four. Lists and starting orders within the two frequency conditions were balanced over the 18 subjects.

Results. The high-frequency list was learned more quickly than the low-frequency list ($\overline{X} = 3.00$ and 5.50, respectively), $F(1, 68) = 12.73, p < .01$. The results of the retention test are presented in Table 3. The forgetting in terms of percentages is not great (approximately 14 percent), but the effect of the delay is significant, $F(1, 68) = 7.29, p < .01$. The comparison of the two lists

---

[2] Dennis Bonge and Peggy Saunders assisted with this study and Experiment V.

Table 3.   Mean correct matches.

Interval	Frequency	
	Low	High
Immediate	11.83	11.06
24 Hours	9.39	10.17
% Forgetting	20.6	8.0

shows a difference in the direction opposite to the theory, but the interaction of frequency and interval was not significant, $p > .10$.

Discussion. It is abundantly clear that even under apparently optimal conditions (associative tasks and extreme variations in word frequency), the original expectation of the Underwood-Postman theory, of a direct relationship between word frequency and forgetting, is simply unsupported. In response to this problem, Postman (e.g., 1962a, 1963) has suggested that manipulations of word frequency may result in a *covariation* of facilitation and interference. Briefly, facilitation is a possibility whenever linguistic associations, direct or mediated, correspond to the prescribed associations. The difficulty with the assumption of this covariation lies in obtaining explicit predictions of the effect of word frequency on learning and retention. In the Postman (1962a) experiment, for example, where the retention of paired-associate lists varying in stimulus and response frequency was studied, forgetting and stimulus frequency were *inversely* related; this finding suggested that "there is greater conservation of facilitation than there is recovery of interference" (Postman, 1963, p. 41).

Another way of investigating the reality of unit-sequence interference is to manipulate interword associations *directly*, rather than by the indirect means of varying word frequency. We will consider three experiments in which this direct approach was undertaken. In a serial task, Postman (1967) compared the forgetting of a list of words representing zero interword free-associative strength with a list representing extremely high interword strength (words which all tend to elicit one another on a free-association test). If unit-sequence interference is an important determiner of forgetting, we should certainly expect greater forgetting of the serial list constructed of free associates. On the contrary, Postman's experiment indicated exactly the opposite. This reversal of outcome was interpreted to reflect the facilitation of response *recall* through the operation of the contextual constraint afforded by the list of high associates. Similar conclusions were drawn from experiments with paired-associate lists containing inappropriately paired free associates (Postman, Fraser, & Burns, 1968; Underwood & Ekstrand, 1968).

A question arising from these experiments is the possibility that the operation of unit-sequence interference on forgetting is *masked* by the facilitation of response recall. That is, the very operations assumed to affect unit-sequence interference (variations in associative strength) also may enhance response recall. It is clear, then, that the relationship between forgetting and associative strength in situations, where the relative importance of the two factors and the requirements of the prescribed associations run counter to the normative ones, will depend upon the relative importance of the two factors (unit-sequence interference and facilitation of response recall) and the requirements of the retention test. In the experiments cited in the last paragraph, the retention test required the *recall* of the responses and so both factors may have been operating. The purpose of Experiment IV was to eliminate the recall component so that the possibility of unit-sequence interference could be assessed directly.

Experiment IV: Retention of Serial Order as a Function of Interword Associative Strength

Method. The experiment was patterned after and conducted in conjunction with Experiment II. Subjects were given a 12-word serial list to master. The serial reordering task described previously was used on the test portion of alternating study-test trials. Lists were selected from Postman (1967). In particular, lists consisting of free associates to the words *butterfly* and *command* represented the high-associative material and lists with zero interword associative strengths, matched in word frequency with the words in the high lists, constituted the low (zero) material. Each list was arranged into four serial orders and used equally often as the learning material. Following the criterion of a correct ordering of the 12 words, subjects were given a second test either immediately or 1 week later. There were 8 subjects in the immediate groups and 24 subjects in the delay groups. In all other respects, the experiment was identical to Experiment II.

Results. The two types of lists were learned at nearly identical rates (6.53 and 6.56 trials for the high and zero lists, respectively). The results of the terminal retention test are presented in Table 4. It is clear that the presence of

Table 4. Mean word-word sequences reproduced.

Interval	Interitem Associative Strength	
	Zero	High
Immediate	11.62	10.38
1 week	6.67	6.75
% Forgetting	42.6	35.0

conflicting interword associations in a serial list does not result in accelerated forgetting when retention is assessed by means of an associative test. Other than the comparison of immediate and delay groups, F (1, 60) = 18.90, none of the other comparisons was significant ($F < 1$).

Conclusions. The present experiments and those previously reported in the literature have all failed to demonstrate the operation of unit-sequence interference in forgetting. Even with retention tests which are sensitive to associative factors the theory continues to be unsupported. When word frequency is manipulated, unit-sequence *facilitation* of the sort described by Postman (1962a, 1963) remains a possibility and may explain some of the failures to find differences in forgetting as a function of this variable. But when unit-sequence interference is manipulated directly, with the variation of presumably conflicting interword associations as in Experiment IV, differential loss of an *associative* nature still remains to be demonstrated.

The earlier unsuccessful tests of the Underwood-Postman theory have led to the design of experiments which were thought to be more sensitive to the postulated linguistic interference and to modifications of interference theory. In the first category, we could point to the last three experiments reported in this paper, where an associative retention test replaced the usual recall test. Other examples are experiments in which the purpose was to bring linguistic habits into the laboratory with the hope that the influence of unit-sequence interference on forgetting would now be observed. This has been attempted by presenting a succession of serial (Postman, 1962b) or paired-associate lists (Underwood & Ekstrand, 1967) varying in word frequency, by manipulating the form class of stimuli and responses in paired-associate lists (Underwood & Ekstrand, 1968, Experiment II), and by having subjects supply their own responses to stimuli varying in frequency (Abra, 1968; Postman, 1964). Without an exception, these various experiments have produced negative results as far as the theory is concerned.

In a relatively early paper, Postman (1963) listed a number of factors which would tend to reduce the effect of extraexperimental interference. Following a different tack, Underwood and Ekstrand (1966) suggested that linguistic habits do not influence the forgetting of verbal material learned in the laboratory because of the conditions under which they are acquired in the first place. Using an experimental analogue, they showed a marked reduction in proactive inhibition when the first (or interfering) list was practiced over four days rather than all at once. In a subsequent study, Underwood and Ekstrand (1967a) provided evidence to support the notion that the reduction in proactive inhibition is the result of increased interlist differentiation. If this interpretation is extended to the single list, we would say that the failure of an interference theory based upon the assumption of linguistic interference is a high differentiation existing between the laboratory task and the linguistic habits of long standing. In view of the lack of success endured by an interference theory based upon the intrusion of specific and conflicting linguistic habits, I suggested an alternative theory of forgetting. We will now turn to this explanation and see how well it has survived in the laboratory.

A NONSPECIFIC INTERFERENCE THEORY OF FORGETTING

As outlined in an earlier paper (Keppel, 1968), I proposed (1) that forgetting is largely the result of the subject's linguistic activity during the retention interval (i.e., retroactive inhibition) and (2) that the interference generated by this activity would be nonspecific, i.e., the same for any type of material learned to the same degree of mastery. The Underwood-Postman theory emphasized preexperimental linguistic activity and hypothesized specific interference generated by the conflict of the prescribed associations and strong linguistic habits associated with the elements making up the learning task. In the language of the transfer/retroaction experiment, specific interference might be described as A-B, A-D, where "A" is a word in the list, "B" is the prescribed response, and "D" is the strong linguistic response to "A." (Other transfer paradigms may also be involved, but the A-B, A-D paradigm makes the point.) In contrast, the transfer paradigm for the nonspecific theory is A-B, C-D, where "A-B" represents the prescribed association and "C-D" represents the linguistic activity. In short, the nonspecific theory does not depend upon an overlap of within-list and extra-list associations, while the specific theory does.

Evidence from the laboratory for retroactive (or proactive) inhibition with the A-D paradigm is so compelling that it need not be documented here. In my review published in 1968, there were only a few studies with the C-D paradigm and these were suspect because of the possibility of interlist stimulus similarity resulting from the duplication of letters making up the nonsense syllables in the two lists. Subsequent studies have overcome these difficulties, however, and considerable amounts of retroactive inhibition have been observed under these circumstances (e.g., Keppel, Henschel, & Zavortink, 1969; Postman, Stark, & Henschel, 1969).

Forgetting is attributed to the occurrence of general linguistic activity during the retention interval. The nonspecific nature of this interference accommodates the numerous failures to find specific interference. That is, equivalent amounts of forgetting of lists consisting of low or high frequency words, for example, are due to the fact that the same amount of linguistic activity intervenes between learning and the retention test. It should be noted that a noninterference explanation of forgetting, such as decay theory, can make the same prediction. What is needed is a way of manipulating linguistic activity. One possibility is to fill the retention interval with a period of sleep or of waking activity, which a number of investigators have done (see Ekstrand, 1967). These experiments have shown less forgetting in the sleep condition. The interpretive problem associated with these experiments is the plausibility of noninteference explanations, e.g., reduced decay, increased rehearsal by the sleep subjects, or less disruption of "consolidation" mechanisms in the sleep conditions.

Another approach is to manipulate the linguistic activity directly. Grissom (1966) attempted to do this by comparing the delayed recall of subjects kept in the laboratory under conditions of sensory restriction with that of control subjects allowed to continue their normal activities. Subjects listened to a prose passage and recalled it verbally. Different groups of restricted and nonrestricted subjects were then tested again after 8, 16, 20, or 24 hours. The results indicated less of a loss between the two tests for the restricted subjects and a suggestion of an interaction, the difference between the two conditions increasing with the length of the interval. It is difficult to interpret these data, however, because the groups may not have been equivalent in learning and the restricted subjects may have spent some of their time thinking about the passage presented immediately before their isolation. It seemed useful, therefore, to try a different sort of manipulation of linguistic activity rather than sleep versus awake or sensory restriction versus nonrestriction.

Experiment V: Forgetting as a Function of Verbal Activity

Method. The experiment was modeled after and run at the same time as Experiment III. Briefly, subjects learned lists consisting of high- or of low-frequency words to a criterion of 11/16 correct pairings. An associative-matching procedure was used to assess performance. Following the attainment of criterion, subjects were given 45 minutes of intense verbal activity or an equal interval requiring minimal verbal activity. More specifically, verbal subjects were presented a different prose passage every 15 minutes during which time they were asked to read the passage aloud, to prepare, and to answer questions on the different passages. Subjects in the nonverbal condition were given a different mechanical puzzle to solve every 15 minutes; except for the initial, brief instructions, verbal activity was minimal. At the end of the 45 minutes, all subjects were given a retention test with the same matching procedure. There were 18 subjects in each of the four experimental conditions. The details of the procedure and of the material are outlined in Experiment II. The expectation was that subjects given verbal activity would show more forgetting over the 45-minute period than subjects given the relatively nonverbal tasks. Moreover, since the theory is nonspecific, it was expected to find an equal deficit for the high- and low-frequency lists.

Results. As in Experiment III, the high list was acquired more rapidly ($\overline{X}$ = 3.75 and 4.69, respectively), but the difference this time is not significant, $F(1, 68) = 2.27, p > .10$. The results of the terminal matching test are presented in Table 5. A statistical analysis of these data draws a blank: the largest effect is associated with a probability of $p > .25$. The interpolation of verbal activity failed to affect retention performance.

Table 5. Mean correct matches.

Activity	Frequency	
	Low	High
Verbal	10.67	11.78
Nonverbal	11.11	10.89

Discussion. Where does one go from here? It is always possible that a longer retention interval (and/or more verbal activity) will produce an effect. A comparison of these results with the level of recall of the subjects given an immediate matching test in Experiment III indicates that virtually no deficit was observed over the 45-minute interval. Additionally, perhaps if retention had been assessed by recall rather than by matching, differences would have appeared. These are all possibilities that can be explored in new experiments.

We should mention an experiment by Birnbaum (1970) which is relevant to this question. Basically, she contrasted the recall of subjects given a pattern-selection task (control) with subjects asked to read and to rate various passages on a number of dimensions. The learning material consisted of 10 pairs of high-frequency nouns. One half of the pairs specifically appeared in the interpolated prose passages; the nouns were always paired with new words in these sentences. Birnbaum argued that if the influence of the reading activity is nonspecific, recall performance on pairs appearing and pairs not appearing in the activity will be equally affected, while if it is specific, only those pairs appearing in the passages would be affected. She found essentially no effect of the verbal activity on recall, but differences in response latencies did appear. Specifically, pairs not appearing in the passages were recalled by the experimental subjects just as quickly as the corresponding pairs were recalled by the control subjects ($\bar{X} = 3.0$ and 2.7 seconds, respectively), while pairs appearing in the passages were recalled more slowly than the control pairs ($\bar{X} = 4.3$ and 2.7 seconds, respectively).

Birnbaum concluded that the reading does interfere with the recall of verbal material and that this interference is specific. Although only response latency was affected in her experiment, she argued that an extension of the length of the interval or an increase in the frequency with which the words appear in the passages, will result in the eventual loss of responses.

It would seem important to conduct this suggested experiment because of the susceptibility of response latencies to factors other than loss of associative strength. But suppose that future experiments do show an actual response loss as a result of the reading activity, we will still be left with the same puzzles. That is, Birnbaum's study indicates that the reading activity induces a *specific* loss. If we consider the verbal activity which normally fills the retention interval and correlate this activity with the material learned in the laboratory, we must reach the conclusion that word frequency and forgetting *should* be positively related.

To amplify, only high-frequency words stand any reasonable chance of being experienced during a retention interval and if the loss is specific, then only high-frequency material should show any forgetting. As we have overwhelmingly documented, word frequency and forgetting are *not* directly related.

In summary, the possibility of nonspecific interference being responsible for the forgetting of subjects who learn and recall a single list in the laboratory is still a real one. The amount of forgetting which needs to be explained is not large and the amount of verbal activity engaged in by the college sophomore is considerable. Grissom's (1966) experiment suggests a reduction in forgetting over relatively long periods of time (up to 24 hours) when subjects are in a restricted environment. The 45 minutes of verbal activity given the subjects in Experiment V may simply not have been enough to show a difference. Birnbaum's (1970) study provides positive evidence, but as we have argued, her finding of a specific loss does not square with the retention data present in the literature.

POTENTIAL MECHANISMS OF FORGETTING

We have examined in detail theories of forgetting which have been based upon the classical interference paradigms of proaction and retroaction. The Under-wood Postman theory of extraexperimental sources of interferences represented a natural extension of these interference paradigms to the explanation of forgetting in the situation where a single list is learned and then subsequently recalled. As we have painfully indicated, the theory has not been upheld. The less precise nonspecific interference theory, considered in the last section, cannot be rejected (or accepted) on the basis of the meager evidence available to date. In this last section, we will discuss several factors which either singly or in combination may provide the answer to the important question with which we began this paper: Why do we forget?

Basic Considerations

It is useful to keep in mind the magnitude of the explanatory job we have before us, i.e., to consider the amount of forgetting that needs to be explained. Ever since Underwood's (1957) demonstration that earlier estimates were greatly influenced by proactive inhibition from materials previously learned in the laboratory, expectations now fall in the range of 10–20 percent forgetting over 24 hours when a subject learns a single list to a criterion of one perfect recitation. This value is not excessively large—a point which made the Underwood-Postman theory, which was based on the postulation of linguistic interference, reasonable and plausible. In view of the lack of success of this general theoretical approach, however, the value has proved to be an elusively small amount! Still, the point remains that mechanisms which may be proposed do not have to be especially powerful ones—even "modest" mechanisms may be sufficiently strong to account for the forgetting actually observed in an experiment.

A second consideration is the fact that mechanisms of forgetting will generally have to be nonspecific in nature. What leads us to this statement is the long line of research which continues to echo the conclusion that task variables, e.g., frequency (or meaningfulness), intralist similarity, and form class, simply do not affect rate of forgetting. Whatever the cause of forgetting, it does not appear to depend upon the specific nature of the material being learned and recalled. This is not to deny the possibility that at the level of the individual item in a list of verbal items forgetting will be attributable to specific characteristics of the particular pair lost. What seems to be needed are mechanisms which are not influenced by variations in the characteristics of the material—at least those characteristics which have been studied as to date. Perhaps future linguistic analyses will identify hitherto uncontrolled, i.e., manipulated, characteristics and provide a potential key for understanding forgetting. For the time being, it seems advisable to search for nonspecific sources of forgetting. With these thoughts in mind, then, we will examine four potentially important mechanisms of forgetting.

Nonspecific interference

We have already mentioned the possibility in the last section that general linguistic activity occurring during the retention interval produces forgetting. As we indicated, only a few attempts at controlling a subject's linguistic activity have been reported. While we were unable to accelerate forgetting by increasing verbal activity (Experiment V), the use of longer retention intervals may be more successful. In this regard, consider Grissom's (1966) experiment varying sensory restriction up to 24 hours and Ekstrand's (1967) contrast of subjects who are asleep or awake during the retention interval. Whether the findings from these latter types of manipulation are reasonably interpreted in terms of differences in verbal activity, of course, is not yet known, but the mere possibility that they may does add a certain amount of credibility to the notion.

Change in environmental context

Whereas nonspecific interference, at least as described in this paper, implies a nonreversible loss from memory, the two mechanisms we will consider next view forgetting as a failure to provide the critical stimulus cues at the time of testing. The implication is, of course, that forgetting is not a loss from storage, but instead, an inability to revive a memory on the critical test. The first mechanism considers nonspecific contextual cues and their role in supporting recall after a retention interval of some duration.

Environmental or contextual cues have entered into the theoretical thinking of a number of researchers. For example, the "contextual association" has been considered a mechanism underlying the response-learning stage of paired-associate learning and as a contributor to retroactive inhibition in a number of transfer paradigms (cf. McGovern, 1964). In free-recall learning, Tulving (1968) uses the concept to allow a way for the subject to initiate recall at the end of the study trial. One line of evidence offered in support of the proposition that contextual stimuli are of some importance for learning and memory are the experiments of Bilodeau and Schlosberg (1951) and of Greenspoon and Ranyard (1957). Briefly, these studies showed that retroactive inhibition can be reduced when the interfering list is learned in an experimental setting which is greatly changed from that in which the critical first list is learned. These findings are usually interpreted to mean that the overlap of environmental cues from one list to the next is an important factor in producing inteference. This interpretation has been questioned in a recent experiment by Strand (1970) who demonstrated that an equivalent reduction in interference could be obtained by simply taking a walk with the subject and returning to the *same* experimental room as was found by journeying him to a *different* room.

The question to which we want to address ourselves here concerns the possibility that nonspecific contextual cues, stimulus cues present during the training session, become associated with the material being learned and that their absence at recall can contribute to the forgetting observed over the retention interval. [It may be noted that Underwood (1969, p. 568) offers a similar proposal for a contextual attribute of memory.] There is some indirect evidence for this speculation in the change-of-context experiments mentioned in the last paragraph. To be more specific, Greenspoon and Ranyard (1957) included conditions in which the context in which the first list was learned and subsequently recall was varied. If the two contexts are labeled "A" and "B" and the three successive contexts (first list, second list, and recall of the first list) are represented by these letters, we can summarize the results of the recall test as follows: AAA (3.47) versus AAB (1.79) and ABA (7.12) versus ABB (3.91). In both comparisons, a change in the context at the time of the retention test markedly reduced recall. A similar result for the second contrast was reported by Gottlieb and Lindauer (1967), i.e., ABA (3.30) versus ABB (2.30). In this case, context was manipulated by varying the color and shape of a geometrical patch surrounding number-nonsense syllable pairs in the two lists. Less compelling results were reported by Lehr and Duncan (1970) who obtained recall of *both* lists under the same conditions as studied by Gottlieb and Lindauer, i.e., ABA and ABB; they also obtained recall with different groups of subjects either immediately following or 14 minutes following second-list learning. Context was manipulated by changing the color of the stimulus terms. For first-list recall, the expected effect was obtained on the immediate test (corresponding to the sort of procedure followed by Greenspoon and Ranyard and by Gottlieb and Lindauer), while just the reverse was found on the delayed test. For second-list recall, there was no difference between the two groups on the immediate test, but higher recall for the "no change" group (ABB) on the delayed test.

As we have indicated, these experiments have been interference situations and, consequently, the context effect may represent a change in interference rather than a lowering of recall per se. There is one experiment in the literature which does consider the effect of contextual factors in the recall of a single list. Specifically, Rand and Wapner (1967) varied what they called "postural status," an aspect of the subject's *internal* environmental context.[3] Subjects were given a serial list of six nonsense syllables to learn and then to relearn 15 minutes later. The learning or relearning sessions were accomplished either in an erect or a supine position. These two variables (learning versus relearning; erect versus supine) were combined factorially to result in two conditions in which the same position was required of the subject in learning and relearning (erect-erect and supine-supine) and two conditions in which different positions were required (erect-supine and supine-erect). The amazing outcome was that relearning (to one perfect recitation) was accomplished significantly faster when the learning-relearning postures were congruent than where they were not ($\bar{X} = 3.25$ and 4.45 trials, respectively).

Although these findings are supportive of the general proposition that change of context can depress recall, it is surprising that any effect was found at all in view of the short retention interval (15 minutes) and the fact that memory was assessed by relearning. Since subjects served in all four treatment combinations, it is also possible that the effect was dependent upon the development of differential amounts of proactive inhibition stemming from the serial lists learned and relearned previously. In any case, the findings of Rand and Wapner are certainly suggestive and are worthy of replication with subjects serving in only one condition and perhaps tested after a longer interval, e.g., 24 hours.

The number and variety of potential contextual cues which might aid and influence retention performance are great. The evidence cited above is positive, showing that retention performance is depressed when the external or internal environment present during learning is deliberately changed at recall. To use these findings as a basis for a general theory of forgetting requires the assumption that there is a sufficient contextual change between learning and recall, e.g., over a 24-hour period, to produce a disruption in performance. Obviously, it is not yet possible to say whether this presumed contextual change is sufficient to account for all of the forgetting observed in an experiment. On the other hand, the loss to be explained is not all that large. In addition, it is possible in some learning tasks for even a small loss, due to contextual change, say, to be magnified during the recall trial, e.g., the "snowball" effect of an item missed at the beginning of a serial list or the occasional loss of a word which is the retrieval cue for a "subjective unit" in a free-recall task.

[3] The importance of internal environmental cues has been recognized for some time in the animal-learning literature. The research areas most relevant for this discussion are the studies concerned with state-dependent learning where the physiological state of the animal is changed through the administration of drugs.

Change in stimulus encoding

We have come to accept the assumption that subjects rarely use the total amount of information available in the stimulus term when attempting to learn a paired-associate list. If the stimulus term is a nonsense syllable, subjects may use the first letter as a cue provided this letter is capable of performing the cueing function unambiguously (e.g., Postman & Greenbloom, 1967). This process has been called "stimulus selection" and has emphasized the transformation of the "nominal" stimulus, the stimulus term offered the subject by the experimenter, into the "functional" stimulus, the stimulus configuration which is actually responsible for cueing the correct response. [Richardson in his chapter reviews this literature in detail.] A related, but theoretically different point of view is one which has been called stimulus "encoding" (Martin, 1968). It is not the intention of this paper to press the distinctions between these two notions, but instead to indicate how the idea of a transformation of the nominal stimulus to a functional stimulus may be used to explain the forgetting of verbal material.

By either notion, a subject learns a paired-associate list by forming an association linking the response to the functional stimulus. Presumably, forgetting can occur if the critical stimulus encoding is not made by the subject at the time of the retention test. Since associative probability has been formed between the response and the functional stimulus, any change in the transformation will result in "random" responding (unless, of course, the subject has multiply encoded the stimulus a sufficient number of times to allow for some associative strength to accrue to the alternative encoding). In experiments dealing with stimulus selection, rarely do we see complete consistency across all subjects and all pairs in the elements of the stimuli shown to be effective in eliciting the correct response. If subjects are not consistent at the end of learning, it is not unreasonble to assume that they were variable during learning. That is, the selection process is probably characterized by a series of selection attempts, the basis for selection for any pair often changing from trial to trial. For Martin (1968), this "encoding variability" is a critical part of his theory of learning. He proposed that any given stimulus term may be responded to (i.e., encoded) in a number of ways, the probability of any particular encoding being dependent upon its probability density over the entire set of possible encodings for that stimulus.

If learning requires the establishment of a stable stimulus transformation, forgetting may be the result of the reactivation of some of the alternative encodings at the time of recall. With a change in the encoding, the chances of the correct response being given are greatly diminished. The critical question now, of course, is to account for the return to the "prelearning" state of encoding variability. Perhaps the changes in environmental context, discussed in the preceding section, may sufficiently "jolt" the subject so that the variability is introduced. Perhaps encoding variability can never be eliminated during the course of learning so that the alternative encodings "recover" from this extinction or suppression "spontaneously." (In accounting for spontaneous recovery in the retroaction design, Martin actually speaks of the external "disinhibition" of alternative encodings.) Whatever the case, the possibility that forgetting may be in part the result of a return of encoding variability implies the potential recovery of associations "forgotten" for this reason. The small, but consistently observed appearance of pairs previously missed upon the repeated application of the stimulus terms (cf. Richardson & Gropper, 1964) may be due to the reactivation on successive presentations of the successful encoding, i.e., the encoding to which the correct response is associated.

The focus of our discussion has been the identification of nonspecific sources of forgetting and it would be a simple matter to assume that the recovery of encoding variability will be the same for different types of stimulus characteristics, either properties of individual stimuli, e.g., meaningfulness or form class, or of stimuli within a list, e.g., intralist stimulus similarity. An important postulate in Martin's theory, however, is the assumption that encoding variability is inversely related to meaningfulness. That is, stimuli of low meaningfulness are assumed to display more encoding variability than do stimuli of high meaningfulness. Martin used this assumption to account for a number of learning and transfer phenomena. An obvious prediction in a retention experiment, then, would be to find greater forgetting with stimuli of low meaningfulness than with stimuli of high meaningfulness. As we have seen, however, evidence for this expected outcome has been mixed. It may be that stimulus meaningfulness has not been varied sufficiently to produce a significant difference in encoding variability. [A respectable, but nonsignificant difference (20.6 percent and 8.0 percent forgetting for low and high pairs, respectively) was found in Experiment III where meaningfulness, defined in terms of word frequency, was represented by two widely-separated extremes on the dimension.] Another possibility is that the process of bringing lists of low and high meaningfulness to the same degree of learning results in the conditioning of some of the alternative stimulus encodings in addition to the one of highest probability. (Martin assumes that the conditioning of additional encodings occurs at later stages of learning.) Thus, even with a greater increase in encoding variability over the retention interval for stimuli of low than of high meaningfulness, equivalent amounts of forgetting may still be observed.

Recovery of interpair interference

The final mechanism of forgetting we will consider is a factor which is the result of having subjects learn and recall *lists* of pairs instead of single paired associates. Tulving and Arbuckle (1963) have clearly shown that recall probability is inversely related to the number of inputs (new pairs presented for study) and/or outputs ("old" stimuli presented for test) appearing between the study and test of any given pair. Thus, one reason why a subject cannot master a list of 10 paired associates in a single trial is that the pairs in the list are subjected to retroaction from input/output events which are interpolated during the study and test portions of a learning trial. (Interference may be generated from proactive sources as well, i.e., earlier input events if we are considering the initial learning trial, but we will not add this possibility to our discussion.) In short, a single study-test trial is a complicated affair, involving acquisition as well as interpair interference generated within the study-test sequence. The picture is much more complicated when the list is presented for more than one study-test sequence as is done in the usual learning-retention study. The same sort of interference is potentially present, however.

As I have described it, interpair interference is nonspecific. Although there is evidence for the recovery from nonspecific interference in a multilist situation, where unrelated pairs make up successive lists (Postman, Stark, & Henschel, 1969), it is not clear what the consequences may be for nonspecific interference generated *within* a list. More specifically, if the main effect of interpair interference is to reduce the recallability of a given pair, recovery then would produce an *increase* in response strength for this pair. Moreover, *all* pairs in the list should show this type of recovery. The expectation, then, might be for *reminiscence*, an uncommon, but occasionally observed phenomenon [e.g., Keppel and Underwood (1967); Peterson (1966)]. But we are looking for a mechanism that will produce forgetting, not reminiscence!

Of course, interpair interference need not be nonspecific nor operate in the manner we have just described. With regard to the first point, we have been assuming that the pairs in the list are unrelated semantically, conceptually, and physically. If relatively common words are used for the learning material, it will be virtually impossible to construct a list of 10 pairs, say, where the similarity between the stimulus term (or the response term) of a given pair and the other stimuli and responses is zero. For nonword stimuli or responses (e.g., nonsense syllables), an experimenter can avoid the duplication of specific elements (i.e., the individual letters), but there is still the possibility of acoustic similarity and associative similarity stemming from strong alphabetical habits. If we can safely assume the presence of a certain amount of intralist similarity in any list constructed for a paired-associate task, some portion of the interpair interference will reflect retroactive and proactive inhibition of a specific sort involving other stimuli and responses in the list. With the recovery of this sort of specific interference within the list, forgetting may result.

The similarity of this mechanism to Gibson's (1940) recovery of intralist generalization is obvious. Because of this similarity, the present explanation loses some of its appeal for one of the same reasons that Gibson's theory has fallen into disrepute, namely, the failure of intralist *similarity*, manipulations where similarity is *explicitly* varied among stimulus-response terms, to influence rate of forgetting (cf. Underwood, 1961). On the other hand, it is possible that the presence of small amounts of intralist similarity involving small numbers of pairs, as would be the case in the typical experiment, *may* be responsible for the forgetting. We cannot reject this possibility until an experiment with this sort of manipulation is conducted.

Earlier in this discussion, we indicated that interpair inteference might not operate in the manner proposed. Battig (e.g., 1966, 1968) has suggested that learning occurs in part through the operation of a number of mechanisms which are brought into play when the intratask interference is present. Loss of the end products of these mechanisms, e.g., interpair grouping, use of mediated and extralist associations, and additional stimulus learning, would result in a return of interpair interference and hence forgetting. Battig did not, however, address himself to the question of why these losses might occur over a retention interval.[4]

CONCLUSION AND SUMMARY

We began this paper with a review of recent research dealing with an interference interpretation of forgetting. This interpretation, stemming from the Underwood-Postman (1960) theory, focused upon extraexperimental, linguistic sources of interference which were said to be responsible for forgetting. Letter-sequence interference was generated when the learning material consisted of uncommon combinations of letters, while unit-sequence interference resulted when integrated units such as words were formed into combinations which were in conflict with other combinations involving these units. Evidence for letter-sequence interference was presented first. The only positive outcome was an experiment by Amster et al. (1970) and the reason for this success is not known. An experiment designed to pinpoint the belated success of the theory and to extend the analysis to response-term interference (Experiment I) failed to do either. Thus, we are left with the same puzzles as before.

We then turned our attention to the unit-sequence portion of the Underwood-Postman theory. Three experiments were reported (Experiments II, III, and IV), in which learning and retention were assessed by means of tests emphasizing associative factors. All three experiments were negative with respect to the general proposition that increased forgetting results when the prescribed associations are at variance with linguistic associations either within the list, manipulated by varying preexperimental interitem associative strength (Experiment IV), or primarily outside of the list, manipulated by varying word frequency (Experiments II and III). There is essentially no experiment which supports the theory.

In view of these negative outcomes of the theory of extraexperimental interference, an alternative theory was considered in which the influence of linguistic activity on forgetting was assumed to be retroactive and nonspecific in nature. Only a few experiments have been conducted testing this notion and the

[4] He has suggested that one reason variables such as meaningfulness and intralist similarity do not affect forgetting is the covariation of intratask interference in learning and intratask facilitation at recall (cf. Battig, 1968, pp. 165–166).

results of these have been mixed. Still, given the small amount of forgetting observed over a 24-hour period and the relatively short intervals of linguistic activity attempted (less than 1 hour), the notion has not been given a reasonable test.

The final section of the paper was devoted to a consideration of alternative sources of forgetting. In addition to the operation of nonspecific interference described previously, three additional mechanisms were mentioned: changes in internal and external environmental cues, an increase in the variability of stimulus encoding over the retention interval, and the recovery of interpair interference. Whether these suggestions fare any better than have the proposals of the Underwood-Postman theory awaits the merciless scrutiny of the laboratory. One mechanism we have not considered in any detail is the possibility of autonomous decay of the memory trace. The reason for this is that it is not obvious how this notion may be brought to direct experimental test and so proponents of this explanation merely need to wait in the background until the last of any alternative processes (the ones presented here and others proposed in the future) have failed to be verified by experimental manipulations.

The prognosis should not be considered all *that* gloomy! What we are striving for is the ability to account for a small amount of forgetting. As we have indicated, the percentage forgetting over 24 hours is not large and the influence of a particular mechanism may be greater than the specific loss seems to imply (i.e., the "snowball" effect). Finally, we may find that no one mechanism is responsible for forgetting. Perhaps different mechanisms operate on different items for any given subject or even on different subjects. Under these circumstances, the total amount of forgetting would be a sum total of the toll extracted by the separate mechanisms. On the other hand, it is conceivable that no one mechanism is sufficiently important to produce forgetting when studied by itself. Instead, it may be necessary for two or more mechanisms to converge upon a particular member of a list before any forgetting is observed. If this latter view is correct, it will be rather difficult to find any mechanism which in isolation can be shown to influence forgetting. Let us hope that this will not be the case and that we will be able to identify at least one independent variable which will influence retention and will also provide the basis for an understanding of the forgetting process.

REFERENCES

Abra, J. C. Acquisition and retention of consistent associative responses with varied meaningfulness and similarity of stimuli. *Journal of Verbal Learning and Verbal Behavior*, 1968, 7, 647—652.

Amster, H., Keppel, G., & Meyer, A. Learning and retention of letter pairs as a function of association strength. *American Journal of Psychology*, 1970, 83, 22—39.

Battig, W. F. Facilitation and interference. In E. A. Bilodeau (ed.), *Acquisition of Skill*. New York: Academic Press, 1966. Pp. 215–244.

Battig, W. F. Paired-associate learning. In T. R. Dixon & D. L. Horton (eds.), *Verbal Behavior and General Behavior Theory*. Englewood Cliffs, N. J.: Prentice-Hall, 1968. Pp. 149–171.

Bilodeau, I. McD., & Schlosberg, H. Similarity in stimulating conditions as a variable in retroactive inhibition. *Journal of Experimental Psychology*, 1951, 41, 199–204.

Birnbaum, I. M. Recall of a word list after interpolated reading. *American Journal of Psychology*, 1970, 83, 412–419.

Ekstrand, B. R. Effect of sleep on memory. *Journal of Experimental Psychology*, 1967, 75, 64–72.

Gibson, E. J. A systematic application of the concepts of generalization and differentiation to verbal learning. *Psychological Review*, 1940, 47, 196–229.

Gottlieb, W., & Lindauer, M. S. The effect of contextual stimuli on retroactive inhibition. *Psychonomic Science*, 1967, 9, 331–332.

Greenspoon, J., & Ranyard, R. Stimulus conditions and retroactive inhibition. *Journal of Experimental Psychology*, 1957, 53, 55–59.

Grissom, R. J. Facilitation of memory by experiential restriction after learning. *American Journal of Psychology*, 1966, 79, 613–617.

Johnson, R. E. Meaningfulness and retention of a single paired associate. *Psychological Reports*, 1964, 14, 951–957.

Keppel, G. Retroactive and proactive inhibition. In T. R. Dixon & D. L. Horton (eds.), *Verbal Behavior and General Behavior Theory*. Englewood Cliffs, N. J.: Prentice-Hall, 1968. Pp. 172–213.

Keppel, G., Henschel, D. M. & Zavortink, B. Influence of nonspecific interference on response recall. *Journal of Experimental Psychology*, 1969, 81, 246–255.

Keppel, G., & Underwood, B. J. Reminiscence in the short-term retention of paired-associate lists. *Journal of Verbal Learning and Verbal Behavior*, 1967, 6, 375–382.

Lehr, D. J., & Duncan, C. P. Effect of priming on spontaneous recovery of verbal lists. *Journal of Verbal Learning and Verbal Behavior*, 1970, 9, 106–110.

Martin, E. Stimulus meaningfulness and paired-associate transfer: an encoding variability hypothesis. *Psychological Review*, 1968, 75, 421–441.

McGovern, J. B. Extinction of associations in four transfer paradigms. *Psychological Monographs*, 1964, 78, No. 16.

Peterson, L. R. Reminiscence in short-term memory. *Journal of Experimental Psychology*, 1966, 71, 115–118.

Postman, L. Extra-experimental interference and the retention of words. *Journal of Experimental Psychology*, 1961, 61, 97–110.

Postman, L. The effects of language habits on the acquisition and retention of verbal associations. *Journal of Experimental Psychology*, 1962, 64, 7–19. (a)

Postman, L. The temporal course of proactive inhibition for serial lists. *Journal of Experimental Psychology*, 1962, 63, 361–369. (b)

Postman, L. Does interference theory predict too much forgetting? *Journal of Verbal Learning and Verbal Behavior*, 1963, 2, 40–48.

Postman, L. Acquisition and retention of consistent associative responses. *Journal of Experimental Psychology* 1964, 67, 183–190.

Postman, L. The effect of interitem associative strength on the acquisition and retention of serial lists. *Journal of Verbal Learning and Verbal Behavior*, 1967, 6, 721–728.

Postman, L. The California Norms: association as a function of word frequency. In L. Postman & G. Keppel (eds.), *Norms of Word Association*. New York: Academic Press, 1970. Pp. 241–320.

Postman, L., Fraser, J., & Burns, S. Unit-sequence facilitation in recall. *Journal of Verbal Learning and Verbal Behavior*, 1968, 7, 217–224.

Postman, L., & Greenbloom, R. Conditions of cue selection in the acquisition of paired-associate lists. *Journal of Experimental Psychology*, 1967, 73, 91–100.

Postman, L., Stark, K., & Henschel, D. Conditions of recovery after unlearning. *Journal of Experimental Psychology Monograph*, 1969, 82, No. 1., Part 2.

Rand, G., & Wapner, S. Postural status as a factor in memory. *Journal of Verbal Learning and Verbal Behavior*, 1967, 6, 268–271.

Richardson, J., & Gropper, M. S. Learning during recall trials. *Psychological Reports*, 1964, 15, 551–560.

Strand, B. Z. Change of context and retroactive inhibition. *Journal of Verbal Learning and Verbal Behavior*, 1970, 9, 202–206.

Thorndike, E. L., & Lorge, I. *The Teacher's Wordbook of 30,000 Words*. New York: Teachers College, Columbia University, 1944.

Tulving, E. Theoretical issues in free recall. In T. R. Dixon & D. L. Horton (eds.), *Verbal Behavior and General Behavior Theory*. Englewood Cliffs, N. J.: Prentice-Hall, 1968. Pp. 2–36.

Tulving, E., & Arbuckle, T. Y. Sources of intratrial interference in immediate recall of paired associates. *Journal of Verbal Learning and Verbal Behavior*, 1963, 1, 321–334.

Turnage, T. W. Unit-sequence interference in short-term memory. *Journal of Verbal Learning and Verbal Behavior*. 1967, 6, 61–65.

Turnage, T. W., & McCullough, T. A. Letter-sequence and unit-sequence effects during learning and retention. *Journal of Experimental Psychology*, 1968, 76, 141–146.

Underwood, B. J. Interference and forgetting. *Psychological Review*, 1957, 64, 49–60.

Underwood, B. J. An evaluation of the Gibson theory of verbal learning. In C. N. Cofer (ed.), *Verbal Learning and Verbal Behavior*. New York: McGraw-Hill, 1961. Pp. 197–217.

Underwood, B. J. Degree of learning and the measurement of forgetting. *Journal of Verbal Learning and Verbal Behavior*, 1964, 3, 112–129.

Underwood, B. J. Attributes of memory. *Psychological Review*, 1969, 76, 559–573.

Underwood, B. J., & Ekstrand, B. R. An analysis of some shortcomings in the interference theory of forgetting. *Psychological Review*, 1966, 73, 540–549.

Underwood, B. J., & Ekstrand, B. R. Studies of distributed practice: XXIV. Differentiation and proactive inhibition. *Journal of Experimental Psychology*, 1967, 74, 574–580. (a)

Underwood, B. J., & Ekstrand, B. R. Word frequency and accumulative proactive inhibition. *Journal of Experimental Psychology*, 1967, 74, 193–198. (b).

Underwood, B. J., & Ekstrand, B. R. Linguistic associations and retention. *Journal of Verbal Learning and Verbal Behavior*, 1968, 7, 162–171.

Underwood, B. J., & Keppel, G. Retention as a function of degree of learning and letter-sequence interference. *Psychological Monographs*, 1963, 77, No. 4.

Underwood, B. J., & Postman, L. Extraexperimental sources of interference in forgetting. *Psychological Review*, 1960, 67, 73–95.

Underwood, B. J., & Schulz, R. W. *Meaningfulness and Verbal Learning*. Philadelphia: Lippincott, 1960.

Walen, S. R. Recall in children and adults. *Journal of Verbal Learning and Verbal Behavior*, 1970, 9, 94–98.

Young, R. K., Saegert, J., & Linsley, D. Retention as a function of meaningfulness. *Journal of Experimental Psychology*, 1968, 78, 89–94.

5 | Methods for Inferring Process Similarity in Different Learning Tasks

KENNETH L. LEICHT
Illinois State University, Normal

The starting point for what follows is a question raised by those whose academic backgrounds are heavily saturated with learning and learning-related courses and whose teaching assignment is consequently likely to include a course in learning. What approach, what general tack is to be taken in teaching the course? The modal answer is indicated by what is so often included in learning courses: a description of operations defining commonly employed learning tasks, description of phenomena generated by the tasks, and a listing of variables known to be relevant to performance on the tasks. Some of our most widely used texts are even geared to the approach (e.g., Hall, 1966; Marx, 1969).

If the teacher does adopt the task-descriptive strategy, his decision will not be free of doubt and recrimination. For one thing, the teacher may wonder whether a national data bank is necessary for implementation of his goal. The number of variations on paired-associate learning alone is rather extensive. And, just restricting ourselves to Underwood's work on determination of variables relevant to paired-associate performance, we could find enough to fill a good many class periods. There are so many studies on so many learning tasks that a voracious reader equipped with an abacus might not do. There is also the search for simplicity to consider. Surely there are not so many learning processes as there are learning tasks. Cursory comparison of many learning tasks (e.g., frequency-discrimination and probability-learning) suggests that many tasks are tapping the same kind of learning.

Being overwhelmed by the vast number of learning studies and being parsimony seeking are not likely to be sufficient grounds for dropping the task-survey approach. When we attempt across-task integration, we know full well that superficial task similarities are often just that, analogies without substance. Task-procedure variations, no matter how slight they appear, can produce different effects, suggesting, of course, that process differences are operative. The Grice and Hunter (1964) report that the effects of CS intensity in classical conditioning depend upon whether we employ a random-groups or within-subject design documents the precaution. Secondly, we really do not have a very extensive literature in learning attempting to establish across-task integration or commonalities. Work such as Young's (e.g., Young, 1962) dealing with transfer from serial to paired-associate learning is exceptional. Finally, there may be little payoff from attempts to relate two learning tasks which taken individually are not well understood. We should, as Underwood (1964) argued, identify the relevant variables and the subcomponents or subprocesses comprising performance on each of a set of tasks before we attempt the across-task integration. In short, there are plenty of arguments for treating tasks singly in catalogue fashion.

The title of this paper makes apparent that task inventories are not advocated here. One option, at least, must be considered. The data bank may make information on different tasks situationally quite accessible. We like something more long standing though, conceptual-theoretical systems which aid a reader in organizing a great number of seemingly disparate findings. I do not think it is misreading the current scene to say that there is clamoring for theories and models which will make findings from disparate tasks jell in a psychologically tractable manner. Theories seem almost to have their counterpart in category relationships among words presented for memorization. Dissimilar events (task findings) can be grouped under single superordinates and principles which are the statements in theories. Nevertheless, new miniature theories and models seem to occur with each twitch of the data, a situation treated in humorous yet educating fashion by Tulving and Madigan (1970). Also, theories with minimal empirical support across tasks seem to increase rather than reduce information load.

Despite the somewhat negative comments about theory, accept that theories serve a useful role in summarizing and organizing across-task findings within a relatively simple framework. We may still ask whether generation of theories is an adequate approach to the many reports of new learning tasks, variants of old tasks, and parametric studies of learning. The question is raised because a step seems to have been missed in the logical sequence of inquiry. The step between description of different tasks and their associated findings and a theory integrating the tasks involves focusing upon methodological rather than substantive questions. A more appropriate order would be, first, to determine whether there is reason to think that procedurally different learning tasks involve different learning processes. Given that reasons for believing such are identifiable, then a common theory or set of principles could be intelligently formulated. To reduce redundancy across tasks, to delimit the number of theories and models, examination of the bases permitting a judgment that task-procedure differences do not result in process differences seems in order. Again, the bases involve methodological rather than substantive considerations.

Before considering the methodological grounds for deciding when procedurally different tasks are process similar, the question should be put in its historical form. In perspective, the question reduces to how many types of learning are extant in the tasks we study. Hull (1943, 1952) consistently talked of the relationship between reinforced practice and learning as exponential in form and considered all learning accomplished through drive reduction, two assertions making Hull a uniprocess theorist. In the search for a simple, elegant theory, he neglected the varied effects corresponding to differences in the nature of reinforced practice. Tolman (e.g., Tolman, 1949) was not so tidy, suggesting six types of learning. Mowrer (1947) fell twixt Hull and Tolman. More recently, Gagne (1970) has suggested eight types of learning; Seligman (1970) suggests there are as many learnings as there are degrees of associability between events. The issue here is by no means new.

BASES FOR INFERRING PROCESS SIMILARITY

Methods for arriving at decisions about process similarity and the issues associated with their use are a heterogeneous lot. A brief outline plus some general commentary on what follows may provide the mediators to link the diverse subcomponents of the paper.

One set of methods relies upon comparison of intrinsic features of learning data. We are not interested in how some outside variable affects learning performance. Some feature(s) of the practice-performance relationship is selected for comparison among different learning tasks.

A second set of methods requires intervention upon the part of the experimenter, the intervention consisting of his manipulation of conditions extrinsic to the learning situation. That is, variables other than practice are involved. In turn, the intervention can take two forms. The first is to examine what effect a common manipulation has on performance in different learning tasks. The second method within this set involves a transfer setup. By building the proper history into the organism, we hope to be able to make conclusions about the process involved in a given learning task.

A third set of methods calls for examination of the types of errors occurring in different learning tasks. Briefly, if there are differences in the types of errors which occur across tasks, we may be able to glean what is different among the tasks. The error discontinuity analysis stems from a particular conception of learning, a conception which seems to have been converged upon by a number of experienced learning researchers within the past few years or so. A description of the particular formulation of learning will wait.

A fourth approach has been widely used, but its relation to the issue of inferring process similarity has not always been made explicit. At base, the approach asks whether predictions from a given theory of learning are generalizeable across learning tasks. The approach goes under various tags—construct validation and establishing nomological networks are two.

As for the general commentary, a first point is that, whatever the method, we should keep in mind a rule so heavily emphasized in experimental psychology. If you want any kind of definitive research conclusion you must restrict the sources of variation. If effects of task variation proper are of interest than the same indices of behavioral change must be present across tasks. The goal is not always easy to achieve. Quite appropriately, we may wish to seek out commonalities between serial and free-recall learning. If we make the comparison, observed differences may be attributable to differences in conditions of presentation (fixed versus varied presentation order) or to differences at recall (ordered versus unordered recall). Learning tasks have too often been the convenient vehicles for studying the effects of various "outside" variables, great effort having been expended in insuring that extraneous outside variables were not affecting the results. The same prescription should apply when task variation is focused upon.

The second general point is that we can no longer ignore the role of individual differences in learning. That individual differences can be fruitfully and systematically dealt with in learning studies is now more than an assertion. Consider, for example, that an entire symposium was devoted to the topic just a few years ago (Gagné, 1967). The role of individual differences in the problem of inferring process similarity will be treated in detail. For the moment, though, it will simply be asserted that it may not even be possible to study the problem of process similarity in a productive way unless we look at subjects by trials interactions as more than error variance.

1. **Intrinsic features of learning data.**   The usual description of learning as a behavioral change attributable to practice is nondifferentiating with respect to the process-similarity question. If production of behavioral change were the sole interest of learning studies, all learning tasks would be judged process similar. A more analytical approach of emphasizing specific features of practice-performance relationships is necessary. Four features which seem promising by reason of historical interest or other criteria are initial performance level or origin, final performance level or asymptote, rate of change in performance, and shape of the learning curve.

When specific learning-function features are emphasized, a great deal of prior work aimed at determining process similarity must be questioned. The interests exhibited in the literature are shared here and not at issue. The previous studies attempted to determine (1) whether different measures from the same learning task were reflective of the same learning process, (2) whether comparison of the same measure on different tasks indicated process similarity, or (3) whether different populations exhibited the same learning process(es) via comparison of the groups on the same task and with the same performance measure. The present focus is on (2), although the points to be made apply to all three interests. That some previous studies have overlapped in terms of present interests is personally gratifying; but, again, many of the extant studies have ignored specific data features and must be judged unanalytical on this account. Consider some illustrations. Jensen and Rohwer (1968) wished to determine whether different learning *rates* were present between retardates and normal-intelligence individuals. Groups were compared with respect to number of correct responses in two trials on a paired-associate task. Differences in total correct responses may reflect differences in rate or in any of the other features of learning data noted above. Thus, to talk of differences in learning rate when total recall is compared is unwarranted. A second example is from Allen (1968), a study concerned with whether trial-by-trial gains in recall were attributable to trial-by-trial increments in structuration or subjective organization. The question indicates that we look at the form of the relationship between trials and the two measures. One line of evidence given by Allen was that significant correlations were obtained between total recall and total organization scores. The Trial classification was ignored, so that conclusions about similarity of form of learning function for the two measures were unjustified. Composite scores gotten by summing across separate trial entries reflect the mix of so many contributing sources as to be the grossest of indices. Yet, they are so common that Hall (1966) took time in an introductory learning text to show that the form of the learning curve for different measures may be quite similar despite slight correlations between total scores on the measures. The procedure of examining correlations among total scores may have arisen because of the predictive fruitfulness of correlating total scores on various ability tests, each test consisting of a number of subtests. That correlating composite scores on ability tests seems to have been useful does not give sanction to such an approach in learning studies.

No special malice was intended for the investigators in the above illustrations. Most investigators, myself included, have made the same or similar mistakes. Although it may not take much talking to convince a person that it is necessary to look at specific features of the practice curve, the individual will eventually ask whether choice among features is completely arbitrary. Some of the arbitrariness may be removed after considering the pros and cons of various learning-curve features.

The first feature to be considered is initial performance level. Initial performance levels would normally be assessed through comparison of mean performance on the first trial of different learning tasks. Less seldom, functions are fitted to learning curves from different tasks, so that the Y intercept can be used as the indicator of initial proficiency.

Arguments relating to examination of initial performance levels are of two varieties, the rational sort and a criterion-validity type. One rational argument against using initial performance level as the basis for comparison is that our literary definition of learning as a change in behavior with practice suggests we avoid static conceptions of learning. Since there is nothing in comparison of initial performance levels which reveals in what fashion or how rapidly performance changes with practice, we should avoid their comparison. Secondly, initial performance levels may be given rational interpretation without recourse to the Trials effect, one such interpretation being that initial proficiency reflects prior organism history and, as such, is not an index of learning proper. A second rational interpretation is that initial performance level reflects some organismic invariance, such as memory span (cf. Murdock, 1960). A criterion-validity approach asks that initial performance level be more strongly related to variables extrinsic to the learning situation (e.g., intelligence score) or to other features of learning data than are other features of the learning curve. The Gagné (1967) conference on individual differences in learning, particularly the Glaser paper, indicates that the evidence is equivocal here. In some instances, initial performance levels correlate more highly with ability-test performance than do other features of the learning curve. In other instances, the evidence is less favorable. At least under some boundary conditions, initial performance level is less strongly related to amount of performance gain over trials than is final level of performance. The weight of argument, if not of evidence, suggests that initial performance levels are inappropriate bases for comparison.

Turning to final performance level, there is not a great deal of evidence, since too few studies have carried practice to a point where performance leveled off. Probability-learning studies (cf. Anderson, 1960) and studies of the effects of reward magnitude (Pubols, 1960) would qualify as exceptions. What is usually termed final performance level is whatever level of proficiency was achieved when practice was arbitrarily terminated.

The argument against use of initial performance level because it implied a static conception of learning also applies to comparison of final performance levels. Further, one rational interpretation of final performance level is that it reflects "capacity," the amount of the learning process which is achievable, rather than differences in type of learning process. For learning tasks with a heavy motor component, final performance level might be associated with a physiological limit. Prior workers (e.g., Hull, 1952; Pubols, 1960) have indicated that final performance levels should be identified with motivational rather than learning factors; their reasons for associating final performance level with motivational factors are sufficiently well grounded but too lengthy to detail here. When the criterion validity of final performance level is examined, the evidence is again equivocal. Whether final performance level correlates better with outside variables or with other features of the practice-performance relationship than does initial performance level will depend upon the particular learning tasks chosen for study and upon a host of boundary conditions (again see Gagné, 1967). Perhaps the most compelling reason for not selecting final performance level as the basis for comparison is that it appears to be confounded with other features of the learning curve. Specifically, if initial performance levels differ, despite constancy of learning rate and the type of learning function involved, final performance levels will differ. The latter problem might be handled through covariance analysis on the data from the trial at which performance leveled off, with initial performance level serving as the concomitant variable. A second possible solution requires computation of partial correlation coefficients, where the variable which is held constant is initial performance level (see Glaser, 1967). An intuitive weighing and summing of arguments for and against final performance level as the basis for comparison leads to its rejection.

A number of individuals have insisted that comparison of rate parameters of learning functions is the appropriate tack in seeking clues to process similarity. Murdock (1960) argues that examination of how rapidly performance changes with practice is a natural consequence of our literary definitions of learning. Seligman (1970) also seems to argue for analysis of rates, although Seligman's manner of talking about rate and his particular arguments differ considerably from Murdock's. Relying almost completely upon results from conditioning studies, Seligman shows that organisms are "prepared to associate certain events, unprepared for some, and contraprepared for others." In particular, in classical conditioning preparedness refers to the number of CS-UCS pairings which are necessary before a criterion of reliable occurrence of the CR is reached. Trials to criterion varies considerably with particular choices of CS and UCS. According to Seligman, differences in degree of preparedness are evidence against a general or uniprocess view of learning. Thus, he asserts that differences in rate mean that different learning processes are operative.

A most compelling argument against use of rate as the basis for comparison is that rate parameters are not meaningful unless different learning tasks generate the same type of learning function. One of the difficulties with Woodrow's massive research effort at relating learning performance to ability-test score (Woodrow, 1946) is that rate was defined in terms of differences between initial and final performance levels. This would be satisfactory were linear relationships always obtained, since rate could be computed by dividing differences between initial and final performance by trials (average rate). However, since there are across-task variations in the type of function which may be fitted to the learning data, differences in rate will not be meaningful. Incidentally, Woodrow reported that correlations between ability-test score and learning rate as he defined it were generally nonsignificant and close to zero. Correlations for initial and final performance levels were generally significant. Choice of rate would indeed be poor were criterion validity the sole standard.

The string of exclusions seems to leave shape of the learning curve as the base for comparison. Historically, more concern has been shown over the shape of learning curves than over all the other features combined, interest in shape going at least as far back as Thurstone (1930). Whether comparing learning in different populations (Zeaman & House, 1963) or predicting the form of the learning curve from a set of theoretical assumptions (Estes, 1959), many researchers have found reason to look at the shape of the learning curve.

There are two questions relevant to comparison of shapes of learning curves. We must first ask what merit it has relative to comparison of the other features which might be examined. Because there are reasons for rejecting the other features as bases for comparison and because there is widespread interest in the shape of the learning curve are rather tenuous grounds for making shape comparisons. However, if we keep in mind that a basic purpose of most disciplines is discovery and interpretation of functional relationships, shape is the logical choice. The second question is how we decide when two learning curves are the same shape. The criterion adopted here is one suggested by Tucker (1966), namely, that two curves will be said to have the same shape if they may be superimposed after a linear transformation of one of the curves. The criterion is arbiratry but would probably be judged an intuitively good one by most individuals to whom the question was put. Statistically, to decide whether the criterion has been met is troublesome; statistical problems associated with the decision will be put aside for the moment.

2. "Manipulative" methods. Recall that this set of methods requires manipulation of conditions or variables other than those associated with practice proper. The first method of the set asks whether a given experimental procedure or independent variable has a like effect on performance in different learning tasks, occurrence of a like effect increasing confidence that the tasks are process similar. The approach has been previously described (Underwood, 1964; D'Amato, 1969). However, Underwood' S (1964) observation that the method has not been applied in any programmatic way is less applicable today, so that illustrations of the method will be given.

In the first illustration, an operation which is critical in defining one type of conditioning task (operant) is performed in order to modify behaviors typically altered through a different conditioning procedure (classical). The critical operation in operant studies is making some outcome, the reinforcing stimulus, contingent upon occurrence of the desired behavior. The contingency is absent in classical conditioning in that occurrence or absence of a CR does not determine whether environmental events presumed significant (UCSs) are presented. If it can be shown that establishing a contingency between a classically conditionable behavior and some event alters the behavior, we have grounds for thinking that we are not dealing with two different types of conditioning. A study by Miller and Carmona (1967) is one of the many now available (cf. Kimmel, 1967) indicating a convergence of classical and operant conditioning. In one condition, thirsty dogs were rewarded with water when they showed spontaneous bursts of salivation. In a second condition, water was given during periods in which salivation was not occurring. Briefly, dogs rewarded for salivating showed an across-days increase in amount of salivation, while salivation in the second condition showed a decline over days.

In the second illustration, we ask whether a given independent variable which is not integrally involved in the operations defining either of two learning tasks has a like effect on performance in the tasks. Bourne and Bunderson (1963) varied the interval between a subject's reply as to whether a stimulus was an instance of the correct concept and the experimenter's feedback about the correctness of the reply. The counterpart of delay of information feedback in instrumental-conditioning studies is delay of reward. While Bourne and

Bunderson found delay of feedback an ineffective variable, the usual finding in instrumental conditioning is that the greater the delay of reward the poorer the performance (e.g., Logan, 1960). The different effects of delay of reward and its counterpart in concept attainment argue that concept attainment and instrumental conditioning involve different types of learning.

In the final example, we deal with only one task, free recall, and assume that more than one memory process or system underlies free-recall performance. More specifically, a test is made of the assumption that free-recall recency effects are mediated by a memory system capable of holding a unit for no more than several seconds in the absence of recirculation or rehearsal of the unit. The primacy effect is attributed to the operation of a long-term memory system capable of holding units for intervals of the magnitude studied in the traditional long-term retention studies. The basic rationale of the method is to find an independent variable which is known to be effective in long-term retention studies (e.g., presentation rate) but which should have no effect on the short-term memory system (cf. Glanzer & Cunitz, 1966; Leicht, 1968). If the variable affects the magnitude of the primacy effect but leaves recency unaltered, the suspicion that free-recall performance involves more than one memory process is supported. Although the last example of the method does not involve across-task comparison, it could be useful in task comparisons provided we know something of the processes or learning strategies operative in one of the compared tasks. That is, if we know that Task A involves a particular learning strategy and that a given variable has an effect on utilization of the strategy, then failure to find an effect of the variable in Task B indicates some degree of process independence for the two tasks.

Pitfalls with the method of seeking like effects of a given operation or variable were nicely described by Underwood (1964). Their restatement in the context of the above variants of the method may still be useful in preventing unwarranted conclusions. The second illustration of the method forcibly raises the first problem. Can we be assured that varying delay of reward in instrumental conditioning is comparable to varying delay of feedback in concept attainment? To argue that we have comparable manipulations because of like effects puts us on a conceptual treadmill. Some independent definition of comparability which does not rely on experimenter intuition is necessary. Practically, it may not be possible to first establish comparability of an independent variable and an "analogous" independent variable. To alleviate some of the pessimism, note that there would be no doubt about comparability of operations in the third illustration. The second problem with the method is the possibility that a given variable can have a like effect in different tasks but for different reasons. Assume that Task A involves Process 1, Task B involving Process 2. It is conceivable that a given variable affects both processes in a similar way. Before leaving the method, it should be pointed out that a subsidiary problem, one of not following the rule about restricting sources of variation, is occasionally encountered. In the second example comparing concept attainment and instrumental conditioning, species differences are present, concept-attainment studies employing human subjects, instrumental studies more often using animal subjects.

Again, it may appear that too much material of the negative sort is on the ledger. With the method of like effects of a manipulation, what is required in the long run is that the weight of evidence favors the conclusion of process similarity. If, with a variety of variables, we find similar effects, we are compelled to think that different tasks involve similar processes. In short, the programmatic use of the method urged by Underwood is what determines its usefulness. Optimism is justified considering the systematic use of the method with some problems, determination of whether we are dealing with more than one memory system being a prime example of thorough use of the method.

The second type of manipulative method encompasses various transfer paradigms. Although transfer studies are no longer devoid of theoretical assumptions, simple empirical determination that two tasks, A and B, have the same effect on a common third task, C, may be a useful first step in establishing that learning of A and learning of B include the same strategies or processes. The reasoning is essentially the same as that accompanying use of factor analysis: If A and C are related, and B and C are related, then A and B have something in common. If the tasks are uniprocess tasks, there is no problem with the method. However, component analysis of transfer effects (cf. Underwood, 1964) reveals that even "simple," rote-learning tasks ordinarily involve a number of subprocesses, compounding in intricate fashion to determine overall performance. Assume that Processes 1 and 2 are both present in learning of Task C and of equal importance in contributing to overall performance on C. Secondly, assume that Process 1 underlies performance on Task A, Process 2 underlying performance on Task B. Given these assumptions, it is apparent that A and B, although process different, can have a like effect on C.

Transfer arrangements are often accompanied by presumptions about the specific subprocesses involved in successive tasks. Recurrent in the literature is a sequence of events which runs as follows: A logical analysis of the types of learning necessary for performance on some task is undertaken. Then, prior to learning of the task in question, practice is given on some task which incorporates one or more of the types of learning deemed necessary for performance of the focal task. If the reasoning behind the sequence is correct, it should not be possible to perform the focal task in the absence of experience with the first task. A milder form of the argument is that, assuming the two tasks involve one or more of the same types of learning, performance on the focal task will be facilitated. The argument reduces to a statement that positive transfer can be expected when assumptions that successive tasks are process similar are correct.

In a first illustration of the method, implications of Spence's (1956) emphasis on the role of classical conditioning in operant conditioning were tested. Spence's account held that classical conditioning of the anticipatory goal reaction, r_g, provided an additional source of motivation for performance of the instrumental behavior. Thus, Trapold and Winokur (1967) reasoned that conditioning of the r_g prior to operant conditioning would facilitate acquisition of the operant. Specifically, they assumed that conditioning of r_g by pairing a CS with food delivery would hasten subsequent training of a discriminative bar-press to the CS. The prediction was supported, suggesting that the type of learning occurring in classical conditioning is a component of the total learning occurring in operant conditioning.

The second instance of the method stems from analysis of paired-associate learning into response-learning and associative-learning stages (Underwood, Runquist, & Schulz, 1959). Logically, before an individual can master a paired-associate list, he must (1) have list response terms available at recall and (2) know which stimulus term each response term had been paired with. Those processes entering into (1) were termed response learning by Underwood et al. To produce response learning prior to paired-associate learning proper, response terms were presented singly a number of times with a free-learning procedure prior to their being inserted into the paired-associate list. Relative to an irrelevant familiarization control, prefamiliarization of response terms facilitated later paired-associate learning, indicating that paired-associate learning includes a subprocess akin to what occurs during free-recall learning.

Perhaps because of its simplicity, a transfer arrangement in conjunction with logical analysis of learning processes has been used frequently, and fruitfully so. In addition to the above instances, the power of the method is visible in studies of stimulus predifferentiation (cf. Ellis, 1969), investigations attempting to establish the functional stimulus in serial learning (cf. Young, 1968), as well as in attempts to establish taxonomies of learning (Gagné, 1970).

I do not know of any method which has been more productive in permitting conclusions about the strategies and processes involved in various learning tasks than the latter method. Nevertheless, two considerations detract from the method. First, when we attribute positive transfer to sharing of a specific, identifiable learning strategy or process, we must recognize that the transfer might have been obtained by reason of overlap of processes other than those specified. Secondly, the method presumes that we know a good deal about the processes involved in successively learned tasks before we initiate the transfer arrangement. In effect, the method seems to presuppose what Underwood (1964) advocated—a thorough understanding of tasks taken individually. If we have studied two tasks in serial fashion and have reached a definitive conclusion that the two tasks share a given learning strategy, a finding that learning of one task affects learning of the second task seems superfluous. Practically, the last criticism of the method is not so decisive. Serial investigation, no matter how thorough the study of the separate tasks, seldom permits an uncontested conclusion that two tasks share a given process. Thus, a finding of positive transfer between tasks presumed to be process similar is ordinarily a desirable confirmation.

3. Error discontinuity analysis.   Numerous studies have been instigated to determine whether a distinction between short-term and long-term memory is functionally justified. The alternative view (cf. Melton, 1963) is that there is one memory system, although we operationally separate short- and long-term memory. One line of evidence supporting functional discontinuity is that recall errors in short-term retention studies consist of reporting units which sound like presented units, whereas recall errors in long-term retention studies are semantically related to presented units (Adams, 1967). At a conceptual level, proponents of functional discontinuity have accepted that different properties or presented units are critical in short- and long-term retention studies. The hypothesis is readily subsumed under a new view of learning (Horowitz & Prytulak, 1969; Underwood, 1969; Wickens, 1970) which holds that learning is the internalization or storage of different properties or attributes of repeated events. Within the new framework, recall is viewed either in terms of inference of what an event must be on the basis of knowledge of attributes of the event or from an associationistic position. The associationistic position holds that event attributes serve as retrieval cues for the event proper through connections between the event proper and its attributes. Returning to task comparisons, if error types differ across tasks, it may be inferred that different attributes are relevant, i.e., that what is learned differs across tasks.

Error analysis has been used to determine relevant recall cues for a particular task (Underwood & Freund, 1968), to study developmental changes in encoding processes (Bach & Underwood, 1970), and to determine whether differences in learning instructions are effective in drawing attention to different event properties (Wallace, 1968). In the Underwood and Freund study, 40 words were presented under free-recall memorization instructions. Following presentation, subjects were asked to identify presented words in a recognition task. Included in the recognition task were the 40 presented words, 40 words which sounded like the presented words, 40 associates of presented words, and 40 words which were not related to presented words in any systematic way. The greatest proportion of errors consisted of judging that associates of presented words had been presented, indicating that associative attributes are dominant under free-recall memorization instruction.

The above studies attest to the potential gain from thorough error analyses. However, methodical use of error discontinuity analysis in cross-task comparisons has not yet occurred. If and when error discontinuity analysis is extensively applied in task comparisons, its value will probably be disputed. Some will argue that its use depends upon adoption of a particular conceptualization of the nature of what is learned. Although error comparisons are suggested by the conceptualization of learning outlined above, they may still be made in the absence of theoretical assumptions. Also, hindsight based upon logical analyses and numerous studies will establish the value of a particular view of learning. There is no quick way to establish the validity and heuristic value of hypotheses and theories. A second anticipated problem arises with a particular variant of error discontinuity analysis. Differences in relative frequency of error types may not be obtained if we do not permit certain types of errors to occur. The point is illustrated by the Underwood-Freund study. The recognition list was such that only three types of errors were possible. When cross-task comparisons are to be made, a sufficiently large number of error types must be permitted by experimental procedures to allow for error discontinuities to reveal themselves. The problem may be peculiar to recognition tasks.

4. Role of theory in inferring process similarity. The earlier presented conviction that theory construction should be preceded by determination of whether tasks are process similar should not be equated with rejection of what theories have to contribute to the issue. In what follows, the term *theory* is intended to denote a set of formal or explicit statements relating internal processes.

Hullian theory will provide the illustrations. Although Hull's work in its classic form is now defunct, it is still representative of the degree of sophistication exhibited in behavioral theories. Both illustrations of the use of theory will focus upon the Hullian statement that Drive and Habit combine multiplicatively. The illustrations differ with respect to the extent that operations inducing Drive are judged comparable.

First, consider the case in which we can be assured that Drive has the same defining operations across learning tasks. Here, Drive is defined as the interval of deprivation from some needed substance. If Drive so defined combines with Habit in the same fashion in procedurally different tasks, there is confidence that the same type of learning is occurring in the different tasks. As predicted by the multiplicative formulation, Drive as hours of deprivation from food interacts with practice in both the free-operant (Perin, 1942) and the discrete-trial operant setting (Barry, 1958), indicating comparability of learning processes for the discrete-trial and free-operant tasks.

A first reaction to the above use of theory is that it can contribute no more than simple determination of whether an experimental manipulation has a like effect in different learning tasks. The reaction has partial validity. The validity of the reaction stems from the fact that it is possible that Drive interacts with many different learning processes, the counterpart of the argument that an operation can have a similar effect for different reasons. Where does the validity of the reaction break down? A theory of merit will explicitly relate internal processes, ultimately, through sets of equations. In turn, the specific form of the relationship between practice and some outside variable, such as deprivation, is dictated. Such detail is ordinarily not encountered when we ask whether an independent variable has a like effect in different tasks. Were we typically to demand that the relationship between practice and some outside variable be thoroughly detailed, theory could contribute no more than looking for like effects of an independent variable. When the latter demand is met, utilization of theory is equivalent to a well planned convergent operationalism (cf. Campbell & Fiske, 1959).

The second illustration of theory has its analogue in the situation in which we look for like effects of a manipulation but cannot be assured that the manipulation is carried out in the same way in different learning tasks. That is, we cannot be completely assured of comparability of operations. Remember the flurry of studies in the late 1950s and early 1960s when Spence was asking whether Drive defined in terms of differences in Taylor Manifest Anxiety Scores interacted with practice in the manner specified by Hull. More recently, Fowler (1967) asked whether Drive defined as time of exposure to a monotonous environment (curiosity drive) interacted with practice, where practice consisted of runs to a changed environment and the performance measure was running speed. The work of Spence and of Fowler represents the development of one segment of the nomological network discussed by Cronbach and Meehl (1955), the total network being all of the interrelationships among intervening variables in the Hullian system. Is the demanded convergence of obtaining a $D \times H$ interaction, in light of the disparate definitions of Drive, realized? The interaction was obtained by Fowler, evidence for presence of the interaction when Drive is defined in terms of Manifest Anxiety scores being more tenuous (Prokasy, 1967). But accept the favorable evidence in the latter case. Other conceptualizations of the learning processes induced by the divergent definitions of practice and the processes associated with the divergent definitions of Drive could conceivably account for the consistency of results. However, considering the potentially large number of alternative conceptualizations, we conclude that it is no accident that the interaction is obtained across divergent operations.

ROLE OF INDIVIDUAL DIFFERENCES

Absence of a differential psychology of learning is attributable to a desire for general laws of learning and to inflexible application of statistical models, the latter reason having had the greater impact. Analysis of Variance has been used almost exclusively in learning studies but has not been applied in ways that permit study of individual differences. In the simplest learning study, we have n subjects exposed to k trials in a particular learning task, a Subjects by Treatments Analysis of Variance then being applied. If we are interested in general laws of learning and presume that a single function adequately describes the practice-performance relationship, we are likely to presume that the structural model underlying the Subjects by Treatments analysis does not include a component associated with Subjects by Trials interaction. The particular investigator may be more flexible and adopt the nonadditive model in which Subjects by Trials interaction contributes to performance of an individual on a given trial. The latter model, while more inclusive, still does not permit testing whether the Subjects by Trials interaction is systematic. So, individual differences in the Trials effect are either ignored or cannot be evaluated.

Three statistical techniques will be presented. The first will illustrate that performance of an individual learner can be meaningfully studied with simple correlational procedures. With the second technique, a suggestion as to how extant Analyses of Variance models might be used to study individual differences in learning will be made. The third technique is factor-analytic in nature and has already proved its worth.

The first technique (Mintz, 1970) was designed for study of trends in the data of a single subject. An individual's trial scores are correlated with orthogonal coefficients for, say, linear trend. Significance of the correlation is tested in the usual fashion

$$t = r \sqrt{N - 2} \over \sqrt{1 - r^2}.$$

The test of significance ignores trend components other than those tested for. However, significance of the difference between correlations for different trend components may be tested for. In the past, tests for trend components in the relationship between mean performance and trials have been common. Mintz's analysis would seem best adapted to single-subject research in the Skinnerian tradition. Its relevance to the process-similarity question can be established, however. Performance of a single subject is assessed in two different learning tasks. Correlations between trial scores and coefficients for a particular trend are computed for each task. A test is made to determine whether the correlations differ. What use of a single subject means is that task differences in trend are not confounded with subject factors.

When the Trials effect is compared in different learning tasks or treatments, the Task by Trials interaction can be evaluated with Analysis of Variance. Since Subjects is a random variable, the Trials by Subjects/Tasks *MS* provides the appropriate error term. But there is still no way of evaluating the Trials by Subjects interaction. Whether there are individual differences in the Trials effect is not ignored here; the individual-differences component just cannot be assessed. A solution is possible if we rearrange our thinking so that each subject is viewed as a different treatment or level of an independent variable. Focus is upon the Trials by Subject (Treatment) interaction. What is needed to evaluate the source is some random variable. The need is met by randomly assigning lists to subjects, the counterpart of randomly assigning subjects to treatments. Among-Subject variation in the usual analysis becomes Among-List variation in the present analysis. The Trials by Subjects/Treatments in the usual analysis has its counterpart in the Trials by Lists/Subjects in the proposed analysis. Since an appropriate error term is now available (the Trials by Lists/Subjects term), we can test for significance of the Trials by Subject interaction. The above design is not new (see Edwards, 1964, pp. 115—117), but I don't believe it has been used to study individual differences in learning. What must the above analysis reveal before it contributes to solution of the process-similarity problem? Hopefully, the null hypothesis is accepted (no Trials by Subject interaction). If so, it is concluded that learning processes are equivalent for the subjects we have sampled. At a later time, the same subjects are tested in a second learning task. A difference in the Trials effect for the two learning tasks cannot be attributed to individual differences, since the first-task analysis indicated equivalence of learning processes across subjects.

Tucker (1966) factor analyzed Gardner's (1958) data from a probability-learning task, with the conclusion that three learning curves would be necessary to describe the data from one condition of Gardner's study. The mean learning curve did not adequately describe the data of individuals contributing to the means. Before giving a cursory description of the model underlying the Tucker analysis, an indication of what can be accomplished with the method is in order. Already intimated is that the method tells us whether the mean learning curve is an adequate representation of the Trials effect. If a single factor is recovered, it may be concluded that a single learning curve, the mean learning curve, will do. The number of retained factors equals the number of learning curves necessary to describe the data. The different learning curves associated with the different factors are linearly independent vectors. That is, they cannot be expressed as linear transformations of one another. In terms of the earlier discussion of the shape of the learning curve, when more than one factor is recovered, two or more learning curves which differ in shape are necessary to describe the data. Hence, the method determines how many learning curves differing in shape are appropriate.

The decomposition model underlying the analysis is as follows: The score of Individual i on Trial j, X_{ij}, is the sum of two or more orthogonal components, each component being the cross product of the individuals's factor score on a factor and the factor loading of the given trial on the factor. More formally,

$$X_{ij} = y_i w_j + x_i z_j + \ldots,$$

where y_i and x_i refer to Individual i's factor scores on Factors w and z, respectively, and where w_j and z_j refer to the factor loadings of Factors w and z on Trial j. As with Analysis of Variance, scores are treated as linear composites of orthogonal components. Unlike Analysis of Variance in which components are specified a priori, how many components are retained in the model depends upon the number of recovered factors. Analysis of Variance models have a single component corresponding to the Trials effect. Many components (factors) may be associated with performance on a given trial in the Tucker model. A least-squares criterion is used to decide the value of the factor scores and factor loadings, with deviations of scores formed from summing the cross products of factor scores and factor loadings from the raw scores in the Subjects by Trials matrix being minimized.

The Tucker analysis most impressed me when it was applied to serial-position data. At Robert Rumery's urging and with his aid, free-recall serial-position effects were analyzed with the Tucker method. Each subject had been presented a number of lists, with recall scores summed across lists for each position. The cross-product matrix of serial-position scores was factored. Two factors were of sufficient magnitude to be retained according to the guidelines set up by Tucker. Hence, we concluded that two serial-position curves were necessary to describe the data. The results really got interesting when put into the context of current theories about the operation of short-term and long-term memory systems in free recall. The overall serial-position curve is supposed to be a composite of two curves, each curve reflecting the output of a different memory system. The curve reflecting the operation of long-term memory supposedly declines from the start to the end of the list, the long-term system mediating the primacy effect. The second curve presumably declines from the end to the start of the list and reflects the operation of short-term memory, the short-term system being responsible for the recency effect. Figure 1 shows the plot of factor loadings against serial position. Notice that factor loadings for Factor I are highest for initial positions and decline over subsequent positions.

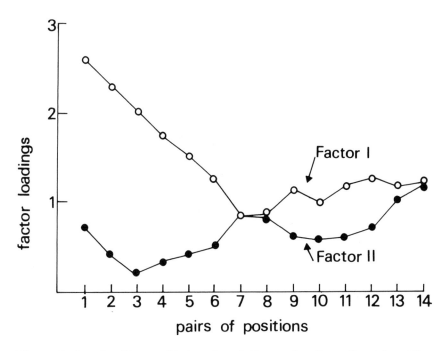

Figure 5—1.   Loading on Factors I and II as a function of serial position.

Factor loadings for Factor II are highest for terminal positions and seem to show an overall increase from initial to end positions.

The results got interesting because of the convergence of conclusions arrived at through the Tucker analysis and the conclusions derived from more traditional analysis procedures.

A restatement of the benefits of factor-analytic procedures in the context of the process-similarity question is necessary to make the procedures more than an esoteric exercise for those of us raised in a bivariate experimental tradition. The above analysis permits determination of how many learning curves which differ in shape are necessary to account for the data from a given learning task. When the factor loadings for the recovered factors are plotted against trials, some clue as to the learning strategies underlying performance may appear. We may find one factor with largest loadings for later trials (corresponding to late learners), a second factor with largest loadings on initial trials (corresponding to early learners). Clusters of individuals differing in the extent to which a given factor is operative can be identified. Directly relevant to the process-similarity issue is the number of factors operative in different tasks. If two tasks vary in the number of retained factors, they differ to some extent in process overlap. Further, the individual-difference component may be removed in across-task comparisons. We locate a cluster of individuals who have high factor scores on one factor but low factor scores on the remaining factors operative in a given task. Individuals within the cluster are homogeneous with respect to learning strategy or process. When the performance of these individuals in a second learning task is examined, the task comparison is not confounded with subject factors.

CONCLUSION

This paper started with the conviction that across-task integration was presently advisable and that integration would occur primarily through methodological means (manipulative and statistical) rather than through understanding of substantive issues. The conviction about achievement through methodological means cannot be too far afield. Courses in Experimental Psychology are directed at exposition of methods of inquiry which are generalizable across content areas. Further, although we do not decide questions by vote in a formal discipline, the fact that students in learning courses ask about similarities and differences among the learning tasks we describe (repeatedly so) would seem sufficient goad to seek commonalities.

One source of annoyance associated with the conviction that methodology should be emphasized in across-task comparisons deserves mention for those who have not already anticipated it. To ask whether two learning tasks involve similar learning processes implies an adequate definition of process. A literary definition of a learning process as a change in the state of the organism under conditions of relative enviromental invariance may not suffice. However, there is no definition of learning, other than one of a literary variety, of any great generality currently available. To dismiss defining a learning process as a mere academic exercise is not justifiable, as can be readily seen from Underwood's (1969) attributes-of-memory conception of learning. If different event properties are internalized in operationally different tasks, we might argue for process differences. On the other hand, a single process, attribute storage, could be argued for just as readily. At least in some instances, then, there may be a search for commonality when it is not known what is being compared.

REFERENCES

Adams, J. A. *Human Memory*. New York: McGraw-Hill, 1967.

Allen, M. Rehearsal strategies and response cueing as determinants of organization in free recall. *Journal of Verbal Learning and Verbal Behavior*, 1968, 7, 58–63.

Anderson, N. H. Effect of first-order conditional probability in a two-choice learning situation. *Journal of Experimental Psychology*, 1960, 59, 73–93.

Bach, M. J., & Underwood, B. J. Developmental changes in memory attributes. *Journal of Educational Psychology*, 1970, 61, 292–296.

Barry, H. III. Effects of strength of drive on learning and on extinction. *Journal of Experimental Psychology*, 1958, 17, 47–65.

Bourne, L. E., Jr., & Bunderson, C. V. Effects of delay of informative feedback and length of postfeedback interval on concept identification. *Journal of Experimental Psychology*, 1963, 65, 1–5.

Campbell, D. T., & Fiske, D. W. Convergent and discriminant validation by multitrait-multimethod matrix. *Psychological Bulletin*, 1959, 56, 81–105.

Cronbach, L. J., & Meehl, P. E. Construct validity in psychological tests. *Psychological Bulletin*, 1955, 52, 281–302.

D'Amato, M. R. Instrumental conditioning. In M. H. Marx (ed.), *Learning: Processes*. London: Macmillan, 1969.

Edwards, A. L. *Expected values of discrete random variables and elementary statistics*. New York: Wiley, 1964.

Estes, W. K. The statistical approach to learning theory. In S. Koch (ed.), *Psychology: A Study of a Science*, Vol. 2. New York: McGraw-Hill, 1959.

Fowler, H. Satiation and curiosity. In K. W. Spence & J. T. Spence (eds.), *The Psychology of Learning and Motivation*, Vol. 1. New York: Academic Press, 1967.

Gagné, R. M. (ed.), *Learning and Individual Differences*. Columbus: Merrill, 1967.

Gagné, R. M. *The Conditions of Learning*. New York: Holt, Rinehart, & Winston, 1970.

Gardner, R. A. Multiple-choice decision-behavior. *American Journal of Psychology*, 1958, 71, 710–717.

Glanzer, M., & Cunitz, A. R. Two storage mechanisms in free recall. *Journal of Verbal Learning and Verbal Behavior*, 1966, 5, 351–360.

Glaser, R. Some implications of previous work on learning and individual differences. In R. M. Gagné (ed.), *Learning and Individual Differences*. Columbus: Merrill, 1967.

Grice, G. R., & Hunter, J. J. Stimulus intensity effects depend upon the type of experimental design. *Psychological Review*, 1964, 71, 247–256.

Hall, J. F. *The Psychology of Learning*. Philadelphia: Lippincott, 1966.

Horowitz, L. M., & Prytulak, L. S. Redintigrative memory. *Psychological Review*, 1969, 76, 519–531.

Hull, C. L. *Principles of Behavior*. New York: Appleton-Century-Crofts, 1943.

Hull, C. L. *A Behavior System*. New Haven: Yale University Press, 1952.

Jensen, A. R., & Rohwer, W. D., Jr. Mental retardation, mental age, and learning rate. *Journal of Educational Psychology*, 1968, 59, 402–403.

Kimmel, H. D. Instrumental conditioning of autonomically mediated behavior. *Psychological Bulletin*, 1967, 67, 337–345.

Leicht, K. L. Differential rehearsal and primacy effects. *Journal of Verbal Learning and Verbal Behavior*, 1968, 7, 1115–1117.

Logan, F. A. *Incentive*. New Haven: Yale University Press, 1960.

Marx, M. H. (ed.), *Learning: Processes*. London: Macmillan, 1969.

Melton, A. W. Implications of short-term memory for a general theory of memory. *Journal of Verbal Learning and Verbal Behavior*, 1963, 2, 1–21.

Miller, N. E., & Carmona, A. Modification of a visceral response, salivation in thirsty dogs, by instrumental training with water reward. *Journal of Comparative and Physiological Psychology*, 1967, 63, 1–6.

Mintz, J. A correlational method for the investigation of systematic trends in serial data. *Educational and Psychological Measurement*, 1970, 30, 575–578.

Mowrer, O. H. On the dual nature of learning: a re-interpretation of "conditioning" and "problem-solving." *Harvard Educational Review*, 1947, 17, 102–148.

Murdock, B. B., Jr. The immediate retention of unrelated words. *Journal of Experimental Psychology*, 1960, 60, 222–234.

Perin, C. T. Behavior potentiality as a joint function of the amount of training and degree of hunger at the time of extinction. *Journal of Experimental Psychology*, 1942, 30, 93–113.

Prokasy, W. F. Do *D* and *H* multiply to determine performance in human conditioning? *Psychological Bulletin*, 1967, 67, 368–377.

Pubols, B. H., Jr. Incentive magnitude, learning, and performance in animals. *Psychological Bulletin*, 1960, 57, 89–115.

Seligman, M. E. P. On the generality of the laws of learning. *Psychological Review*, 1970, 77, 406–418.

Spence, K. W. *Behavior Theory and Conditioning*. New Haven: Yale University Press, 1956.

Thurstone, L. L. The learning function. *Journal of General Psychology*, 1930, 3, 469–493.

Tolman, E. C. There is more than one kind of learning. *Psychological Review*, 1949, 56, 144–155.

Trapold, M. A., & Winokur, S. Transfer from classical conditioning and extinction to acquisition, extinction, and stimulus generalization of a positively reinforced instrumental response. *Journal of Experimental Psychology*, 1967, 73, 517−525.

Tucker, L. R. Learning theory and multivariate experiment: illustration by determination of generalized learning curves. In R. B. Cattell, *Handbook of Multivariate Experimental Psychology*. Chicago: Rand-McNally, 1966.

Tulving, E., & Madigan, S. A. Memory and verbal learning. *Annual Review of Psychology*, 1970, 21, 437−484.

Underwood, B. J. The representativeness of rote verbal learning. In A. W. Melton (ed.), *Categories of Human Learning*. New York: Academic Press, 1964.

Underwood, B. J. Attributes of memory. *Psychological Review*, 1969, 76, 559−573.

Underwood, B. J., & Freund, J. S. Errors in recognition learning and retention. *Journal of Experimental Psychology*, 1968, 78, 55−63.

Underwood, B. J., Runquist, W. R., & Schulz, R. W. Response learning in paired-associate lists as a function of intralist similarity. *Journal of Experimental Psychology*, 1959, 58, 70−78.

Wallace, W. P. Incidental learning: The influence of associative similarity and formal similarity in producing false recognition. *Journal of Verbal Learning and Verbal Behavior*, 1968, 7, 50−54.

Wickens, D. D. Encoding categories of words: An empirical approach to meaning. *Psychological Review*, 1970, 77, 1−15.

Woodrow, H. A. The ability to learn. *Psychological Review*, 1946, 53, 147−158.

Young, R. K. Tests of three hypotheses about the effective stimulus in serial learning. *Journal of Experimental Psychology*, 1962, 63, 307−313.

Young, R. K. Serial learning. In T. R. Dixon & D. L. Horton (eds.), *Verbal Behavior and General Behavior Theory*. Englewood Cliffs: Prentice-Hall, 1968.

Zeaman, D., & House, B. J. The role of attention in retardate discrimination learning. In N. R. Ellis (ed.), *Handbook of Mental Deficiency: Psychological Theory and Research*. New York: McGraw-Hill, 1963.

6 | In Search of Associative Symmetry

SLATER E. NEWMAN
North Carolina State University, Raleigh

This paper describes a number of experiments, each of which derived from our concern with the question "are associations symmetrical?" The answer to this question has appeared to us to be of interest not only in its own right but as Ekstrand (1966) has also suggested, because of its possible implication for the explanation of transfer (e.g., McGovern, 1964), of mediation (e.g., Horton & Kjeldergaard, 1961), and of retroactive and proactive effects.

Originally our position, like that of Asch and Ebenholtz (1962a), was that associations are symmetrical and that what looked like associative asymmetry was an artifact of the procedure ordinarily used in paired-associate learning experiments. This procedure, it seemed to us, was more likely to foster stimulus selection in a stimulus-term than in a response-term. The results from a number of experiments, however, led us to modify our position. This research is described here.

At the outset let me make clear how I will use certain terms. I shall refer to what has commonly been called the stimulus-term as the A-term, and to what has commonly been called the response term as the B-term. The so-called forward association will be called the A-B pair, and the so-called backward association will be called the B-A pair. Associative symmetry will be said to occur if, following A-B learning, B-A strength, as indicated by the number of B-A pairs, is found to be equal to A-B strength, as indicated by the number of A-B pairs. If the number of A-B and B-A pairs is found to be unequal, then associative asymmetry will be said to occur—A-B asymmetry if A-B exceeds B-A, and B-A asymmetry if B-A exceeds A-B. Finally, aided recall will refer to recall of A-terms with B-terms persent or recall of B-terms with A-terms present, while free (or unaided) recall will be used to designate recall of A-terms without B-terms present or of B-terms without A-terms present.

Early in the history of research on memory, the question was asked "are backward associations established during forward learning?" Ebbinghaus (1913)

Support for a number of the experiments reported here was provided by the Office of Naval Research under Contract Nonr 486(08) and by the National Science Foundation under Grant GB-6044. I appreciate the comments of Keith Wollen and Sam Brown on an earlier version of this manuscript.

phrased the question this way: "As a result of the previous learning of a, b, c, d, the sequences, a, b, c, a, c, e, are more easily learned than any grouping of equal length of syllables previously unknown such as p, q, r. . . . Is the same thing true of the sequences, c, b, a and e, c, a? As a result of manifold repetition of a series are associations also formed in the reverse order?" (p. 110) This question was, as you probably know, answered in the affirmative by Ebbinghaus and by others through experiments on serial recall, on serial learning, and on paired-associate learning (McGeoch & Irion, 1952). The results of most of these experiments seemed to show also that associations are asymmetrical and that A-B strength exceeds B-A strength.

OUR INITIAL EXPERIMENTS

My interest in experimentation on backward associations was stimulated by my reading of the paper by Feldman and Underwood (1957) entitled "Stimulus Recall Following Paired-Associate Learning." Feldman and Underwood were interested in studying the effects of similarity among stimulus terms and among response terms on A-B learning and on B-A recall. Thus they had their Ss learn seven trigram-adjective pairs to a criterion of 2 successive perfect trials. Then each S was tested for B-A recall. Feldman and Underwood reported that approximately 50 percent of the A-terms were given correctly during B-A recall. The results of this experiment appeared to accord with those from previous experiments in showing that B-A pairs do get learned during A-B learning and that B-A strength may not be as great as A-B strength. It seemed reasonable to us, however, that at least part of the difference in strength between A-B and B-A pairs may have been due to the use of trigrams as A-terms and the use of adjectives as B-terms. A fairer test, we thought, would be to use the same type of items as A-terms as were used as B-terms. I hasten to add here that Feldman and Underwood did not design their experiment to deal primarily with the question of associative symmetry. That question appeared to be incidental to their main interest in studying the effects of A-term and B-term similarity on A-B learning and on B-A recall.

Not long after this, one of my students replicated the Feldman and Underwood experiment (Buckhout, 1958; Newman & Buckhout, 1962). One important difference, however, was in the type of B-terms he used. He used low-association value (Glaze, 1928) trigrams both for the A-terms and for the B-terms. Thus it was possible for him to vary similarity in the same way among each set of terms. This he did by using 4 consonants or 8 consonants in forming the CVC trigrams. In this experiment Buckhout gave his Ss 39 anticipation trials at a 3:3 rate to learn the seven trigram pairs. Then each was tested twice for B-A recall, first at a 5-second rate and then without a time limit. Spelling the items was required on all tests. The results for this experiment appear in Table 1. In this table, the first letter refers to similarity among A-terms—High or Low—and

Table 1. Mean correct responses during and after A-B training (after Buckhout, 1958).

Treatment	N	A-B test (Trial 39)	B-A test (Trial 40)	B-A test (Trial 41)
HH	20	2.65	.55	1.25
HL	20	3.70	.85	1.65
LH	20	2.55	1.10	1.60
LL	20	5.60	2.00	3.00

the second letter refers to similarity among B-terms—High or Low. These results in Table 1 show that in all four treatments B-A pairs were established during A-B learning. They show also, as did Feldman and Underwood, that performance on the B-A tests was not as good as performance on the immediately preceding A-B test.

One finding from this experiment was of much greater interest to us. In examining the data for each S we noticed that one of the fastest learners in the LL treatment (a treatment in which each stimulus-term began with a different letter) had learned all seven of the pairs by the 20th trial. He had then gotten all seven pairs correct on almost all of the subsequent 20 trials, from Trial 20 through Trial 39. However, when we looked at his performance in B-A recall, we found that he had given correctly only the first letter of each of the A-terms. Data from his postexperimental inquiry accorded with the interpretation that he had used the first letter of each A-term as the cue to which he had associated its response.

These results suggested to us that the usually observed differences in A-B and B-A performance could have been due to an artifact deriving from a difference in the way in which A-terms and B-terms had usually been treated in the paired-associate learning experiment.

During paired-associate training, as you know, S ordinarily calls out (e.g., spells or pronounces the B-terms but not the A-terms. This difference in treatment could, it seemed to us, lead to better learning of the entire B-term than of the entire A-term. This difference in learning would occur since, during acquisition, S could respond to a part of the A-term, but he had to respond to the entire B-term.[1] Thus, at the end of training, performance on the A-B test on which the entire B-term had to be given was likely to be better than performance on the B-A test on which the entire A-term had to be given. And that, of course, is what seems to have been observed.

We looked again at the literature on backward associations, this time more closely than we had before. Our analysis indicated that the evidence of apparent

[1] We assumed (Newman, 1961) that training would lead to a change in the dominant response of the hierarchy for the A-term but not for the B-term. At the beginning of training the dominant response would be to the entire A-term (e.g., pronouncing or spelling), whereas at the end of training the dominant response would be to a part of it (e.g., first letter). For the B-term, however, the dominant response would more likely be to the entire B-term both at the beginning and end of training.

asymmetry between A-B and B-A pairs was equivocal. There appeared to us to be no experiment in which the conditions for the B-A test were the same as those for the A-B test. Thus, a thesis experiment was done by Ward (1960) in an attempt to provide such a test.

In this experiment, Ward exposed his Ss to a list of eight paired-associates made up of trigrams of medium association value. Half the Ss learned one list and the rest learned the same list, but with the A- and B-terms reversed. In this experiment, the anticipation procedure was used with a 2:2 rate, and with spelling the required response. Ss were given 8, 16 or 24 A-B trials of anticipation training. Then half of the Ss in each treatment were given an A-B test followed by a B-A test; and the rest of the Ss were tested first for B-A and then for A-B. A 2-second rate was used on the test with spelling again the response required.

The results of Ward's experiment appear in Table 2. The data have been collapsed across amount-of-practice and lists. Table 2 shows a much higher mean for A-B pairs than for B-A pairs, independent of which test came first. When the data for individual Ss were examined, Ward found that of the 48 Ss, 36 gave more A-B than B-A pairs, 11 gave the same number of each, and only one of the 48 Ss gave more B-A pairs than A-B pairs. These results seemed to indicate that the procedure that was ordinarily used in paired-associate training experiments led to better A-B than B-A performance.

The next experiment was reported in a 1961 thesis by Cunningham. This experiment was done to find out whether the procedures ordinarily used for paired-associate training, differentially affect the learning of A-terms and of B-terms. Free recall was used to measure A-term and B-term learning.

In this experiment, Cunningham used the same procedure during acquisition that had been used by Ward. Ss were given a fixed number of anticipation trials to learn the same list of eight trigram pairs. Then, half of the Ss were tested for B-term recall, and then for A-term recall. The remaining Ss had A-term recall first and then B-term recall. Both free recall trials lasted 45 seconds.

The results of this experiment are presented in Table 3. Again the data have been collapsed across amount of practice and lists. Table 3 shows that more B-terms than A-terms were recalled whether B-terms were recalled first or second. When the data for individual Ss were examined, 23 of the 24 Ss were found to give more B-terms than A-terms, and only 1 S of the 24 gave more A-terms than B-terms. These results were taken to mean that the procedure ordinarily used for paired-associate training, led to better B-term learning than A-term learning (Cunningham, 1961; Newman, Cunningham, & Gray, 1965).

Table 2. Mean correct responses after A-B training (after Ward, 1960).

Treatment	N	A-B test	B-A test
A-B, B-A	24	2.33	.50
B-A, A-B	24	2.04	.71

Table 3. Mean correct responses after A-B training (after Cunningham, 1961).

Treatment	N	B-term recall	A-term recall
B-term, A-term	12	4.83	1.67
A-term, B-term	12	4.83	1.58

EFFECTS OF PRONOUNCEABILITY

The results of these experiments were replicated in a series of experiments done in collaboration with Clifton Gray (Newman & Gray, 1964; Gray & Newman, 1966). In the first experiment of this series, Ss were given 21 study-test trials to learn a 6 item list of easy-to-pronounce (EP) trigrams. At the end of training, half of the Ss were tested for A-B and then for B-A; and the rest were given the B-A test first. In all four experiments in this series two lists were used in each treatment (one the mirror-image of the other), a 2-second rate was used on all study and test trials, and S was required to spell the responses on the tests.

The results of this first experiment are presented in the upper third of Table 4. These results are like Ward's in showing the A-B mean to be higher than the B-A mean, regardless of which test came first. Of the 40 Ss in this experiment, 26 had higher A-B and B-A scores, 2 had higher B-A scores, and 12 were equal in A-B and B-A performance.

In the next experiment of this series we used the same procedure, but we added another variable—pronounceability. We predicted that the difference between A-B and B-A performance would be greater for hard-to-pronounce pairs than for easy-to-pronounce pairs. This prediction was based on the assumptions that: (1) when the A-term is hard to pronounce, S is more likely to respond to a

Table 4. Mean correct responses after A-B training (after Newman & Gray, 1964).

Experiment	Treatment	N	A-B test	B-A test
I	EP-A-B, B-A	20	3.15	1.90
	EP-B-A, A-B	20	3.35	1.65
II	EP-A-B, B-A	20	3.30	2.50
	EP-B-A, A-B	20	4.15	2.55
	HP-A-B, B-A	20	.45	.05
	HP-B-A, A-B	20	.80	.05

Experiment	Treatment	N	B-term recall	A-term recall
III	EP-B-term, A-term	20	4.45	1.85
	EP-A-term, B-term	20	3.65	2.75
	HP-B-term, A-term	20	1.60	.20
	HP-A-term, B-term	20	1.45	.10

part of it than when the A-term is easy to pronounce; (2) the B-terms will be learned whether they are easy- or hard-to-pronounce, since S has to produce each B-term during training; (3) this difference in A-term and B-term learning will be directly reflected in a difference in A-B and B-A performance.

Again as in the previous experiment, Ss were given 21 study-test trials. They were then tested for A-B and B-A strength or for B-A and then A-B strength. Half the Ss in each treatment had the same six easy-to-pronounce trigram pairs as in the first experiment. The rest of these Ss had six hard-to-pronounce trigram pairs. The results are presented in the middle third of Table 4. They show, as in the previous experiments, that the A-B mean is higher than the B-A mean, no matter which test came first. They show also, and the analysis of variance verified, that the difference between A-B and B-A performance was not related to pronounceability of the two items of a pair. Again, also, the within subject comparisons accorded with these findings. In The EP treatments, 25 Ss had higher A-B scores, five had higher B-A scores, and ten performed equally well on A-B and B-A tests. For the HP groups, the results were similar: 19 had better A-B scores, four had higher B-A scores, and 17 did equally well on both. The results of this experiment, then, though replicating the asymmetry observed in previous studies, did not support the prediction that this asymmetry is a function of the pronounceability of the items of the pair.

The third experiment in this series was the same as the second except that Ss were tested for unaided or free recall rather than for aided or associative recall. Thus, at the end of training half of the Ss were tested for B-term recall followed by A-term recall; whereas the rest of the Ss were tested first for A-term recall. Each free recall test lasted 30 seconds. Again, as in the prior experiment, pronounceability was varied, half the Ss being exposed to the list of easy-to-pronounce pairs, and the others exposed to the list of hard-to-pronounce pairs.

The results for this experiment appear in the bottom of Table 4, where it may be seen that B-term recall was better than A-term recall at both levels of pronounceability, and no matter which test came first. Again, however, the difference between B-term recall and A-term recall did not appear to be strongly related to the pronounceability of the terms of the pairs. The within-subjects data also showed better B-term than A-term recall at both levels of pronounceability and independent of which test came first. However, there did appear to be a tendency for this difference to be greater for the hard-to-pronounce pairs than for the easy-to-pronounce pairs. Thus, for the EP Ss, 20 had higher B-term recall, 16 did equally well on both, and four had higher A-term recall; for the HP Ss, 31 had higher B-term recall, nine performed equally well on both, and no S did better on A-term recall. These results, combined with the data from the postexperimental inquiry which showed that a substantially greater number of Ss in the HP treatments than in the EP treatments reported responding to a part of the A-term, suggested to us that if HP Ss were given more A-B training, the hypothesis that asymmetry in recall is a function of pronounceability, might be supported.

Accordingly, the fourth and final experiment in the series was run (Gray & Newman, 1966). Again it was predicted that asymmetry in both aided recall and unaided recall would be greater for HP pairs than for EP pairs. The training procedure was the same as for the first three experiments in the series except that each list had four rather than six pairs, and Ss learned to one perfect trial rather than to a trials criterion. Following acquisition, all Ss were tested for eight seconds either in aided recall (A-B then B-A or B-A then A-B) or in unaided recall (B-term then A-term then B-term). Aided recall was paced, unaided was not.

In this experiment each prediction (i.e., greater asymmetry for HP than EP pairs) was tested in two analyses. One was a between-Ss comparison and the other was a within-Ss comparison. The data are presented in Table 5. For aided recall, the results from neither analysis supported the prediction. A-B recall exceeded B-A recall about equally in each pronounceability condition and about equally whether the A-B test or the B-A test came first.

For the between-subjects analysis the results for unaided recall were the same as for aided recall. B-term recall exceeded A-term recall about equally at each level of pronounceability. For the within-Ss analysis, however, the effects of pronounceability were as predicted—the difference between B-term and A-term recall was greater for HP Ss than for EP Ss. For all four comparisons in this experiment, the data were in the predicted direction—that is there was greater asymmetry under HP conditions; in only one of the four comparisons, however, the within-S comparison for unaided recall, was the asymmetry statistically significant.

Up to this point, then, we had established that the procedures that were ordinarily used for paired-associate training resulted in B-A pairs also being learned. We had found also that following A-B training, A-B performance was better than B-A performance and B-term recall was higher than A-term recall. Finally we had found that neither the asymmetry in aided recall nor the asymmetry in unaided recall are dependent on the order of the recall tests, nor are they strongly dependent on the pronounceability of the terms of the A-B pairs. We interpreted this set of findings as supporting our analysis that associative asymmetry results from better learning of the entire B-term than of the entire A-term.

Table 5. Mean correct and difference scores after A-B training (After Gray & Newman, 1966).

Pronounce-ability[1]	A-B test	B-A test	Within-S Difference[2]	B-term recall	A-term recall	Within-S Difference[2]
Easy	2.1	1.1	1.1	2.3	1.8	1.3
Hard	1.3	0.0	1.5	2.3	0.2	2.7

[1] Total N = 96, 12 Ss per treatment.

[2] Not reproducible from other figures in this table, which are for performance on the first test only.

EFFECTS OF INSTRUCTIONS AND READING ORDER

Our analysis of apparent associative asymmetry turned out to be similar to an analysis proposed by Solomon Asch and Sheldon Ebenholtz (1962a) in a paper entitled "The Principle of Associative Symmetry." Associations are symmetrical, they said; what looks like associative asymmetry can be explained by assuming that (1) in an association test, either an A-B test or a B-A test, the term to be given as a response must be available, and (2) the procedure ordinarily used in paired-associate training experiments leads to the B-term of a pair becoming more available than its A-term.

If these two assumptions are correct then performance on the A-B test will be better than performance on the B-A test, since more B-terms will be available than A-terms. Thus, according to Asch and Ebenholtz (1962a), what looks like associative asymmetry is due to an asymmetry of availability.

One implication of their analysis and of our analysis was clear. If an experiment was designed in which the availability of the A-terms were equal to the availability of the B-terms, associative symmetry would be observed.

We designed several experiments to meet these requirements. The first two were done in collaboration with Ralph Campbell. These experiments (Newman & Campbell, 1971) were modeled after several experiments done by Keith Wollen (Wollen, 1968; Wollen & Allison, 1968). In order to control availability in the experiments we took several precautions: we used single digits as A-terms and as B-terms; we told Ss that the A-terms were odd numbers and the B-terms were even numbers, or vice versa as the case happened to be, and we tested them on their knowledge of this; we had Ss read both items aloud during study trials; finally we used only study trials during acquisition. There were no intervening tests.

These experiments were done to study the effects of test instructions and of reading order on A-B and B-A performance following A-B training. Both were done to evaluate a proposal made by Wollen and Allison (1968) to help explain better A-B than B-A performance. Wollen and Allison pointed out that an unexpected shift from A-B learning to B-A recall could interject what they called a "surprise effect" that might tend to attenuate recall for the B-A Ss. Thus, Wollen and Allison carried out an experiment in which they had each S tested in the direction in which he was told he would be tested. Ss who were told that they would be given an A-B test were given an A-B test; and Ss who were told that they would be given a B-A test were given a B-A test. Wollen and Allison assumed that doing this would eliminate, or at least minimize the "surprise effect." The results from their experiment were, however, the same as from experiments in which all Ss were given A-B test instructions; namely, A-B performance was found to be significantly better than B-A performance.

Our first experiment was the same as theirs except that we added the two missing cells in the 2 X 2 design. Half of the Ss in each treatment were told that the test would be an A-B test, and the rest were told that the test would be a B-A test. Thus, half of the Ss in each treatment were tested in the direction in which they were told they would be tested; the rest were tested in the opposite direction.

The main features of the procedure for this experiment appear in Table 6. In Table 6 note first that all subjects were given a preliminary task to get them accustomed to the nature of the criterion task. On this preliminary task, five single-letter pairs were shown at a one-second rate on the memory, drum. S was instructed to read each pair aloud from left to right. There were three such study trials with no intertrial interval and no test.

Then came the criterion task. The criterion task was similar to the preliminary task. On the criterion task, all Ss were given six study trials on five single-digit pairs (either an odd-even list or an even-odd list). Again the pairs were presented at a one-second rate and Ss read each pair aloud from left to right. At the beginning of training half the Ss were told that they would be given an A-B test and the rest were told that they would be given a B-A test. At the end of training half the Ss in each treatment were given an A-B test and the rest were given a B-A test. On the test, each item was presented for one second, during which Ss pronounced the given item aloud and then produced the missing item if he could. The memory-drum window used for the test was not the same as the windows used during the study trials. Each test item appeared in the middle of the window. There were two tests with no interval between them. The responses for each S were tape-recorded and later scored. There were 80 Ss, 20 in each of the four cells of the experiment.

Table 6. Procedure for each experiment (after Newman & Campbell, 1971).

Experiment I

A. Preliminary task	B. Criterion task	C. Criterion test
1. 5 single-letter pairs	1. single-digit pairs (odd-even or even-odd)	1. half the Ss in each treatment given A-B test; rest given B-A test
2. 1 sec. rate	2. 1 sec. rate	2. Test–1 sec. rate
3. S read each pair aloud from left to right	3. S read each pair aloud from left to right	3. S says aloud presented item; then supplies omitted item
4. 3 pairing trials	4. 6 pairing trials	4. Each pair tested twice
	5. half the Ss told test would be A-B; rest told would be B-A	

Experiment II

A. Same procedure as in Experiment I–but half the Ss in each treatment read items aloud during pairing trials from right to left; the rest read items aloud from left to right, as in Experiment I.

Table 7. Mean correct for each treatment – experiment I (after Newman & Campbell, 1971).[1]

	Test Direction	
Test Instructions	A-B test	B-A test
A-B	6.80	3.90
B-A	6.90	5.55

[1] Total N = 80, 20 Ss per treatment.

The results for this experiment (the mean number of correct responses on the test) are presented in Table 7. The analysis of variance of these data showed that the F for Direction of Test was significant at the .001 level. Neither the F for Instructions nor for the Interaction of Instructions and Direction of Test was significant. As can be seen in Table 7, the A-B mean exceeded the B-A mean for each type of instruction S was given about the test. These data thus accord with those from the experiments by Wollen and suggest that A-B performance is better than B-A performance independent of the type of test that S is told he will get.

It seemed possible to us, however, that the asymmetry we obtained in this first experiment may have resulted, at least in part, from the left-right location of the terms responded to first on the study trials. Thus, in our next experiment (Newman & Campbell, 1971), we had half our Ss in each treatment read the items aloud from right to left; the remaining Ss in each treatment read the items aloud from left to right, just as had all the Ss in Experiment I. In all other respects the procedure for Experiment II was the same as for Experiment I. On the preliminary task, each S read the items aloud in the same order as he would on the criterion task.

The design, then, was a 2 X 2 X 2; two reading orders (A-B and B-A), two types of test instructions (A-B and B-A), and two types of test (A-B and B-A). A total of 160 Ss was run, 20 in each of the eight cells of the experiment.

The results for this experiment appear in Table 8—in terms of the mean correct responses for each treatment. In the analysis of variance the only significant F was for the interaction of Reading Order and Test Order. For Ss who read the items aloud from left to right, the A-B mean was higher than the B-A mean, while for Ss who read the items aloud from right to left the B-A mean was higher than the A-B mean.

The results of these experiments appeared to indicate that even with the availability of A-terms and B-terms equated, A-B asymmetry occurs, and that this asymmetry is independent both of the type of test S is told he will get, and of the left-right location during study trials of the term S overtly responds to first. The major factor determining asymmetry in these experiments appears to have been the temporal order in which the two terms of a pair were responded to during study trials; performance was better when the item more recently responded to was the one to be given on the test.

Table 8. Mean correct for each treatment—experiment II (after Newman & Campbell, 1971).[1]

	A-B Reading Order		B-A Reading Order	
Test Instructions	A-B test	B-A test	A-B test	B-A test
A-B	7.40	5.85	4.80	6.20
B-A	6.25	5.75	5.85	6.55

[1] Total N = 160, 20 Ss per treatment.

EFFECTS OF ITEM PRONUNCIATION ON AIDED AND FREE RECALL

We turn now to a set of experiments in which we studied the effects of pronouncing the A-terms and the B-terms during training on performance in aided and free recall. In these experiments we did again what we could to control the availability of the A-terms and the B-terms. Thus, we used only study trials with no intervening tests. We gave only one test, and that was at the end of training; we used words both as A-terms and as B-terms to reduce the likelihood that stimulus selection would occur; finally, we controlled overt occurrence of A-terms and of B-terms by having the subject pronounce the A-term, the B-term, both, or neither, throughout paired-associate training. Results from experiments by Hakes (1965) and by Murray (1965) had led us to expect that the overt pronunciation of a term would increase its availability.

The three experiments were the same except that one tested for association and the other two tested for availability. Availability, according to Asch and Ebenholtz (1962b), can be evaluated by performance on a free recall test.

First we carried out one of the availability experiments (Newman, 1969). In this experiment (as in the other two of this series) Ss were given four, eight, or 16 trials to learn a list of 14 pairs of dissyllables. All items had an "m" value greater than 3.20 (Noble, 1952). During training Ss pronounced the A-terms (Treatment A), the B-terms (Treatment B), both (Treatment AB), or neither (Treatment N), on all study trials. Ss in each treatment were exposed to a list of 14 A-B pairs, or to the same list but with the A- and B-terms reversed. A two-second rate was used on all study trials.

At the end of training, Ss were given test instructions (lasting 98 seconds). Then half the Ss in each treatment were tested for free recall of the A-terms and the rest were tested for free recall of the B-terms. On the recall test (which was paced) S was asked to call out a different term each time the memory-drum turned. The drum turned every two seconds.

Although a 4 (Pronunciation) X 3 (Trials) X 2 (Test) X 2 (List) design was used, we shall concern ourselves in this paper mainly with the predictions comparing B- and A-term recall for each pronunciation condition. We derived four predictions, and these appear in the third column of Table 9.

Table 9. Treatments, predictions, and results for the paced availability experiment (after Newman, 1969).

Treatment[1]	Term(s) Pronounced	Predictions	Results
N	Neither	B = A	B (5.00) > A (4.06)*
A	A	B < A	B (4.33) = A (4.78)
B	B	B > A	B (4.56) = A (4.16)
AB	A and B	B = A	B (4.56) = A (4.16)

[1] Total N = 144, 18 Ss per treatment.

*$p < .01$

These predictions were based on the assumptions that (1) at the beginning of training the A-terms and B-terms are equally available, (2) pronouncing a term increases its availability, (3) the increase in availability will be the same for A-term pronounciation as for B-term pronunciation, and (4) availability is measured by free recall.

For Treatment N, in which no term was pronounced during training, we predicted no difference between A-term and B-term recall. We made the same prediction—that is, no difference between A-term and B-term recall—for Treatment AB in which both of the terms of each pair were pronounced. Thus, for both Treatment N and Treatment AB we predicted symmetry of availability. We expected, however, that the level of availability for both A-terms and B-terms would be greater for Treatment AB than for Treatment N.

We predicted asymmetry of availability for Treatment A and for Treatment B. For Treatment A, where the A-terms were pronounced, we expected better A-term recall than B-term recall; and we predicted better B-term than A-term recall under Treatment B where only the B-terms were pronounced.

The results for this experiment appear in the fourth column of Table 9. Only one of the four predictions was supported, the prediction for Treatment AB. When both terms were pronounced the number of A-terms recalled was equal to the number of B-terms. But none of the other three predictions was supported. Also contrary to expectation, pronouncing a term did not appear to enhance its availability nor did an increase in the number of study trials from four to 16.

We were, of course, surprised (particularly in light of the results from Underwood, Runquist, and Schulz, 1959) that recall was not affected by the number of study trials. We were surprised also by the rather small number of items recalled in each of the treatments of this experiment. We wondered whether, if we tested for association rather than for availability, the results would be the same as in this paced availability experiment.

Our next experiment was an association experiment (Newman, 1968). In this experiment we used the same materials and followed the same procedure as in the availability experiment, except that at the end of training, (1) Ss were tested for association rather than for availability and (2) we reduced to 45 seconds the interval between the last pairing trial and the test, anticipating that test performance would thereby be faciliated. In this experiment, half the Ss were given an A-B test, and the rest were given a B-A test. A two-second rate was used on the test.

Rather than base our predictions for this experiment on the results from the paced availability experiment, we derived our predictions from the same first three assumptions that we had used in deriving the predictions for the availability experiment. In addition we assumed that (1) associations are symmetrical, (2) pronouncing the A-term or the B-term does not affect the A-B or the B-A association, and (3) symmetry or asymmetry of availability is directly reflected in performance on association tests.

The predictions for this experiment are presented in the third column of Table 10. Note that we expected that symmetry would be observed in Treatments AB and N, those treatments in which both terms of a pair were treated in the same way. In Treatment B, however, we expected that A-B performance would exceed B-A performance, while in Treatment A, we expected B-A performance to exceed A-B.

The results for this experiment appear in the fourth column of Table 10. The data do not accord with any of the four predictions.[2] Symmetry was observed only under Treatment B in which the B term was pronounced aloud throughout training. In the other three treatments, however, A-B asymmetry was observed. Further examination of the data revealed that, as expected, performance on both the A-B and the B-A tests improved with practice. Again, however, contrary to expectation, pronouncing a term overtly did not enhance performance on either test.

Table 10. Treatments, predictions, and results for the association experiment (after Newman, 1968).

Treatment[1]	Term(s) Pronounced	Predictions	Results
N	Neither	A-B = B-A	A-B (10.33) > B-A (8.80)*
A	A	A-B < B-A	A-B (8.97) > B-A (7.16)*
B	B	A-B > B-A	A-B (8.27) = B-A (8.47)
AB	A and B	A-B = B-A	A-B (9.00) > B-A (6.97)**

[1] Total N = 240, 30 Ss per treatment.

*$p < .05$.

**$p < .01$.

[2] Had the results from the paced availability experiment been used as a basis for predictions for this experiment, two rather than none of the four predictions would have been supported (i.e., the prediction that A-B asymmetry would occur in Treatment N, and that symmetry would occur in Treatment B).

It was obvious that one and perhaps more of the assumptions on which these predictions were based was wrong. In devising an ad hoc explanation for the asymmetry in Treatments N, A, and AB, and for the symmetry in Treatment B, we continued, however, to hold to the assumption that associations are symmetrical, contending that what looked like associative asymmetry (in Treatments N, A, and AB) could derive from an asymmetry of availability.[3] Our problem, then, became one of explaining how asymmetry of availability could occur in Treatments N, A, and AB, and how symmetry of availability could occur in Treatment B. Our explanation emphasized the effect that pronouncing a term might have on S's eye movements during the study trials rather than (as before) the effect of the pronounciation itself.

To us it seemed reasonable that in Treatments N, A, and AB, S would be more likely to look first at the A-term and then at the B-term. If the availability of a term were directly related to its recency, the B-term of a pair would be more likely to be available than the A-term. If, as we had assumed previously, symmetry (or asymmetry) of availability were directly reflected in performance on an association test, A-B asymmetry might thus be expected to occur in each of these three treatments.

A further assumption was required to deal with the symmetry observed in Treatment B. Thus we proposed that requiring Ss to pronounce the B-term increases the likelihood that S would look first at it, and then at the A-term. The tendency for A-term availability to exceed B-term availability would thus be increased. Concomitantly, the tendency for A-B asymmetry to occur would decrease, and symmetry or perhaps even B-A assymmetry might be observed.

One way to test this explanation is to study the effects of A-term and B-term pronunciation on eye movements during paired-associate training (cf. McCormack & Haltrecht, 1965). A second, though somewhat less direct, way to evaluate this explanation is to see whether the results from an availability experiment paralleled those from the association experiment. Since the equipment for studying eye movements during paired-associate training was not available to us, we chose this less direct way.

We decided, then, to try once more to study the effect of pronouncing a term on its availability. Though the results from the paced availability experiment suggested that the availability results would not parallel those of the association experiment, it appeared conceivable that paced free recall may have been an infelicitous technique for assessing availability. In addition, the use of different intervals between the end of training and the test in the two experiments (i.e., 98 seconds in the paced availability experiment, 45 seconds in the association experiment) led to noncomparability of their results. Thus, our next experiment (Newman, 1970) was the same as the paced availability experiment except that, (1) the test was unpaced, S being given 28 seconds to

[3] This experiment was done prior to those reported by Newman and Campbell (1971).

call out as many of the 14 different A-terms or B-terms as he could, and (2) 45 seconds (rather than 98 seconds) separated the end of the last study trial from the beginning of the test, just as in the association experiment.

The predictions for this experiment appear in the third column of Table 11. These predictions are derivable from the results of the association experiment, and concomitantly from the explanation for these results. Thus, asymmetry of availability was predicted for Treatments N, A, and AB: B-term recall to exceed A-term recall in each of these treatments. Symmetry of availability was predicted for Treatment B. We expected also that the level of performance in this experiment would be better than in the paced availability experiment, since the test was unpaced (cf. Ekstrand & Underwood, 1963) and there was a shorter interval between training and test.

The results for this experiment appear in the fourth column of Table 11. This time two of the predictions were supported. As predicted, no differences were observed in A-term and B-term recall in Treatment B, whereas in Treatment N more B-terms than A-terms were recalled. Contrary to expectation, however, the asymmetry predicted for Treatments A and AB was not observed. In each case, A-term recall was slightly, though not significantly, higher than B-term recall.

The assumptions used in deriving predictions for the paced availability experiment (cf. Table 9) can also be used to derive the same predictions for this experiment. Thus, symmetry would be predicted for Treatments N and AB, asymmetry for Treatment B (B > A), and for Treatment A (A > B). The results of this experiment are, however, similar to those for the paced experiment. Only one of these four predictions was supported, the symmetry in Treatment AB. For Treatments A and B, where directional predictions were made, the differences are small though in the predicted direction. The results of this experiment are like those of the paced experiment in that pronunciation was not found to enhance availability, the number of items recalled in each treatment was quite low, and increasing the number of study trials from four to 16 had relatively little effect.

Table 11. Treatments, predictions, and results for the unpaced availability experiment (after Newman, 1970).

Treatment[1]	Term(s) Pronounced	Predictions	Results
N	Neither	B > A	B (5.60) > A (4.53)**
A	A	B > A	B (4.93) = A (5.40)
B	B	B = A	B (4.67) = A (4.97)
AB	A and B	B > A	B (4.70) = A (4.83)

[1] Total N = 240, 30 Ss per treatment.

**p < .01.

Thus, the results of this experiment were not strikingly in accord with the predictions whether based on the assumption that (1) the pronounciation of an item enhances its availability or that (2) pronouncing an item influences the order in which S responds to it, thus affecting availability in that the item later responded to is the more available.[4]

FREE RECALL AS A MEASURE OF AVAILABILITY

One assumption that we had made in designing this set of experiments is that free recall measures availability. We had taken a strong position on this; namely, that if an item is available, it will be given in free recall, and that if an item is not given in free recall, it is not available. One implication of this position—an implication which appeared to us to accord both with the two-stage analysis of paired-associate learning proposed by Underwood, Runquist, and Schulz (1959), and with the separation of availability from association proposed by Asch and Ebenholtz (1962a), is that performance in free recall will always be equal to or greater than performance in aided recall.

It occurred to us that it would be possible to test this implication by comparing the results from the association experiment with results from the unpaced availability experiment, since the only difference between these two experiments was that a free recall test was used in one and an aided recall test was used in the other. There were 24 treatments in each experiment, permitting 24 between-experiment comparisons between free and aided recall. The results of these comparisons appear in Table 12.

Table 12 shows that in 22 of the 24 comparisons, performance in aided recall exceeded performance in free recall. This occurred even though free recall was unpaced, and aided recall was paced, and even though a stringent criterion (i.e., number correct) was used in assessing performance in aided recall. Table 12 shows also that these differences appeared to be greater for B-term recall than for A-term recall, and seemed to increase with training.

Table 12. Differences between means for comparable treatments (association versus unpaced availability) (after Newman, 1968; 1970).

	(A-B) minus B			(B-A) minus A		
	Trials			Trials		
Treatment	4	8	16	4	8	16
N	3.1	5.7	5.4	3.5	5.5	3.8
A	1.7	3.8	6.6	− .7	1.9	3.9
B	2.5	3.3	5.0	2.4	3.5	4.6
AB	1.4	5.1	6.4	− .7	2.3	4.8

[4] If both of these effects are combined and given equal weight in making predictions for the unpaced availability experiment, the data from that experiment would support three of the four predictions (i.e., all but the results from Treatment AB would be predicted).

Table 13. Mean correct on each test after A-B training (after Newman & Logan, 1970).

Treatment	N	1st test	2nd test	3rd test
W	10	*A-B 7.20	A-B 6.50	A-B 6.20
X	10	A-B 7.50	B 4.90	A-B 7.00
Y	10	**B 4.90	A-B 8.30	A-B 8.80
Z	10	B 4.30	B 4.70	A-B 10.30

*Aided recall.

**Free recall.

Since these comparisons were done between experiments, we designed another experiment (Newman & Logan, 1970) so that free and aided recall could be compared within the same experiment. The materials and procedure were the same as in the previous three experiments of this series. The free recall test was paced to make it comparable in this respect to the aided recall test. We used only one of the 24 treatments, recall of the B-terms following eight pairing trials. Neither term was pronounced aloud during study trials.

The design for this experiment appears in Table 13. In this experiment, all Ss were given eight study trials to learn the 14 word-pairs. Then half the Ss (Treatments Y and Z) were tested for free recall of the B-terms, paced at a two-second rate; the rest of the Ss (Treatments W and X) were tested for aided recall at a two-second rate. After this first test, half of the Ss (X and Z) in each of the two treatments were tested for free recall and the rest (W and Y) were tested for aided recall. Again, both tests were paced at a two-second rate. Finally, all Ss were tested for aided recall, also at a two-second rate.

The results for this experiment appear in Table 13. Again for aided recall a stringent criterion was used. Even so, on Test 1 the mean for aided recall was higher than the mean for free recall ($p < .01$). The results for Test 2 are the same and this is independent of the kind of test S was given first. Finally, when within-subject comparisons were done for Groups X, Y, and Z, the mean for aided recall was in each case higher than the mean for free recall. Within-subject analysis showed also that those items which occurred in free recall also occurred in aided recall, no matter which test came first.

The results from this experiment, and the results from several experiments in which performance in free recall has been compared with performance in cued recall (Thomson & Tulving, 1970; Tulving & Osler, 1968), indicate that S does better when A-terms which have been present on study trials are also present on the test. The results from Gray and Newman (1966), and Underwood, Runquist, and Schulz (1959) suggest, however, that this may not always be so.[5]

We interpret the results of this experiment not as infirming the two-stage analysis of paired-associate learning proposed by Underwood, Runquist, and

[5] Results from a recently completed experiment (Newman & Logan, 1971) show that with A-terms of high formal similarity, paced free recall of B-terms was substantially ($p < .001$) higher than aided recall of B-terms; however, with low formal similarity among A-terms, performance in free and aided recall of B-terms did not differ ($p > .05$).

Schulz (1959), nor the separation of association and availability proposed by Asch and Ebenholtz (1962a) and also by us. Rather, the better performance in aided than free recall suggests that under some conditions B-term availability (i.e., response learning) during paired-associate training is imperfectly measured either by paced free recall (cf. Ekstrand, 1966) or by unpaced free recall (cf. Underwood, Runquist, & Schulz, 1959). One challenge for research is to identify what those conditions are, perhaps through identifying the conditions under which performance in free and aided recall differs, and the conditions under which it is the same.

CONCLUDING STATEMENT

In our search for associative symmetry we have observed asymmetry almost everywhere we have looked: whether Ss were told that the test would be A-B or B-A; whether the A-term was on the left or on the right; whether the items were words or digits or trigrams of low or high pronounceability; whether the anticipation or the study-test procedure was used; whether performance was measured early or late in training; whether a within- or a between-subjects comparison was used; and whether S pronounced both terms, neither term, or just the A-term during training. Only when the B-term was pronounced during training were A-B and B-A performance found to be equivalent.

Asymmetry was also observed in free recall. Thus, B-term recall was better than A-term recall whether the items were easy- or hard-to-pronounce trigrams; whether the anticipation or the study-test procedure was used; whether S was tested early or late in training; whether a within- or a between-S comparison was used; and when S was not required to pronounce either term aloud during study trials. However, when S pronounced the A-term, the B-term, or both during study trials, no difference was observed between A-term and B-term recall, whether recall was paced or unpaced.

Our original position (Newman, 1961), like that of Asch and Ebenholtz (1962a), was that "associative asymmetry" derived from an asymmetry of availability due to the greater likelihood of stimulus selection in A-terms than in B-terms. Though our early experiments provided support for this position, the results from later experiments (Wollen, 1968; Newman & Campbell, 1971) seemed to us to make such a position untenable.

If associations are symmetrical, the asymmetry observed in these later experiments does not appear to be easy to explain. This is particularly the case since well-learned, highly available sets of items were used both as A-terms and as B-terms.

One possible explanation (though to us it does not seem a likely one) derives from the assumption that the B-term of a pair is more available than its A-term since it is the more recently responded to. Thus, the asymmetry observed in these and in other experiments could still be due to an asymmetry of availability. To account for the symmetry observed when B-term pronunciation occurred during study trials, a further assumption would be necessary (cf. page 144); namely that pronouncing the B-term increases the likelihood that the B-term will be responded to first. Information about (1) the effect of item pronunciation during study trials on eye movements and (2) the relationship between such eye movements and subsequent A-B and B-A performance could prove useful in evaluating this assumption.

The above assumptions could be used also to account for all findings from the free-recall experiments except the symmetry when the A-terms were pronounced during study trials either alone or with the B-terms. We have proposed, however, that free recall appears to have been an imperfect measure of availability under the conditions of these experiments. Thus, it is not appropriate to expect an explanation for these free-recall results in terms of the effect of pronunciation on availability.

There are other results from the two later free-recall experiments which continue to puzzle us—the failure of the item pronunciation during study trials to enhance recall, and the rather small changes in free-recall performance which accompanied the increase from four to 16 study trials. In addition, we would like to know more about those conditions under which performance in aided and free recall differ and those conditions under which it is the same, and we hope to continue to delineate those conditions under which symmetry, A-B asymmetry, and B-A asymmetry (cf. Asch & Lindner, 1963) occur. We hope that further experimentation in our laboratory will prove useful in dealing with these questions.

REFERENCES

Asch, S. E., & Ebenholtz, S. M. The principle of associative symmetry. *Proceedings of the American Philosophical Society*, 1962, 106, 135–163. (a)

Asch, S. E., & Ebenholtz, S. M. The process of free recall: evidence for non-associative factors in acquisition and retention. *Journal of Psychology*, 1962, 54, 3–31. (b)

Asch, S. E., & Lindner, M. A note on "Strength of Association". *Journal of Psychology*, 1963, 55, 199–209.

Buckhout, R. The effect of variation in degree of similarity among stimulus terms and among response terms on recall of the stimulus term during R-S retention measurement. Unpublished M.S. thesis, North Carolina State University, 1958.

Cunningham, J. W. S-term and R-term recall as functions of S-R training. Unpublished M.S. thesis, North Carolina State University, 1961.

Ebbinghaus, H. *Memory: A Contribution to Experimental Psychology*. (Translated by H. A. Ruger and C. E. Bussenius). New York: Teachers College Press, Columbia University, 1913.

Ekstrand, B. R. Backward association. *Psychological Bulletin*, 1966, 65, 50–64. (a)

Ekstrand, B. R. A note on measuring response learning during paired-associate learning. *Journal of Verbal Learning and Verbal Behavior*, 1966, 5, 344–347. (b)

Ekstrand, B. R., & Underwood, B. J. Paced versus unpaced recall in free learning. *Journal of Verbal Learning and Verbal Behavior*, 1963, 2, 288–290.

Feldman, S. M., & Underwood, B. J. Stimulus recall following paired-associate learning. *Journal of Experimental Psychology*, 1957, 53, 11–15.

Glaze, J. A. The association value of nonsense syllables. *Journal of Genetic Psychology*, 1928, 35, 255–269.

Gray, C. W., & Newman, S. E. Associative asymmetry as a function of pronounceability. *Journal of Experimental Psychology*, 1966, 71, 923–924.

Hakes, D. T. Stimulus articulation and backward learning. *Psychonomic Science*, 1965, 3, 47–48.

Horton, D. L., & Kjeldergaard, P. M. An experimental analysis of associative factors in mediated generalization. *Psychological Monographs*, 1961, 75 (11, Whole No. 515).

McCormack, P. D., & Haltrecht, E. J. Two-stage paired-associate learning and eye movements. *Science*, 1965, 148, 1749–1750.

McGeoch, J. A., & Irion, A. L. *The Psychology of Human Learning*. (2nd ed.) New York: Longmans, Green, 1952.

McGovern, J. B. Extinction of associations in four transfer paradigms. *Psychological Monographs*, 1964, 78 (16, Whole No. 593).

Murray, D. J. Vocalization-at-presentation and immediate recall with varying presentation rates. *Quarterly Journal of Experimental Psychology*, 1965, 17, 47–56.

Newman, S. E. A mediation model for paired-associate learning. Technical Report Number 1, 1961, North Carolina State University, Contract Nonr 486(08), Office of Naval Research, (A shorter version appears in De Cecco, J. P. *Educational Technology*. New York: Holt, Rinehart and Winston, 1964, 174–184).

Newman, S. E. S-R and R-S performance as functions of S-term and R-term pronunciation. Paper presented at meeting of the Psychonomic Society, St. Louis, November, 1968.

Newman, S. E. Paired-associate learning. Final Report, June 30, 1969, North Carolina State University, Grant NSF GB-6044, National Science Foundation, p. 5.

Newman, S. E. Effects of A-term and B-term articulation on recall following paired-associate training. Paper presented at the meeting of the Southeastern Psychological Association, Louisville, April, 1970.

Newman, S. E., & Buckhout, R. S-R and R-S learning as functions of intralist similarity. *American Journal of Psychology*, 1962, 75, 429–436.

Newman, S. E., & Campbell, R. T. A-B and B-A performance as functions of test instructions and reading order. *Journal of Experimental Psychology*, 1971, 88, 57–59.

Newman, S. E., Cunningham, J. W., & Gray, C. W. Asymmetry in stimulus term and response-term recall following paired-associate training. *Psychonomic Science*, 1965, 2, 297–298.

Newman, S. E., & Gray, C. W. S-R vs. R-S recall and R-term vs. S-term recall following paired-associate training, *American Journal of Psychology*, 1964, 77, 444–450.

Newman, S. E., & Logan, G. W. Aided and unaided recall of B-terms following A-B training. Paper presented at meeting of the Psychonomic Society, San Antonio, November, 1970.

Newman, S. E., & Logan, G. W. Effect of formal similarity among A-terms on aided and unaided B-term recall. Unpublished manuscript, North Carolina State University, 1971.

Noble, C. E. An analysis of meaning. *Psychological Review*, 1952, 59, 421–430.

Thomson, D. M., & Tulving, E. Associative encoding and retrieval: weak and strong cues. *Journal of Experimental Psychology*, 1970, 86, 255–262.

Tulving, E., & Osler, S. Effectiveness of retrieval cues in memory for words. *Journal of Experimental Psychology*, 1968, 77, 593–601.

Underwood, B. J., Runquist, W. N., & Schulz, R. W. Response learning in paired-associate lists as a function of intralist similarity. *Journal of Experimental Psychology*, 1959, 58, 70–78.

Ward, S. W. Strength of S-R and R-S pairs as a function of number of S-R trials. Unpublished M.S. thesis, North Carolina State University, 1960.

Wollen, K. A. Effects of maximizing availability and minimizing rehearsal upon associative asymmetry in two modalities. *Journal of Experimental Psychology*, 1968, 77, 626–630.

Wollen, K. A., & Allison, T. S. Latency and frequency of S-R and R-S associations as a function of recall time. *Journal of Verbal Learning and Verbal Behavior*, 1968, 7, 895–899.

7 | Stimulus Selection in Associative Learning

JACK RICHARDSON

State University of New York at Binghampton

Underwood (1963) specified the difference between the nominal and functional stimulus in verbal learning and emphasized that human Ss may select part of a compound verbal stimulus as the functional stimulus. He pointed out some of the implications of stimulus selection for verbal learning and transfer and noted that selection comparable to that in concept learning may occur at a low level in rote paired-associate learning.

Since 1963, not only has there been an increased experimental interest in stimulus selection but it has been used to interpret the results of a variety of studies. For instance, stimulus selection has been used to interpret the differences between forward and backward recall (Houston, 1964; Nelson, Rowe, Engle, Wheeler, & Garland, 1970; Young, Farrow, Seitz, & Hays, 1966), some effects of formal stimulus similarity (Runquist, 1970), false stimulus recognition (Martin, 1968), the effects of interpolated learning on recall (Goggin & Martin, 1970; Schneider & Houston, 1968, 1969; Weaver, 1969), the effects of similarity of meaningfulness within compound stimuli (Solso & Trafimow, 1970), and to investigate differences between retardates and normal children (Baumeister & Berry, 1968; Baumeister, Berry, & Forehand, 1969). It seems possible that the interpretative use of stimulus selection may be exceeding our investigation of the basic processes and that stimulus selection is in danger of becoming, with the mediating response, "a theory looking for a body of data" (Wickens, 1963, p. 379).

Studies of stimulus selection in paired-associate learning are concerned with the what-how-why and degree of differential effectiveness of the redundant components of compound stimuli as cues for learning. The task is simple. A paired-associate list with compound stimuli is presented to Ss until they learn to some specified criterion. The original compounds and the individual components are then presented separately as cues for recall or as stimuli for a transfer

This research was supported by National Science Foundation Grants GB 5876 and GB 17614. Elizabeth A. Jones, Sara K. Stanton, Janet Keyes, Jon R. C. Hobrock, Anita J. Gavazzi, and Alan Trager assisted in the collection of the data. The author is grateful to Delos D. Wickens and Ann K. Wolfgang for their comments on an earlier draft of this paper.

learning task in which the responses are the same as were previously paired with the components. Stimulus selection is defined by the differential effectiveness of the components as cues for recall, or as stimuli in the transfer list. The most effective component of the compound is said to be "selected" or "dominant." In addition, the lists tend to have certain characteristics which help distinguish studies of stimulus selection from other areas of research. The stimuli are usually compounds which are easily analyzed into components instead of components which Ss tend to integrate (cf. Shepard, 1963, for a discussion of this problem). The components are easily distinguishable (e.g., letters, words, trigrams) and the responses are usually simple ones which require a minimum of integration and are readily available for recall. The compound stimuli always consist of at least two redundant components, i.e., it is possible to learn each pair in the list by using either, or both, components as the functional stimulus.

As in any area of research, the proper controls and inferences depend upon the conception of underlying processes. In a recent review (Richardson, 1971), Underwood's conception that stimulus selection is the result of an active process under the control of S was adopted and, in addition, it was assumed that selection is the result of some sort of time-sharing device. The time-sharing may be the result of a peripheral mechanism, such as an orientation which focuses on the one component and reduces stimulation from the other components, or it may be more central, such as differential rehearsal time. At any rate, the conception of stimulus selection as the result of a time-sharing device under the control of S has certain methodological implications. Demonstrating that redundant components are differentially effective as cues for recall following learning with the compounds as stimuli does not necessarily demonstrate stimulus selection. It may simply be easier to learn the responses to one set of the components than to the other. For instance, if the compounds consist of words and low-meaningfulness trigrams, the fact that more correct responses are recalled to the words following learning than to the compounds may be due to the fact that the responses are easier to learn to the words than to the trigrams, and not to any differential time sharing. This conception also implies that the proper controls for stimulus selection studies are lists in which single components from the compounds are paired with the same responses and learned under the same conditions as the compound list. That is, the maximum selection should result if S effectively eliminates all components except the selected one. The learning of the component-response list, under the same conditions as the compound-response list, should provide the baseline for maximum stimulus selection. If stimulus selection is the result of a time-sharing device, any learning to one component of the compound should reduce the learning to other components and this leads to the need for some measure of *efficiency*, i.e., a measure of the extent to which learning is limited to only one component of a compound.

In reviewing the literature (Richardson, 1971), it seemed that in many experiments the selected components could be identified by a simple rule which permitted differentiation of the selected from the nonselected components but did not distinguish among selected components or among nonselected components. The selected components could be described as the first of three letters, the word surrounded by a colored rectangle, etc. Investigation of this rule behavior requires a measure of *consistency* which designates the extent to which an individual S selects according to a rule and which is not dependent upon the extent to which all Ss select according to the same rule. For example, following paired-associate learning with CCCs as stimuli, a group of Ss will recall some correct responses to letters from each of the three positions but much more to letters from the first position. This may mean that all Ss select the first letters as functional stimuli and that learning to the other two letters is due to lack of efficiency. On the other hand, it could mean that selection is completely efficient and that most, but not all, Ss select the first letter as the functional stimulus. Some measure of individual consistency is necessary to distinguish between these possibilities.

EXPERIMENTAL PROCEDURES

Several general objectives were considered in designing the five experiments which are presented here. One objective was to determine the usefulness of the time-sharing, consistency, and efficiency concepts when applied to studies of stimulus selection. A second objective was to determine the limits of efficiency and consistency of stimulus selection, i.e., what level of efficiency and consistency can be expected with optimum conditions. A third was to investigate selection in "rote paired-associate learning." The latter probably requires further comment. It is assumed that rote learning designates learning which is accomplished by rehearsal or repetition and does not include organization, mediation, elaboration, or other special devices which can aid learning.

The objectives of the experiments required a task which is relatively easy to learn, minimizes response learning, and has easily distinguished stimulus components which Ss do not tend to integrate into a unit. There should be a minimum of preexperimental associations among the stimuli and among the stimuli and responses, so that the component-response pairs tend to be of equal difficulty and thus minimize the problem of distinguishing difficulty from selection. The task should offer minimum opportunity and incentive for organization although, of course, the stimuli must be compounds.

Consonant trigrams with.no duplication of letters and arbitrarily paired with single-digit responses seemed to be the verbal material most likely to meet these criteria. As with any verbal material, Ss can give associations to numbers and letters, encode CCCs as words, imbed the trigram and digit in an image, etc. It was assumed that the paired-associate learning and six CCC-digit pairs would offer little incentive for such encoding. It was known that strong letter selection occurs with CCC stimuli and there seemed to be no systematic way to classify the component letters except on the basis of the position in the trigram. The same six trigrams were used in all of the experiments; TLN, BQD, CFP, XJM, ZSG, and RKH. The digits 2 through 7 were the responses.

The amount of transfer from learning with the compounds as stimuli to learning with the components as stimuli is sometimes used as a basis for inferring stimulus selection during original learning. This transfer procedure was avoided because it gives Ss an opportunity to apply a strategy to second-list learning. In order to compute individual measures of efficiency or consistency, it is necessary that Ss learn with *all* components as cues following learning to the compound. Even if the component-response pairs are equally difficult, there may be faster second-list learning for some components because Ss select these components for early learning in the second list, and not because they were more effective cues in first-list learning. Thus, cue effectiveness may be incorrectly attributed to selection during the compound-list learning when it is due to the use of a strategy during second-list learning. In the present series of experiments all Ss were given three successive recall trials to the 18 component letters from the 6 CCCs. It seemed possible that the results on a single recall trial might be unduly affected by guessing. Of course, there is the problem of the effect of successive recall trials on recall but evidence on this point will be presented later.

The general procedure was very similar in all five experiments. The paired-associate lists of six pairs were presented by the study-test method and Ss learned to a criterion of two successive perfect trials. The stimuli for the learning trials were presented on IEE display units in Experiments I-III and on memory drums in Experiments IV and V. Unless specified otherwise, the material on both the study and test cycles was presented at a 2-sec. rate and with a 4-second intercycle interval.

Following the learning of the paired-associate list, all Ss were given three recall trials with the single letters as stimuli. This was accomplished with three decks of 18 cards. Each card in a deck contained one of the 18 letters from the 6 CCCs. The order of the letters within a deck was counterbalanced for position of the letters in the CCCs. Each deck started with a letter from a different position and an equal number of Ss within each condition started recall with each of the decks. The Ss were given a deck of 18 cards, required to turn them up one at a time, say the letter on that card aloud, and attempt to say the digit that had been paired with the letter during paired-associate learning—guessing if they did not know. This procedure was repeated for the second and third decks so that each S attempted three recalls to each of the 18 component letters. No feedback was given to S during the three recall trials and E recorded the responses as they were given by S.

The conditions were listed in counterbalanced orders for each experiment and this sequence was used to assign Ss to conditions as they appeared at the laboratory. The Ss were college students from introductory psychology courses. The Ss in Experiment I were not necessarily naive with respect to verbal learning, but none had previously served as an S in a stimulus selection experiment. The Ss in Experiment II through V had not previously served as Ss in any type of verbal learning experiment.

The measures of consistency and efficiency are critical to the interpretation of the results of the studies, so the method of computing these will be specified at this point. On a recall trial S can give the correct response to 0, 1, 2, or 3 of the letters from a CCC. The number of different correct responses will designate the number of the six CCC letter sets which result in at least one correct response, i.e., the number of different digits given to one or more of the three letters for which it is the correct response. The letters "selected" from the CCCs will be specified for each experiment but the consistency score is always the percentage of different correct responses which are also recalled correctly to the selected letters, i.e., for each S the number of responses correctly recalled to one or more of the three letters from a trigram is divided into the number of correct responses to the selected letters and the result multiplied by 100. It should be noted that correct recall to the two nonselected letters does not affect this score unless the recall to the selected letter is not correct, and that items which do not have a correct recall response to any of the three letters do not enter into the computations. Regardless of the recall to the nonselected letters, the consistency score is 100 if the recall to all six selected letters is correct.

The efficiency score is the number of different correct responses divided by the total number of correct responses and multiplied by 100. This score gives the percentage of the total correct recall responses which would be necessary to give a single correct response to each trigram from which one or more of the three letters elicit the correct recall response. It should be noted that the efficiency score does not depend upon specifying the selected letters and that any trigram set of three letters for which there is no correct recall does not enter into the computation.

Some examples may help clarify the computations of the consistency and efficiency scores. Consider the following protocols of a single recall trial to the 18 letters for two different Ss:

	S 1			S 2	
T +	L +	N +	T +	L −	N −
B −	Q +	D −	B +	Q −	D −
C +	F −	P +	C −	F −	P +
X +	J −	M +	X −	J −	M +
Z −	S −	G −	Z +	S −	G +
R −	K −	H −	R +	K −	H −

The letters in each row are from a single CCC and are in the same sequence as during the paired-associate learning. The plus or dash following each letter indicates whether the recall response to that letter was correct or incorrect. Assume that the letters in the first position are the selected letters for both Ss. S 1 has one or more correct responses in four rows so that four is the number of different responses. Three of these four rows have correct responses to letters in the selected (first) position. The consistency score is the number of correct responses to letters in the selected position divided by the number of different correct responses and multiplied by 100, i.e., $(3/4)(100) = 75$. The efficiency score it the number of different correct responses divided by the total correct responses to all 18 letters and multiplied by 100, i.e., $(4/8)(100) = 50$. The corresponding consistency and efficiency scores for S 2 are $(4/6)(100) = 66.7$ and $(6/7)(100) = 85.7$.

EXPERIMENT I

The major purpose of the first experiment was to determine the usefulness of the consistency and efficiency measures in specifying important aspects of stimulus selection. There were four basic conditions. Let T represent the six CCCs and S represent the six letters from one of the three positions in the six CCCs. The four conditions were S-S, S-T, T-S, and T-T with the first letter specifying the stimuli on the study cycles and the second specifying the stimuli on the test cycles of the paired-associate learning. The digit paired with, or correct for, a single letter was always the same as that for the corresponding CCC. These four conditions vary in the opportunity afforded S for variations in consistency and efficiency.

The S-S condition was simply paired-associate learning by the study-test method with six single letters as stimuli. Stimulus selection is considered to be the result of some type of time-sharing mechanism which is under the control of S. Thus, if selection is perfect, the learning to compound stimuli should be the same as that produced by presenting only the selected components to S for learning. In this sense, the S-S is the basic control condition; S learns the responses to the single components and the learning, consistency, and efficiency should be maximum. The Ss in the S-S condition, as in all other conditions, were presented all 18 letters from the CCCs as cues on the three recall trials. The results from attempting to recall to the 12 letters which were not presented during learning should help control for any guessing biases.

In the S-T condition the same six letters from a single position in the trigrams were presented paired with the digit responses on each study cycle and the six trigrams were presented alone on the test cycles. In this case, the responses must be learned to the single letters during the study cycles so consistency should remain at a maximum, as in the S-S condition. The trigrams were presented on the test cycles and S could learn that certain letters were presented together or, after learning the response to the single letter, could learn the response to the letters presented only on the test cycles. However, it seemed that these possibilities were rather remote and that efficiency might also be high in the S-T condition.

In the T-S condition the six trigrams were paired with the digit responses on the study cycles and same six letters from a single position in the trigrams were presented on each test cycle. The S was free to learn the response to any or all of the letters of a trigram on the study cycle but was forced to produce the response to a single letter on the test cycle. Thus, consistency should remain at a maximum because the test cycles force learning to single letters, but efficiency could be lower because S has an opportunity to learn the response to other letters on the study cycles.

The T-T condition was ordinary paired-associate learning by the study-test method with the CCCs as stimuli on both study and test cycles. This condition is the one commonly used in studies of stimulus selection and S is free to learn the response to any or all of the letters in a trigram. Consistency and/or efficiency may be lower under these conditions.

Within the four basic conditions various controls were introduced. Consider the six CCCs (TLN, CFP, ZSG, XJM, BQD, and RKH) as consisting of three sets of six letters; those in the first position in the trigrams, those in the second position, and those in the third. These three sets of letters were used to construct two additional sets of trigrams. The same letters were used within a trigram but the order was changed so that each set of six letters occurred once in each position in the trigrams. For instance, TLN was LNT in the second set and NTL in the third. These three sets of trigrams were used equally often as T stimuli and the three sets of letters were used equally often as S stimuli. This procedure should control for differences in difficulty of specific letter sequences and permit determination of the relative difficulty of the component-response pairs in the S-S condition. In addition, there were two different pairings of the digits 2 through 7 with the stimulus terms.

The four basic conditions contained different numbers of subconditions and different numbers of Ss. The three sets of six letters were used equally often as stimuli in the S-S condition and there were two different letter-digit pairings for a total of 6 subconditions and 24 Ss. The three sets of trigrams were used equally often in the T-T condition and, with two response pairings, there were a total of 6 subconditions and 24 Ss. In the S-T and T-S conditions each of the three sets of trigrams was used equally often and the six S letters were equally often from each position in the trigrams. With two response pairings this gave 18 subconditions and 72 Ss for the S-T and for the T-S condition. In addition to the 192 Ss who completed the experiment, 2 Ss were dropped because of E errors.

The Ss in the S-S and T-T condition were given the usual paired-associate learning instructions. In addition to the usual instructions, Ss in the T-S and S-T condition were told about the differences between the study- and test-cycle stimuli and the position in the trigrams the S letters would occupy. The Ss were not informed that there would be recall trials following learning. After learning the paired-associate list to the criterion of two successive perfect trials, all Ss were given three recall trials to the 18 component letters. Following recall to the single letters, all *S*s were given a deck of six cards containing the six trigrams, asked to read the three letters in the trigram aloud, and to give the digit that had been paired with one or more of the letters. The three sets of trigrams were used equally often for recall by *S*s in the S-S condition while *S*s in the other three conditions recalled to the trigrams as they had appeared during the learning trials.

Learning. A variety of analyses were computed on the subconditions but the resuls may be summarized very briefly. Neither the order of the letters in the CCCs, the specific set of letters used as S terms, the position of the S terms in the CCCs, the particular pairings of the stimuli with the responses, nor the interactions containing any of these variables approached statistical significance. Since there were no effects of particular letter set in the S-S or S-T conditions, it is reasonable to assume that the letter-response difficulty does not differ among the letter sets and that differences in recall to different sets of letters in the T-T condition are the result of selection rather than differential difficulty. Since the letter sets from the three positions had no detectable effect on learning in the T-S condition, it is reasonable to assume that selection of letters from a particular position in a CCC is an *S* preference and is not determined by differential difficulty of learning to letters in different positions.

The mean trials required to attain the criterion of two successive perfect trials (T/C) include the two criterion trials and are presented in Table 1 along with the mean trials per item to the last error (T/LE). The T/LE was computed for each *S* by summing the number of the trial on which the last error occurred for each of the six items and dividing the result by six. Although it seems that T/LE should be less influenced by unusually difficult pairs than T/C, the two measures show the same trends. The S-T and T-T conditions tend to be more difficult than the S-S condition but the differences are not significant at the .05 level for either measure. Condition T-S was more difficult than S-S by both measures; $t(94) = 4.13$ and 5.16 for T/C and T/LE respectively, $p < .001$. In general, these trends agree with previous findings that paired-associate learning with compound stimuli tends to be more difficult than with component stimuli (cf. Richardson, 1971, for a review). However, there is no obvious reason why the T-S condition should be more difficult than the T–T.

Table 1. Experiment I: Mean trials to criterion (T/C) and mean trials per item to the last error (T/LE) for the paired-associate learning.

Condition	n	T/C		T/LE	
		M	$\hat{\sigma}$*	M	$\hat{\sigma}$
S–S	24	5.67	2.53	1.64	1.25
S–T	72	5.72	2.48	2.07	1.92
T–S	72	9.18	5.68	4.68	4.52
T–T	24	6.21	1.82	2.08	1.15

*Estimate of the standard deviation of the population.

Recall. All *S*s were required to give one of the digits 2 through 7 on each trial to each of the 18 letters presented for recall, even if they did not know the correct response. Some *S*s used a strategy which obviously biased the recall results. These *S*s chose one digit from the six possibilities and consistently gave this digit as a response to the letters from two of the three positions in the trigrams. Since this digit was always given correctly to the appropriate letter in the other position, this procedure resulted in correct responses to all three letters from one trigram on each recall trial. This recall is about guessing level if each trial is considered but it also results in correct responses to the same trigram letters on all three recall trials and the number correct to a higher criterion, on two or three of the recall trials, is much greater than chance. The use of this strategy apparently was not related to speed of learning or to the total number of correct responses on the recall trials. The data from *S*s who consistently gave the same digit as the response to letters from two of the three positions for two of the three recall trials was not included in any of the recall analyses. This changed the number of *S*s in the conditions and this number will be specified in each case. It may be worth noting that this guessing strategy was used less often in the T-S and T-T conditions than in the S-S and S-T.

The amount of recall to the component letters of the trigrams is the critical data and will be presented in considerable detail. The six S letters were designated the selected letters in the S-S, S-T, and T-S conditions, and the set of six letters from the position for which *S* gave the most correct responses during recall was designated the selected set of letters in the T-T condition. Although there were three sets of trigrams with different letter orders in the T-T condition, all 24 *S*s selected the set of letters which was in the first position in the trigrams. The *S*s in the S-S, S-T, and T-S conditions always gave more correct recall responses to the S letters than to either of the other two sets of letters. Thus, the selected letters were always the set of six letters which produced the most correct responses during recall.

Table 2 presents the mean recall measures for each condition on each of the three recall trials. The correct responses on the recall trials are divided into those given to letters from the selected position (SP) and those given to letters from the other two positions (OP). Table 2 also presents the number of different responses (DR), i.e., the number of digit responses that were correct for one or more of the three letters from a trigram. Careful examination of Table 2 shows that the differences among trials are small and unsystematic for all of the recall measures. The 178 *S*s gave 8.57, 8.47, and 8.48 mean total correct responses on Trials 1, 2, and 3 respectively. There is no indication that recall varies systematically as a function of successive recall trials. There were more correct recall responses given in the T-S and T-T conditions and this consisted of fewer correct responses to the letters from the selected position and more correct responses to letters from other positions.

Table 3 presents the same recall measures but the left half of the table gives the means when a response is considered correct only if it is correct on at least two of the three recall trials, and the right half gives the means when a response

Table 2. Experiment I: Correct responses for the three recall trials; the mean number of correct responses to letters from the selected positions (SP), to letters from other positions (OP), and the mean number of different correct responses (DR).

Condition	n	Trial 1			Trial 2			Trial 3			Total
		SP	OP	DR	SP	OP	DR	SP	OP	DR	SP & OP
S–S	20	5.55	2.40	5.70	5.50	2.05	5.75	5.50	2.30	5.50	23.30
S–T	65	5.62	2.48	5.72	5.69	2.34	5.78	5.66	2.18	5.75	23.97
T–S	69	5.32	3.55	5.54	5.41	3.46	5.61	5.26	3.64	5.55	26.64
T–T	24	4.92	4.58	5.50	4.58	4.67	5.25	5.04	4.54	5.42	28.33

Table 3. Experiment I: Mean correct responses to letters for the two or more correct out of three recall criterion (2/3), to letters for the three correct out of three recall criterion (3/3), and to the trigrams; recall to the letters is presented for the letters from the selected positions (SP), for letters from other positions (OP), and for the number of different responses (DR).

Condition	n	2/3 Trials				3/3 Trials				Trigrams
		SP	OP	Total	DR	SP	OP	Total	DR	
S–S	20	5.75	1.35	7.10	5.85	5.00	.50	5.50	5.10	5.50
S–T	65	5.80	1.38	7.18	5.80	5.20	.46	5.66	5.28	5.80
T–S	69	5.49	2.94	8.43	5.61	4.74	1.48	6.22	4.84	5.55
T–T	24	5.00	4.04	9.04	5.42	3.92	2.50	6.42	4.54	5.67

is considered correct only if it is correct on all three recall trials. The mean number of correct recall responses decreases as the criterion of correct recall becomes more strict, but this is accomplished by an increased difference between the mean number correct to letters from the selected position and the mean number correct to letters from other positions. In the S-S condition, the difference between SP and OP is 3.15, 4.40, and 4.50 for Trial 1, 2/3 correct, and 3/3 correct respectively.

The trigrams were presented as stimuli for recall following recall to the letters, and the mean numbers of correct recall responses to the trigrams are given in the last column of Table 3. Differences among conditions are small and 82 percent of the 178 Ss gave only correct responses to the trigrams. In the S-S condition, the mean number of correct responses to the trigrams is the same as the mean number correct on all three recall trials to the single letters.

The above results suggest that requiring a correct response on all three recall trials may be the best criterion of learning. There is no systematic effect of successive recall trials. In the S-S condition, the responses were learned only to the S, or selected, letters and were never paired with the other letters presented during recall. In this condition, the 3/3 criterion minimizes the correct recall to letters which have never been paired with the responses and maximizes the difference between the correct recall to letters which have, and have not, been paired with the responses. Accordingly, the statistical tests are presented only for the mean number of correct responses for the 3/3 criterion of recall and all comparisons are with respect to the S-S condition. The S-T and S-S conditions gave essentially the same results in all respects. The T-S and T-T conditions produced more total correct responses and fewer different correct responses but these trends are not significant. The trend for fewer correct responses to letters from the selected position is significant for T-T, $t(42) = 2.45$, $p < .05$, but not for T-S. Many of the recall scores to letters from other positions were zero and the number of zeros (12) in the S-S condition was used to compute an expected frequency for the other conditions. Only in the T-T condition was the number of zeros (4) significantly different, $\chi^2(1) = 17.02$, $p < .01$.

Consistency. Examination of Tables 2 and 3 shows that there were some correct recall responses to letters from the positions which were not selected. However, these tables do not reveal to what extent these correct responses occur when the selected letters also produce correct responses or to what extent they are violations of the consistent use of letters from the selected position as cues for correct recall. The consistency score specifies the percentage of cases in which the correct recall occurred to the selected letter if it occurred to any of the three letters from a trigram. The mean consistency scores for each condition are presented in Table 4 for each recall trial and for the 2/3 and 3/3 recall criterion. Since a large proportion of the Ss were perfectly consistent, the percentage of scores of 100 are also presented in each case. Although the scores vary somewhat from trial to trial, there is no indication of any systematic

Table 4. Experiment I: Mean consistency scores and percentage of Ss with perfect scores for each recall trial, the two or more correct out of three recall criterion (2/3), and the three correct out of three recall criterion (3/3).

Condition	n	Trial 1		Trial 2		Trial 3		2/3 Correct		3/3 Correct	
		M	% 100	M	% 100	M	% 100	M	% 100	M	% 100
S–S	20	96.9	85	95.2	75	94.4	80	97.2	85	98.2	90
S–T	65	97.6	89	98.6	92	98.7	92	100.0	100	98.4	92
T–S	69	96.2	81	95.9	78	94.0	75	98.0	90	98.1	91
T–T	24	88.8	46	87.7	54	91.7	58	92.3	62	85.1	46

Table 5. Experiment I: Mean efficiency scores for each recall trial, the two or more correct out of three recall criterion (2/3), and the three correct out of three recall criterion (3/3); the percentage of Ss with perfect scores is presented for the 2/3 and 3/3 recall criteria.

Condition	n	Trial 1	Trial 2	Trial 3	2/3		3/3	
		M	M	M	M	% 100	M	% 100
S–S	20	73.6	79.8	75.6	84.8	30	94.6	65
S–T	65	73.6	74.6	75.9	82.6	26	94.9	77
T–S	69	66.5	68.1	67.8	71.7	10	85.8	51
T–T	24	63.1	61.1	59.8	64.0	4	76.1	33

variation with trials. As with the difference between recall to selected and nonselected letters, the mean consistency tends to increase with the more strict recall criteria and this is another indication that guessing has more effect on correct responses to nonselected than to selected letters. The mean consistency with the 3/3 recall criterion is about 98 and about 91 percent of the Ss are perfectly consistent except in the T-T condition. The proportion of the perfect scores in the S-S condition was used to compute the expected number of 100 scores for the T-T condition. Significantly fewer Ss scored 100 in the T-T condition at the 3/3 criterion, $\chi^2(1) = 47.23$, $p < .01$, but it should be noted that the expected number of scores less than 100 was only 2.4.

Efficiency. Tables 2 and 3 show that there were more total correct responses than different correct responses at recall. These measures may be used to compute a group efficiency score. For instance, the mean Total and DR correct for the 3/3 criterion are given in Table 3. Dividing the DR by the Total and multiplying by 100 gives group efficiency scores of 93, 93, 78, and 71 for conditions S-S, S-T, T-S, and T-T respectively. Efficiency scores were computed for each S in the same fashion and the mean efficiency scores are presented in Table 5. The number of perfect scores on the individual trials was too small to be meaningful but the percentage of Ss with perfect efficiency is presented for the 2/3 and 3/3 criteria. Again, there seems to be no systematic variation with trials and the use of a more strict recall criterion increases the mean efficiency score in the S-S condition. Statistical tests were computed on the scores from the 3/3 criterion and the proportion of Ss with perfect scores in the S-S condition was used to compute expected values for the other three conditions. Significantly fewer Ss scored 100 in the T-S condition, $\chi^2(1) = 5.50$, $p < .02$, and the T-T condition, $\chi^2(1) = 9.23$, $p < .01$. The S-T superiority did not reach significance, $\chi^2(1) = 3.60$, $p > .05$, and, since S-S is assumed to be maximally efficient, any increase must be attributed to sampling error.

Summary. Experiment I shows that the material and techniques are reasonable ones to use in studies of stimulus selection. There were no appreciable differences in learning produced by the three sets of letters when they were used alone as stimuli in the S-S condition or when they were used as S terms in the S-T and T-S conditions. This indicates that selecting letters from a specified position in the CCCs in an S preference and is not due to differential difficulty of the sets of letters or to the position in which they occur.

The S-S and S-T conditions produced about the same results in all cases but learning tended to be more difficult in the T-S and T-T conditions. The increased difficulty was accompanied by a tendency for less recall to the selected letters and more recall to the nonselected letters. This tendency is reflected in the lower efficiency scores. The T-S and T-T conditions also tended to produce more total correct recall responses. These results suggest that the greater difficulty of learning usually produced by the use of compound stimuli may be due to the fact that Ss are not perfectly efficient and tend to learn unnecessary component-response pairs when presented compound stimuli.

The successive recall trials had no systematic effect on recall. It was shown that the use of a strict criterion of learning, correct on all three recall trials, increased the difference in the number of correct recall responses given to the selected and nonselected letters, as well as increased consistency and efficiency. It is to be expected that a higher criterion would give fewer correct recalls but the reason for the differential effect on selected and nonselected stimuli is not as obvious. This difference is interpreted to mean that guessing benefits the nonselected items more than the selected and that the amount of selection may be underestimated when based on only one recall trial.

The consistency and efficiency scores seem to reflect aspects of recall which are not obvious from the examination of the mean recall scores. As was expected from the task demands of the conditions, the mean consistency was about the same for all conditions except the T-T, where there was nothing to enforce the consistent use of letters from only one position as the functional stimuli. In this case, the mean consistency was reduced from about 98 to 85 and only 46 percent of the Ss were perfeclty consistent as compared to about 91 percent in the other conditions.

The mean efficiency was about 95 in the S-S and S-T conditions but it was lower in the two conditions where the CCCs were presented on the study trials. The lower efficiency in the T-S and T-T condition is not forced by the task but the opportunity is present for Ss to learn to more than one of the letters from the trigram.

Tables 4 and 5 show that, at the 3/3 criterion, 46 percent of the T-T Ss had perfect consistency scores and 33 percent had perfect efficiency scores. An attempt was made to relate consistency and efficiency to the speed of the paired-associate learning by dividing the T-T Ss into four groups based on whether the consistency and efficiency scores were 100 or less than 100. The results suggest that consistency is more strongly related to speed of learning, with low consistency and slow learning tending to appear together. However, there were only four Ss in each of two of the four categories; consequently these results cannot be considered reliable. This question will be considered again in a later experiment.

EXPERIMENT II

This experiment was a partial replication of Experiment I but the selected letters were emphasized by underscoring them and Ss were instructed to learn to the underscored letters. It was expected that this procedure would make the lists for the various conditions equally difficult to learn and that the consistency and efficiency in the T-S and T-T conditions would be equivalent to that in the S-S condition.

The paired-associate lists were part of those used in Experiment I and the four basic conditions were the same (S-S, S-T, T-S, and T-T). With the exception of the two stimulus-response pairings, the subconditions were eliminated. Only one set of trigram orders was used (TLN, BQD, CFP, XJM, ZSG, and RKH) and the S letters were always the letters from the third position in the trigrams. The S letters, either alone or as the third letter of the trigram, were always underscored. The Ss in the S-T, T-S, and T-T conditions were instructed to learn to the underscored letters and to ignore the other letters. The other procedures for learning and recall were the same as in Experiment I. Twenty-four Ss were assigned to each of the four conditions.

Learning. The two stimulus-response pairings differed significantly in difficulty but did not interact with conditions. The mean trials required to learn to the criterion of two successive perfect trials and the mean trials per item to the last error are presented in Table 6 for each of the four conditions. The Ss learned somewhat slower than did those in Experiment I but the relationships are the same. The S-T and T-T conditions seem to be more difficult than the S-S but the differences do not approach significance. The T-S condition was more difficult than the S-S by both learning measures; t (46) = 2.15 and 2.27, $p < .05$, for T/C and T/LE respectively. Underscoring the S letters and instructing Ss to learn to the underscored letters did not equate the difficulty of learning in the S-S and T-S conditions.

Recall. The data from nine Ss was eliminated from the recall analyses because these Ss consistently gave the same digit as the response to all of the nonselected letters on two of the three recall trials. The mean correct recall responses for the remaining 87 Ss was 7.47, 7.63, and 7.57 for Recall Trial 1, 2, and 3 respectively. As in Experiment I, there was no apparent systematic effect of recall trials on the number correct.

The selected letters were the third letters of the trigrams in all conditions, and the recall to the letters is presented according to the position of the letters. The mean number of correct recall responses for Recall Trial 1 and for the 2/3 correct criterion are presented in Table 7. Table 8 presents the mean correct

Table 6. Experiment II: Mean trials to criterion (T/C) and mean trials per item to the last error (T/LE) for the paired-associate learning.

Condition	T/C		T/LE	
(n = 24)	M	$\hat{\sigma}$	M	$\hat{\sigma}$
S–S	7.08	3.41	2.94	2.62
S–T	7.25	3.53	3.20	3.15
T–S	11.04	8.34	6.73	7.76
T–T	7.50	4.93	3.03	3.20

Table 7. Experiment II: Correct responses for recall Trial 1 and the 2/3 recall criterion; the mean number of correct responses to the letters from each position and the mean number of different correct responses (DR) are presented for each criteria.

Condition	n	Trial 1					2/3 Correct				
		Position					Position				
		1	2	3	Total	DR	1	2	3	Total	DR
S–S	21	1.05	.62	5.57	7.24	5.71	.52	.71	5.57	6.81	5.67
S–T	19	1.37	.89	5.74	8.00	5.79	.68	.58	5.63	6.89	5.68
T–S	24	1.04	.75	5.50	7.29	5.75	.50	.67	5.46	6.62	5.71
T–T	23	1.00	.91	5.52	7.43	5.70	.83	.74	5.70	7.26	5.78

Table 8. Experiment II: Mean number of correct responses to the letters for the 3/3 correct recall criterion and to the trigrams; the recall to the letters is presented separately for each position and for the number of different responses.

Condition	n	Position							DR		Trigram	
		1	2	3		Total						
		M	M	M	$\hat{\sigma}$	M	$\hat{\sigma}$		M	$\hat{\sigma}$	M	$\hat{\sigma}$
S–S	21	.19	.09	4.86	1.20	5.14	1.35		4.90	1.22	5.52	1.03
S–T	19	.21	.11	5.21	1.23	5.53	1.43		5.26	1.24	5.47	1.02
T–S	24	.17	.08	4.75	1.54	5.00	1.53		4.79	1.53	5.38	1.06
T–T	23	.39	.13	5.13	1.01	5.65	1.30		5.22	.90	5.83	.65

recall responses for the 3/3 correct criterion and the mean correct recall responses to the trigrams. Inspection of Table 7 and 8 shows that the differences among conditions are small. As in Experiment I, the difference between the mean correct recalls to the selected and nonselected letters in the S-S condition increases with the use of the more strict criteria. The same analyses as in Experiment I were computed on the recall scores at the 3/3 criterion but none of the conditions was significantly different from the S-S condition. Recall to the trigrams was consistently high and 77 percent of the 87 Ss gave perfect recalls to the trigrams.

Consistency and efficiency. The mean consistency and efficiency scores are presented in Table 9 for Trial 1, the 2/3 criterion and the 3/3 criterion. The percentages of Ss who were perfectly consistent or efficient are also presented. The mean consistency and mean efficiency scores are somewhat higher in the S-S condition than in Experiment I, but the consistency and efficiency of the S-T and T-S conditions in this experiment are very similar to that in the S-S condition. The T-T condition is slightly less consistent and efficient than the S-S but comparisons of the number of Ss who had perfect scores on the 3/3 criterion did not approach significance.

Summary. Underscoring the selected letters and instructing Ss to learn to these letters produced equivalent recall in all conditions. The consistency and efficiency scores were very similar in the four conditions and this demonstrates that S can focus on a designated letter in a trigram during learning and produce essentially perfect selection of that letter as the functional stimulus.

Although emphasis and instructions produced essentially perfect selection, the paired-associate learning of the T-S list remained much more difficult than the learning of the S-S list. There is no apparent reason why Ss in the T-S condition cannot learn as fast as those in the T-T condition and it is not clear what, if anything, the T-S Ss are learning during the additional trials. Although the T-S Ss required about 55 percent more trials to learn to criterion than did the S-S Ss, the mean total correct responses on all three recall trials was the same; 21.81 for the S-S and 21.88 for the T-S condition.

EXPERIMENT III

Paired-associate learning was more difficult in the T-S condition of Experiment II even though the S letters were underscored and Ss were instructed to learn only to the underscored letters. There is no obvious reason why Ss can not learn as fast under the T-S condition as under any of the other conditions. Experiment III was an attempt to force attention to a single letter in each trigram and to make the selection more overt by requiring S to read the selected letters aloud each time they appeared during learning.

Table 9. Experiment II: The mean consistency and efficiency scores for recall Trial 1, 2/3 correct criterion, and 3/3 correct criterion.

Condition	n	Consistency						Efficiency				
		Trial 1		2/3 Correct		3/3 Correct		Trial 1	2/3	3/3		
		M	% 100	M	% 100	M	% 100	M	M	M	% 100	
S–S	21	97.4	86	98.1	90	99.2	95	80.5	85.6	96.1	76	
S–T	19	99.0	95	98.3	95	99.1	95	75.2	84.5	96.2	74	
T–S	24	95.5	83	94.8	79	99.2	96	80.2	87.8	95.9	79	
T–T	23	97.0	87	98.4	91	98.0	91	82.0	81.8	93.8	70	

The four basic conditions and the lists were the same as in Experiment II, except the S letters were not underscored. All Ss were required to say a single letter aloud each time a stimulus, either a trigram or a single letter, appeared during learning. The S-S Ss read the letter and digit aloud on the study cycles and read the letter aloud before saying one of the digits on the test cycles. The S-T and T-S Ss read the S letters aloud and read the third letters in the trigram aloud before saying the digits. In the T-T condition, S were told that they should learn the number to a single letter from the trigram. They were instructed to say the letter they had selected from the trigram each time it appeared and were required to read the digits aloud on the study cycles. However, they were free to select whatever letters they wanted and to change letters during the course of learning.

The procedure for learning was the same as in the previous experiment except the test cycles were S paced by presenting the next test stimulus only after S read a letter and said a digit aloud. The three recall trials to the single letters were given as usual but Ss were not required to recall to the trigrams. Instead, a letter matching task was administered following recall to the letters. The letter matching for the S-S, S-T, and T-S Ss consisted of displaying six cards, each containing one of the S letters, on a table. The S was given a deck of 12 cards containing the other letters from the trigrams and asked to construct six three-letter items by placing two cards from the deck with each card on the table. The procedure for the T-T Ss was the same except that the set of six letters placed on the table was determined by which letters S said aloud on the last test cycle. The six letters were from the same position in the trigrams as the majority of the letters S said aloud on the last test cycle. Twenty-four Ss were assigned to each of the four conditions.

Learning. The mean trials to criterion and the mean trials per item to the last error are presented in Table 10. The mean trials required to learn the S-S list is comparable to that in Experiment II and the means are essentially the same for the S-S, S-T, and T-S conditions. Apparently, when S is forced to pay attention to the S letters, the T-S condition is no more difficult than the S-S. As

Table 10. Experiment III: The mean trials to criterion (T/C), and mean trials per item to the last error (T/LE) for the paired-associate learning.

Condition	T/C		T/LE	
(n = 24)	M	$\hat{\sigma}$	M	$\hat{\sigma}$
S–S	7.04	3.54	2.67	2.58
S–T	6.96	3.90	2.85	2.68
T–S	6.71	3.29	2.97	2.42
T–T	9.00	5.47	4.40	4.55

in the previous experiments, the T-T condition tends to be more difficult than the S-S but the difference is not significant.

Recall. The recall data from 8 of the 96 Ss was eliminated because of the consistent guessing strategy. The remaining 88 Ss gave 7.78, 7.64, and 7.60 mean correct responses on Trial 1, 2, and 3 respectively. The selected letters were defined as the S letters in the S-S, S-T, and T-S conditions and as the letters from the position of most of the letters spoken aloud on the last test trial in the T-T condition. In every case, the set of letters in the selected position produced the most correct recall responses. The mean number of responses correct on all three recall trials to letters from the selected position and to letters from other positions are presented in Table 11. The mean numbers of different responses correct on all three recall trials are also presented. The mean total responses correct on all three trials is about the same for the four conditions. However, compared to the S-S condition, there are fewer mean correct responses to the selected letters in the T-T condition, $t(43) = 2.73, p < .01$, and fewer Ss fail to give any correct responses to letters from other positions, $\chi^2(1) = 11.34$. There is also a tendency for fewer different correct responses in the T-T condition, but this is not significant, $t(43) = 1.94, p < .10$.

Consistency and Efficiency. The consistency and efficiency scores for Trial 1 and for the 2/3 and 3/3 criteria are presented in Table 12. All of the Ss in the S-S condition were perfectly consistent so the usual comparison of number of perfect scores cannot be made. However, consistency is high in the S-S, S-T, and T-S conditions and seems comparable to that in Experiment II. The consistency in the T-T condition is appreciably less than in the other conditions and somewhat less than in Experiment II.

The superior efficiency of the S-T and T-S conditions approaches significance with $p < .10$, but this must be attributed to sampling error. The superiority of the S-S to the T-T condition, in terms of number of Ss with perfect efficiency, is not significant at the .05 level, but the tendency for T-T efficiency to be lower is consistent with the results of Experiment I.

The mean consistency and efficiency scores in the T-T condition are appreciably larger than the corresponding scores in Experiment I. This suggests that instructing Ss to select a single letter and say it aloud each time the trigram is presented may increase the consistency and efficiency of selection during learning.

Selection in the T-T condition. The Ss in the S-S, S-T, and T-S conditions were instructed to read the S letters aloud and all Ss in these conditions followed the instructions on both study and test cycles. The instructions permitted the T-T Ss to select letters from different positions and to change the letters selected. The fact that these Ss gave more correct recall responses to the set of letters said aloud most often on the last test cycle shows that the letters said

Table 11. Experiment III: Correct responses for the 3/3 correct recall criterion; the mean number of correct responses to letters from the selected positions (SP), to letters from other positions (OP), and the mean number of different correct responses (DR).

Condition	n	SP M	SP $\hat{\sigma}$	OP M	Total M	Total $\hat{\sigma}$	DR M	DR $\hat{\sigma}$
S–S	21	5.00	.77	.33	5.33	.86	5.00	.77
S–T	21	5.14	.79	.14	5.29	.90	5.14	.79
T–S	22	4.77	1.34	.23	5.00	1.38	4.91	1.27
T–T	24	4.00	1.59	.96	4.96	1.85	4.38	1.50

Table 12. Experiment III: The mean consistency and efficiency scores for recall Trial 1, 2/3 correct criterion, and 3/3 correct criteiron.

Condition	n	Consistency Trial 1 M	Trial 1 % 100	2/3 M	2/3 % 100	3/3 M	3/3 % 100	Efficiency Trial 1 M	2/3 M	3/3 M	3/3 % 100
S–S	21	99.2	95	100	100	100	100	72.4	77.1	94.3	71
S–T	21	98.2	90	99.2	95	100	100	77.5	83.9	97.8	90
T–S	22	94.6	82	98.2	91	97.0	86	79.2	85.0	98.7	91
T–T	24	88.8	58	91.0	62	91.2	71	69.2	76.5	90.4	58

aloud were selected. However, not all Ss in the T-T condition selected letters from a single position in the trigrams. Examination of the learning trials shows two types of performance on letter selection. Thirteen of the 24 Ss selected letters from a single position on the first study cycle and 12 of these said the same letters from the same position throughout learning. The thirteenth S changed a single letter during learning. Six of the 13 Ss selected letters from the first position, 5 selected letters from the second position, and 2 from the third. This position selection suggests that requiring Ss to say a letter aloud or instructing them to select one letter may change the position selected since all 24 Ss in the T-T condition of Experiment I selected letters from the first position.

The other 11 Ss from the 24 in the T-T condition did not select letters from a single position on the first study cycle and all of them changed some letters during learning. The letter changes during learning resulted in selection from a single position by the end of learning by 5 of the Ss but the other 6 were still selecting letters from more than one position at the end of learning.

The mean trials to criterion and the mean efficiency scores for the 3/3 criterion of recall are presented in Table 13 for each of the two T-T subgroups. It is clear that Ss who consistently selected letters from a single position on the first study cycle perform very much as the S-S Ss (cf. Table 10 & 12). They learn rapidly and are very efficient. The other Ss, who were not consistent on the first study cycle and who changed letters during learning, learn more slowly and are more variable, as well as being less efficient.

Letter matching and recall. Following recall to the letters, all Ss were presented the selected letters and required to match two additional letters with each one. Position of the matched letters was ignored and the nonselected letters, which were matched correctly and incorrectly with the selected letters, were tabulated in conjunction with whether they had, or had not, produced a correct recall response on two or more of the three trials. The probabilities resulting from these frequency counts are presented in Table 14. The T-T Ss are separated into those consistent and not consistent in the selection of letters from a single position on the first study cycle. The CM column shows that Ss presented the trigrams on the study cycles, T-S and T-T, learned something about which letters were presented together but in the T-T condition this is

Table 13. Experiment III: The mean trials to criterion and the mean efficiency scores at the 3/3 recall criterion for the T–T subgroups that were consistent (C) and not consistent (C̄) in the letter selection on the first study cycle.

Subgroup	n	T/C		3/3 Efficiency	
		M	$\hat{\sigma}$	M	% 100
C	13	6.38	2.75	94.4	69
C̄	11	12.09	6.35	85.6	45

restricted primarily to Ss who were not consistent on the first study cycle. The CR column shows no appreciable 2/3 recall to the nonselected letters except in the T-T subgroup which was not consistent. This is also the only group for which the contingent probabilities show any appreciable relationship between correct matching and correct recall.

Summary. The technique of requiring Ss to say the selected letters aloud seems to be a useful one. From all indications, the Ss in the S-T and T-S conditions focused their attention on the S letters and learned about the same things to the same degree as Ss in the S-S condition, i.e., the letter selection was essentially perfect. Apparently, the slower learning in the T-S condition found in the previous experiments was caused by Ss' failure to concentrate on the S letters.

The 13 Ss in the T-T condition, who selected letters from a single position on the first study cycle, used the same selected letters throughout learning and performed much like the S-S Ss. They learned rapidly and selection was essentially perfect. The 11 Ss in the T-T condition, who selected letters from more than one position on the first study cycle, all changed letters during learning, learned more slowly, and were less efficient.

The results from the matching task show that the T-S Ss learned, to some extent, which letters were presented together but this was not accompanied by any additional associative learning to the nonselected letters. Only for T-T Ss, who did not select letters from a single position on the first study cycle, was there increased associative learning to nonselected letters and decreased efficiency. Only these Ss showed any appreciable relationship between correct matching and correct recall to the nonselected letters. The increased recall to the nonselected letters may be mediated by the selected letters or the correct matching may be on the basis of the common responses. There is no way that the results in this experiment can distinguish between these possibilities and direct associative learning.

Table 14. Experiment III: The probabilities associated with the nonselected letters; the probability of a correct match (CM) with the selected letters, the probability of 2/3 correct recall (CR), and the probability of a 2/3 correct recall contingent upon a correct or incorrect match.

Condition	Probabilities			
	CM	CR	CR/CM	CR/IM
S–S	.139	.163	.114	.171
S–T	.155	.099	.154	.089
T–S	.208	.095	.127	.086
T–T C	.192	.128	.100	.135
T–T C̄	.273	.288	.444	.229

The results of this experiment suggest that the tendency for paired-associate learning to be more difficult with compound stimuli than with component stimuli may be due to the failure of some Ss to use a consistent rule for selection from the beginning of learning. These Ss learn to give correct responses to more than one component in a compound and this learning requires time without a corresponding increase in performance on the paired-associate task.

EXPERIMENTS IV AND V

The Experiments III T-T results showed that failure to use the strategy of selecting letters from a single position of the CCCs from the beginning of learning was associated with slower learning and lower efficiency. There was also a positive relationship between correct recall to the nonselected letters and the correct matching of the nonselected with the selected letters. If these results are indeed due to not using a consistent rule for selection, presenting the T-T list in a fashion which prevents the use of a simple consistent rule should produce the same results. In Experiment IV, the order of the letters within the trigrams was changed on each cycle so that selecting letters from a single position could not be an effective rule for component selection.

The pairs of items used in Experiment IV were the same as the T-T pairs in the previous experiment except that in one condition (U) the third letter in each trigram was underscored while in the other condition no letters were underscored ($\bar{U}$). Each of the six possible permutations of a trigram was used in one of six different orders of the study stimuli and of the test stimuli. The same permutation of a trigram did not appear on adjacent cycles and the same letter was always underscored in the $\bar{U}$ condition regardless of the position in the permutation. An equal number of Ss started learning with each of the six study cycle orders.

The Ss in the U condition were instructed to read the underscored letter aloud each time before they said the digit and to learn to give the response to the underscored letter. The Ss in the $\bar{U}$ condition were instructed to learn the response to a single letter and to read the letter they had selected aloud each time the trigrams were presented before saying the digit. Both groups were informed that the three letters presented together would be the same on each cylé and that the order of the letters would change on each cycle. The other procedures were the same as in Experiment III; the study stimuli were presented at a 2-second rate; the test stimuli were S paced; the intercycle interval was 4 seconds; all Ss learned to a criterion of two successive perfect trials; and all Ss received the three recall trials to the single letters before the letter matching task.

Thirty-six Ss were assigned to the underscored (U) condition and 108 to the not underscored ($\bar{U}$) condition. There was quite a problem getting Ss in the $\bar{U}$ condition to say both a letter and a digit aloud within the 2-second study cycle.

In addition to the 144 Ss who completed the experiment, there were 15 Ss who were dropped from the $\bar{U}$ condition. Twelve of these Ss failed to say the letter and digit for many of the study cycle presentations and 3 failed to learn the paired-associate list in 50 trials.

Because of the excessive number of Ss dropped from the $\bar{U}$ condition in Experiment IV, and because many of the retained Ss did not say all the letters and digits on every study cycle, Experiment V was conducted to check the results of Experiment IV. It was the same as Experiment IV in every respect except the study stimuli were presented at a 3-second rate to give Ss more time to respond and there was a 6-second intercycle interval. In Experiment V, 24 Ss were assigned to the U condition and 72 to the $\bar{U}$.

Learning and recall. The mean T/C, T/LE, and total correct responses on all three recall trials are presented in Table 15. In both Experiments IV and V there is a tendency for Ss in the U condition to learn faster and recall fewer responses than those in the $\bar{U}$ condition. The differences in T/C and T/LE are not significant at the .05 level in Experiment IV but in Experiment V, $t(94) = 2.01$ and 2.12, $p < .05$, for T/C and T/LE respectively. The superior total recall in the $\bar{U}$ condition is significant in both experiments, $t(142) = 5.34$ and $t(94) = 4.49$ for Experiments IV and V respectively.

The order of the letters within a trigram changed on each cycle so position could not be used as an effective rule for selection. In the $\bar{U}$ condition of Experiment IV, there were 35 Ss who selected all letters from the same position on the first study cycle and 50 who selected from more than one position. The other 23 Ss did not say one or more letters on the first study cycle. The 35 Ss who selected letters from a single position on the first study cycle required a mean of 9.91 trials to criterion while the 50 Ss who selected from more than one position required a mean of 9.72. The results were much the same in Experiment V with 7.85 mean trials to criterion required for the 27 Ss who selected from a single position on the first study cycle and 7.40 for the 45 Ss who did not select letters from a single position. In contrast to the results from Experiment III, where the trigram letters were in the same sequence on each cycle, there was no relationship between using a consistent rule of selection on the first study cycle and speed of learning.

Selection. The underscored letters were designated as the selected letters in the U conditions and the letters said aloud on the last test cycle were designated the selected letters in the $\bar{U}$ conditions. The mean consistency and efficiency scores for the 3/3 criterion of correct recall are presented in Table 15. As expected, efficiency is high in the U condition, where Ss could simply select the underscored letters from each trigram, and is considerably lower in the $\bar{U}$ condition, which did not allow the use of any simple rule for selection. The probabilities of correctly matching the nonselected letters with the selected

Table 15. Experiments IV & V: The mean leraning, recall, consistency, and efficiency scores.

Condition		n	T/C		T/LE		Total Recall		3/3 Consistency		3/3 Efficiency	
			M	$\hat{\sigma}$	M	$\hat{\sigma}$	M	$\hat{\sigma}$	M	% 100	M	% 100
Exp. IV	U	36	7.75	6.40	3.82	5.62	22.42	4.09	90.8	81	90.7	76
	Ū	108	10.00	7.32	5.26	5.87	27.76	7.66	93.9	79	78.6	29
Exp. V	U	24	6.08	2.73	2.03	1.61	22.08	3.78	100	100	93.2	92
	Ū	72	7.57	4.07	3.01	2.75	26.35	4.70	94.2	81	84.3	38

letters and of a 2/3 correct recall to the nonselected letters are presented in Table 16 along with the contingent probabilities. It appears that the U condition produces little learning of which letters are presented together and little associative learning to the nonselected letters. On the other hand, the $\bar{U}$ condition produces learning of both varietes and there is a positive relationship between the correct matching of the components and the 2/3 correct recall.

Although the letter position could not be used as a basis for selection in the $\bar{U}$ condition, there were some Ss who constantly selected the same letters throughout learning. The constant Ss were defined as either those who continued to say aloud the same letters selected on the first study cycle or those who changed only one letter for a single cycle. The rest of the Ss were classified as not constant. There were 20 constant Ss in Experiment IV and 23 in Experiment V. The various learning and selection measures for the constant (C) and not constant ($\bar{C}$) Ss in each of the two experiments are presented in Table 17. The C Ss learn faster and are slightly more consistent and efficient than the $\bar{C}$ Ss. However, the probabilities show that both groups of Ss match the nonselected and selected letters about the same and have about the same positive relationship between the 2/3 correct recall and the correct matching. Although there may be large differences in the learning ability of the two groups, these results do suggest that much of this learning occurs during the search for the selected letters rather than prior to the selection.

Summary. Changing the order of the letters within the trigrams on each cycle without underscoring one of the letters removes the possibility of selection according to a simple rule. This makes learning somewhat more difficult and reduces efficiency. The Ss in the $\bar{U}$ condition also learn, to some extent, which letters are presented with the selected letters and this is related to correct recall to the nonselected letters. The lack of a simple rule of selection produced results

Table 16. Experiments IV & V: The probabilities associated with the nonselected letters; the probability of a correct match (CM) with the selected letters, the probability of a 2/3 correct recall (CR) and the probability of a 2/3 correct recall contingent upon a correct or incorrect match.

Condition		n	Probabilities			
			CM	CR	CR/CM	CR/$\overline{\text{CM}}$
Exp. IV	U	36	.167	.136	.229	.117
	$\bar{U}$	108	.360	.296	.611	.176
Exp. V	U	24	.184	.090	.189	.068
	$\bar{U}$	72	.323	.216	.419	.120

Table 17. Experiments IV & V: The learning and selection means and the probabilities in the $\bar{U}$ conditions for Ss constant (C) and not constant ($\bar{C}$) in the selection of the same letters throughout learning.

Condition		n	T/C	Total Recall	3/3 Consistency		3/3 Efficiency		Probabilities			
					M	% 100	M	% 100	CM	CR	CR/CM	CR/CM
Exp. IV	C	20	6.50	27.85	100	100	83.6	35	.358	.233	.477	.097
	$\bar{C}$	88	10.80	27.62	92.5	74	77.5	27	.360	.311	.518	.194
Exp. V	C	23	6.13	26.09	97.3	87	87.3	43	.261	.185	.403	.108
	$\bar{C}$	49	8.24	26.47	94.6	78	83.0	35	.352	.231	.425	.126

similar to those obtained in Experiment III with the T-T *S*s who did not use the single position rule of selection.

The results from $\bar{U}$ *S*s who constantly selected the same letters throughout learning suggest that learning about the nonselected letters occurs during the search for the selected letters.

DISCUSSION

The S-S condition, with single letters as stimuli for the paired-associate learning, was the control condition in Experiments I-III. It was shown that a criterion of correct recall on all three of the recall trials was best for distinguishing between letters which had, and had not, been used as stimuli during learning. With the 3/3 criterion, the 62 *S*s who served in the control condition in the first three experiments gave a mean consistency score of 99 and 95 percent of the *S*s were perfectly consistent. The mean efficiency score for these *S*s was 95, and 71 percent were perfectly efficient. The consistency and efficiency scores varied in a reasonable fashion with the various conditions and seem to reflect important aspects of behavior in the selection of redundant relevant components from compound stimuli during paired-associate learning.

In Experiment I, the compound-response list (T-T condition) was presented in the usual fashion without special instructions. The mean consistency score was 85 with 46 percent of the *S*s perfectly consistent and the mean efficiency score was 76 with 33 percent of the *S*s perfectly efficient. In Experiment II, the lower consistency and efficiency scores in the T-T condition were shown to reflect an *S* strategy rather than any necessary result of compound stimuli; underscoring the letters in a single position of the CCCs and instructing *S*s to learn only to those letters increased the consistency and efficiency scores to a level comparable to that in the control condition. The idea that the lower consistency and efficiency is the result of an *S* strategy, received additional support in Experiment III where *S*s were instructed to learn to a single letter from the trigram and to say that letter aloud. Although the instructions increased consistency and efficiency somewhat, compared to the same condition in Experiment I with no special instructions, the consistency and efficiency scores were still lower than in the control condition. It was shown that the decreased efficiency was produced primarily by *S*s who did not select letters from a single position on the first learning trial. In Experiments IV and V, the changed position of the letters within a trigram on each cycle prohibited selection on the basis of position. The increased difficulty of learning and reduced efficiency was attributed to the lack of a simple rule for selection.

In Experiments II and III, the learning in the T-T condition tended to be more difficult than in the control condition. These differences were not significant but the trend for a list with compound stimuli to be more difficult to learn than a list with component stimuli is consistent with most previous research (cf. Richardson, 1971). In each case the increased difficulty of the compound list was accompanied by a decreased efficiency. This suggests that the greater difficulty of compound lists is produced by an S strategy which results in decreased efficiency, i.e., part of the learning has no effect on performance during paired-associate learning. However, the T-S condition in Experiment II was an exception to this; high efficiency was accompanied by increased difficulty of learning. It is not clear what, if anything, Ss were learning during the additional trials required to reach the learning criterion in this condition. The idea of selection being the result of a time-sharing device receives overall support in this series of experiments but the evidence is not completely consistent.

The data from the experiments offers little help in interpreting the relationship between correctly matching the nonselected with the selected components and correct recall to the nonselected components. As Postman and Greenbloom (1967) point out, a correct recall to a component may be mediated by another component rather than being the result of a direct component-response connection. In the present experiments, any appreciable recall to the nonselected components was accompanied by correct matching of selected and nonselected components (Experiments III, T-T $\bar{C}$; IV, $\bar{U}$; and V, $\bar{U}$), so some mediation by the selected components remains possible. Wichawut and Martin (1970) used words as components and found essentially no probability of recalling one component, with another component as a cue, unless the response was also recalled. They conclude that the components do not become directly associated but become related through their common response, i.e., recall of a component with another component as a cue is response mediated. In the most comparable condition in this series of experiments (Experiment III, T-T), the conditional probability of correctly matching the nonselected and selected components, given that the 2/3 recall to the nonselected component was incorrect, is .36. This is considerably larger than the corresponding conditional probability of .15 for the control condition (Experiment III, S-S). Of course, there are many differences in procedures but it is not obvious why any of these should produce the differences in learning to the nonselected components.

The data from the Ss in Experiments IV and V, who constantly used the same selected components throughout learning, shows that learning to the nonselected components does occur during the search for the selected components. However, it is not clear to what extent learning to the nonselected components occurs prior to the consistent identification of the selected component. A large number of Ss were assigned to the nonunderscored condition of Experiments IV and V in the hope that the letters spoken aloud during learning could be related to the recall. The number of different letters spoken aloud, the number of times that the same letter was spoken aloud, and the number of trials to criterion were all so variable that it was not possible to relate the nonselected letters spoken aloud to recall to those letters. Some other method must be found to evaluate the effect of any stimulus processing which occurs prior to the consistent identification of the selected component. After the first few trials, James and Greeno (1967) found no additional learning to nonselected components until after the list was mastered. They suggest that Ss probably attend to the entire stimulus compound early in learning and then attend more selectively as learning proceeds. It also seems possible that Ss select early in learning but change to different components later in learning. Thus, it may not be the amount of selection, but the component that is selected, which changes as learning proceeds. It also seems possible that later learning to the selected component may effectively cancel part of the early learning to nonselected components.

The remainder of the discussion will be devoted to presenting a tentative framework which seems consistent with the data from studies of stimulus selection.

There is a strong tendency to select one component, from among the redundant relevant components of a compound stimulus, as the functional stimulus for associative learning. The selection serves the function of reducing the difficulty of the associative learning and, insofar as the selection is effective, the difficulty is equivalent to learning with a single component as the stimulus. There are at least two types of stimuli which differ in the possible efficiency of the selection.

One type of stimulus, such as the CCCs with the letters in a different position each time the CCC is presented, provides no means of identifying the selected component except by comparing it with the nonselected components. The selection with this type of stimulus is not efficient and consequently the associative learning is difficult. There may be learning to nonselected components prior to consistent identification of the selected component, but there is also learning to nonselected components after consistent identification and use of the selected component. This continued learning results from Ss scanning the components each time the compound is presented in order to identify the selected one. The selection is accomplished by differential rehearsal and the basis of the identification of the selected component is the differential frequency of the components similar to that in a verbal discrimination task (Ekstrand, Wallace, & Underwood, 1966). If the basis of identification is similar to that in verbal discrimination, it is to be expected that the components become associatively connected (Zechmeister & Underwood, 1969).

The second type of compound stimulus is constructed so that one component can be identified without effectively processing the other components. Examples of this type of compound are CCCs with the letters in a constant position, CCCs with the letters changing positions with each presentation but the same letter is always underscored, and words with one word surrounded by a rectangle (Harrington, 1969). With this type of stimulus, Ss can learn the response to a selected component without any learning to the nonselected components. If, from the beginning of learning, S uses the selection rule, selection is highly efficient and learning is rapid. If S does not use the available rule, the learning is similar to that with the other type of stimulus, efficiency is low and learning is slow. Learning to the nonselected components does not occur after S consistently applies the rule which enables the component selection. Some Ss do not use the available rule of selection under the usual paired-associate learning conditions, but various instructions and component emphasis can induce more Ss to select according to the rule.

The use of certain procedures, such as requiring S to name each component in the compound each time it is presented (Jenkins, 1963), may force further processing of the nonselected stimuli even though the Ss are selecting according to the available rule. In this case, the decreased efficiency should be similar to that with the first type of compound.

There may be some compounds for which a simple rule of selection is available but which necessarily result in learning to nonselected components. For instance, compounds consisting of words printed in distinctive colors permit consistent selection on the basis of a rule but the words and the color are presented so that both components must register visually at the same time. The maximum efficiency of selection with this type of compound may be less than with compounds consisting of spatially separated components.

REFERENCES

Baumeister, A. A., & Berry, F. M. Context stimuli in verbal paired-associate learning by normal children and retardates. *Psychological Record*, 1968, 18, 185–190.

Baumeister, A. A., & Berry, F. M., & Forehand, R. Effects of secondary cues on rote verbal learning of retardates and normal children. *Journal of Comparative and Physiological Psychology*, 1969, 69, 273–280.

Ekstrand, B. R., Wallace, W. P., & Underwood, B. J. A frequency theory of verbal-discrimination learning. *Psychological Review*, 1966, 73, 566–578.

Goggin, J., & Martin, E. Forced stimulus encoding and retroactive interference. *Journal of Experimental Psychology*, 1970, 84, 131–136.

Harrington, A. L. Effects of component emphasis on stimulus selection in paired-associate learning. *Journal of Experimental Psychology*, 1969, 79, 412–418.

Houston, J. P. S-R stimulus selection and strength of R-S association. *Journal of Experimental Psychology*, 1964, 68, 563–566.

James, C. T., & Greeno, J. G. Stimulus selection at different stages of paired-associate learning. *Journal of Experimental Psychology*, 1967, 74, 75–83.

Jenkins, J. J. Stimulus "fractionation" in paired-associate learning. *Psychological Reports*, 1963, 13, 409–410.

Martin, E. Recognition and correct responding mediated by first letter of trigram stimuli. *Journal of Verbal Learning and Verbal Behavior*, 1968, 7, 703–704.

Nelson, D. L., Rowe, F. A., Engel, J. E., Wheeler, J., & Garland, R. M. Backward relative to forward recall as a function of stimulus meaningfulness and formal interstimulus similarity. *Journal of Experimental Psychology*, 1970, 83, 323–328.

Postman, L., & Greenbloom, R. Conditions of cue selection in the acquisition of paired-associate lists. *Journal of Experimental Psychology*, 1967, 73, 91–100.

Richardson, J. Cue effectiveness and abstraction in paired-associate learning. *Psychological Bulletin*, 1971, 75, 73–91.

Runquist, W. N. Structural effects of letter identity among stimuli in paired–associate learning. *Journal of Experimental Psychology*, 1970, 84, 152–163.

Schneider, N. G., & Houston, J. P. Stimulus selection and retroactive inhibition. *Journal of Experimental Psychology*, 1968, 77, 166–167.

Schneider, N. G., & Houston, J. P. Retroactive inhibition, cue selection, and degree of learning. *American Journal of Psychology*, 1969, 82, 276–279.

Shepard, R. N. Comments on Professor Underwood's paper. In C. N. Cofer & B. S. Musgrave (eds.), *Verbal behavior and learning*. New York: McGraw-Hill, 1963.

Solso, R. L., & Trafimow, E. S. Stimulus competition as a function of varying stimulus meaningfulness. *Psychonomic Science*, 1970, 18, 103–104.

Underwood, B. J. Stimulus selection in verbal learning. In C. N. Cofer & B. S. Musgrave (eds.), *Verbal behavior and learning*. New York: McGraw-Hill, 1963.

Weaver, G. E. Stimulus encoding as a determinant of retroactive inhibition. *Journal of Verbal Learning and Verbal Behavior*, 1969, 8, 807–814.

Wichawut, C., & Martin, E. Selective stimulus encoding and overlearning in paired-associate learning. *Journal of Experimental Psychology*, 1970, 85, 383–388.

Wickens, D. D. Summary and evaluation. In C. N. Cofer & B. S. Musgrave (eds.), *Verbal behavior and learning*. New York: McGraw-Hill, 1963.

Young, R. K., Farrow, J. M., Seitz, S., & Hays, M. Backward recall with compound stimuli. *Journal of Experimental Psychology*, 1966, 72, 241–243.

Zechmeister, E. B., & Underwood, B. J. Acquisition of items and associations in verbal discrimination learning as a function of level of practice. *Journal of Experimental Psychology*, 1969, 81, 355–359.

8 | Intralist Interference and Stimulus Similarity

WILLARD N. RUNQUIST

University of Alberta, Edmonton, Alberta, Canada

In cued-recall situations, as distinct from free-recall situations, the learner is asked to remember specific events associated with specific cues. One experimental paradigm often used to simulate cued-recall learning in the laboratory is paired-associate learning. Thus, a theory of paired-associate performance is essentially a theory of cued recall.

Central to any discussion of paired-associate learning is the concept of interference. At a descriptive level, interference simply refers to the existence of decrements in performance which are attributable to the learning of other materials and hence represents a ubiquitous set of phenomena to be explained rather than an explanatory concept.

This paper is concerned with a subset of interference phenomena, namely, the effects of formal similarity among the stimulus terms in paired-associate learning. With few exceptions, paired-associate lists in which stimulus terms share letters are more difficult than those in which stimulus terms contain no letters in common (e.g., Runquist, 1968c; Underwood, 1953). The theoretical problem in accounting for these effects is straightforward, and consists of two subproblems: (1) What are the mechanisms by which the interference occurs? and (2) How does the learner overcome interference in order to master the material?

In a discussion of several general issues in verbal learning, Underwood (1964) considered some tentative answers to the above questions. At the same time, he pointed out that little was actually known about the mechanisms involved in interference production and reduction. Nevertheless, several concepts adopted from Underwood's discussion may serve as a framework for the analysis of similarity produced interference. It is apparent, moreover, that the study of such effects may provide some general indication of how learners process stimuli in cued-recall type situations.

Most of the research conducted by the author and reported herein was supported in part by Grant APA-88 from the National Research Council of Canada and by Grant GB-6166 from the National Science Foundation.

The basic concepts may be illustrated by considering the psychological events assumed to occur when a cue stimulus is presented to the learner and recall of the unit associated with it is requested. It is assumed that the presentation of the cue stimulus produces a sequence of implicit responses which serve to encode the information present in the physical stimulus. That is, a sequence of stimulus codes is activated. The general notion is that the to-be-recalled item exists in some form in memory along with codes representing the stimulus. The exact nature of the cue code and the exact meaning of the term "along with" need not be of present concern. The term *code* refers to the state resulting from the implicit responses, and is psychologically describable in terms of various physical and symbolic attributes of the stimulus.

Recall, then, depends upon the activation of critical and distinctive cue codes. An important distinction between two kinds of implicit responses was made by Underwood (1965). The first response made to a verbal unit involves the basic perception of the unit, which has been called the representational response (Bousfield, Whitmarsh, & Danick, 1958). Although Underwood (1964) states that the representational response, or more appropriately the code it produces, is some kind of neural representation of the stimulus, its psychological properties are of more direct interest. The most pertinent characteristic of the representational responses is that they encode only information concerning the physical properties of the presented stimulus and that they have stimulus properties in the sense that the resulting codes can lead to other responses. Theoretically, then, it should be possible for the learner to form associations directly to codes resulting from the representational response.

There is a second class of implicit responses which are produced by these representational codes. Underwood (1965) calls these implicit associative responses (IAR) and restricts his attention to word associates, but he also makes it clear that other kinds of elaborative responses to the representation are possible. Given that learners seem to have proclivities for constructing complex mediational devices for recalling information (Runquist & Farley, 1964; Underwood & Schulz, 1960), it is likely that these secondary implicit responses are usually involved in coding the association with the to-be-recalled item, and thus, in some sense these codes represent the functional stimulus for recall.

Elaborative responses may encode information in several different forms. When based on the formal properties of the representation, they may result in selected attributes of a compound stimulus (Underwood, Ham, & Ekstrand, 1962), selected letters (Postman & Greenbloom, 1967), or rearranged letters (Underwood & Keppel, 1963). At a more abstract and symbolic level, elaborative codes may consist of word associations to the representation (Underwood, 1965), category codes (Bousfield, 1953), affective codes (Osgood, Suci, & Tanenbaum, 1957), or images (Paivio, 1971).

Essentially, then, the recall process consists of the successive activation of two classes of stimulus codes: representational codes and elaborative codes, either of which may be used to "cue off" recall. While the above discussion considers these mediational states as resulting from responses, it should be made clear that the use of this term does not indicate any a priori commitment to the mechanism by which these codes are activated. The encoding responses are responses only in the sense that they result from the presentation of a cue stimulus or the activation of a particular code.

The application of this analysis to the problem of interference resulting from stimulus similarity is uncomplicated. Formal intralist stimulus similarity produces inhibitory effects because the representational response results in identical or similar representational codes. Thus, the resolution of interference may occur either by developing an unique representational code or by elaborative coding of the representational code resulting in distinctive functional cues for recall (Underwood, 1964).

The remainder of this paper will be concerned with an elaboration of these two basic points.

REPRESENTATIONAL RESPONSES

While there is considerable research on the coding of to-be-recalled items in memory, particularly over short time intervals, there has been little explicit research on stimulus or cue coding. Nevertheless, one might expect a number of principles to be identical for the two kinds of coding systems, so that some general hypotheses may be advanced concerning the processes involved in representation.

There is a great deal of evidence which indicates that the perceptual representation of verbal stimuli involves acoustic or articulatory (phonemic) attributes; that is, the process of reading a verbal stimulus results in a transformation of the visual input to a representation which is at least in part phonemic.

The postulation of an essentially phonemic representational response is not meant as a denial that visual information in stimuli may not be part of the representation (e.g., Posner, Boies, Eichelman, & Taylor, 1969) and certainly some classes of nonverbal stimuli appear to be represented by visual codes (Bates, 1967). Nevertheless, it would appear that well-established reading habits in the adult would lead to predominately phonemic codes for even visually perceived words.

The argument is in part inferential. Children initially learn the meanings of words through phonological rather than graphic presentation. Thus, by the time he attends to written words, the child has already established a large vocabulary of sound-meaning associations. In fact, it is likely that once he has mastered the system for transforming graphic symbols into familiar phonemic representations he can "read" and understand words he has never seen via phonemic mediation. The persistence of this system is hard to estimate, but occasional direct evidence of its existence may be obtained even in adults by recording covert activity of the speech musculature during silent reading and other language processing tasks (McGuigan, 1970). Indeed, one author (Edfeldt, 1960) argues that such activity is a concomitant of all silent reading, even though it is more marked in poor readers and when difficult material is used.

At a more experimental level, it has been shown that word perception accuracy depends upon the correspondence of letter sequence to English pronunciation rules (Gibson, Pick, Osser, & Hammond, 1962; Gibson, Osser, & Pick, 1963), a fact which has been interpreted to mean that the basic unit of word perception is a cluster of letters that corresponds to a pronounceable sound.

It would be possible that representational codes are primarily acoustic-articulatory but that such attributes play little role in memory. This does not, however, appear to be the case.

A large amount of research (see, e.g., Neisser, 1967) has shown that phonemic properties of to-be-recalled items produce interference in immediate recall. More to the point of the present concern, however, would be a demonstration of interference based on phonemic similarity among stimuli in cued-recall learning. Short-term recall of items paired with similar sounding stimuli has been shown to be impaired (Bruce & Murdock, 1968), although the similar sounding stimuli were also similar visually in most cases. Runquist (1970a) attempted to control for identical letters by comparing lists where the stimuli sound similar when pronounced with lists where the stimuli sound different because the terminal consonant changes the vowel sound (e.g., HEM, HEN, HEP versus HEM, HEW, HER). Lists containing similar sounding stimuli were clearly more difficult.

On the basis of this research, letter identity, the traditional operational definition of formal similarity, would seem to produce its effects largely because it is correlated with phonemic similarity. Whether this is the sole source of interference is problematical. Critical experiments relating graphic characteristics to interference have not been done. Nevertheless, research on pattern recognition has been unambiguous in indicating that human observers are capable of abstracting visual information from letter displays (Posner & Taylor, 1969). The question is whether such information is part of the representational code for stimuli in memory tasks and if it is, does it produce interference? Although Runquist (1970a) found no difference in interference between vowel-identical and vowel-different when the pronunciation was different (e.g., HEM, HEW, HER versus HAM, HOW, HER), for a variety of reasons these data are not conclusive. Furthermore, some graphic information must be able to be utilized in the representational process or it would be impossible for Ss to learn lists in which different stimuli have identical acoustic representations (BARE, BEAR).

While overall phonemic similarity seems to be a basic source of interference when pronounceable and meaningful units serve as stimuli, the situation must be different when letter strings which serve as stimuli are not pronounceable (e.g., low *m* CCC). It is likely that the representational response consists of spelling the unit. Thus, interference produced by similar or partially identical spelled representations would result specifically from identical elements in the representational code.

The role of phonemic attributes in producing this interference is not as clear-cut as it seems to be in the case of pronounceable meaningful stimuli. A series of experiments (Runquist, 1971c) which varied the phonemic similarity of letters comprising CCC stimuli failed to produce evidence that interference is generally greater when the letters are similar (B, D, T) as opposed to when they are dissimilar (B, R, H). Not only is this true when they are CCC but it is also true when they are single letters or CCC which demand letter selection for discriminative coding.

On the other hand, there seems to be at least one set of conditions under which phonemic similarity of letters will produce greater interference. If a set of stimuli all share the same two letters, and the "discriminative" letters are phonemically similar to the identical letters as well as to each other, interference is enhanced (Dobbs & Jesswein, 1972). In addition to implicating phonemic coding for analyzed CCC items, this result is important in another context and will be discussed below.

Regardless of the content of the stimulus code, there are other explicit features of the coding process which are assumed. Perhaps the most critical property is the sequential nature of the activation of the two states. That is, formal attributes and the more elaborative attributes are not considered to be part of a single code but represent separate and in some sense independent cue systems. Secondly, the elaborative codes are assumed to be activated by the representational code and are not derived directly from the physical stimulus. Thus, there are two critical theoretical issues which are somewhat interrelated: (1) Are there two independent coding systems? and (2) If there are two systems, is the elaborative code activated by the representational code or by the physical stimulus directly? There are no clear answers to these questions. The usual argument for separate independent systems is to point to data which show that the effects of phonemic and semantic factors differ as a function of various variables.

Several studies have shown that phonemic similarity among to-be-recalled items exerts effects after short intervals, but not after long intervals (Baddeley, 1966; Kintsch & Buschke, 1969; Levy & Murdock, 1968). On the other hand, semantic similarity effects seem to occur primarily after longer retention intervals (Baddeley & Dale, 1966). Similarly, Bregman (1968) provided retrieval cues of various types in a running recall task and showed that phonemic, semantic, and orthographic cues are differentially effective for retrieval at different retention intervals. While it is undoubtedly incorrect to assume that short-term (primary) memory involves only formal attributes and long-term memory elaborative attributes, the data clearly implicate differential temporal effects for semantic and phonemic attributes. This conclusion is not mitigated by the fact that occasionally differences have not been obtained (Craik & Levy,

1970); the point is that interactions have been obtained even if the boundary conditions for these interactions are not clearly understood.

Variables other than retention interval also interact with semantic and phonemic attributes. Bruce and Crowley (1970) have demonstrated that enhanced recall of phonemically related words from a long-term memory system depends upon them being presented contiguously during learning, while semantically related items do not demand this condition for enhanced recall. Wickens (1970) summarized the effects of a number of different attributes on the PI release phenomenon. In general, it was apparent that changes within semantic attributes (e.g., shift in conceptual category, change in semantic differential value, etc.) produce large recovery from PI, while changes in formal characteristics (articulatory locus, number of syllables, etc.) produced considerably smaller changes. Finally, Crowder (1970) has recently shown that the effects of adding a redundant prefix to a to-be-recalled or being recalled series of items are localized differently within the series depending upon whether the presentation involved vocalization at input or silent study. He interpreted this result according to a dual-system theory.

Temporal parameters other than retention interval also appear to interact with phonemic-semantic variations; namely, study time and time allowed for recall. These variables are of special interest, since the postulated sequential nature of representational and elaborative codes suggests what kinds of interactions must occur. The basic notion is that shortening either study time or test time should restrict the time allotted for either formation or reactivation of elaborative codes.

Several facts appear to be consistent with this assumption. Many of the paired associate experiments conducted at the University of Alberta have used the anticipation method with a fairly rapid 1.5: 1.5 sec. presentation rate. Under these conditions, many "semantic" variables such as intralist stimulus synonymity, associative overlap among stimuli, and concreteness of stimuli have produced only small and often nonsignificant effects (Runquist, 1968b; Runquist, 1971c). Occasionally, evidence of elaborative responses involving letter selection has not appeared even when similarity relations among the stimuli make this a highly viable means of coping with interference (Runquist, 1968c; 1970b, 1971a).

More direct evidence comes from a recent experiment in which Ss learned lists consisting of several sets of three paired associates (Runquist, 1971c). Each set of stimuli consisted of words such as CRAZY, INSANE, LAZY. When learned with a 1-second anticipation interval, the phonemically similar stimulus (LAZY) produced slower learning than the semantically similar item (INSANE), but when the anticipation interval was 3-seconds, the difference disappeared. Furthermore, switching from a 3- to a 1-second interval after partial learning, allowed the differences in performance on the two kinds of pairs to reappear while changing from a one- to a 3-second interval resulted in equal performance. Thus, it appears as if limiting the recall (anticipation) time forces Ss to use phonemic representations for attempted recall, thereby resulting in interference from that source, while at longer times semantic elaboration of the stimulus enables Ss to avert phonemic interference.

In a second experiment, Ss learned lists in which stimuli were all phonemically similar (rhymes), semantically similar (common conceptual category), or dissimilar. When recall time was restricted to 1-second, the phonemic similarity produced substantially more interference than semantic similarity. With a 3-second recall time, both effects were reduced, but phonemic similarity Ss gained more from added time than did semantic similarity Ss.

In this experiment, the results were independent of whether a 3-second or 1-second study period was used. Schulman (1970), on the other hand, has demonstrated that phonemic and semantic codes depend on the study time of to-be-recalled items in a short-term memory task.

The available data are encouraging, albeit not definitive. While it is clear that semantic and phonemic codes are often affected differently by various variables, and that the temporal interactions are at least consistent with the successive encoding hypothesis, the data admit to other interpretations.

For example, it is possible that there are separate coding systems, a representational code and elaborative codes, but they are activated in parallel, with representational coding occurring more rapidly. Alternately, there may be a single coding system in which various attributes are added, subtracted, or utilized for recall according to different temporal laws and task demands. It is thus apparent that the mere presence of differences in the characteristics of supposed representational codes and elaborative codes is not sufficient to distinguish between alternative conceptions of coding systems. Presumably, more sensitive designs, and a more clearly formulated conceptual analysis is necessary. Furthermore, and most important for the present formulation, most research and theory has been concerned with the coding of the to-be-recalled items, and there is no guarantee that the same functions are involved in processing cue stimuli.

ELABORATIVE RESPONSES AND INTERFERENCE REDUCTION

The most commonly held notion of interference is response competition. That is, in some sense the presented cue stimulus results in the recall of items associated with other stimuli, which either block or replace the recall of the correct item. By making an analogy to successive discrimination or differential conditioning procedures, it is possible to conceptualize the reduction of interference as extinction of incorrect associations resulting from the nonreinforcement of either overt or implicit errors. The analogy might also be made to some forms of the theory of interlist interference (Keppel, 1968) in which interfering responses from one list are supposed to undergo a similar extinction process during the learning of a second list.

Evidence relating to this issue is scarce. In one experiment (Runquist, 1971c), Ss learned lists in which the stimuli consisted of two sets of four formally similar trigrams. After varying numbers of trials, half the response terms were repaired within the set, while half were repaired between sets. Repairing within the set was always easier with the difference increasing with the amount of first list practice. Since overt errors were primarily from within the set, as learning increased the extinction of these errors should have made within-set repairing more difficult. It clearly did not.

In a second study (Runquist, 1971c), Ss who learned the same lists as above were asked after learning to give the first two responses from the list which occurred to them. As amount of first-list practice increased, the percentage of within-group errors also increased relative to between-group errors, despite the fact that such errors were presumably being extinguished.

Also relevant is the continued failure to demonstrate poorer long-term recall of lists of high formal similarity (Underwood, 1961; Joinson & Runquist, 1968), thus providing lack of evidence of spontaneous recovery of the presumably extinguished intralist interferences.

None of these results is alone definitive, as one can readily think of alternative interpretations. Nevertheless, it is significant that no study has as yet demonstrated that intralist error tendencies are weakened and become less available. Thus, it would appear that when Ss are faced with formally similar or identical cue representations, the problem is resolved by establishing and utilizing discriminative elaborative codes, and not by the direct weakening of competing responses to the similar representations. So, any condition which delays or increases the difficulty of establishing stable discriminative elaborative codes should allow formal similarity to exert its powerful inhibitory effects. The focus of theoretical interest then shifts to the process by which the learner acquires the disposition to encode beyond the representational level.

A conceptual distinction may be made between the elaborative coding response and the code it produces. The coding response may be conceptualized as the mechanism by which distinctive codes are produced. For example, when coding occurs by letter selection, the act of selecting a particular letter is the *coding response*, while the particular letter selected (or more properly its psychological representation) is the *code* for that stimulus.

In order to reduce interference, coding responses must be acquired which generate distinctive codes. Furthermore, it is clear that coding responses are not merely mediating responses which are associated with specific stimulus representations but function more like "rules" or means of generating distinctive codes which may be applied to any stimuli.

Two recently completed experiments throw some light on this problem. One experiment (Runquist, 1971c) was essentially a short-term memory experiment using the probe method (Murdock, 1963). The S was presented with two CVC trigram-noun pairs, then counted backwards for 10-seconds after which one of the two stimuli was presented for recall of the associated noun. Each S was tested on 49 different sets. In one group, the two CVCs used within a set had no letters in common. In another group, they shared one or two letters, but the shared letters were never in the same position from set to set. A third group also had stimuli which shared letters, but they were always in the same position. The results of interest were changes in recall with successive sets. All groups showed improvement over sets, but the low similarity group was initially obtaining more correct recalls than either of the two groups where letters were duplicated. In the group where position of the identical letters kept changing, performance was less accurate throughout all 49 sets, but for the group which had duplicated letters in the same position, performance equalled that of the low similarity group by set 35. The gradual reduction of interference over sets when discriminative letters are always in the same position may be attributed to the acquisition of a specific letter selection coding response since the specific code changes with each set.

It is also possible to demonstrate the transfer of letter selection responses separate from specific stimulus codes. Dobbs and Carlson (1971) had Ss learn lists in which the stimuli consisted of sets such as XJQ, XJM, BKT, BKS, PLZ, PLD. When transferred to lists consisting of new stimuli but with identical similarity structure, such Ss showed positive transfer, when compared with Ss who had learned a first list in which the "selection rule" differed for the different sets of two stimuli, i.e., the distinctive letter was in different positions (XJQ, XJM, BKT, BST, PLZ, KLZ).

The fact that coding responses appear to act like general rules for generating particular codes suggests that the most important factor in interference reduction is the availability of discriminative codes. That is, interference resulting from formally similar representations will be less persistent, when distinctive codes are more readily available.

With respect to letter selection codes, availability will be in part a function of the structure of the set of stimuli. When a single selection rule is more salient or if fewer selection rules are necessary to code the entire set, interference should perseverate less. These generalizations are unequivocally supported by the data.

A set of CCC stimuli, all of which have the same two letters in common and in which these shared letters are in the same position for each stimulus, is as easy as a set in which the stimuli have no common letters. That is, shared letters produce no additional interference under this condition (Runquist, 1970b). If the positions of the common letters are scrambled, however, difficulty increases considerably even though the discriminative letter maintains in the same position in all stimuli (Runquist, 1970b, 1971b, 1971c). If the position of the discriminative letter is different for each stimulus, again there is an increase in interference, but curiously enough this interference is no greater than that produced by variation in the position of the shared letters, and does not increase when the latter are also scrambled (Runquist, 1971c).

Moreover, it would appear that the increase in difficulty produced by letter identity combined with structural complexity results directly from difficulty in attaining a stable code and not from an increase in stimulus confusion at the representational level. In almost all studies using CCC stimuli, the ratio of overt errors to opportunities has been remarkably constant across conditions varying widely in difficulty. That is, it appears that changing positions of either discriminative letters, shared letters, or both results in difficulty in "discovering" a distinctive coding rule or rules.

This principle also suggests why phonemic similarity of "spelled out" consonants seems to have effects only when the distinctive letter is similar to the shared letters (Dobbs & Jesswein, 1972). The confusion manifests itself in the choice of the code letter, not in confusion among codes for different stimuli.

A second factor which appears to be involved is pronounceability. Generally, when a single letter selection rule is available, low *m* CVC and word stimuli will produce considerable interference when similarity is high while CCC stimuli will not (Runquist, 1968c, 1970b). This suggests that a spelled representation may facilitate the occurrence of letter selection responses while a pronounced representation makes selection coding more difficult.

While low *m* CVC appear ultimately to be coded by letter selection, it is possible to reduce interference among formally similar words by meaning coding. As is the case with letter selection coding, any condition which makes meaning codes more difficult to produce should make learning more difficult. On the other hand, part of the difficulty with similar CCC comes from the fact that not any letter selection code will suffice, i.e., the learner may produce a coding response which generates a nondistinctive code.

In the case of meaning coding, however, the latter source of interference would not seem to be important, unless there is also semantic similarity among the stimuli. That is, even though CAT and HAT have highly similar formal representations it appears unlikely that *any* semantic coding response would ever generate the other's meaning code, or even similar meaning codes in the absence of perceptual failure. Thus, almost any semantic code would be distinctive. Therefore, in terms of interference reduction, it should be sufficient merely to produce a semantic code, and the conditions which increase the difficulty of letter selection coding (i.e., structural complexity of the list) should be unimportant. Indeed, this seems to be the case as interference from formal similarity with trigram words appears to be primarily a function of overall similarity and is unrelated to variations in the number of potential letter selection rules necessary to discriminately code the stimuli (Runquist, 1970b). However, there are other conditions which would seem to make the generation of meaning codes difficult (e.g., time pressure, low familiarity) and these conditions should result in greater interference among formally similar word stimuli.

This analysis is not meant to imply, however, that meaningful words are always processed in wholistic fashion and coded exclusively by meaning. There are many examples of situations where *S*s selectively respond to parts of words (e.g., Haslerud & Clark, 1957; Horowitz, Chilian, & Dunnigan, 1969). Moreover, Nelson and Rowe (1969) have shown that with trigram word stimuli, letter identity in different positions produces differential interference with the order of importance being first, third, second.

One might argue that these results simply mean that similarity among phonemic representations depends upon position of identity for reasons which have nothing to do with selective processing. Several lines of data deny this argument. Notably, both Runquist (1968d) and Nelson and Nelson (1970) had *S*s rate word trigram pairs for similarity, with the latter study actually instructing *S*s to attend to phonetic properties. In neither case did ratings correspond to the relative interference produced in the Nelson and Rowe (1969) experiment. Secondly, the series of experiments in the Alberta laboratory has consistently failed to produce differences in interference as a result of identity in different positions (Runquist, 1968c, 1970b, 1971a). Thus, locus of identical letters does not always produce the effects it should, particularly in ratings and in learning situations where phonemically produced interference seems to predominate.

It would seem more likely, then, that differential interference resulting from identity in different positions will result from conditions producing letter selection coding. That is, the appearance of position effects in the Nelson and Rowe (1969) experiments, or conversely, the failure of such effects to occur in the Runquist (1968c, 1970b, 1971a) experiments may be based on the fact that Nelson and Rowe's procedures favored letter selection coding of words, while Runquist's did not. Exactly what these conditions are is not clear, but it is interesting to note in this respect, that Runquist (1971a) is able to demonstrate the differential position effects with CCC stimuli under his experimental conditions where he does obtain other evidence of letter selection coding. Perhaps the safest conclusion at the present time was offered by Nelson, Peebles, and Pancotto (1970), who point out quite conservatively that a large number of dimensions may be used for coding words, and that the code which is actually established depends upon the task demands. For example, letter selection coding may be produced with word stimuli by using response terms which begin with one of the letters in the stimulus (RAG-GHOST). Under such conditions, stimuli which contain two letters in common in identical positions do not interfere with one another more than stimuli which do not share letters, whereas manipulation of the position of identical and discriminative letters, which ordinarily has little effect on performance with word stimuli, results in considerable interference. In short, words can be made to be processed as if they were CCC. Moreover, CCC stimuli can be made to produce the pattern usually found with words by using pairs which are meaningfully related and CCC which can easily be translated into meaningful words (e.g., QCK-SPEED). Under such conditions structural variations in position of discriminative letters should not be effective, and indeed they are not (Runquist, 1971b).

ADDITIONAL DISCUSSION

This paper has been addressed to two questions concerning interference produced by formal similarity among cue stimuli in paired associate performance: (1) How does interference occur? and (2) How is it reduced?

At a very general level, Underwood (1964) answered the first question when he stated that interference results from similar representations. Current theorizing and some data have suggested that it is the phonemic (acoustic or articulatory) attributes of these representational codes which are important in producing this interference. Yet, the basic nature of the mechanism by which interference is produced remains obscure.

Traditionally, interference is presumed to occur by the interaction of associations at recall, in which presentation of a cue stimulus more or less simultaneously activates several associations. Those which are incorrect thus block or replace correct associations. Similarity among stimuli increases interference by stimulus generalization, or generalization among representational codes. It is possible, however, that interference does not involve associative interaction at all. Results with CCC stimuli have suggested that similarity acts indirectly by making it difficult to generate elaborative codes (letter selection) which are distinctive, thus producing a kind of generalized suppression of learning. Secondly, it is possible that confusion in stimulus recognition or inappropriate coding of cue stimuli at recall could result in activation of incorrect associations or failure of recall without simultaneously activating the correct association. There are no data bearing on this latter issue, although recent research and theory implicating stimulus recognition in the cued-recall process indicates the viability of such an approach. Bernbach (1967), Martin (1967), and Schulman (1970) have pointed out how such a theory might explain some of the effects of similarity on short-term memory.

With respect to the nature of interference reduction, Underwood's (1964) interpretation is again generally appropriate. Interference from formally similar representational codes is reduced not by the direct weakening of erroneous associations but by the production of mediating responses which distinctively encode the stimuli. Thus, when general learning conditions make either the acquisition or utilization of distinctive codes difficult, interference is produced. The effects of a number of different variables, e.g., list structure, pronounce-ability, meaning, and temporal factors therefore have predictable effects on the amount of interference produced by formal similarity.

In any event, it is becoming quite apparent from research on interference that the specific elaborative coding responses involved in interference reduction have the property of control processes rather than structural processes (Atkinson & Schiffrin, 1968) in that a particular coding response is highly dependent upon the specific experimental paradigm, the task demand, and the particular material being learned. Consequently, it does not seem to be particularly edifying to attempt to catalogue all of the possible attributes of similarity which produce interference and to identify all of the specific codes by which this interference is reduced.

A more fruitful approach might be directed toward an understanding of the way the coding system operates both to produce and reduce interference. Aided by Underwood's (1964) analysis, some general principles have begun to emerge and several other critical problems are being brought into focus.

REFERENCES

Atkinson, R. C., & Schiffrin, R. M. Human memory: a proposed system and its control processes. In K. W. Spence, & J. T. Spence (eds.) *The Psychology of Learning and Motivation*, Vol. 2, New York: Academic Press, 1968.

Baddeley, A. D. The influence of acoustic and semantic similarity on long-term memory for word sequences. *Quarterly Journal of Experimental Psychology*, 1966, 18, 302–309.

Baddeley, A. D., & Dale, H. C. A. The effect of semantic similarity on retroactive interference in short- and long-term memory. *Journal of Verbal Learning and Verbal Behavior*, 1966, 5, 417–420.

Bates, G. A. The effect of parastimulus verbal interference on short-term visual retention. Unpublished master's thesis, University of Alberta, 1969.

Bernbach, H. A. Stimulus learning and recognition in paired associate learning. *Journal of Experimental Psychology*, 1967, 75, 513–519.

Bousfield, W. A. The occurrence of clustering in the recall of randomly arranged associates. *Journal of General Psychology*, 1953, 49, 229–240.

Bousfield, W. A., Whitmarsh, G. A., & Danick, J. J. Partial response identities in verbal generalization. *Psychological Reports*, 1958, 4, 703–713.

Bregman, A. S. Forgetting curves with semantic, graphic and contiguity cues. *Journal of Experimental Psychology*, 1968, 28, 538–546.

Bruce, D., & Crowley, J. J. Acoustic similarity effects of retrieval from secondary memory. *Journal of Verbal Learning and Verbal Behavior*, 1970, 9, 190–196.

Bruce, D., & Murdock, B. B. Acoustic similarity effects on memory for paired associates. *Journal of Verbal Learning and Verbal Behavior*, 1968, 7, 627–631.

Craik, F. I. M., & Levy, B. A. Semantic and acoustic information in primary memory. *Journal of Experimental Psychology*, 1970, 86, 77–82.

Crowder, R. G. The role of one's own voice in immediate memory. *Cognitive Psychology*, 1970, 1, 157–158.

Dobbs, A. R., & Carlson, D. Transfer of stimulus selection coding rules, 1971, (unpublished).

Dobbs, A. R., & Jesswein, I. Acoustic similarity and stimulus selection. (unpublished).

Edfeldt, A. W. *Silent speech and silent reading.* Chicago: University of Chicago Press, 1960.

Gibson, E. J., Osser, H., & Pick, A. D. A study in the development of grapheme-phoneme correspondences. *Journal of Verbal Learning and Verbal Behavior*, 1963, 2, 142–146.

Gibson, E. J., Pick, A. D., Osser, H., & Hammond, M. The role of grapheme-phoneme correspondence in the perception of words. *American Journal of Psychology*, 1962, 75, 554–570.

Haslerud, G. M., & Clark, R. E. On the redintegrative perception of words. *American Journal of Psychology*, 1957, 70, 97–101.

Horowitz, L. M., Chilian, P. C., & Dunnigan, K. P. Word fragments and their redintegrative power. *Journal of Experimental Psychology* 1969, 80, 392–394.

Joinson, P. A., & Runquist, W. N. Effects of intralist stimulus similarity and degree of learning on forgetting. *Journal of Verbal Learning and Verbal Behavior*, 1968, 7, 554–559.

Keppel, G. Retroactive and proactive inhibition. In T. R. Dixon & D. L. Horton (eds.) *Verbal behavior and general behavior theory.* Englewood Cliffs: Prentice-Hall, 1968.

Kintsch, W., & Buschke, H. Homophones and synonyms in short-term memory. *Journal of Experimental Psychology*, 1969, 80, 403–407.

Levy, B. A., & Murdock, B. B. The effects of delayed auditory feedback and intralist similarity in short-term memory. *Journal of Verbal Learning and Verbal Behavior*, 1968, 7, 887–894.

Martin, E. Relation between stimulus recognition and paired associate learning. *Journal of Experimental Psychology*, 1967, 74, 500–505.

McGuigan, F. J. Covert oral behavior during the silent performance of language tasks. *Psychological Bulletin*, 1970, 74, 309–316.

Murdock, B. B. Short-term retention of single paired associates. *Journal of Experimental Psychology*, 1963, 65, 433–443.

Neisser, U. *Cognitive Psychology.* New York: Appleton-Century-Crofts, 1967.

Nelson, D. L., & Nelson, R. L. Rated acoustic (articulatory) similarity for word pairs varying in number and ordinal position in common letters. *Psychonomic Science*, 1970, 19, 81–82.

Nelson, D. L., Peebles, J., & Pancotto, F. Phonetic similarity as opposed to informational structure as a determinant of word encoding. *Journal of Experimental Psychology*, 1970, 86, 117–119.

Nelson, D. L., & Rowe, F. A. Information theory and stimulus encoding in paired associate acquisition: ordinal position of formal similarity. *Journal of Experimental Psychology*, 1969, 79, 342–346.

Osgood, C. E., Suci, G. J., & Tanenbaum, P. H. *The measurement of meaning.* Urbana: University of Illinois Press, 1957.

Paivio, A. *Imagery and verbal processes.* New York: Holt, Rinehart & Winston, 1971.

Posner, M. I., & Taylor, R. L. Subtractive method applied to separation of visual and name components in multi-letter arrays. *Acta Psychologica*, 1969, 30, 104–114.

Posner, M. I., Boies, S., Eichelmann, W., & Taylor, R. L. Rentention of visual and name codes of single letters. *Journal of Experimental Psychology Monographs*, 1969, 79, No. 1, Part 2.

Postman, L., & Greenbloom, R. Conditions of cue selection in the acquisition of paired associate lists. *Journal of Experimental Psychology*, 1967, 73, 91–100.

Runquist, W. N. Reversal vs. non-reversal repairing in categorized paired associate lists. *Canadian Journal of Psychology*, 1968, 22, 285–293. (a)

Runquist, W. N. Functions relating intralist stimulus similarity to acquisition similarity to acquisition performance with a variety of material. *Journal of Verbal Learning and Verbal Behavior*, 1968, 7, 549–553. (b)

Runquist, W. N. Formal intralist similarity in paired associate learning. *Journal of Experimental Psychology*, 1968, 78, 634–641. (c)

Runquist, W. N. Rated similarity of high *m* CVC trigrams and words and low *m* CCC trigrams. *Journal of Verbal Learning and Verbal Behavior*, 1968, 7, 967–968. (d)

Runquist, W. N. Acoustic similarity among stimuli in paired associate learning. *Journal of Experimental Psychology*, 1970, 83, 319–322. (a)

Runquist, W. N. Structural effects of letter identity among stimuli in paired associate learning. *Journal of Experimental Psychology*, 1970, 84, 152–163. (b)

Runquist, W. N. Ordinal position of letter identity among stimuli in paired associate learning. *Journal of Experimental Psychology*, 1971, 87, 270–273. (a)

Runquist, W. N. Stimulus coding and intralist interference. *Journal of Experimental Psychology*, 1971, 87, 373–377. (b)

Runquist, W. N. Intralist Interference in Paired Associate Learning. Psychology Research Bulletin No. 1, University of Alberta, 1971. (c)

Runquist, W. N., & Farley, F. H. The use of mediators in the learning of verbal paired associates. *Journal of Verbal Learning and Verbal Behavior*, 1964, 3, 280–285.

Schulman, H. G. Encoding and retention of semantic and phonemic information in short-term memory. *Journal of Verbal Learning and Verbal Behavior*, 1970, 9, 499–508.

Schulman, H. G. Similarity effects in short-term memory. *Psychological Bulletin*, 1971, 75, 399–415.

Underwood, B. J. Studies of distributed practice VIII. Learning and retention of paired nonsense syllables as a function of intralist similarity. *Journal of Experimental Psychology*, 1953, 45, 133–142.

Underwood, B. J. An evaluation of the Gibson theory of verbal learning. In C. N. Cofer (ed.) *Verbal Learning and Verbal Behavior*, New York: McGraw-Hill, 1961.

Underwood, B. J. The representativeness of rote verbal learning. In A. W. Melton (ed.) *Categories of human learning*. New York: Academic Press, 1964.

Underwood, B. J. False recognition produced by implicit verbal responses. *Journal of Experimental Psychology*, 1965, 70, 122–129.

Underwood, B. J., Ham, M., & Eckstrand, B. Cue selection in paired-associate learning. *Journal of Experimental Psychology*, 1962, 64, 405–409.

Underwood, B. J., & Schulz, R. W. *Meaningfulness and verbal learning*. Chicago: Lippincott, 1960.

Underwood, B. J., & Keppel, G. Coding processes in verbal learning. *Journal of Verbal Learning and Verbal Behavior*, 1963, 1, 250–257.

Wickens, D. D. Encoding categories of words. An Empirical approach to meaning. *Psychological Review*, 1970, 77, 1–5.

9 | Mediation

RUDOLPH W. SCHULZ
University of Iowa, Iowa City

In 1964, a programmatic research effort was initiated in our laboratory to study the process of mediation. The main thrust of this research has been to attempt to describe and understand the manner in which mediational processes function. More specifically, we have concerned ourselves largely with mediation in verbal paired-associate (PA) learning where the associations which are potentially available to be utilized as mediating associations have been acquired in the laboratory. It should be noted, however, that the choice of the PA situation was a tactical one; our aim was not the understanding of PA learning qua PA learning. Thus, we have used the PA situation as a "tool" to reveal the manner in which mediational processes were affected by specifiable variations in antecedent conditions. The choice of the PA situation has facilitated our efforts in this regard because the PA situation is a reasonably analytic one in which the parameters affecting performance have been rather fully determined. This strategy may be seen as akin to the one being employed by Kendler and Kendler (1962) in their use of the reversal-shift paradigm in discrimination learning as a vehicle for making inferences regarding the development of mediational processes in children.

Reports of most of the research completed in the earlier phases of this program have been published; hence, it is upon the recently completed studies which the present discussion will, in the main, focus. Similarly, it seems unnecessary to review at length the published research literature concerned with mediation because this literature has been reviewed in detail frequently (Earhard & Mandler, 1965; Horton, 1967; Jenkins, 1963; Kjeldergard, 1968) and recently (Postman, 1971).

The research which will be discussed in this paper may be grouped, roughly, as having been addressed to the following general methodological, empirical, and theoretical issues: (1) The development of materials and procedures to produce

This research was supported by Grants GB2835 and GB8392X from the National Science Foundation. I am also indebted to the students, graduate and undergraduate, who have assisted me in the conduct of this research program. In this regard special thanks are due Bruce Britton, James Cooper, Lee Dahle, Allen Dobbs, Arthur Firl, Catherine Henigbaum, Marda Higdon, Ronald Hopkins, Michael Maus, Constantine Poulos, Michael Shea, George Weaver, and Philip Zitzelman.

stable, persistent, and reproducible differences in PA performance which can be interpreted unequivocally as reflecting facilitation of performance due to utilization of mediating associations. (2) The evaluation of the merits of maintaining that it is theoretically fruitful to distinguish between the discovery of a mediating association and its utilization. (3) Exploration of the circum- stances in which mediating associations may interfere with PA performance. (4) An attempt to ascertain the acquisition and retention parameters which affect PA performance in which mediating associations could be utilized. These four topics may be seen then as providing the focal points in the description and discussion of the results of various studies which will be reported here. While the somewhat separate consideration of each topic provides a convenient expository framework, it should be clear that these four issues are interrelated and that a given experiment may have had implications for more than one of them.

One additional orienting remark seems pertinent; namely, the reader may find the theoretical orientation underlying the research reported in this paper to be in a sense inconsistent. Thus, at times the orientation will seem much closer to an associationistic S-R view while on other occasions the theoretical view will more nearly approximate what might be termed a relational-cognitive interpreta- tion. At still other times, the orientation will be largely an empirical, phenomenon-oriented one, an orientation characteristic of the functionalist approach. Thus, the approach is eclectic. Inasmuch as a comprehensive theoretical articulation of the facts pertaining to mediational processes is in the longrun quite unlikely to be *exclusively* either associative or cognitive, an eclectic stance which is responsive to a number of viewpoints seems clearly justified, if not demanded, at this point in time.

DEVELOPMENT OF MATERIALS AND PROCEDURES

To study a phenomenon effectively, it must first be possible to produce the phenomenon reliably and produce enough of it to permit detection of changes that occur as the result of having manipulated one or another theoretically pertinent independent variable. Without attempting to document this assertion in detail, I believe it is fair to say that, taken as a whole, the research concerned with mediation in the PA situation available to us at the time the present project was begun had not been successful in delineating a method that gave the investigator the level of "control" of the phenomenon that we deemed requisite. Indeed, as Jenkins put it, "In an extensive series of experiments in our laboratories we have found more ways *not* to get the equivalence (mediation) effects than we have found ways to achieve them" (1965, p. 85). Moreover, this state of affairs seemed particularly characteristic of attempts to produce mediation via associations acquired in the laboratory. Therefore, our *first objective* was to develop materials and procedures which would produce large, sustained, and reliable differences in performance between a condition allowing mediation and one serving as a suitable control even though all the requisite associations were acquired in the laboratory.

This objective was first achieved for the phenomenon of mediated facilitation employing the materials and procedures described in detail by Schulz, Weaver, and Ginsberg (1965). The essentials of their methods are outlined in Table 1. The two basic conditions shown there are the A-B, B-C, A-C forward-chaining facilitation (FC), and A-B, D-C, A-C control (FCC) paradigms which are defined by three successively learned PA lists. The A-terms of the lists are paralogs, the B- and D-terms nouns, and C-terms CVC (Consonant-Vowel-Consonant) trigrams. Each list was learned by the study-test method. As may be seen in Table 1, an S (Subject) in Condition FC learned lists containing pairs such as *Zonad-Soldier* in Stage I (A-B), then *Soldier-BIW* in Stage II (B-C), and finally in Stage III *Zonad-BIW* (A-C). An S in Condition FCC learned the same lists in Stage I and in Stage III; however, the "chain" was broken in Stage II where he would have learned a list consisting of pairs such as *Hand-BIW* (D-C) in which the nouns had not appeared in Stage I. Test trials in Stage I required *recall* of B to A. In Stages II and III test trials consisted of the presentation of A-terms as stimuli along with four C-terms as response alternatives, the correct C-term, and three other C-terms. The C-terms were numbered 1, 2, 3, and 4. The S gave as his response the number beneath the C-term he had chosen. Thus, test trials were multiple-choice recognition tests involving four alternatives. Training in the form of alternating study and test trials in Stages I and II was taken to a criterion of two successive perfect trials. Stage III consisted of a constant number of alternating study and test trials.

Mediated facilitation was inferred when Stage III A-C performance in Condition FC reliably exceeded that in Condition FCC, in that Ss in Condition FC may be presumed to have utilized B as a mediator in learning A-C because of the A-B-C associative chain acquired in Stages I and II. With the methods outlined above, the requisite superiority of Condition FC over Condition FCC in A-C performance has been observed in all of the experiments we have conducted involving these conditions; but more importantly, this difference is a clear one and persists throughout Stage III A-C performance (Schulz, Weaver, & Ginsberg, 1965). Furthermore, there is a high degree of consistency from one experiment to another in terms of the magnitude of the FC-FCC difference in A-C performance, with no more than 20 Ss per group being required to achieve this consistency. Namely, the level of correct responding in ten Stage III trials, overall, under Condition FCC ranges from 45 to 55 percent, while that under Condition FC ranges from 70 to 80 percent in spite of variations in S population, degree of S naïvete, list length, pairing of S and R terms, and a variety of other minor procedural alterations. In short, the FC-FCC difference is a stable and reproducible one. The curves in Figure 1 are typical of those obtained in Stage III acquisition under FC and FCC conditions with the methods described above. Additionally, it has now been rather convincingly established that this difference can, indeed, be interpreted as having resulted from the

Table 1. General description of materials and procedures employed to study mediation, the forward-chaining paradigm *via* associations acquired in the laboratory.

	Chaining Condition	Material S R		Control Condition	Material S R	Task
A-B	Stage I	Zonad-Soldier	A-B	Stage I	Zonad-Soldier	PA Learning by Study-Test Method to Two Successive Perfect Recitations
B-C	Stage II	Soldier-BIW	D-C	Stage II	Hand-BIW	PA Learning by Study-Test Method with Multiple-Choice Test Trials to Same Criterion as in Stage I
A-C	Stage III	Zonad-BIW	A-C	Stage III	Zonad-BIW	Ten Trials of PA Learning by Study-Test Method with Multiple-Choice Test Trials

A-Terms: Low M Taylor (1959) paralogs.

B & D Terms: Common nouns having AA T-L frequencies and minimal associative overlap in the Russell and Jenkins (1954) norms.

C Terms: Low M Archer (1960) CVC trigrams.

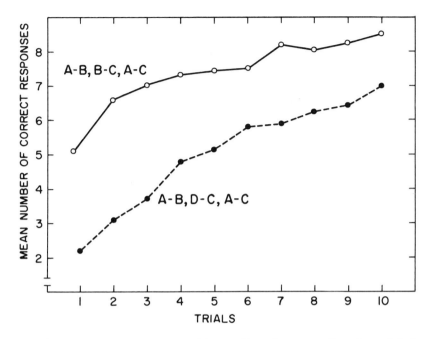

Figure 9–1. Mediated facilitation of Stage III performance. Data from Schulz, Weaver, and Ginsberg (1965).

utilization by Ss of the A-B-C associative chain under Condition FC. That is, our research has ruled out the two main "contending" alternative interpretations.

One of these alternatives has been proposed by Mandler and Earhard (1964). They maintain that superior performance on A-C under Condition FC may be due not to mediation but to a decrease in interference from A-B associations by virtue of the weakening of B-A associations, via unlearning, during the acquisition of B-C in Stage II. A second alternative is the one suggested by Schwenn and Underwood (1965). Though the learning of B-C is again implicated as the mechanism, its role is assumed to be quite different from the one assigned it by Mandler and Earhard. That is, B, via the backward association B-A, is presumed to elicit A in the presence of C and, as a result, direct A-C associations can be formed during Stage II B-C performance which will transfer positively to Stage III A-C performance. In sum, there are then for the same empirical result three alternative interpretations, one involving mediation, one decreased interference and, a third, direct association.

Even though the pseudomediation and direct-association hypotheses specify quite different mechanisms to account for the FC-FCC difference in Stage III, the processes operative during the learning of B-C in Stage II are critical for both hypotheses; therefore, experiments designed to evaluate one of these hypotheses have almost inevitably had implications for the evaluation of the other as well.

With one exception, this has been the case in our research. The exception is an experiment by Schulz, Weaver, and Ginsberg (1965) which was relevant only to the pseudomediation issue. It included, along with an FC and FCC condition, conditions designed to produce pseudomediation. Mandler and Earhard (1964) had neglected to include an FC and an FCC condition in their design. Hence, even if pseudomediation was responsible for some of the FC-FCC difference in Stage III A-C performance, it need not follow that all of this difference could be so attributed. As it turned out, no pseudomediation effect was observed under the present conditions. Subsequently, Goulet and Postman (1966) obtained similar results.

Additional evidence unfavorable to both the pseudomediation and direct-association hypotheses has been obtained in several other experiments. First, Schulz, Liston, and Weaver (1968) showed that, testing for recall of A-B following A-C performance, the recall of Ss in Condition FC was reliably superior to that for those in Condition FCC. Horton and Wiley (1967a 1967b) have also recently reported similar results as has Dobbs (1968). The pseudomediation hypothesis predicts just the opposite. Moreover, recall of A-B in Condition FC was also superior to that under conditions where the paradigm was A-B, B-C, E-F, suggesting that A-B strength was maintained at a level above the one involving "normal" forgetting as the result of the utilization of the A-B portion of the A-B-C chain during Stage III A-C performance in Condition FC.

In sum, it would appear that we have developed successfully a method which will allow the investigation of verbal mediational processes, based on associations acquired entirely in the laboratory, to be carried out in a flexible and controlled manner with the forward-chaining paradigm. It is unnecessary to belabor the matter of materials and procedures in respect to this paradigm further since the results of experiments to be described subsequently will attest further to the adequacy of these methods. However, before leaving the present discussion, it should be noted that the methods and procedures just described are basically the same as those employed in most of the experiments which will be reported in this paper; hence, the reader will want to be sure that he understands them fully.

Though the forward-chaining paradigm may be assumed to be widely applicable to situations in which mediational behavior obtains, there are clearly numerous additional ways in which implicit associative networks may be organized. For example, the stimulus-equivalence and the response-equivalence paradigms have long been prominent in theoretical analyses of mediational behavior (Jenkins, 1963). However, as in the case of the forward-chaining paradigm, previous investigations of these paradigms in the PA situation have, in general, failed to achieve a degree of control that would permit a thoroughgoing analysis of them (Kjeldergaard, 1968). In view of our success in gaining control of the mediation effect in the forward-chaining paradigm, we have recently attempted to determine whether similar levels of control could be achieved in the stimulus-equivalence, response-equivalence, and backward chaining paradigms.

Experiment 1

The three paradigms described above were investigated along with our "standard" forward-chaining paradigm. For the stimulus-equivalence paradigm, the condition in which mediation could occur to facilitate performance in Stage III involved the list sequence A-B, C-B, A-C, and will be called Condition SE. The control list sequence was A-B, D-B, A-C, and will be called Condition SEC. Similarly, for the response-equivalence paradigm, we had Condition RE (B-A, B-C, A-C) and its control Condition REC (B-A, D-C, A-C). In the case of the backward-chaining paradigm, the mediation condition was Condition BC (B-A, C-B, A-C) and the control was Condition BCC (B-A, D-B, A-C). Conditions FC and FCC, as defined previously, constituted the forward-chaining paradigm.

In addition to studying the effects of paradigms, the effects of presence (study test) versus the absence of study trials (test only) in Stage III on A-C performance were studied. This was done for three reasons: (1) To enable us to compare the present results with those obtained by Peterson, Colavita, Sheahan, and Blattner (1964) who used a test-only procedure in studying the relative effectiveness of the present paradigms under "mixed-list" conditions. (2) To shed additional light on the usefulness of distinguishing between discovery and utilization processes, a topic to be considered later in this paper. (3) Because we have found the test-only procedure to be particularly useful in other phases of the present program, but we had not compared the two procedures explicitly within the context of the same experiment; our previous comparisons were of the "between-experiment" variety and involved only the forward-chaining paradigm.

Method. Except for the changes in procedure dictated by the purposes of this study, only a few minor additional changes were made. In their essentials the methods employed here were comparable to those described earlier (Cf., p. 207). Briefly, they were as follows: (1) Six-pair lists were used in all stages. (2) The study interval was 2.0 seconds per pair. (3) The test-interval was 2.0 seconds in Stage I and 3 seconds in Stages II and III. (4) There were 12 alternating study and test trials for all Ss in Stage I (recall method) and Stage II (multiple choice). (5) Stage III (multiple choice) consisted of either 6 alternating study-test trials (half the Ss) or 3 test-only trials followed by 3 alternating study and test trials (other half of the Ss). (6) All Ss were shown the responses of the first list prior to learning it so that S could choose a comfortable pronunciation for the paralogs which were the response terms of the B-A Stage I list in Conditions RE, REC, BC, and BCC. The Ss in the other conditions pronounced the nouns of their A-B Stage I list. (7) A total of 160 Ss, 10 per condition, who were naïve in respect to studies of mediation, were assigned to conditions according to a block-randomization condition schedule.

Results. The only source of differential treatment in Stage I was whether S learned List A-B or List B-A. The mean total numbers of correct responses given during the 12 Stage I test trials by *S*s learning A-B was 51.10 and for those *S*s learning B-A it was 48.74. The difference between these means is not a statistically reliable one, $F(1,152) = 1.19, p > .05$.

The means of subgroups learning List A-B were compared with one another and found not to differ significantly, $F(7,72) = 1.68$, $p > .05$. A similar comparison of the List B-A subgroups showed them not to differ reliably, $F(7,72) = 1.78$, $p > .05$. Thus, the *S*s in the various subgroups may be considered to be of comparable ability.

In Stage II *S*s can be partitioned in terms of differential treatment as follows: (1) Stage I, A-B or B-A. (2) Stage II, B-C, D-C or C-B, D-B. (3) Stage II, mediation or control. Mean total numbers of correct responses served as the dependent variable. Generally, it may be said of the differences between Stage II means that they were small in absolute terms. However, since the variability in performance in Stage II was also small, a number of statistically reliable differences were obtained. Only those differences having possible consequences for the interpretation of the Stage III data will be discussed here.

Performance was slightly poorer in the mediation ($\bar{X} = 58.14$) than in the control conditions ($\bar{X} = 62.00$), $F(1,152) = 9.29, p < .01$. Those *S*s who learned List A-B in Stage I ($\bar{X} = 57.78$) learned their lists in Stage II slightly slower than the ones who learned List B-A in Stage I ($\bar{X} = 62.36$), $F(1,152) = 13.11$, $p < .01$. Two other sources of variance in Stage II approached significance. These two were related in that noun-trigram lists (B-C and D-C) were learned slightly faster than trigram-noun lists (C-B, D-B), especially so in the conditions where the Stage I list was List A-B.

The analyses of interest in the critical stage, Stage III, were preceded by an analysis of the total number of responses, correct as well as incorrect, which were emitted. This was done to insure that differences in performance under test-only conditions could not be attributed to differential responsivity of the *S*s in the various conditions. That is, even though *S*s were encouraged to guess in the test-only phase, they might have made fewer attempts to respond in some conditions than they did in others. If this occurred it would lead to differences in the *chance frequency* of responding correctly with the present multiple-choice procedures. The preceding analysis was performed separately for Trials 1–3 and Trials 4–6 of Stage III. No statistically reliable differences in level of responding were obtained in either analysis.

Attention is now shifted to performance in Stage III in terms of mean total numbers of correct responses on Trials 1–3. The relevant data are presented graphically in Figure 2. It can be seen that under test-only conditions performance under mediation conditions was superior to that under control conditions. With one exception, the stimulus equivalence paradigm, the same result obtained under study-test conditions. Statistically, the following sources of variance were reliable ones during Trials 1–3: (1) Study-test ($\bar{X} = 9.10$) performance was superior to test-only ($\bar{X} = 6.21$), $F(1,144) = 26.96, p < .01$. (2) More correct responses were given in the mediation ($\bar{X} = 10.32$) than in the

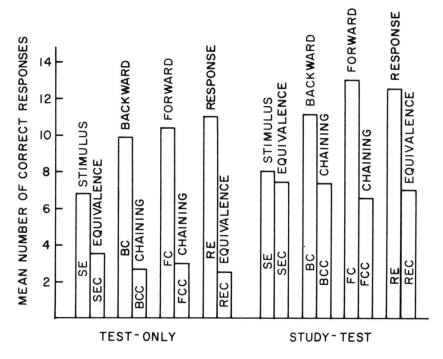

Figure 9–2. Stage III performance in terms of mean total numbers of correct responses over Trials 1–3 as a function of paradigms and the presence versus the absence of study trials.

control ($\overline{X} = 4.99$) conditions, F (1,144) = 92.12, $p < .01$. (3) The Ss who learned B-C and D-C lists in Stage II performed better ($\overline{X} = 8.22$) than those learning C-B and D-B lists in Stage II ($\overline{X} = 7.09$), F (1,144) = 4.18, $p < .05$. (4) There was less difference between mediation than between control conditions for study-test versus test-only performance F (1,144) = 4.95, $p < .05$. (5) A larger difference in performance obtained between mediation and control conditions when Lists B-C and D-C were learned in Stage II than when Lists C-B or D-B were learned in Stage II, F (1,144) = 8.41, $p < .01$. Findings 1, 2, 3, and 4 above remained significant sources of variance during Trials 4–6 and no new sources of variance emerged.

Since the results for Trials 4–6 did not differ from those for Trials 1–3, save in one respect described as Finding 5 above, the remaining analyses will be restricted to the Trials 1–3 data. Pairwise comparisons between the means of the mediation and those of the control conditions revealed that significant amounts of mediated facilitation could be inferred in all paradigms under both test-only and study-test conditions except in the case of the stimulus equivalence paradigm with the study-test method. Furthermore none of the differences among the study-test ($F < 1$) or among the test-only ($F < 1$) control condition

214   Rudolph W. Schulz

means were reliable ones, these means being 6.5, 7.0, 7.4, and 7.3 for study-test and 3.0, 2.5, 3.5, and 2.7 for test-only in Conditions FCC, REC, SEC, and BCC, respectively. In the case of the mediation conditions, the mean for Condition SE differed significantly from those of the other conditions in both the test-only and the study-test mode, while the means of the other conditions did not differ from one another, with means of 13.0, 12.5, 8.0, and 11.1 having been obtained for study-test, and 10.4, 10.9, 6.8, and 9.9 for test-only under FC, RE, SE, and BC conditions, respectively. Finally, though the means for test-only mediation conditions have consistently lower values than those for study-test, the difference between them in any given condition does not exceed the "critical" difference of 3.1 required for significance at the .05 level. The same trend is, of course, apparent in the control condition means; additionally, it is a statistically reliable trend in all of these conditions.

Discussion. What is to be concluded from the results of this study? First, it is apparent that the present materials and procedures seem well suited to the investigation of the mediation process in paradigms other than the forward-chaining paradigm. However, the test-only procedure would seem preferable over the study-test procedure if the stimulus equivalence paradigm is of interest since mediated facilitation failed to obtain in this paradigm with the latter procedure.

Second, the forward-chaining, response-equivalence, and backward-chaining paradigms appeared to be about equally efficacious from the standpoint of the extent to which performance in Stage III was facilitated in the mediation conditions. The significant trend for the mediation-control difference to have been larger when the Stage II tests were B-C or D-C rather than C-B or D-B seems to have resulted in the main from the nominal amounts of mediated facilitation obtaining in the stimulus-equivalence paradigm. That is, since the backward-chaining paradigm which also involved C-B and D-B tests in Stage II did not differ from the forward-chaining and response-equivalence paradigms, it would seem unlikely that the nature of the Stage II list per se was a prominent factor in producing this result and, by implication, associative directionality in Stage III of the relationship between B and C terms was not a central factor. This interpretation is consistent with the fact that the directionality of the Stage III relationship between A and B terms clearly failed to influence Stage III performance in that performance in response-equivalence (Stage I: B-A) and (Stage I: A-B) forward-chaining paradigms did not differ in Stage III. Additionally, it may be noted that performance was poorest in Stage II in Condition SE, poorer than in Condition RE, even though the *transfer relation* between Stage I and II in the latter conforms to an A-D paradigm (B-A, B-C) while the former involves the C-B paradigm (A-B, C-B). This suggests more interference may have been present in Stage II in Condition SE than in Condition RE, a suggestion which at first glance seems not to be a sensible one. However, it should be recalled (Table 1) that Condition RE though nominally an A-D paradigm probably was not one functionally because of the change in the class of materials constituting the response terms in the two stages, paralogs in Stage I and trigrams in Stage II. Such a change would minimize the likelihood of interference from Stage I responses during Stage II acquisition (Postman, 1971). In short, the prospects for the unlearning of A-B during the learning of C-B in Condition SE may, indeed, have been greater than those for the unlearning of B-A during B-C learning in Condition RE.

Third, Condition BC has not usually fared as well in other studies as a "producer" of mediated facilitation as it did in the present one, both when the potential mediating associations were acquired in the laboratory (Horton & Kjeldergaard, 1961; Peterson et al., 1964) and when they were based on language habits (Cramer, 1967). Here too, the nature of the materials may have been a factor. Also, the multiple-choice format of the test trials in Stage III may have played a role; namely, the multiple-choice format may have increased the likelihood that Ss would proceed backwards from C to B to A rather than beginning with A as they would be required to do with a recall procedure. However, since Peterson et al. (1964) also used a multiple-choice format, it does not seem that this format, in and of itself, was crucial. A more likely explanation of Condition BC's equivalence to Conditions FC and RE is that it resulted from the combination of this format with an extremely high degree of Stage I-II learning, the latter having resulted from 12 trials given all Ss in each stage on lists containing only 6 pairs. The median numbers of trials to reach a 6/6 criterion was 6.38 in Stage I and 3.97 in Stage II; thus, most Ss overlearned these lists to a considerable degree.

While on the topic of degree of learning, it is worth noting that differences in the Stage I and Stage II degrees of learning among the four paradigms were nominal, the presence of statistically significant trends notwithstanding (the means of p. 212).   Thus, it would appear safe to assume that these nominal differences in Stage I-II degree of learning were not important determiners of performance in Stage III. This interpretation is also consonant with the results in our studies of degree of learning which will be reported at a later point in this paper.

Having speculated at some length regarding the comparative effectiveness of the various paradigms in the production of mediated facilitation, it is probably unproductive to speculate further until there are data at hand from research designed explicitly to address itself to this question. Nevertheless, the foregoing speculations should serve, at the very least, to suggest some of the directions in which further explorations might proceed profitably.

A final point to be noted regarding the present data relates to one made earlier in the dicussion of the transfer relation between Stage I and II in Condition RE. It will be recalled from the results section that the performance of the study-test control conditions in Stage III did not differ from each other. The point is this. The Stage I-Stage III transfer relation conformed to the A-D relation in Conditions FCC and SEC but not in Conditions REC and BCC; hence, a difference in performance favoring the latter over the former conditions would be anticipated. Such a difference did not obtain. Consistent with our earlier interpretation, the failure to find the performance in Conditions FCC and SEC inferior to performance in Conditions REC and BCC may be attributed to the change in class of materials which served as response terms in the two stages, nouns in Stage I, and trigrams in Stage III. The fact of such changes in class of materials represents an important difference between our studies and most other studies of mediation.

Concluding Comments on Materials and Procedures

No attempt has been made to evaluate explicitly all of the various aspects of our method; however, informal evaluations via numerous pilot studies, our previous failures to obtain clear-cut mediation effects under certain conditions (Schulz & Lovelace, 1964), and contrasts of our procedures with those used by others who either failed entirely to obtain, or at best obtained marginal, evidence for mediation, suggest that the following five main factors or principles, account, at least in part, for the uniformity of results obtained with the methods described earlier: (1) The presumed mediator (B) is readily discovered or elicited during the learning of A-C on Stage III because the A-B association has been learned under recall conditions and, being a common noun, it is not likely to be forgotten in a context of materials which include no other meaningful words. (2) Because both A and C are very low in meaningfulness, the likelihood is also very low that Ss have available to them idiosyncratic natural-language mediators or direct language associations to link A with C in Stage III. (3) Since mediation is an associative-phase phenomenon in the context of Underwood and Schulz's (1960) two-phase conception, the use of multiple-choice test trials in the A-C stage precludes the possibility of Ss having failed to utilize a mediating association by virtue of their having forgotten the terminal overt response (C), the necessity for response learning in Stage III is eliminated. (4) The length of the Stage III A-C test interval is long enough to permit effective utilization of a mediating association (Schulz & Weaver, 1968). (5) The gross dissimilarity between B (nouns) and C (CVC trigrams) largely neutralizes negative transfer from A-B to A-C under control conditions (Schulz, Liston, & Weaver, 1968; Poulos, 1970); thus, negative transfer need not be counteracted by the effects of mediation in facilitation conditions and, by the same token, the possibility that such transfer will inhibit Ss from adopting a mediational strategy is minimized.

Throughout the remainder of this paper, when the results of an experiment are reported, the report will not include the Stage I and II data unless they happen to be pertinent for the interpretation of the Stage III data. Furthermore, it may be assumed that a comparison of Stage I performance has been made to insure that the performance of the groups of Ss who were treated differentially in subsequent stages was comparable.

DISCOVERY AND UTILIZATION

Sometime ago we proposed (Schulz & Lovelace, 1964) that it might be productive, theoretically, to consider the process of mediation as consisting of at least two subprocesses: discovery and utilization. That is, discovery of a mediational rule as distinguished from the utilization of such a rule to determine the choice of response. Mandler (1967) has adopted a similar distinction in his model for the processing of verbal information in respect to the rules presumed to govern the manner in which Ss transform stimulus inputs.

Initially, two experiments (Schulz & Weaver, 1968) were conducted to evaluate further the merits of the duoprocess conception of mediation. They were based on the following rationale. The length of the Stage III A-C test interval (TI) was tentatively identified as one of the crucial determinants of the utilization process because presumably the utilization of mediating responses would require more time than is required when the association process does not involve such intermediate events. Similarly, it was postulated that the likelihood of discovering a mediating association would be, at least in part, contingent upon the length of the Stage III A-C study interval (SI). Accordingly, these two intervals were varied factorially employing the forward-chaining paradigm and the materials and procedures outlined earlier for experiments in which Stage III involved alternating study and test trials. It was found, as predicted, that magnitude of the mediation-control difference in A-C performance was a direct function of TI duration. However, optimum conditions for discovery (long SI) when coupled with conditions unfavorable for utilization (short TI) failed to have the anticipated consequences for A-C performance. That is, A-C performance was a direct function of the length of SI under both mediation and control conditions whereas we had expected a short TI to inhibit A-C performance under mediation conditions when SI was long. Moreover, these findings were replicated in a second experiment.[1] Nevertheless, an analysis of S's responses to questions regarding the methods employed by them in learning the A-C list revealed that the ability to report the relationship between A and B and C in mediation condition was a function of SI. Thus, 84 percent of the Ss reported using B when SI was 2.5 seconds but only 52 percent reported its use when SI was 1.0 second. A comparable 1.5 seconds' increase in length of TI increased reported use of B only 11 percent, suggesting clearly that merely allowing S more time on test trials is not equivalent to providing him with additional time to study. However, we have also found (Weaver, Hopkins, & Schulz, 1968) that mediated facilitation can be readily produced even though *no*

---

[1] Two experiments were conducted because in one an attempt was made to vary A-B strength and in the other B-C strength. These manipulations were unsuccessful. This aspect of these experiments will be considered at a later point in this paper.

study trials are present in Stage III–"0 sec. SI." Moreover, it is now clear, based on the results of our more recent studies such as Experiment I described in the preceding section of this paper, that it is generally the case that study trials are largely superfluous in the demonstration of mediated facilitation. Evidently then, discovery can be accomplished either during the SI and/or the TI. However, S's ability to utilize the TI for discovery was undoubtedly enhanced by the fact that our test-trials were of the multiple-choice variety; hence both the initial element A and the terminal element C of the A-B-C mediational chain in mediation conditions were physically present on test trials. It would be interesting to know whether or not Ss could also discover and utilize this associative chain in the absence of Stage III study trials if test trials required the recall of C-term, not merely their recognition.

In sum, it may be concluded that the length of TI can, indeed, be a critical factor in determining whether or not a mediating association can be utilized effectively. Additional and very convincing evidence regarding this matter has also been reported by Richardson (1967). As Postman (1971) has put it in his recent review of the literature in this area, "It is apparent that the time available for mediation can have an important influence on transfer; the exact conditions under which this factor becomes critical remain to be determined" (p. 1080).

It does not appear that the length of SI is an equally critical determinant of the discovery process, at least under the present conditions. Nevertheless, if the finding, discussed earlier, that an S's ability to verbalize (postexperimentally) the A-B-C relationships increases as the length of SI increases is to be acknowledged, then it may be premature to conclude that the length of SI can be ruled out unequivocally as playing a role in the discovery process.

Most of our experiments had been conducted with homogeneous-list designs on the assumption that a mixed-list design might impair the discovery process or inhibit utilization or both. However, in the present context of attempting to ascertain the merits of the discovery-utilization notion, a comparison of the homogeneous and mixed-list designs seemed to be an ideal way to shed further light on this assumption. That is, if discovery consists of the detection of an associative relation between the stimulus and response terms of the Stage III pairs, then the absence in some pairs of such a relation should reduce the probability that S will discover this relation when it is present in other pairs, relative to the probability of making such discoveries in a homogeneous list. Thus, less mediated facilitation would be expected to obtain if both the FC and FCC conditions of the forward-chaining paradigm are embodied in a single, mixed Stage III list than when separate mediation and control lists are employed.

By the same logic, embodiment in a single list of both the interference A-B, B-C_r, A-C and control A-B, D-C_r, A-C portions of the forward-chained interference paradigm should lead to less mediated interference than when homogeneous interference and control lists are used to define a forward-chained interference paradigm. The subscript r is used above to denote that the stimulus and response terms of the B-C and D-C lists of the FC and FCC conditions have been repaired in the interference paradigm.

Lastly, if mediated facilitation and mediated interference pairs are combined into a single mixed list then facilitation should be reduced still further and interference should be amplified relative to the homogeneous case. This is to be anticipated because adoption of a mediational strategy will have incompatible consequences, on the one hand, facilitating performance and on the other, leading explicitly to the choice of an incorrect response alternative. Therefore, S must either abandon the mediational rule or he must learn rapidly to discriminate between pair types. The latter discrimination and decision process is not required under homogenous list conditions.

Experiments 2, 3, and 4

Three experiments were conducted to determine if there was any empirical support for the foregoing expectations. Though these experiments were not conducted simultaneously, the results obtained from them can be compared directly inasmuch as a common Stage I list was employed in all of them and performance on this list was comparable among conditions within and across experiments.

General method. The design of these experiments was patterned after the one used by Twedt and Underwood (1959) in their comparison of mixed and homogeneous list effects in two-stage transfer paradigms. That is, the subforms of the mixed lists were such that when taken together they represented "reconstituted" versions of the homogeneous lists, thus eliminating possible differences in item difficulty as a source of confounding.

The three homogeneous-list conditions consisted of a mediated-facilitation condition (A-B, B-C, A-C), a mediated-interference condition (A-B, B-C$_r$, A-C), and a control condition (A-B, D-C, A-C). The requisite mixed-list conditions were defined through selection of suitable Stage II pairs from the homogeneous-list conditions. The Stage I and Stage III lists were the same for the mixed and homogeneous conditions. Thus, a Stage II list containing four B-C and four B-C$_r$ pairs defined the mixed facilitation-interference condition. The mixed facilitation-control condition learned a Stage II list containing four B-C and four D-C pairs. The Stage II list for the mixed-interference control condition contained four B-C$_r$ and four D-C pairs. In all other essential respects the method and procedures were the same as the study-test procedures of Experiment 1, Schulz et al. (1965) and Schulz and Weaver (1968).

The exposition will be facilitated by considering the results of the three experiments together, focusing upon the manipulations which distinguish them from one another as these become pertinent during the course of the discussion of the results. The number of Ss per condition was 40 in some conditions and 20 in the others. The reason for this is not important.

Results and discussion. The focus of Experiment 2 was on mixed-list effects. The results for Stage III in terms of total numbers of correct responses expressed as percentages of the total possible number correct are shown in Table 2. As may be seen in Table 2, the trends in the data for the mixed-list conditions are only partially in agreement with the expected ones. Thus, while mediated facilitation was dampened somewhat in both mixed-list conditions, it was not dampened to a greater extent in the facilitation-interference than in the facilitation-control conditions. The latter trend is contrary to expectations. Performance on interference pairs in the mixed facilitation-interference condition was inferior to that in the homogeneous-list interference condition as had been predicted. However, in the case of all of these trends, save for the one showing mediated facilitation to have been present in all conditions, the magnitude of the differences is disappointingly small, so small that statistical analysis revealed that they could have arisen by chance. Furthermore, these conclusions apply not only to performance in Stage III considered overall but to performance as a function of trials as well.

Even though support for the duoprocess notion was not strongly apparent in the present results, several features of these results merit comment in terms of their implications for the manner in which S must be dealing with the problems posed for him by a mixed-list in Stage III. Namely, the tendency for performance on facilitation pairs to have been inhibited less when they were combined with interference pairs than when they were combined with control pairs, suggests that Ss were able to learn rapidly to discriminate between facilitation and interference pairs. In line with this suggestion is the fact that performance on interference pairs was only slightly poorer in the mixed-list condition than in the homogeneous-list condition. Had Ss adopted a general mediational strategy, they should have been particularly vulnerable to interference in the mixed-list condition. Conversely, had Ss abandoned a mediational strategy entirely, performance on facilitation pairs in the mixed interference-facilitation condition should have been decremented dramatically. What emerges then is a picture of S as highly selective in his utilization of mediating

Table 2. Stage III performance in Experiment 2, contrasting percentages of correct responses under homogeneous and mixed list conditions.

	Homogeneous Lists		Control-Facilitation		Facilitation-Interference	
	N	%	N	%	N	%
Mediated Facilitation	20	71.62		61.81		66.50
Control	20	54.06	40	53.06	40	
Mediated Interference	20	51.62				48.62

associations, one who carefully discriminates on an item-by-item basis between those occasions on which utilization will facilitate and those on which it will interfere. Accordingly, if S were to be put under "time pressure" at the time the decision to utilize, or not to utilize, is being made, his ability to behave in this highly selective manner should be impaired. Experiment 3 was designed to focus on this issue.

In Experiment 3 the length of the test interval (TI) in Stage III was varied parametrically in half-second steps from 1.5 seconds to 3.0 seconds. The study interval was 2 seconds as in Experiment 2. There were two mixed-list conditions: one was a mixed interference-facilitation condition, the other a mixed control-interference condition. An assumption underlying this choice was that the control pairs would, as was the case in Experiment 2, be influenced minimally by the context in which they were presented, facilitation or interference. There were 20 Ss per condition at each of the four levels of TI. The procedures were otherwise the same as those in Experiment 2.

The results for performance over ten Stage III test trials are summarized in Table 3. Again, the total numbers of correct responses have been expressed as percentages of the total possible number correct.

Two features of these results are of central concern. First, did "time pressure" induced by shortening the duration of TI have any notable effects upon Ss ability to discriminate between facilitation and interference pairs in the facilitation-interference conditions? The answer to this question given by the data in Table 3 and statistically, $F\,(3,64) < 1$, is clearly negative. Second, was there, TI duration aside, any tendency for performance on interference pairs to be poorer in the mixed facilitation-interference condition than in the mixed control-interference condition? The answer to this question is also no except when TI was 1.5 seconds. At the other intervals, the trend is for the reverse to be true. Also, if the performance of the facilitation-interference condition of the

Table 3. Stage III performance in Experiment 3, contrasting percentages of correct responses in mixed facilitation-interference and control-interference lists as a function of test interval length.

	Test Interval (sec.)			
Conditions	1.5	2.0	2.5	3.0
Mixed FC-FC$_r$				
Facilitation	20.38%	53.00%	56.25%	65.75%
Interference	13.50	37.88	46.38	56.38
Mixed FCC-FC$_r$				
Control	26.50	39.25	39.62	57.50
Interference	22.12	34.38	45.12	48.62

present experiment with a 3-second TI is compared with performance under equivalent conditions in Experiment 2 (Table 2), we see that performance on facilitation pairs was again not noticeably dampened when the list contained both facilitation and interference pairs.

In Experiment 4 a change was made in the nature of the Stage III test trials in an effort to increase interference and dampen facilitation effects under dual-rule mixed-list conditions. The facilitation-interference and control-interference conditions (Experiment 3) with a three-second TI were employed (20 Ss per condition). However, we altered the nature of the test trials in Stage III A-C learning for interference pairs. In Experiments 2 and 3, the appearance among test-trial alternatives of a *mediated incorrect alternative* was allowed to occur randomly. This meant that such alternatives occurred about 37 percent of the time among the four choices available to S on test trials with interference pairs. We had ruled out the possibility of having the mediated incorrect C terms present 100 percent of the time in Experiment 2 because of the homogeneous-list interference conditions. We were fearful, particularly on early trials, that S might simply adopt a rule such as "never choose the one you think it is" in order to avoid interference from *mediated incorrect* alternatives. Since such a strategy would be less likely to be effective under mixed-list conditions, we thought 100 percent presence of mediated incorrect responses might increase the amount of interference obtaining. Hence, in Experiment 4 the randomness of the test-trial alternatives for interference pairs was constrained to produce 100 percent presence of the mediated incorrect alternative on test trials in Stage III. This change in test-trial format failed to affect Stage III performance. There were 67.00 percent correct responses on facilitation pairs in Experiment 4, which differs very little from the percentages of 66.50 and 65.75 obtained, respectively, in Experiments 2 and 3 under comparable conditions. For interference pairs performance was slightly better, not worse, with 100 percent presence in that there were 59.00 percent correct responses as compared with 48.62 percent and 56.38 percent correct in Experiments 2 and 3 with 40 percent presence. In the mixed control-interference condition the percentages were 58.50 and 52.00 for control and interference pairs respectively. Again, these percentages do not differ substantially from the comparable ones of Experiment 3, namely, 57.50 and 48.50.

General Discussion of Mixed-List Effects

If the results of all three experiments in this section are taken together, the conclusion seems inescapable that whether one employs mixed or homogeneous versions of FC and FC_r paradigms, the effects of this variation upon the amounts of transfer which obtain in Stage III were negligible with the present methods and materials. Thus, S's behavior in the present 3-stage mediation paradigms is not unlike his behavior in 2-stage transfer paradigms where the effects of mixed vs. homogeneous lists have either been null (Twedt & Underwood, 1959) or, at best, small in magnitude (Postman, 1966).

It may seem, in retrospect, that the mixed-versus-homogeneous-list manipulation was not particularly well suited for the task of ascertaining the merits of maintaining theoretically a distinction between discovery as opposed to utilization of mediating associations. Alternatively, one might say, in light of the very limited correspondence between the predicted and actual outcome of Experiment 2, that this notion should be junked because empirical support for it was not obtained. On the other hand, it could be argued, after the fact unfortunately, that the results of these experiments offer the strongest and clearest support yet obtained for this distinction. That is, if one accepts as prima facie evidence for discovery the fact that mediated facilitation did obtain under mixed facilitation-interference conditions, then the failure to obtain symmetrically equivalent amounts of mediated interference in these conditions must mean that Ss discovered the existence of mediating associations in the interference pairs but chose, wisely, *not to utilize them.*

Postman and Stark (1969a) have also obtained evidence recently that Ss were capable of highly selective utilization of associative mediation in two-stage paradigms. Thus, they found both positive transfer and retroactive facilitation of recall in the A-B, A'-B paradigm but no mediated interference or retroactive inhibition with the A-B, A'-C paradigm. Cramer (1969) has also found evidence that Ss were capable of "turning off" implicit associative responses under interference conditions. There appears to be substantial convergence of evidence from a number of different sources that facilitation and interference effects may be expected to be asymmetrical at least under certain conditions. In short, as Postman and Stark have put it, "it is well to emphasize the relevance to verbal associative learning of the distinction between habits and performance, and more specifically the distinction between potential and functional mediators" (1969a, p. 797).

Though there appears to be agreement that the Ss can be associatively selective, discriminatory in their utilization process, or "turn off" implicit responses, the task that lies ahead is the one of determining more precisely what it means to say that they can do this. That is, we know at present very little about the nature of the mechanism by which this highly selective behavior is achieved. Hence, in the framework of the present program this means specifying more precisely the conditions of which discovery is a function and the manner in which the discovery and utilization processes interact, particularly in relation to the consequences of utilization. We have not made any great strides as yet toward the realization of this objective, but perhaps it is worth describing what we have done in the hopes that by making these data available to others the rate of progress will be accelerated. These efforts have centered in the main around an attempt to discover the conditions which are requisite for the production of mediated interference.

MEDIATED INTERFERENCE[2]

As we have already learned from Experiments 2, 3, and 4, the extent to which mediated interference occurs with the present procedures and materials is, at best, nominal. Additionally, there is another source of data consistent with this conclusion. These data were obtained by Hopkins and Schulz (1967) in an experiment conducted almost simultaneously with Experiment 2. In their study, two of three independent comparisons of interference and control conditions revealed performance in the former to be inferior to performance in the latter condition, but not significantly so. The control condition used differed from the one used in Experiments 2, 3, and 4 in that the interstage relations were A-B, B-E_r, A-C. Also, homogeneous-list conditions were employed throughout. Therefore, it seems justifiable to conclude that the failure to obtain mediated interference in Experiments 2, 3, and 4 was not somehow inherent in those particular materials and conditions; rather, it seems generally the case that mediated interference is difficult to generate under conditions where test-trials in Stage III A-C learning involve recognition rather than recall of C terms. However, as Postman (1971) has pointed out in his recent review of the literature for three-stage paradigms involving associations acquired in the laboratory, the evidence for the demonstration of mediated interference under recall conditions is not uniformly positive either, a fact we had also noted. This led us to undertake Experiment 5.

Experiment 5

Successful demonstrations of mediated interference with the FC_r paradigm (e.g., Horton & Wiley, 1967b) had employed test trials requiring recall in all three stages. It seemed possible, therefore, that our use of recognition procedures in Stage II might in some way have prevented interference from becoming manifest. For example, we had thought, in reflecting upon the results of a study mentioned above (Hopkins & Schulz, 1967), that the C_r terms, CVC trigrams of low meaningfulness, might not have become sufficiently integrated as units during the course of Stage II B-C_r training with multiple-choice test trials to enable them to serve as effective competitors in Stage III. Accordingly, half the Ss learned by the recall method and half by our usual recognition method in Stage II of this experiment.

Alternatively, is it the use of recognition procedures in Stage III A-C learning that allows Ss to avoid mediated interference? That is, would mediated interference become manifest, if S had to recall rather than merely recognize the C-terms in Stage III? Thus, the design of the experiment may be seen as having

---

[2] Though a number of the experiments described in this section were completed prior to the appearance of certain extremely relevant data from 2-stage transfer studies, no attempt will be made to retain a chronological order in the present discussion.

consisted of a factorial manipulation of Stage II and Stage III test procedure, and recall versus recognition.

Method. The control-interference condition lists of Experiment 3 were used. There were 80 Ss, 20 per condition. The remaining procedures (e.g., time intervals, etc.) were our "standard" ones.

Results and discussion. Since Stage II in this experiment involved a new differential treatment, the results for this stage warrant brief comment. The Ss learning their Stage II list by the method of recall required significantly more trials, F (1,76) = 25.00, $p < .01$, to attain criterion ($\bar{X}$ = 12.72) than those learning by the recognition method ($\bar{X}$ = 7.55), a result which is entirely consistent with what might have been expected.

The results for Stage III in terms of total numbers of correct responses over 10 A-C test-trials are shown in Figure 3 expressed as percentages of the total possible number correct. The upper pair of curves denotes performance under recognition conditions in Stage III and the findings correspond precisely to the

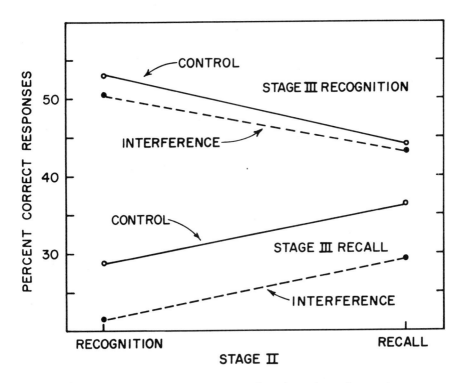

Figure 9—3. Stage III performance in terms of total numbers of correct responses over ten A-C trials expressed as percentages of total possible number of correct as a function of Stage II and III test- procedure and pair-type.

ones we have usually obtained under these conditions. However, when Stage III involved recall on test trials, performance on interference pairs was clearly inferior to performance on control pairs. Statistically, the interaction between pair-type and test-method in Stage III is a reliable one, $F(1,76) = 4.26$, $p < .05$. Also, further F tests reveal that interference and control pairs under Stage II recognition conditions do not differ, $F(1,79) < 1$. Under Stage III recall conditions, the difference between them is highly significant, $F(1,79) = 11.77$, $p < .01$.

As in Stage II, performance in Stage III under recognition conditions was generally superior to performance under recall conditions, $F(1,76) = 34.71$, $p < .01$. Furthermore, as is obvious from Figure 3, method of testing in Stage II interacted with the method employed in Stage III, $F(1,76) = 5.28$, $p < .05$, reflecting a generalized decrement in performance due to a change in method of testing in Stage III. However, this decrement was unrelated to the effects of pair-type since interference and control pairs were affected equally under both recall and recognition conditions in Stage III. Finally, it is to be noted, based upon inspection of the acquisition curves, that all of the effects discussed above were characteristic of performance throughout Stage III.

If it is the case that we demonstrated mediated interference, this fact should be reflected in the type of overt errors which the Ss made. Accordingly, the following analysis was performed. The responses of each S to interference pairs were classified as correct, mediated errors, or nonmediated errors, under both recognition and recall conditions. A similar classification was made of his responses to control pairs except here the mediated error category was replaced by one we have come to term "pseudomediated" errors. A pseudomediated error is an error made on a control pair which *would have been* a mediated error had this pair been serving as an interference pair. It will be recalled that pair-type is defined in Stage II through suitable manipulations of item pairings in this stage. Hence, it is possible to score control items in Stage III *as if* they were interference pairs and thereby derive an empirical baseline, as it were, for the frequency with which "mediated errors" would be made under control conditions. Such a baseline is particularly useful under recognition conditions where S is likely to guess at least part of the time.

The results of the above analysis are shown in Table 4. In Table 4 the data are differentiated only in terms of Stage III test method and pair-type; data from Ss who had recall in Stage II have been combined with those who had recognition in that stage. Both the actual numbers of responses in each classification and these numbers expressed as percentages of the total number of responses (errors + correct) are shown in Table 4.[3] The latter conversion is

---

[3] It should be borne in mind that the percentages of correct responses in Table 4 are not comparable to those reported in Figure 3 or Tables 2 and 3, the latter percentages were based on number correct/total possible number correct including failures to respond. The percentages reported here and subsequently for Experiments 6, 7, 8, 9, and 10 were calculated with failures to respond excluded.

Table 4. Experiment 5: Correct responses, mediated errors, pseudomediated errors, and nonmediated errors expressed as percentages based on total number of responses with failures to respond excluded.

Conditions		Correct Responses	Nonmed. Errors	Pseudo or Med. Errors	Total No. of Responses
Recall					
Interference	f	408	282	95	785
	%	51.97	35.92	12.10	
Control	f	521	308	34	863
	%	60.37	35.69	3.94	
Recognition					
Interference	f	767	337	72	1176
	%	65.22	28.66	6.12	
Control	f	786	309	50	1145
	%	68.65	26.99	4.37	

designed to take into account the higher response rate in recognition than in recall conditions. Inspection of Table 4 reveals with exceptional clarity the "trade-offs" in terms of types of errors which reflect the operation of mediated interference under recall conditions. Fewer responses were attempted on interference pairs, and the percentage of mediated errors increased by approximately the same amount as the percentage of correct responses decreased for these pairs when contrasted with the control pairs. For the recognition conditions, there is only a slight elevation in the percentage of mediated errors and a slightly greater number of response attempts for interference relative to control pairs. Thus explicit evidence for the presence of mediated interference is provided by the analysis of overt errors.

The results of Experiment 5 for the recall conditions confirm, with a mixed-list, those obtained by Horton and Wiley (1967b). At the same time, the results for recognition conditions confirm once again our previous findings under these conditions. An additional feature of the present results which should not be overlooked is the fact that our previous failures to obtain mediated interference would not seem to be attributable in some peculiar way to our choice of task or material parameters, save of course, the mode of testing. What now? Two things.

First, we entertained briefly the hypothesis that we had encountered an instance of the state of affairs which has intrigued and confronted investigators of memory for quite a long time. Namely, it has often been the case during the course of the investigation of the phenomena of memory that results obtained with recognition measures often have differed from those obtained with recall. Indeed, some writers have gone so far as to suggest that recognition and recall may be reflecting two different kinds of memory traces (Adams, 1967) and, hence, it is to be expected that the laws for recognition will differ from those for recall. Accordingly, one might expect that interference processes, mediated or direct, might be mitigated in some way by multiple-choice test procedures. The evidence now available suggests that the latter proposition is false.

Postman and Stark (1969b) have demonstrated, using multiple-choice procedures similar to ours, that the amounts of negative transfer obtaining in two-stage A-C and A-B_r paradigms were as great, if not greater, under recognition as under recall conditions. Furthermore, Poulos (1970) has recently replicated this finding for the A-B_r paradigm. One must continue to wonder, however, how Ss appear to be able in some way to inhibit interfering response tendencies in a three-stage FC_r paradigm while they appear unable to do so in a two-stage A-B_r paradigm, even though the two situations are logically and theoretically isomorphic.

Second, though in retrospect it might have been wiser to have settled for "two memory systems," at least for a time, and to have set about investigating mediated interference with recall procedures, we lacked that wisdom. We proceeded instead to try to find a way to obtain mediated interference under recognition conditions.

Returning to the mixed-list case, we reasoned that there were at least two ways in which S could discriminate between interference pairs and control or facilitation pairs. He may "match" the terminal response of the mediational chain against his "memory" of the A-C pair presented on study trials. If they "match" he chooses C, if they fail to "match" he rejects C_r, and if C_r is present among the alternatives, he chooses the C he thinks it is or guesses among the remaining alternatives. Alternatively, he may base his discrimination upon a "partitioning" of the items into two lists, a "list" in which what you learned before helps you, and a "list" in which what you learned before impairs your performance. Such a discrimination would most likely be based on a discrimination between A and/or B terms. Since in either case, the Ss ability to make a discrimination must be contingent upon the degree of similarity that is present among the to-be-discriminated items, it should be possible to obtain evidence regarding the basis of S's discrimination by manipulating similarity.

Experiment 6

Method. In Experiment 6 similarity among C-terms was manipulated. This was done by replacing the C-terms of the lists used in Experiment 5 with high-similarity C-terms taken from List 3 of Underwood and Schulz (1959). The low-similarity lists were the same as those employed in Experiment 5. Thus, the lists defined mixed interference—control conditions with either high or low formal similarity among C-terms. A total of 48 Ss, 24 per group, was employed. The procedures were, with one exception, the same as those used previously and in Experiment 5. The exception was that Ss were required to push a button beneath the alternative of their choice on test-trials in Stage III.[4]

Results. The outcome that was anticipated according to the notion that high-formal similarity among C-terms would prevent S from successfully discriminating between control and interference pairs was that conditions and similarity would interact.

The groups did not differ in Stage I ($t < 1$). In Stage II, 12.04 trials were required to achieve criterion on the high-similarity as opposed to 7.04 trials for the low similarity lists, $t(46) = 3.82, p < .01$.[5]

The outcome in Stage III was totally unexpected. The data are displayed in Table 5 in a format parallel to the one used in Table 4 to describe the results of Experiment 5 when correct responses, nonmediated, pseudomediated, or mediated errors were examined.

As may be seen in Table 5, the data are very orderly, but there is no evidence that similarity and conditions interacted ($F < 1$). And most surprisingly of all, the reason that they did not interact is that significant amounts of mediated interference, $F (1,46) = 6.22, p < .05$, obtained under both high and

Table 5. Experiment 6: Correct responses, mediated errors, pseudomediated errors, and nonmediated errors expressed as percentages based on total number of responses with failures to respond excluded.

Conditions		Correct Responses	Nonmed. Errors	Pseudo or Med. Errors	Total No. of Responses
High Similarity					
Interference	f	441	216	167	824
	%	53.52	26.21	20.27	
Control	f	538	190	95	823
	%	65.37	23.09	11.54	
Low Similarity					
Interference	f	505	180	169	854
	%	59.13	21.08	19.79	
Control	f	604	169	76	849
	%	71.14	19.91	8.95	

[4] We had intended to measure latency of choice. Unfortunately, the system designed to record latencies malfunctioned soon after the experiment was begun. The experiment was completed with Ss pushing buttons, but the recording of latencies was abandoned.

[5] Interestingly, 13 Ss failed to achieve criterion in Stage II on the high-similarity lists while none failed to achieve it on the low-similarity lists, suggesting that rather substantial S selection had occurred; however, in spite of this selection, the groups had virtually identical first-list means of 8.75 for low, and 8.92 for high similarity.

low similarity conditions. Note also in Table 5, as in Experiment 5 under recall conditions, there is a direct "trade-off" between correct responses and mediated errors. Further, it may be noted that the magnitude of the effect of mediated interference is slightly larger here than it was in Experiment 5 under recall conditions. Finally, as was to be expected, overall performance was poorer under high than low similarity conditions, $F(1,46) = 5.70, p < .05$.

Could these data be telling the truth? Is one to conclude that Ss can inhibit a "slip-of-the-lip," but are incapable of inhibiting a "slip-of-the-finger"? Ridiculous!

Experiment 7

In this experiment we replicated Experiment 6 except that Ss were required to choose their responses on test trials by giving the number below them (the method used in most of our experiments) instead of pushing a button as they had done in Experiment 6. Again, even though no evidence for an interaction between C-term similarity and conditions was evident in Experiment 6, we hoped it might emerge here. That is, because of the entirely unexpected outcome of Experiment 6, we were concerned that it might have been a "fluke" of some kind in respect to the presence of mediated interference under conditions of low C-term similarity.

Results and discussion. The results of Experiment 7 may be seen in Table 6 where Stage III performance has been summarized. While a slight trend toward mediated interference and an interaction of similarity with conditions are evident in these data, these trends are small and statistically nonsignificant. The high and low similarity groups did not differ in Stage I but a significant effect due to similarity was present in Stage II; hence, it is somewhat puzzling that in Stage III C-term similarity failed to be a significant source of variance. If the levels of performance achieved in this experiment with "number-calling" are contrasted with those in Experiment 6 with button-pushing (Table 5 in relation to Table 6) and conditions are disregarded, the overall percentages of correct responses were 62.33 and 62.58 in Experiment 6 and Experiment 7, respectively.

In sum, we are quite frankly at a loss to explain why mode of responding should have such an apparently profound effect upon the likelihood that mediated interference becomes manifest. We are currently in the process of replicating Experiment 6 *with button-pushing.* As far as the discrimination hypotheses which led us to initiate this line of investigation are concerned, it seems clear from the fact that a similarity by conditions interaction was not obtained in either Experiment 6 or Experiment 7 that these hypotheses are untenable—untenable at least insofar as C-terms represent the basis upon which this discrimination is made.

Table 6. Experiment 7: Correct responses, mediated errors, pseudomediated errors, and nonmediated errors expressed as percentages based on total number of responses with failures to respond excluded.

Conditions		Correct Responses	Nonmed. Errors	Pseudo or Med. Errors	Total No. of Responses
High Similarity					
Interference	f	446	176	123	745
	%	59.87	23.62	16.51	
Control	f	482	184	79	745
	%	64.70	24.70	10.60	
Low Similarity					
Interference	f	484	168	125	777
	%	62.29	21.62	16.09	
Control	f	496	188	98	782
	%	63.43	24.04	12.53	

Experiment 8

Our assault on the discrimination hypothesis took several tacks in addition to the one described in Experiments 6 and 7. In Experiment 8 a very short (.70 second) study interval was introduced in Stage III. Also, Ss were "forced" to respond on test trials in Stage III. Our reasoning was that if Ss were not given much time to study the A-C pairs in Stage III and were "forced" to respond on test trials, then at least during the early trials S's ability to discriminate between interference and control, or between interference and facilitation pairs, in the mixed-list situation might be impaired.

Method. The low similarity lists of the previous experiments were employed, one set involving a mixed-list version of facilitation and interference conditions and the other mixed interference-control conditions. The mode of responding on test trials was "number calling"; however, as distinguished from the neutral instructions usually given, Ss were told they must respond to every pair on test trials in Stage III. Also, as already noted, the study-interval in Stage III was .70 second instead of the usual 2 seconds. Otherwise, the method was identical to the one employed in Experiment 7 and most of our previous experiments. There were 12 Ss per group.

Results and discussion. In Table 7, where the results of this study are shown for performance in Stage III, a rather interesting pattern of trends is apparent in the data. First, it may be noted that performance on interference

Table 7. Experiment 8: Correct responses, mediated errors, pseudomediated errors, and nonmediated errors expressed as percentages based on total number of responses with failures to respond excluded.

Conditions		Correct Responses	Nonmed. Errors	Pseudo or Med. Errors	Total No. of Responses
Mixed FC_r-FC					
Interference	f	119	142	187	448
	%	26.56	31.70	41.74	
Facilitation	f	250	123	88	461
	%	54.23	26.68	19.09	
Mixed FC_r-FCC					
Interference	f	145	173	135	453
	%	32.01	38.19	25.80	
Control	f	166	181	110	457
	%	36.32	39.61	24.07	

pairs in the facilitation-interference condition was only very slightly above the *chance level* of 25 percent correct for four alternative multiple-choice tests. A very high percentage of the responses (41.74 percent) were of the *mediated incorrect* variety; indeed, this percentage approximates closely the percentage of opportunities Ss had to make such errors. Performance on facilitation pairs was not only substantially above chance but also well above that on control pairs in the control-interference condition. In short, it appears that Ss under the present conditions adopted a mediational strategy for all pairs in the facilitation-interference condition and were unable (made no effort?) to discriminate between them. The fact that the acquisition functions remained essentially flat across the 10 Stage III trials for both types of pairs is also consistent with this interpretation.

Under interference-control conditions performance on interference and control pairs did not differ reliably, though the difference is in the expected direction. Performance was above chance and improved slowly with trials. Note also that the percentage of mediated incorrect errors for interference pairs was well below that for these same pairs in the facilitation-interference condition and only slightly greater than the percentage for pseudomediated errors on control pairs. These findings have two important implications. First, they suggest that if mediated interference is to occur, a short test interval and forced responding are not sufficient conditions, in and of themselves, to produce mediated-interference. Second, it would appear that Ss simply did not behave as if a mediational strategy were applicable, albeit applicable in a maladaptive sense, under interference-control conditions, as opposed to having in some way discriminated between pair types in order to avoid interference.

The findings of this study suggest that it may be productive in future research to vary systematically the length of the Stage III study interval with mixed lists to determine the point at which it becomes possible for *S* to respond more selectively than he was evidently able to do when this interval was .70 second. Additionally, it seems in retrospect regrettable that a facilitation-interference condition was not included in Experiments 5, 6, and 7. Perhaps, performance in such a condition should be examined in the context of the other manipulations performed in those studies.

Experiment 9

If *S*s base their discrimination between pair-types on the information gained from Stage III study trials, then it should be possible to disrupt this discrimination by introducing a delay or retention interval between study and test trials. The merits of this proposition were assessed in Experiment 9.

Method. Using the materials and procedures (including forced-responding instructions in Stage III) of Experiment 8 but a "normal" two-second Stage III study interval, a 20-second delay interval was interpolated between study and test, and between test and study trials in Stage III. To prevent rehearsal during the delay interval, a recognition-memory task requiring *S*s to designate two-digit numbers as "old" or "new" was made a part of Stage III.[6] The numbers were presented aurally via a tape recorder to *S* who responded "old" or "new" orally. On the average across trials, 50 percent of the digits were new and 50 percent old. A total of 24 *S*s, 12 per condition, was used in this study.

Results and discussion. The data for Stage III are summarized in Table 8. The pattern of trends in these data is much like the pattern for Experiment 8. That is, performance in Stage III was poorest on the interference pairs in the interference-facilitation condition, slightly better on these pairs in the control-interference condition, and best on facilitation pairs, with performance on control pairs intermediate between interference and facilitation pairs. The trend for percentages of mediated errors was also entirely consistent with the one for percentages of correct responses. However, the differences among pair-types are not as large as they were in Experiment 8 either in respect to correct responses or mediated errors. Statistically, performance on facilitation pairs differed reliably from the other pair types, but performance on interference and control

---

[6] We have found, incidentally, that a recognition-memory task of this type can be combined readily with a variety of other tasks to prevent rehearsal, provided of course that *S* is led to believe his performance on both tasks is of equally great interest to us. In fact, *S*s seem to enjoy the change of pace introduced by switching from one task to another. The recognition-memory task can be used, for example, in a Peterson and Peterson (1959) short-term memory study in place of counting backwards (Schulz, 1969) or as a filler task in the Goggin (1966) nominal-lists short-term memory task (Holborn, 1968).

Table 8. Experiment 9: Correct responses, mediated errors, pseudomediated errors, and nonmediated errors expressed as percentages based on total number of responses with failures to respond excluded.

Conditions		Correct Responses	Nonmed. Errors	Pseudo or Med. Errors	Total No. of Responses
Mixed FC$_r$-FC					
Interference	f	231	96	132	459
	%	50.33	20.92	28.76	
Facilitation	f	364	76	32	472
	%	77.12	16.10	6.78	
Mixed FC$_r$-FCC					
Interference	f	257	110	95	462
	%	55.63	23.81	20.56	
Control	f	282	131	47	460
	%	61.30	28.48	10.22	

pairs did not differ significantly. Nevertheless, the trends are suggestive of the possibility that a delay interval impairs S's ability to discriminate between facilitation and interference pairs in the mixed interference-facilitation condition.

Experiment 10

Earlier an effort was made to disrupt S's ability to discriminate between facilitation and interference, or control and interference pairs by making the C-terms highly similar. The logic of the present experiment was the same except that it was the stimulus terms, the A-terms, that were made highly similar. A low-similarity condition was not included in the design because of the anticipated loss of Ss who would fail to master the high-similarity list in Stage I, thus introducing a selection artifact which would have made a high similarity-low similarity comparison questionable. It was in fact the case that the loss of Ss in this study exceeded 50 percent, a figure which is much above the normal loss rate.

   Method. The present lists were simply the "turned-over" versions of the high-similarity lists used in Experiment 7. Thus, in the present lists the A-terms were CVC trigrams high in formal similarity and the C-terms were paralogs. There were 16 Ss in each group. To reduce loss of Ss due to failure to attain criterion in Stage I, the length of the test interval was increased from 2 to

Table 9. Experiment 10: Correct responses, mediated errors, pseudomediated errors, and nonmediated errors expressed as percentages based on total number of responses with failures to respond excluded.

Conditions		Correct Responses	Nonmed. Errors	Pseudo or Med. Errors	Total No. of Responses
Mixed FC_r-FC					
Interference	f	218	129	144	491
	%	44.39	26.27	29.32	
Facilitation	f	384	74	55	513
	%	74.85	14.42	10.72	
Mixed FC_r-FCC					
Interference	f	214	129	116	459
	%	46.62	28.10	25.27	
Control	f	290	132	48	470
	%	61.70	28.08	10.21	

3-seconds. Also, Ss were not "forced to respond" in Stage III. In all other respects, Experiments 7 and 10 were identical.

Results and discussion. The Ss in this study, in spite of being a highly selected sample, required 17.31 and 17.56 trials in the Stage I to attain criterion in the facilitation-interference and control-interference conditions, respectively. Since Stage I usually requires about 10 trials, the effects of high A-term similarity were substantial.

Performance in Stage III has been summarized in the usual manner in Table 9. It is immediately evident from the data in Table 9 that mediated interference was present in both facilitation-interference and in the control-interference conditions. The difference in performance as a function of pair-type was highly significant in the control-interference condition, $t(15) = 3.60$, $p < .01$. However, when these pair types were compared "between-groups" the trend toward interference only approached significance, $t(30) = 1.83$, $p < .10$. The latter occurred because of the variability due to Ss in this comparison, even though the difference in performance was actually slightly larger than the "within groups" interference-control difference. The trend in the data showing mediated facilitation to have obtained was also a reliable one, $t(30) = 2.23$, $p < .05$, when performance on facilitation and control pairs was compared. The trends in the percentages of responses which were mediated or pseudomediated errors were, as before, clearly in line with the trends for percentages of correct responses.

In short, the present data offer strong support for the discrimination hypothesis. And they suggest, further, that the stimulus-terms play a prominent role as the basis for making discriminations between pair types.

General Discussion: Mediated Interference

If one considers only performance on interference pairs in Stage III and uses as a measure of performance the percentages of the total numbers of responses given which were correct ones, then the following factors seem to have been influential in lowering S's level of performance on these pairs. For each factor, the percentage correct on interference pairs is given. (1) A short test interval (1.5 second) under facilitation-interference conditions (44.4 percent). (2) A short study interval (.70 second) under either facilitation-interference (26.6 percent) or interference-control (32.0 percent) conditions. (3) High A-term similarity under both facilitation-interference (44.4 percent) and interference-control conditions (46.6 percent). (4) Delay (20 seconds) between study and test trials under facilitation-interference conditions (50.3 percent). (5) High C-term similarity under interference-control conditions when the mode of response was a button push (53.5 percent). (6) Recall as the mode of response under interference-control conditions (51.9 percent). At all other times the percentage correct on interference pairs ranged from 55.6 percent to 67.0 percent, the average percentage for these fourteen other times being 61.8 percent[7].

Shifting consideration to facilitation pairs, there were only two notable factors affecting performance on these pairs: (1) Short test interval (1.5 seconds) under facilitation-interference conditions (56.9 percent). (2) Short study interval (.70 second) under facilitation-interference conditions (54.2 percent). The average percentage correct on eight other occasions was 77.5. These percentages ranged from 73.5 percent to 82.9 percent.

Treating the control-pair data in a similar fashion, we find only one factor which appears to have drastically affected performance on these pairs. This factor was a short test interval (.70 seconds) in Stage III (36.3 percent). The remaining percentages ranged from 58.4 to 71.1 with the average being 64.2 on 15 other occasions. This is not to say that such factors as test-interval length, delay between study and test trials, A-term similarity, C-term similarity with button-pushing as the mode of response, or recall as the response mode did not have any effect; rather these effects may be regarded as nominal when contrasted with the effect of a short-study interval or when contrasted with the effects of these variables on interference and facilitation pairs.

The above summarization may appear to be a rather gross one which ignores many of the nuances of the outcomes of one or another experiment, nuances which were noted at the time a particular experiment was being discussed. On the contrary, given the broader perspective afforded us by viewing, for the first

[7] Except TI = 2.0 sec. under interference-control conditions in Experiment 3 (53.6 percent) which is inconsistent with data for other TI's in that experiment, e.g., TI = 2.5 or 3.0.

time in this paper, the "forest" as a whole, as it were, it appears we may have spent too much time inspecting the individual "trees." Thus, when one acknowledges the fact that the foregoing summarization involved "summing across" nine different experiments (Experiments 2-10), some of them with numerous conditions with a variety of experimental manipulations, points in time, Es, lists, and procedural variations, it is extremely startling to find that, viewed in this larger perspective, so few of these factors seem to have made a genuine just-noticeable difference in performance. This is particularly true in the case of control and facilitation pairs. Indeed, it appears justifiable to conclude that the percentages of the responses an S will make which are *correct* ones over the course of 10 Stage III test trials in the present situation will be as follows, give or take roughly 5 percent: (1) for interference pairs, 62 percent; (2) for control pairs, 64 percent; and (3) for facilitation pairs, 78 percent. Therefore, any variable or factor having an effect which lowers performance on interference pairs by more than 5 percent or enhances performance by more than 5 percent on facilitation pairs from the levels just stated, while leaving performance on control pairs essentially unchanged, may be viewed as a variable or factor of special significance in relation to the process of mediation, either mediated interference, mediated facilitation, or both.

Further, by way of summarization, it should be noted that performance on interference pairs was inferior to performance on control pairs in *14* of 15 direct, and independent comparisons in Experiments 2-10 where pair-type was the only source of differential treatment. The results of these studies, considered as a whole, suggest that the conditions for impairment of performance due to mediated interference were present quite generally in our experiments even though the degree of impairment was seldom of an order of magnitude such that it could be regarded as statistically reliable. Nevertheless, it seems equally clear that the present results are not easily accommodated in the context of existing theoretical frameworks, either of a cognitive or of an associatve variety.

Given that the mediation paradigms we have been studying may be viewed as being fundamentally a form of a problem-solving or conceptual task, a view we share with Earhard and Mandler (1965), it seems to be of little additional consequence whether the results are interpreted in cognitive or in associationistic terms. The fact which requires explanation is that Ss apparently were often capable of "solving" a relatively complex problem such as the one posed by a mixed facilitation-interference condition in virtually a *single trial.* That is, there was little, if any, evidence in our data of interaction between trials and pair-type.

Cognitively, we may see S as having achieved this solution by adopting two different strategies, utilizing a mediational strategy for some pairs but not for other pairs. Since these strategies have incompatible consequences, S must also be seen as being able to discriminate with a high degree of accuracy, after but a single study trial, between the pair-types to which these two rules apply.

Associatively, one could follow Postman's (1968) lead and account for the asymmetry in the effectiveness of mediated facilitation and mediated interference by acknowledging that Ss have available to them a wide variety of response dispositions or habits which they are capable of performing selectively, depending upon the demands of the task or problem and the consequences of utilizing one or the other response disposition.

In short, we have on the one hand selective strategy utilization and we have on the other selective associative arousal. The key to an understanding of the asymmetry is seen, in either case, to rest with a more precise determination of what it means to say that Ss are selective.

How might one proceed to answer this question more fully? We know, based on the results of Experiment 1, and from other sources (Weaver, Hopkins, & Schulz, 1968), that mediated facilitation will obtain under test-only conditions in Stage III. Consequently, it must follow that were one to compare the FC and FC_r paradigms under these conditions, the facilitation and interference effects must be *symmetrical.* No other outcome is possible unless S is provided with informative feedback regarding the "correctness" and "incorrectness" of his responses. Hence, one might ask what else it does take to enable S to develop the requisite discrimination between pair-types under these conditions, if, indeed, anything will do so.

We also know, based on the present series of studies, that it is possible to disrupt or impair S's ability to discriminate between pair-types so that mediated interference becomes manifest. Moreover, this discrimination seemed to be contingent more directly on the nature of the stimulus terms (Experiment 10) than upon the nature of the response terms (Experiment 7), except possibly when the mode of response was a button push (Experiment 6). Perhaps, similarity manipulations warrant further consideration as a vehicle for determining the conditions under which S's responding is selective and conditions under which he is incapable of being selective?

Equally interesting, but more perplexing, are the following unresolved issues: (1) Why should S, under otherwise comparable conditions, be able to monitor his recognition responses more effectively than his recall responses (Experiment 5)? (2) Why is it that mediated interference was obtained recently in copious amounts with both the A-B, A-B$_r'$ and A-B, A$'$-B$_r$ paradigms when homogeneous—single rule—lists were employed with B-B$'$ and A-A$'$ based on taxonomic similarity (Wickens, Ory, & Graf, 1970)? (3) Why do Ss appear to be incapable of inhibiting interfering response tendencies in two-stage A-B, A-C and A-B, A-B$_r$ transfer situations with multiple-choice recognition procedures virtually identical (Postman & Stark, 1969b) to those employed in our three-stage situation? If S is capable of "turning off" an inappropriate response tendency under one set of circumstances, he should be equally capable of doing so under less challenging circumstances, e.g., in a two-stage homogeneous-lists situation as opposed to three-stage mixed-lists situation. (4) Are the differences in results between two-stage and three-stage transfer situations resolvable in terms of the proposition that the latter induce a "problem-solving set" while the former do not?

Finally, specific questions in the present context aside, a fact which must not be overlooked in the concern with the details of the present research is that the question how organisms monitor their response tendencies is empirically and theoretically a central one for the understanding of behavior generally, and particularly so for the understanding of the problem-solving process. Thus, while investigators of the process of mediation have tended, historically, to concentrate their efforts on the phenomenon of mediated facilitation, seen in the present light it is equally critical to come to understand more fully the phenomenon of mediated interference. As has often been emphasized (e.g., Duncan, 1959; Schulz, 1960; DiVesta & Walls, 1967), one of the crucial dimensions of the problem-solving process involves S's ability to inhibit dominant but inappropriate response tendencies. In short, the ability to develop new response patterns or select more appropriate ones from among available habit patterns, when those that are aroused initially prove ineffective, distinguishes the adaptive organism from a maladaptive one.

DEGREE OF STAGE I AND STAGE II LEARNING

Internal analyses, involving rankings for individual Ss, of A-B and/or B-C items in terms of their strength as indexed by a number of times the correct B or C terms were given on test trials during Stages I and/or II have shown A-C performance to be related to A-B and/or B-C strength under Conditions FC and FCC in a manner that accords with the S-R view. They were directly related in the case of FC and unrelated in the case of FCC (e.g., Schulz, Liston, & Weaver, 1968). However, attempts to duplicate this relationship when strength has been manipulated directly in the laboratory have not been particularly successful (e.g., Horton & Hartmann, 1963; Peterson, 1964; Schwenn & Underwood, 1965; Schulz & Weaver, 1968). Some of the possible reasons for these failures have been discussed elsewhere (Schulz & Weaver, 1968) and need not be reiterated. It will suffice to note that, for one or another reason, the differences in strength that were produced probably were too small to have had detectable effects upon Stage III performance. For additional discussions of the ambiguous state of our knowledge on this topic, cf., Postman (1971), and Saltz (1971).

In the experiments reported below the variations in degree of learning were as wide as they could be made within the constraints imposed by the requirement than an S's participation in them would be limited to a single experimental session whose duration did not exceed 90 minutes.

A second facet of our efforts to determine the effects of degree of learning under FC conditions was that of defining degree of learning in Stages I and II in either of two ways, in terms of the number of trials or in terms of the number of correct responses.

Third, since it apparently had not been attempted by previous investigators, both the degree of Stage I and the degree of Stage II learning were systematically varied within the same experiment in two of the studies reported below.

Experiment 11

The focus in this study was upon the development of wide differences in the degree of Stage I A-B learning in Conditions FC and FCC while degree of Stage II learning remained constant. Degree of learning was defined by the number of trials S received.

Method. Stage I A-B strength was varied in the context of the FC and FCC paradigms by allowing Ss 3, 6 or 22 trials of practice on A-B. The B-C or D-C lists of Stage II were practiced for a fixed number of trials, six, in all conditions. This latter number was chosen for two reasons. First, it permitted the detection of the effects of Stage I degree of learning on performance in Stage II. Second, on the average about six trials are usually required to attain a criterion of two-perfect recitations in these paradigms in our other experiments. Thus, the design was a 3 X 2 factorial combination of degrees of learning and paradigms. There were 16 Ss per cell. A seventh group of 16 Ss, an additional control, received 6 trials on A-B but no interpolated practice on B-C or D-C. This group worked instead on the pyramid puzzle for a period of time equivalent to that which was required in the other conditions to administer 6 Stage II trials.

The status of A-B was assessed immediately prior to the initiation of Stage III A-C practice by giving all Ss an A-B recall test (1.5-second rate). Thus, it was thought it would be possible to examine on an item-by-item basis performance on A-C, conditionalized upon correct or incorrect recall of A-B. Following A-B recall all Ss received five alternating study and test trials on A-C.

In all other essential regards (e.g., materials, presentation rates, and procedures) the methods employed in this experiment were the same as those used in our "standard" FC-FCC experiments.

Results. Performance in Stages I and II does not required detailed consideration. In Stage I Ss given 3 trials on A-B had an average total number of correct responses of 7.24 while those receiving 22 trials averaged 146.94 correct. The FC and FCC conditions did not differ from each other across levels of A-B learning. As has been observed frequently in the past, performance under FC conditions was inferior to that under FCC conditions, $F(1,90) = 33.23, p < .01$, the average difference between Conditions FC and FCC for all levels of A-B learning combined being 8.49 correct responses. However, in spite of the presence of very large differences in degree of A-B learning, neither the learning of B-C nor D-C was affected differentially. The interaction of conditions with degree of A-B learning was nonsignificant, $F(2,90) = 2.38, p > .05$. Degree of Stage I learning was also not significant as a main effect.

The data of main concern here are shown in Table 10. The upper portion of the table contains the means and S.D.'s for recall of A-B prior to Stage III. The lower portion contains the means and S.D.'s for total number of correct responses over the five trials in Stage III on A-C.

Table 10. Means and SDs for correct responses in recall of A-B and performance in Stage III as a function of the number of trials in Stage I and Conditions in Experiment 11.

		Number of Stage I Trials					
		3		6		22	
Conditions		$\bar{X}$	SD	$\bar{X}$	SD	$\bar{X}$	SD
	FC	1.62	1.20	4.31	1.89	7.19	.98
A-B Recall	FCC	2.88	1.47	5.00	1.71	7.62	.62
	C			5.69	2.09		
5 Trials on	FC	17.94	4.42	23.56	9.49	27.50	6.51
Stage III	FCC	15.56	5.44	17.31	3.88	17.87	5.61
	C			16.75	5.36		

The recall of A-B increased as a function of the level of A-B practice under both FC and FCC conditions, $F(2,90) = 213.01$, $p < .01$, indicating that the manipulation of degree of learning had the desired effect. Also apparent in these data are trends both for recall to have been poorer under FC than FCC conditions, $F(1,90) = 7.92$, $p < .01$, but for it to have been decreasingly so as the number of Stage I trials increased, though the latter trend was not statistically reliable. Finally, when the FC and FCC 6-trial conditions are contrasted with the six-trial control condition in which there was no interpolated learning of either B-C or D-C, Condition C in Table 10, it is seen that recall was poorest in Condition FC and intermediate in Condition FCC; however, the differences among these means were not statistically significant, $F(2,45) = 2.03$, $p > .05$.

Turning to performance on A-C in Stage III, it may be seen in Table 10 that performance increased monotonically as a function of number of A-B trials in both the FC and the FCC conditions, $F(2,90) = 7.09$, $p < .01$, and that the increases with trials were greater for FC than FCC. Statistically, this trend toward interaction was only of marginal reliability, $F(2,90) = 2.60$, $.05 < p < .01$. Since this trend is in the expected direction, follow-up comparisons seemed justified. The critical difference for $t(90) < .05$ is 4.41, using the within-groups error term to estimate the standard error of the difference. Thus the difference between the 3 and 6 trial FC conditions (5.62) exceeds the critical value easily, the difference (3.94) between the 6 and 22-trial FC conditions approaches it, and none of the differences for FCC conditions either approach or exceed it. The overall difference between the FC and FCC conditions is a highly reliable one, $F(1,90) = 21.90$, $p < .01$, as usual. Lastly, only in the case of the 3-trial FC and FCC conditions is convergence apparent during the course of the 5 trials of performance on A-C.

Though it had been our intent to utilize the outcome of the A-B recall test prior to Stage III to examine A-C performance when it was conditionalized upon correct versus incorrect recall of A-B, these analyses will not be presented. The main difficulty with them is that the nature and extent to which item and S selection artifacts were present is uncertain. Also, the 22-trial conditions could not be included in these analyses because recall was virtually perfect in these conditions. It seemed preferable, therefore, to utilize the data of Experiment 12, presented next, for this type of analysis because recall did not differ among conditions in that experiment and was low enough to permit all conditions to be included in the analysis.

Discussion. The fact that the amount of mediated facilitation was a monotonic increasing function of the number of A-B trials is consonant with an associative interpretation of the mediation process. The fact that the statistical evidence supporting this conclusion was not strong may be, at least in part, attributable to the attenuation of the interaction as a source of variance as the result of the trend for A-C performance to have increased under FCC conditions with increasing numbers of A-B trials (Table 10), a result which seems puzzling at first glance. However, we have had Ss comment frequently that they utilize B under FCC conditions in combination with A to form the compound stimulus AB thereby "making A more meaningful" in their efforts to associate C with A in Stage III. If just a few Ss, or a number of Ss on a few items, utilized such a strategy with increasing frequency as degree of A-B learning increased, then the increase in A-C performance under FCC conditions in the present experiment would be predicted.

Statistical questions aside, the magnitude of the effect of increases in degree of A-B learning can be seen another way; namely, Ss in Condition FC made 15.06 percent, 47.99 percent, and 53.85 percent more correct responses than those in Condition FCC with 3, 6, and 22 trials on A-B, respectively.

Experiment 12

This experiment was conducted by Schulz, Weaver, and Dobbs (1968). In Experiment 11 the focus was on A-B strength; in this experiment it was on B-C strength. The two experiments were in the main parallel in design.

Method. In this study Ss received three, six, or 22 trials on B-C or D-C in the FC and FCC conditions, respectively. A test for A-B recall at a 1.5-second rate preceded the initiation of practice on A-C. All Ss received five alternating study and test trials on A-C. There was also a condition which did not practice B-C or D-C; instead, the Ss in this condition worked on the pyramid puzzle for 16.5 minutes. This was the amount of time required to complete Stage II in the 22-trial FC and FCC conditions. The reason for equating this group with the 22-rather than the six-trial groups (Experiment 11) need not concern us here.

The Ss in the 3- and 6-trial FC and FCC conditions also performed the pyramid puzzle for a period of time required to equate their A-B retention interval with that of the 22-trial FC and FCC conditions. In short, the interval between the end of A-B practice and the test for recall of A-B was equivalent for all Ss (16.5 minutes). The learning of A-B was to a criterion of 2 perfect recitations in all conditions. There were 16 Ss in each condition. In all other respects the procedures, materials and presentation rates were our "standard" ones.

Results. Performance in Stage I did not differ among the various groups. The means for trials to reach the 2 perfect criterion ranged from 8.50 to 11.25. As usual in Stage II, performance under FC conditions was inferior to that under FCC conditions. In the former conditions the mean total numbers of correct responses were 11.25 after 3 trials and 154.19 after 22 trials, while they were 17.56 after 3 and 161.31 after 22 trials in the latter conditions.

Table 11 shows the means and SDs for the numbers of correct responses on the A-B recall test and for the total number correct during five trials of A-C performance. Inspection of the upper half of Table 11 reveals that the recall of A-B was not affected to any large extent by the wide differences in B-C or D-C practice. Statistically, neither the effect of conditions, number of Stage II trials, nor the interaction of these factors proved to be reliable sources of variance, all $ps > .10$. When the recall in the pyramid control was compared with the other conditions combined the resulting $t(110)$ was less than unity. In short, the type and amount of interpolated activity did not affect A-B recall.

The means in the lower half of Table 11 reflect the expected trend for mediated facilitation to increase with increasing numbers of trials on B-C. This trend is a reliable one statistically. Both the main effect of paradigm, $F(1,90) = 56.62$, $p < .01$, and interaction of paradigm with number of Stage II trials, $F(2,90) = 4.80$, $p < .05$, were statistically significant. Pairwise comparisons revealed the differences between 3 and 22 trials and 6 and 22 trials under FC

Table 11. Means and SDs for correct responses in recall of A-B and performance in Stage III as a function of the number of trials in Stage II and conditions in Experiment 12.

		Number of Stage II Trials							
		0		3		6		22	
Conditions		$\bar{X}$	SD	$\bar{X}$	SD	$\bar{X}$	SD	$\bar{X}$	SD
	FC			6.00	1.10	5.50	1.63	5.50	1.10
A-B Recall	FCC			5.81	2.20	5.86	1.46	6.50	1.63
	C	6.31	1.74						
5 Trials	FC			23.00	6.56	25.25	5.52	29.75	4.63
on	FCC			18.13	6.70	17.06	6.80	15.94	4.30
Stage III	C	14.94	6.60						

conditions to have exceeded the critical difference of 4.04, $p < .05$. None of the differences among FCC conditions even approaches significance.

As noted earlier, it was possible to examine A-C performance conditionalized upon whether A-B was recalled correctly (A-B+) or incorrectly (A-B−) with the advantage that recall of A-B did not differ among conditions. The relevant data are presented in Figure 4. First, it may be seen that the mean number of correct responses per item did not vary systematically with number of Stage II trials under FCC conditions. This is true of both the A-B+ and the A-B− curves. In contrast, and as expected from mediational theory, the mean number correct per item increased directly with increases in Stage II practice under FC conditions. The values for A-B+ consistently exceeded those for A-B− and both of these curves were above the FCC curves.

One final bit of interesting information was obtained from the 3-trial FC condition data. Items were partitioned in two ways: (1) Was A-B + or −? (2) B-C never given correctly in Stage II versus B-C being given one or more times

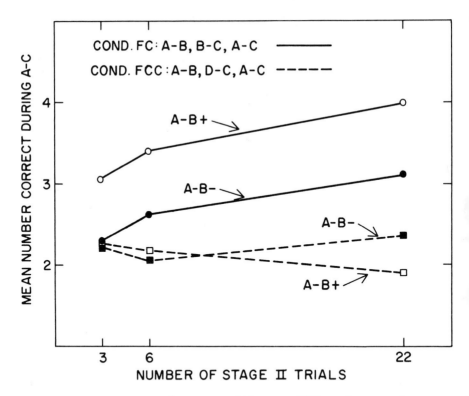

Figure 9—4. Stage III performance in FC versus FCC conditions and varying numbers of Stage II trials when items have been partitioned as to whether A-B was recalled (A-B+) or not recalled (A-B−) immediately prior to beginning Stage III.

correctly. When B-C had never been given correctly there was no difference in A-C performance for A-B+ and A-B− items, $\overline{X} = 1.88$ and 1.80, respectively. However, if B-C had been given correctly then A-C performance for A-B+ ($\overline{X} = 3.46$) was superior to that for A-B− ($\overline{X} = 2.41$). This analysis could not be carried out in six-and 22-trial conditions because all B-C items were given correctly at least once. Nevertheless, the above analysis emphasizes the crucial role of the B-C link for the facilitation of A-C under FC conditions.

Discussion. The results of this study are congruent with those obtained in Experiment 11. The interaction between levels of Stage II degree of learning and conditions (FC versus FCC) was a statistically reliable one because A-C performance under FC conditions increased monotonically with increases in B-C strength, while the number of Stage II trials on D-C failed to produce statistically reliable differences in A-C performance under FCC conditions. However, just as we noted a slight increase for A-C performance in Condition FCC with increases in A-B degree of learning in Experiment 11, there is a slight systematic decrease across levels of Stage II learning in the present FCC data. While we were able to offer a tenable explanation for the trend in Experiment 11, a similar explanation is not apparent for the present data.

One feature that is specially intriguing about the present data is the finding that A-C performance and number of Stage II trials were directly related both for A-B+ and A-B− items. This finding could be interpreted as representing evidence favorable to the notion that A and C became associated in Stage II, the direct-association hypothesis of Schwenn and Underwood (1965, p. 6) via the backward association from B to A. Thus, one would conclude that both Stage III chaining and direct-associations transferred from Stage II to facilitate A-C performance, the former to a greater extent than the latter. However, a corollary of the direct association hypothesis is that A-B should be extinguished, or unlearned, as A becomes associated with C during Stage II. Thus, the absence of differences in overall A-B recall following Stage II (Table 11) is not in accord with the direct-association hypothesis. The latter finding coupled with our previous failure (Schulz, Liston, & Weaver, 1968) discussed earlier in this paper (p. 210) leads us to favor an alternative interpretation. Namely, an S's ability to discover and utilize an A-B-C chain may have been imperfectly indexed by the stringent requirements of the heavily paced (1.5-second rate) overt recall of A-B. And, given that A and C were jointly present on both study and test trials in Stage III, S may have been able to recall Bs that he could not recall when A alone was the cue for recall in the A-B recall task preceding Stage III.

Experiment 13

Experiments 11 and 12 demonstrated that strength of A-B and B-C, respectively, when defined by the number of acquisition trials, affected A-C performance in Condition FC in the predicted manner. The increases in mediated facilitation observed there could have arisen either because the number of items for which an A-B-C mediation chain was established increased with increasing numbers of trials in Stage I or II, or because the chain remained intact, was not forgotten, for increasing numbers of items as the number of trials in Stage I or III increased. Similarly, it was not possible to assess fully the possible interaction between A-B and B-C strength because, while one varied, the other remained fixed. That is, are some combinations of A-B and B-C strength better, or worse, than others for the production of mediated facilitation? The present experiment was designed to provide a more complete and analytic assessment of the effects of A-B and B-C strength in Condition FC. To this end, A-B and B-C strength were manipulated factorially with strength defined by the number of times S correctly recalled or recognized a response, not by the number of trials the S received.

Method. The strength criteria were 1, 3, or 7 correct responses per item. The criterion for a given item in Stage I and in Stage II was specified in advance by E, thus eliminating item selection artifacts. The lists for Stage I and II in Conditions FC and FCC consisted of nine critical items, one item defining each of the nine cells of the 3 X 3 factorial (1–1, 1–3, 1–7, 3–1, 3–3, 3–7, 7–1, 7–3, and 7–7) where Stage I strength is designated by the first number and Stage II by the second. The items were counterbalanced across Ss so that each item served equally often at each strength level. A "drop-out" procedure was used for critical items. That is, as soon as S achieved the desired criterion in Stage I or Stage II on a critical item, it was removed from the list and replaced by a filler item; thus, the list always contained nine pairs. The Ss were told to anticipate the changes in items and that they were to devote equal effort to all items, whether they were old or new. Presentation of the materials, which were our "standard" ones, was via a Carousel Slide Projector utilizing a small Polacoat Screen and rear projection. The intertrial interval in Stages I and II was 60 seconds to allow E to change slides. The Ss worked on arithmetic problems during these intervals. The remaining intervals were the same as those we have usually employed: (1) Stage I, 2:2 seconds, (2) Stage II, 2:3 seconds, and (3) Stage III, 2:3 seconds. The Ss recalled these responses in Stage I, while Stages II and III involved multiple-choice recognition. All stages involved alternating study and test trials.

All S learned an A-B list in Stage I, those in Condition FC learned a B-C list and those in Condition FCC a D-C list in Stage II. In Stage III all Ss learned an A-C list for ten trials which contained only the *nine critical pairs.* In short, except for the changes in procedure required by the manipulation employed in this experiment, the procedures were our usual ones.

Results. Performance in Stage I was comparable in Conditions FC and FCC. The mean numbers of trials required to achieve the respective criteria of one, three, and seven correct on critical items were 2.74, 5.38, and 9.34 in the combined FC and FCC conditions, $F(2,284) = 1657.05, p < .01$. The pattern of performance in Stage II was also the expected one, the Ss in Condition FC requiring slightly more trials than the Ss in Condition FCC to achieve criterion levels of performance, $F(1,142) = 17.88, p < .01$, (Condition FC $\overline{X}$ = 4.71 and Condition FCC $\overline{X}$ = 4.26). The average numbers of trials to reach the respective criteria of 1, 3 and 7 correct were 1.74, 4.06, and 8.00 in Condition FC and 1.48, 3.61 and 7.68 in Condition FCC, $F(2,284) = 4644.22, p < .01$.

There were two other significant sources of variance in the Stage II data: (1) Stage I strength, $F(2,284) = 3.69, p < .05$. (2) Interaction of Stage II strength with FC vs. FCC, $F(2,284) = 3.60, p < .05$.

Stage III, A-C performance, was not affected differentially under FC and FCC conditions by either Stage I or Stage II strength in a statistically reliable manner. The trends in the data were directionally appropriate but the differences were too small to be statistically significant. The mean differences between Conditions FC and FCC were .64, .94, and .85 for Stage I and .75, .89, and .79 for Stage II at strength criteria 1, 3, and 7, respectively. This was true for performance measured early in Stage III (Trials 1–5) and for performance throughout all 10 Stage III trials. The relevant data are shown in Figure 5, those for Stage I strength in the upper half and those for Stage II strength in the lower half. Only the data for Trials 1–5 have been presented because they are theoretically the most sensitive to the effects under consideration here. Moreover, the data for Trials 1–10 simply mirror them. As may be seen in Figure 5, mediated facilitation is evident at all strength levels, $F(1,142) = 29.26$, $p < .01$. Since the maximum possible number correct was 5.00, it seems doubtful that a "ceiling effect" was responsible for the failure of the effects of strength to have become manifest to a substantial degree.

Numerous subsidiary analyses (e.g., fast versus slow Ss, etc.) failed to reveal the operation of any factors which might have counteracted the expected effects of strength under the conditions of this experiment.

Discussion. The absence of a reliable effect of differences in associative strength surprised us, to say the least, in light of the findings obtained in Experiments 11 and 12. Though it was anticipated that A-B and B-C strength in Condition FC would interact, no such interaction was apparent in the data. That is, one might have thought that if either A-B or B-C were very strong (correct 7 times in Stage I or II), this would have helped S recover a weak associative link for B-C or A-B. Evidently, this did not occur because the interaction of conditions with Stage I and Stage II strength did not even approach significance. It seems unlikely, therefore, that the effects of strength were attenuated in this fashion. Similarly, examination of the extremes of variation in strength (1–1 versus 7–7) shows the performance difference between Conditions FC and FCC to be independent of strength.

It will be of interest to discuss the present results in relation to those obtained in Experiments 11 and 12. However, this discussion shall be deferred until the results of two additional experiments which bear directly upon this issue have been presented.

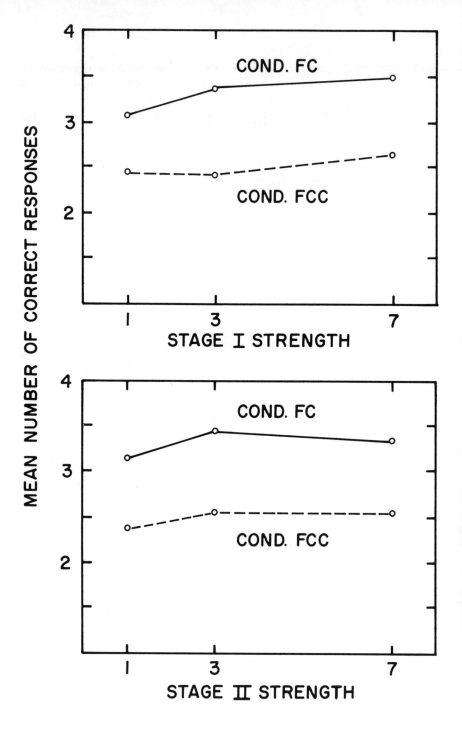

Figure 9—5. Mean total numbers of correct responses during five study-test Stage III trials in Conditions FC and FCC as a function of three levels of Stage I and Stage II strength.

Experiment 14

Method. The design of this experiment paralleled the design of Experiment 13 exactly as far as Stages I and II were concerned. Stage I-II strength was varied factorially in Conditions FC and FCC. The performance criteria were 1, 3, and 7 correct responses. Immediately following the completion of Stage II half the Ss in each condition were tested for *recall* of the *critical* A-B association, the other half received a multiple-choice *recognition* test for the *critical* B-C or D-C associations. These tests were given to ascertain that the strength manipulations had produced requisite differences in associative availability. This would permit us to rule out the possibility that the failure to obtain strength effects in Stage III of Experiment 13 was due to the fact that 1, 3 and 7 correct responses as strength criteria had not actually produced differences in the availability of the links of the A-B-C associative chain even though we had assumed that they would. The presentation rate for these tests was the same as it had been during acquisition, 2 seconds for recall and 3 seconds for recognition. To insure that an adequate number of observations would be obtained there were three successive tests of each type. In short, the results of Experiment 14 should tell us whether or not the associative relations, A-B and B-C, did in fact differ in strength just prior to the test for mediated facilitation in Stage III of Experiment 13.

Though it had been our intent originally that Experiment 14 would be terminated following the retention tests, after some of the data had been collected it was decided to add some tests for mediated facilitation using the Stage III A-C list of Experiment 13. However, since our main concern, at least at the time, continued to be with the retention data, we did not reduce the number of retention tests to, say, a single test, even though it seemed that we might risk attenuating the effects of strength on A-C performance by continuing to give three successive retention tests.

It may be recalled that in previous experiments reported in this paper (e.g., Experiment 1) that a procedure referred to as the test-only method was employed. This is the procedure we employed for Stage III of Experiment 14. In Experiment 13 Stage III had consisted of alternating study and test trials. In Experiment 14 it consisted of three test-only trials on the A-C list. It was reasoned that when study trials were present as in Experiment 13 only very nominal levels of associative strength may have been required to discover and utilize a mediating associative strength while with the test-only procedure performance may be more heavily dependent upon the availability in memory of the links in the A-B-C associative chain. In all other essential respects the materials and procedures were the ones we have employed previously.

In brief, this experiment may be seen to have involved two treatments defined between Ss, conditions (FC versus FCC) and type of retention test (recall versus recognition), and two treatments defined within Ss, Stage I (1,3, or 7 correct) and Stage II (1, 3, or 7 correct) strength. A total of 108 Ss was employed, 27 per between-Ss treatment.

Results. Performance in Stage I on critical items was slightly better in Condition FCC overall ($\bar{X}$ = 5.72) than in Condition FC ($\bar{X}$ = 6.38). Even though this difference was statistically significant, it is small in magnitude and favors the control rather than the mediation condition. The mean numbers of trials required to achieve 1, 3, and 7 correct responses were 3.18, 5.42 and 9.56, respectively, F (2,208) = 1067.60, $p < .05$, for the combined FC and FCC conditions. These values approximate those obtained in Experiment 13. Also, as in Experiment 13, Condition FC required slightly more trials in Stage II ($\bar{X}$ = 4.91) than Condition FCC ($\bar{X}$ = 4.30), F (1,104) = 17.93, $p < .05$, to reach criterion performance levels on critical items. In Condition FC it took on the average 1.83, 4.38 and 8.51 trials to reach criterion levels of performance of 1, 3, and 7 correct, while the means for the same criteria in Condition FCC were 1.52, 3.71 and 7.67, F (2,208) = 2518.71, $p < .05$. Again these values are very similar to those observed in Experiment 13. Finally, as in Experiment 13, Stage I strength and the conditions by Stage II strength interaction were also significant.

The correct response data obtained from the tests of A-B recall and B-C or D-C recognition contained the following significant sources of variance ($p < .05$) as main effects: (1) Recall performance ($\bar{X}$ = 1.88) was poorer than recognition performance ($\bar{X}$ = 2.52). (2) Performance was an increasing function of Stage I strength ($\bar{X}$ = 1.74, 2.27 and 2.59 for criteria 1, 3, and 7, respectively). (3) Performance was an increasing function of Stage II strength ($\bar{X}$ = 2.07, 2.21 and 2.31 for criteria 1, 3, and 7, respectively). (4) Performance in Condition FC ($\bar{X}$ = 2.09) was lower than in Condition FCC ($\bar{X}$ = 2.30). The maximum number of correct responses an S could have made was three.

In addition to the main effects identified above there were three significant ($p < .05$) first-order interactions. Two of these interactions involved the method of testing retention (recall versus recognition) and strength, Stage I strength in one case and Stage II strength in the other. Recall performance increased while recognition performance decreased as Stage I strength increased. Similarly, recognition performance increased but recall decreased as Stage II strength increased.

The third interaction, one involving Stage II strength and Conditions FC versus FCC, was a bit more difficult to interpret. In Condition FC there was no difference in retention performance for strength criteria 3 and 7 while in Condition FCC a lack of difference obtained for criteria 1 and 3. It is not clear from the present data why this outcome was obtained.

Performance under test-only conditions in Stage III may now be examined in light of the demonstrated differences in associative strength for the A-B and B-C portions of the A-B-C associative chain which the preceding analysis revealed. If A-C performance under test-only conditions in Condition FC was a function of A-B, B-C, or both A-B and B-C strength, it would be reflected in a reliable interaction of strength with Condition FC versus Condition FCC. The relevant data are summarized in Figure 6. The trends in the means in Figure 6 are clearly the anticipated ones and statistically they are dependable ones, F (2,208) = 14.39 and F (2,208) = 8.57, p's $< .05$, for the Stage I and Stage II

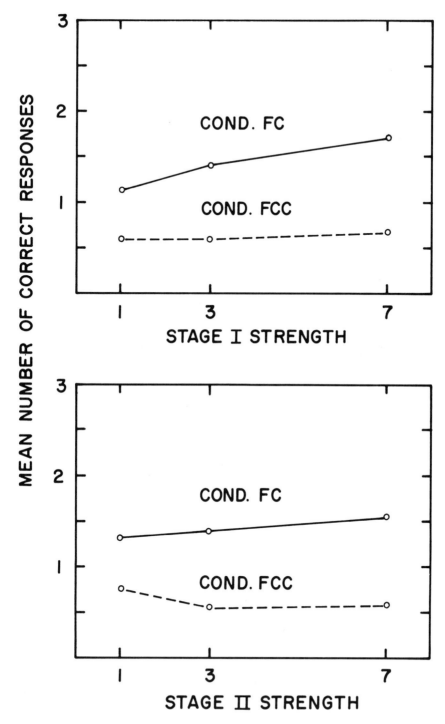

Figure 9–6. Mean total numbers of correct responses during three test-only Stage III trials in Conditions FC and FCC as a function of three levels of Stage I and Stage II strength.

strength by conditions interactions, respectively. The second-order interaction involving these three factors was also significant, F (4,416) = 7.62, $p < .05$, because the FC-FCC difference and the differences under FC conditions due to Stage I strength were not the same at each level of Stage II strength. The effect of Stage I strength increased as a function of increases in Stage II strength.

Returning to the data in Figure 6, it may be noted that the effects of A-B and B-C strength on A-C performance were approximately symmetrical when they are inferred from the mean FC-FCC differences, which is the usual basis for inferences regarding amounts of mediated facilitation. These differences were .55, .84, and .96 for Stage I and .52, .82, and 1.01 for Stage II at criteria 1, 3, and 7, respectively. It is particularly important to look at the FC-FCC differences because there was a curious anomaly in the present data which the analysis of variance failed to detect. In both Conditions FC and FCC, for the Ss who received three recognition tests after Stage II there was a decrement in A-C performance as Stage II strength increased. The presence of this trend in the FC condition A-C data attenuated the effects of B-C strength, viewed solely from the standpoint of increases in A-C performance as a function B-C strength in that condition. We are at a loss to explain this result. Overall, performance under FC conditions was superior ($\overline{X} = 1.41$) to that under FCC conditions ($\overline{X} = 0.63$), F (1,104) = 87.30, $p < .05$.

Two other first-order interactions manifested themselves in the A-C test-only data. Both involved type of retention test (recall versus recognition) and strength, Stage I strength in one instance, F (2,208) = 3.31, $p < .05$, and Stage II strength in the other, F (2,208) = 9.01, $p < .05$. Performance on A-C increased as A-B Stage I strength increased, more if S had been tested for multiple-choice recognition than if he had been tested for recall. A parallel state of affairs obtained for Stage II strength in that here the A-C performance of those Ss who had recalled A-B was an inverse function of Stage II strength while it was a direct function of Stage II strength if S had been tested for recognition. These trends evidently reflect the effects of differential availability of A-B and B-C in Condition FC indirectly, since the same trends were observed in the retention data.

Finally, when the correct response data for Stage III were expressed as percentages of the total number of responses attempted, they differed by a constant amount from their expression in terms of total possibilities to respond. Hence, the results cannot be attributed to guessing biases which might have resulted from the use of the test-only method in this stage. Even though no study trials were given, it was also apparent that performance in Stage III in Condition FC improved across the three successive tests. Such improvements did not occur generally in Condition FCC since all that Ss could do in this condition was guess. This result is fully consistent with those obtained in our other studies where Stage III involved the test-only method. In fact, the levels of A-C performance under FC Conditions equalled or exceeded the levels achieved by

FCC Ss of Experiment 13 on their first three study-test trials except when A-B strength was at the once-correct level.

Discussion. The results obtained here agree with those obtained in Experiments 11 and 12 in showing mediated facilitation to be a function of the associative strength of the links A-B and B-C. Additionally, they imply that the process of mediation can be enhanced by overlearning of the components of the mediating chain.

The retention tests following Stage II indicated that the failure to obtain effects due to strength in Experiment 13 was probably not due to the absence of requisite strength differences prior to the initiation of Stage III. Clear and significant differences in the availability of A-B and B-C were found to exist immediately following the completion of Stage II in the present experiment. A more likely cause of the failure to detect strength effects in Experiment 13 was the use of the study-test procedure in Stage III which afforded S the opportunity to reinstate into memory a temporarily inaccessible mediating association through the use of either A or C, or both A and C as retrieval cues, the latter being vastly more difficult under test-only conditions where the correct A-C pairs were never shown in the absence of other C-term distractors.

On the other hand, it is also perfectly clear that the presence or absence of study-trials cannot have been the sole determiner of whether or not strength effects became manifest in A-C performance, since such effects were observed in Experiments 11 and 12 where Stage III consisted of alternating study and test trials. However, in those experiments some of the effect, particularly in the case of 3 versus 6 trials, was undoubtedly due to the establishment of increasing numbers of suprathreshold associative relations in combination with any effects due to overlearning. In the present experiment, save possibly in the cases where the once-correct criterion was achieved by chance, the effects that were observed must have been in the main due to overlearning. It is also possible that the longer interval between Stages II and III in this experiment than in Experiment 13, which was occasioned by the three interpolated recall and recognition tests, may have contributed to the finding of effects due to strength. As Dobbs (1968) has shown in an experiment which will be described subsequently, mediating associations follow the same laws of forgetting as any other associative relation. Indeed, it would be interesting to repeat Experiment 13 and vary the length of the intervals between successive stages to assess the effects of differences in degree of learning on the retention of the links in the mediating chain.

Experiment 15

About the same time that we were conducting Experiment 14, we also followed up Experiment 13 from a somewhat different angle. We had been particularly struck by the fact that even for the most extreme difference in strength in

Experiment 13, once correct on A-B and B-C (1−1) versus seven times correct on A-B and B-C (7−7), the difference between Conditions FC and FCC seemed to have remained largely unaffected. We were interested in seeing whether this result would also obtain when Stage III involved recall rather than multiple-choice recognition and when the critical items were homogeneous in strength, not mixed strength as they had been in Experiment 13.

Method. The method was in all essential respects the same as that used in Experiment 13, except as noted above, strength was a between-Ss variable. For half the Ss the criterion was 1−1 and for the other half 7−7. Also, all the Ss received three successive tests on critical A-B items immediately following Stage II. This was done to insure that the strengths were indeed different at least for A-B. In short, the design was a 2 (Condition FC versus FCC) by 2 (1−1 versus 7−7) factorial. There were 10 Ss in each cell.

Results and discussion. Aside from having taken a little longer to achieve criterion strength level here than in Experiments 13 and 14, the results for Stages I and II were the same as those obtained in those experiments. The recall of A-B was markedly superior for 7−7 ($\bar{X} = 24.00$) as opposed to 1−1 ($\bar{X} = 9.30$) Ss, F (1,36) = 119.86, $p < .05$. The levels of recall for Conditions FC and FCC did not differ reliably. The maximum possible number correct was 27.00 for the three successive tests on A-B.

Performance in Stage III over 5 alternating study and test trials was better under FC than FCC conditions at both strength criteria, the mean total numbers correct being 8.20 and 17.40 in the former and 4.80 and 6.20 in the latter for 1−1 and 7−7 criteria, respectively. The interaction of strength with conditions was significant, F (1,36) = 4.24, $p < .05$.

While the results of this study obviously do not isolate the reasons for the failure to have obtained larger strength differences in Experiment 13, they do illustrate once more than such strength differences are demonstrable and thereby enlarge the conditions under which these differences have been observed.

General Discussion of Degree of Learning

The ambiguities of the previous literature on this topic notwithstanding, the present series of studies demonstrates that the mediation process can be affected by the strength of the associative relations upon which it is contingent. At the same time it seems clear that the discovery and utilization of mediating associations is not primarily determined by the strength of the associative relations which play a role in the mediation process. If the latter were the case, then an outcome such as the one obtained in Experiment 13 would be perplexing, indeed. We know from the retention data of Experiment 14 that the requisite differences in strength must have been present, yet the effects of these differences failed to manifest themselves reliably in A-C performance. A similar state of affairs may have obtained in other previous studies which failed to obtain effects due to strength. The absence in Experiments 13 and 14 of trends suggesting interaction between Stage I and Stage II strength also argues against a simple associationistic model as the proper one for the interpretation of the mediation process.

In brief, it would appear that existence of an associative relation between the components of a mediational chain is a necessary, though not always a sufficient condition, for the discovery and utilization of that relation. The strength of this relation may or may not play a role in performance, depending upon the demands of the task. The present data suggest the following factors will enhance the importance of strength: (1) The absence of study trials in Stage III. (2) Recall as the mode of response in A-C learning. (3) Interpolated activity or a retention interval between Stage II and III. (4) Very wide differences (as in Experiments 11 and 12) in degree of Stage I or Stage II learning. Of these factors 1, 2, and 4 seem most clearly established. Item number (3) above will require additional research to establish it as a factor. Another factor which comes to mind is the length of the test interval in Stage III. It will be recalled from the discussion of the study of temporal factors by Schulz and Weaver (1968), p. 217, that the length of the Stage III test interval affected A-C performance rather profoundly. Therefore, insofar as degree of learning may be expected to shorten the latency with which the constituent associative relations can be utilized, the degree to which these associations have been learned would play an increasingly prominent role in A-C performance as the length of the test interval is decreased in Condition FC.

RETENTION

An interest in the retention of a mediating association can take at least two forms. First, we may ask what happens to an associative relation as the result of its utilization during the course of A-C Stage III performance. It has been theorized that mediating associations "drop-out" (are forgotten?) and come to be replaced by "direct" A-C associations as the degree of A-C learning reaches high levels (e.g., Barnes & Underwood, 1959). Alternatively, one could hold the view that the strength of a mediating association should be maintained, if not increased, through its continued utilization during the course of Stage III A-C performance. The results from a test for retention of A-B subsequent to performance on A-C in a study discussed earlier in this paper (Schulz, Liston, & Weaver, 1968) favored the latter over the former interpretation as did similar studies by Horton and Wiley (1967a, 1967b). A fixed number of A-C trials was employed in these studies.

One could also entertain the hypothesis that both the "drop-out" and the "maintenance" notions are applicable for the understanding of the retention of an associative relation during the course of A-C performance. That is, the retention of A-B, if not already at asymptote, might first increase as the result of its being utilized as a constituent of A-B-C associative chain and then "drop-out," à la Barnes and Underwood. This possibility was investigated by Weaver and Schulz (1968) using our "standard" materials and procedures.[8] The number of trials on A-C was systematically varied so as to permit the retention of A-B to be traced throughout the course of A-C learning. Recall of A-B was measured after 0, 3, 7, and 15 trials of A-C performance.

The results indicated, as shown previously, that performance on A-C under FC conditions was reliably superior to that under FCC conditions—mediated facilitation. Also, recall of A-B did not differ for these conditions prior to A-C learning, i.e., after zero A-C trials. Thereafter, A-B recall as a function of A-C trials remained constant under FC conditions and decreased under FCC conditions. Additional analysis showed, among other things, that initially weak A-B associations were strengthened while those which were strong initially first increased and then decreased in strength (mediator "drop-out") as a result of their having been utilized in acquiring A-C rapidly. Under FCC conditions, unlearning of A-B was the rule regardless of the initial strength of A-B or the ease with which A-C was acquired. There is in these data a suggestion that both drop-out and maintenance processes may be operative during A-C performance in Condition FC. However, in order to reach a firm conclusion on this point, it will clearly be necessary to study the matter further.

A second focus for the investigation of the retention of mediating associations is to study their retention as a function of the temporal interval between the point at which they have been acquired and the point at which they are to be utilized, as well as their susceptibility to sources of retroactive and proactive interference. Surprisingly, the investigation of this aspect of mediational phenomena had been almost entirely neglected until Dobbs (1968) undertook his extensive study of it in our laboratory. He studied the retention of mediating associations and the effects of retroactive (RI) and proactive interference (PI) under FC and FCC conditions. There were three basic conditions: (1) A-B learning preceded by learning A-X (Condition PI). (2) Learning of A-X interpolated between A-B and B-C or D-C learning (Condition RI). (3) Neither interpolated nor prior A-X learning (Condition Rest-Control). Tests for A-B recall were given in all conditions just before and just after A-C learning. The retention interval was 10 minutes or 24 hours. In the Rest-Control conditions, less mediation obtained after 24 hour than after 10 minutes—mediating associations were forgotten. Comparisons of A-C performance in the FC and FCC paradigms for Conditions RI and PI relative to Condition Rest-Control permitted the following inferences with respect to the retention of mediating associations: (1) After 10 minutes, they are subject to both RI and PI, with the

[8] Because A-B recall was the main dependent variable in this study, Condition FCC consisted of A-B, B-E, A-C lists rather than the usual A-B, D-C, A-C lists as added assurance against any confounding due to pseudomediation effects (Mandler & Earhard, 1964).

former being greater than the latter. (2) They are subject to PI but not RI after 24 hours, with the latter decreasing markedly over the interval while the former increased slightly. (3) They recover spontaneously under RI conditions with the amount of recovery being such that more mediation obtains at 24 hours than at 10 minutes under these conditions. The inferences based on A-C performance were fully corroborated by the pre- and post-A-C measures of A-B recall. Thus, it was possible to conclude that the retention of mediating associations was fully in accord with expectations generated by an associative model within the context of an interference theory of forgetting.

Dobbs' results contrast rather strikingly with what appears to be the only other modern study (Horton & Wiley, 1967a) of the retention of mediating associations. Horton and Wiley failed to observe any decrement in A-C performance in Condition FC with a 10-day retention interval. Moreover, with the exception of the use of recall procedures in all three stages by Horton and Wiley, their study and the one by Dobbs were very similar in other respects (e.g., materials, etc.). At this point we are at a loss to explain the discrepancy between their results and his.

CONCLUDING STATEMENT

The study of mediational phenomena in the context of the paradigms discussed in this paper has been likened to the study of a simple form of problem-solving behavior on several occasions when commenting upon the outcomes of some of the experiments reported here. This is specially true in those instances where test-only procedures were employed in Stage III. Thus, A-C is the to-be-solved problem and A-B and B-C are previously acquired component associations requisite for solution when properly integrated and applied to the to-be-solved problem.

Gagné (1964), in his insightful analysis of problem solving, speaks of component processes, simpler processes, as being acquired in hierarchical fashion with the successive steps being paired-associate learning, concept learning, and rule learning. Problem solving is seen to be contingent upon the proper integration of these previously acquired component processes. Furthermore, the mediational model is seen as being applicable to the understanding of the integration processes (Lee & Gagné, 1969). While this is an oversimplified and necessarily brief presentation of Gagné's views, one could conclude that the present studies have been dealing with variables affecting integration processes of a very simple sort. Indeed, Lee and Gagné (1970) have recently reported a study of the effects of the degree of component learning upon the acquisition of a complex conceptual rule which is directly analogous to Experiments 11, 12, 13, 14, and 15 of this paper, save for the fact that A-B was an attribute coding task, B-C a contingent rule task, and A-C a complex rule. Their results were similar to those obtained here in that they supported a mediational interpretation of rule learning which included both associative and nonassociative processes. While this is of course interesting, what interests us most is the possibility of utilizing the results we have obtained in this program and the techniques we have developed here to open exciting new avenues of investigation involving more complex forms of problem-solving behavior than we have heretofore attempted to analyze.

Finally, it is quite obvious that our efforts have to date been concentrated heavily upon the study of variables whose effects would be anticipated to be mainly associative ones. However, there is ample evidence even in these studies of a subtle interplay between associative and nonassociative, cognitive processes. Clearly, it will be necessary in future work to investigate more intensively than we have previously the role of these nonassociative factors.

REFERENCES

Adams, J. A. *Human memory.* New York: McGraw-Hill, 1967.

Archer, E. J. Re-evaluation of the meaningfulness of all possible CVC trigrams. *Psychological Monographs*, 1960, 74 (10, Whole No. 497).

Barnes, J. M., & Underwood, B. J. "Fate" of first-list associations in transfer theory. *Journal of Experimental Psychology*, 1959, 58, 97–105.

Cramer, P. Mediated transfer via natural language association. *Journal of Verbal Learning and Verbal Behavior*, 1967, 6, 512–519.

Cramer, P. The functioning of implicit associative responses in mediated transfer. *Journal of Experimental Psychology*, 1969, 82, 301–309.

DiVesta, F. J., & Walls, R. T. Transfer of solution rules in problem solving. *Journal of Educational Psychology*, 1967, 58, 319–326.

Dobbs, A. R. The effect of retention interval, RI, and PI on mediating associations. Unpublished doctoral dissertation, University of Iowa, 1968.

Duncan, C. P. Recent research on human problem solving. *Psychological Bulletin*, 1959, 56, 397–429.

Earhard, B., & Mandler, G. Mediated associations: Paradigms, controls and mechanisms. *Canadian Journal of Psychology*, 1965, 19, 346–378.

Gagné, R. M. Problem solving. In A. W. Melton (ed.), *Categories of human learning.* New York. Academic Press, 1964.

Goggin, J. Retroactive and proactive inhibition in short-term retention of paired associates. *Journal of Verbal Learning and Verbal Behavior*, 1966, 5, 526–535.

Goulet, L. R., & Postman, L. An experimental evaluation of the pseudomediation hypothesis. *Psychonomic Science*, 1966, 4, 163–164.

Holborn, S. W. Proactive inhibition in short- and long-term memory as a function of acoustic similarity and modality. Unpublished doctoral dissertation, University of Iowa, 1968.

Hopkins, R. H., & Schulz, R. W. The A-B, B-C_r, A-C mediation paradigm: recall of A-B following varying numbers of trials of A-C learning. *Psychonomic Science*, 1967, 9, 235–236.

Horton, D. L. Mediation or pseudomediation: a reply to Earhard and Mandler. *Canadian Journal of Psychology*, 1967, 21, 471–489.

Horton, D. L., & Hartman, R. R. Verbal mediation as a function of associative directionality and exposure frequency. *Journal of Verbal Learning and Verbal Behavior*, 1963, 1, 361–365.

Horton, D. L. & Kjeldergaard, P. M. An experimental analysis of associative factors in mediated generalization. *Psychological Monographs*, 1961, 75, Whole no. 515.

Horton, D. L., & Wiley, R. E. The effect of mediation on the retention and strength of previously formed associations. *Journal of Verbal Learning and Verbal Behavior*, 1967, 6, 36–41. (a)

Horton, D. L., & Wiley, R. E. Mediate association: facilitation and interference. *Journal of Experimental Psychology*, 1967, 73, 636–638. (b)

Jenkins, J. J. Mediated associations: paradigms and situations. In C. N. Cofer & B. S. Musgrave (eds.), *Verbal behavior and learning*. New York: McGraw-Hill, 1963. Pp. 210–245.

Jenkins, J. J. Mediation theory and grammatical behavior. In S. Rosenberg (ed.), *Directions in psycholinguistics*. New York: Macmillan, 1965. Pp. 66–96.

Kendler, H. H., & Kendler, T. T. Vertical and horizontal processes in problem solving. *Psychological Review*, 1962, 69, 1–16.

Kjeldergaard, P. M. Transfer and mediation in verbal learning. In T. R. Dixon, & D. L. Horton (eds.), *Verbal behavior and general behavior theory*. Englewood Cliffs, N. J.: Prentice-Hall, 1968. Pp. 67–96.

Lee, S. S., & Gagné, R. M. Effects of chaining cues on the acquisition of a complex conceptual rule. *Journal of Experimental Psychology*, 1969, 80, 468–474.

Lee, S. S., & Gagné, R. M. Effects of degree of component learnings on the acquisition of a complex conceptual rule. *Journal of Experimental Psychology*, 1970, 83, 13–18.

Mandler, G. Verbal learning. In G. Mandler, P. Mussen, N. Kogan, & M. A. Wallach (eds.), *New directions in psychology III*. New York: Holt, Rinehart and Winston, 1967. Pp. 1–50.

Mandler, G., & Earhard, B. Pseudomediation: is chaining an artifact? *Psychonomic Science*, 1964, 1, 247–248.

Peterson, L. R., & Peterson, M. J. Short-term retention of individual verbal items. *Journal of Experimental Psychology*, 1959, 58, 193–198.

Peterson, M. J. Cue trials, frequency of presentation, and mediating responses. *Journal of Experimental Psychology*, 1964, 67, 432–438.

Peterson, M. J., Colavita, F. B., Sheahan, D. B., & Blattner, K. C. Verbal mediating chains and response availability. *Journal of Verbal Learning and Verbal Behavior*, 1964, 3, 11–18.

Postman, L. Differences between unmixed and mixed transfer designs as a function of paradigm. *Journal of Verbal Learning and Verbal Behavior*, 1966, 5, 240–248.

Postman, L. Association and performance in the analysis of verbal learning. In T. R. Dixon & D. L. Horton (eds.), *Verbal Behavior and General Behavior Theory*. Englewood Cliffs, N. J.: Prentice-Hall, 1968.

Postman, L. Transfer, interference and forgetting. In J. W. Kling and L. A. Riggs (eds.), *Experimental Psychology*. New York: Holt, Rinehart and Winston, 1971.

Postman, L., & Stark, K. The role of associative mediation in retroactive inhibition and facilitation. *Journal of Verbal Learning and Verbal Behavior*, 1969, 8, 790–798. (a)

Postman, L., & Stark, K. Role of response availability in transfer and interference. *Journal of Experimental Psychology*, 1969, 79, 168–177. (b)

Poulos, C. C. Mediated interference, mediated facilitation and negative transfer in a three stage paired associate paradigm with recognition. Unpublished Masters thesis, University of Iowa, 1970.

Richardson, J. Latencies of implicit verbal responses and the effect of the anticipation interval on mediated transfer. *Journal of Verbal Learning and Verbal Behavior*, 1967, 6, 819–826.

Russell, W. A., & Jenkins, J. J. The complete Minnesota norms for responses to 100 words from the Kent-Rosanoff word association test. Technical Report No. 11, 1954, Contract N8-onr-66216, the Office of Naval Research and the University of Minnesota.

Saltz, E. *The cognitive bases of human learning*. Homewood, Ill: Dorsey Press, 1971.

Schulz, R. W. Problem solving and transfer. *Harvard Educational Review*, 1960, 30, 61–77.

Schulz, R. W. Learning of aurally received verbal material: Including comparisons with learning and memory under visual conditions of reception as a function of meaningfulness, abstractness or similarity. Final Report Project No. 50318 Contract No. OE 5-10-018, March 1969.

Schulz, R. W., Liston, J. R., & Weaver, G. E. The A-B, B-C, A-C mediation paradigm: recall of A-B following A-C learning. *Journal of Verbal Learning and Verbal Behavior*, 1968, 7, 602–607.

Schulz, R. W., & Lovelace, E. A. Mediation in verbal paired-associate learning: the role of temporal factors. *Psychonomic Science*, 1964, 1, 95–96.

Schulz, R. W., & Weaver, G. E. The A-B, B-C, A-C mediation paradigm: the effects of variation in A-C study- and test-interval lengths and strength of A-B or B-C. *Journal of Experimental Psychology*, 1968, 76, 303–311.

Schulz, R. W., Weaver, G. E., & Dobbs, A. R. The A-B, B-C, A-C chaining paradigm: the effect on A-C performance of varying numbers of B-C trials. Paper presented at the meeting of the Midwestern Psychological Association, Chicago, May 1968.

Schulz, R. W., Weaver, G. E., & Ginsberg, S. Mediation with pseudomediation controlled: chaining is not an artifact! *Psychonomic Science*, 1965, 2, 169–170.

Schwenn, E., & Underwood, B. J. Simulated similarity and mediation time in transfer. *Journal of Verbal Learning and Verbal Behavior*, 1965, 4, 476–483.

Taylor, J. D. The meaningfulness of 320 words and paralogs. Unpublished doctoral dissertation, Duke University, 1959.

Twedt, H. M., & Underwood, B. J. Mixed vs. unmixed lists in transfer studies. *Journal of Experimental Psychology*, 1959, 48, 111–116.

Underwood, B. J., & Schulz, R. W. Studies of distributed practice: XIX. The influence of intralist similarity with lists of low meaningfulness. *Journal of Experimental Psychology*, 1959, 58, 106–110.

Underwood, B. J., & Schulz, R. W. *Meaningfulness and verbal learning.* Chicago: Lippincott, 1960.

Weaver, G. E., Hopkins, R. H., & Schulz, R. W. The A-B, B-C, A-C mediation paradigm: A-C performance in the absence of study trials. *Journal of Experimental Psychology*, 1968, 77, 670–675.

Wickens, D. D., Ory, N. E., & Graf, S. A. Encoding by taxonomic and acoustic categories in long-term memory. *Journal of Experimental Psychology*, 1970, 84, 462–469.

10 | Arousal in Verbal Learning

BARBARA S. UEHLING

Roger Williams College, Rhode Island

The concept of arousal and its relation to learning and retention has received considerable attention in recent years. Initially, arousal had been introduced by some investigators as a behaviorally-inferred construct (Duffy, 1957; Schlosberg, 1954). Peripheral measures such as heart rate and GSR had been identified as indices of an internal emotional state and the relationship of this state to performance has been usually postulated to be an inverted U-shaped function.

Arousal has also been defined directly as central nervous system activity (Lindsley, 1951; Hebb, 1955). Lindsley defined arousal after the work of Magoun and his co-workers as a pattern of low-voltage, rapid, desynchronous waves in the brainstem and cortex. The term arousal was chosen because this type of brain activity is characteristic of a behaviorally alert organism. Furthermore, as Magoun (1963) relates, investigators found that sensory inputs such as flashes of light, bursts of white noise, and peripheral stimulation administered to a sleeping organism would not only rouse the organism behaviorally but would change the high-voltage, slow synchronous waves characteristic of light sleep to the electrical pattern identified with the aroused organism. Thus, those sensory inputs which have been shown to produce the activated EEG arousal pattern, could be considered appropriate stimulus conditions for the operational definition of arousal.

Problems with the use of these physiological definitions of arousal have since arisen. Dissociation of EEG activation and behavioral manifestations of arousal can occur (Feldman & Waller, 1962). It has also been found that peripheral measures of arousal such as heart rate, palmar conductance, and muscle-action potentials are not highly correlated (Lacey, 1967; Taylor, 1967). Therefore, variables which can be shown to alter anyone of these definitions of arousal may not necessarily be expected to have the same effect on another measure of arousal. Lacey has suggested that the concept of arousal needs drastic revision and has presented a forceful case for separating electrocortical arousal, autonomic arousal, and behavioral arousal, each of which may be different and complex forms of arousal in themselves.

Hypotheses based on a unidimensional concept of arousal have been offered by several researchers relating arousal to verbal learning. In an hypothesis offered

The author is indebted to E. James Archer for his reading of the manuscript.

by Walker (1958) and modified by Walker and Tarte (1963), physiological arousal has been related to immediate and delayed retention. It was hypothesized that the occurrence of any psychological event will set up a perseverative trace which will persist for some period of time. During this time, permanent memory is laid down, but a temporary inhibition of recall will occur ("action decrement") which will serve to preserve the trace and protect it against disruption. High arousal which results from nonspecific activity of the reticular formation (detectable by the EEG pattern described by Lindsley) will result in a more active trace process which will in turn result in greater long-term memory but greater temporary inhibition against recall. Specifically, high arousal in verbal learning should lead to interference in immediate retention as compared with low arousal, but increased long-term retention relative to the low arousal condition. The difference between high and low arousal conditions for long-term retention, it is predicted, may result in differential forgetting or even reminiscence for the high arousal condition.

Berlyne (1967) has offered an alternative view to the consolidation hypothesis regarding effects of arousal on learning and retention. He further develops the idea that an intermediate level of arousal is optimal for the organism and that verbal responses will be most effectively reinforced when arousal is at an intermediate level. However, rather than maintenance at that level, he suggests that changes from either high arousal to intermediate or low arousal to intermediate levels will be reinforcing. A distinction between *learning* and *performance* is necessary according to Berlyne. Short-term recall is influenced both by the influence of arousal on performance and arousal on learning, while long-term retention is influenced only by arousal on learning. He also suggests that differences for arousal effects on short- and long-term retention are due to differences in the particular inverted-U shape functions which relate arousal to performance and to learning.

Malmo (1959) has suggested that arousal is part of the mechanism of drive. Predictions from a Hull-Spence theory of drive can then be made regarding arousal. First, it has been predicted that increases in arousal should increase the likelihood of evocation of dominant responses more than weak responses (Berkowitz & Breck, 1967; Frankel, 1969). Second, high arousal should produce facilitated performance on easy tasks in which few competing responses are available but should interfere with performance on difficult tasks where competing responses are present.

In summary, the predictions which have been made relating arousal to behavior are the following.

(1) Performance is related to arousal by an inverted U-shape function, i.e., maintenance of arousal at an intermediate level will be optimal for performance and learning.

(2) Arousal produces a consolidative neural process which interferes with short-term retention but which will increase long-term retention.

(3) Changes in arousal level from low to intermediate or high to intermediate, rather than maintenance at an intermediate level, will increase learning.

(4) Arousal can be viewed as a generalized drive, hence increases in arousal should increase the likelihood of evocation of dominant responses and should produce facilitation on easy tasks, but interference on difficult tasks.

Reflecting the lack of unidimensionality, a variety of operational definitions have been labeled "arousal." All, however, have two properties in common; first, that they refer to some elevated state of body function, and second, that arousal is noninformational and represents a nonspecific increment in activity. For the present purposes of reviewing the available literature, the operational definitions used will be divided into the following categories: (1) stimulus materials which are judged a priori to be arousing or which have been demonstrated to be arousing by another index such as the GSR; (2) arousal defined as sensory input variables such as white noise, delayed auditory feedback, peripheral shock, and induced muscle tension; (3) alterations in central or autonomic nervous system functions; (4) changes in peripheral measures such as GSR and heart rate; and (5) as personality characteristics of the organism such as introversion-extraversion or anxiety. A sixth possible category excluded in the present paper is arousal defined as the giving of incentives for performance, such as money or shock avoidance. Weiner and Walker (1966) and Weiner (1967) have made predictions from the consolidation theory of the Michigan group (Walker & Tarte, 1963: Kleinsmith & Kaplan, 1963a & 1963b) for the introduction of incentives in verbal learning. They suggest that high incentives produce high arousal which augments consolidative processes over time and therefore should result in increasing resistance to interference over time. In Weiner's studies as well as others (Loftus & Wickens, 1970) varying incentive, a cue is given immediately following the stimulus, signaling a reward condition which is to follow. The incentive thus becomes informational, unlike the other ways of manipulating arousal which have been used.

RESPONSE-INFERRED AROUSAL

Although the apparent logical order in which to discuss the proposed definitional categories would be, first, those involving stimulus manipulations; second, those involving central nervous system manipulations; and third, response-inferred definitions, the order will be changed to discuss response definitions first. The reason for this choice is that many of the studies involving "arousing" stimuli have used stimulus materials from other studies for which a response measure, the GSR, was the index of arousal. Hence, a discussion of these response-inferred arousal studies is appropriate first. Included in this section also, will be those studies using a priori stimulus definitions of arousal if a GSR measure has been used as a check on the choice of items.

Two early studies (Obrist, 1962; Berry, 1962) were concerned with the prediction of an inverted-U shape relationship between arousal and verbal learning. Obrist presented a series of lists to each of 5 Ss and found that for 3 Ss, the basic relationship between performance on the learning task and GSR was indeed an inverted-U shape function. For the remaining 2 Ss, the relationship was a positive linear function. He suggested two alternative interpretations of his data: (1) that the shape of the relationship between performance and learning is not universally curvilinear or linear but rather specific to each S, or (2) that the curvilinear relationship is common to all Ss but not found in the 2 Ss because they were performing on only one side of the optimal level. Berry found that moderate levels of skin conductance in the first minute of a learning session were related to better recall measured 6 minutes later and that moderate levels of conductance in the first minute of the recall period were also optimal for recall performance. Lesser and greater levels of skin conductance produced poorer performance. Some support for the inverted-U shape function relating arousal to verbal learning performance is found in these two studies. However, Kleinsmith, Kaplan, & Tarte (1963b) found that when both a six-minute recall and one-week recall measure were employed, the relationship between recall and skin conductance in the first minute of learning appeared to be an inverted-U shape for immediate retention, but a positive one for long-term retention.

There is a lack of clear support for an inverted-U shape function. In addition, the problem with the hypothesis is that in any study attempting to test the adequacy of the inverted-U shape for describing the relationship between arousal and performance, it may always be argued, after the fact, that not enough points along the arousal dimension were utilized if the predicted function was not obtained. Thus, a positive or a negative, or an inverted U-shape function may all result and be rationalized. Still another problem is that the function relating arousal to learning may appear to be different depending upon whether learning is assessed through short- or long-term recall. For example, in the Kleinsmith et al. (1963b) study, it could be argued that the positive relationship relating arousal to long-term retention and the inverted-U shape relating arousal to short-term retention occurred because arousal values change from short-term recall to long-term recall so that skin conductance in the first minute of learning is not indicative of arousal after one week.

Eisdorfer (1968), interested in the relationship of arousal level of different age groups to verbal learning, has used a different response, viz, level of free fatty acid in the plasma component of the blood. Blood samples were taken from indwelling needles during learning of verbal materials by young and old groups after the 5th, 10th, and 15th learning trails. Eisdorfer concluded from his data, that, contrary to the implicit assumption which has been made that the aged are at a resting state of low internal arousal, the aged, once aroused autonomically, perhaps because of a faulty ability to suppress individual organ responses or altered feedback, appear to function as in high levels of autonomic activity. The learning task increases arousal and produces a deterioration in performance. He further suggests that the inverted U-shape relationship is a reasonable model and consequently a decrease in arousal should facilitate performance by the older person.

The majority of studies using response measures of arousal have been concerned with the prediction of the Michigan group that high arousal produces poor immediate recall but ultimately better recall than low arousal. Studies testing these predictions have used both responses during acquisition and immediate recall as a measure of immediate retention. For purposes of this paper, these will be labeled short-term retention (STR) while later measures will be referred to as long-term retention (LTR). Walker & Tarte (1963) used words which were judged a priori to be high and low in arousal value. Independent groups of *S*s served in one of three arousal conditions, high, low, or mixed, consisting of four high and four low arousal stimuli. Within each list, one group recalled after 2 minutes, one after 45 minutes, and one after 1 week. The results showed that low arousal items were better recalled after 2 minutes while high arousal produced greater recall after 45 minutes and one week. A check was made in this study on the arousal value of the items by recording basal skin resistance levels to each item. Some disagreement with the a priori classification was obtained, since an overlap was reported between mean basal skin resistance levels for the high and low arousal words. Kleinsmith & Kaplan (1963; 1964) and Kaplan & Kaplan (1969), using GSRs to define high- and low-arousal items, employed both words and nonsense syllables in other tests of the differential effect of arousal for STR and LTR. Again, low arousal produced greater recall after 2 minutes while high arousal produced greater recall after 45 minutes, 1 day, and one week.

Butter (1970) replicated the Kleinsmith and Kaplan (1963) study with improved procedures to control for serial position effects and GSR habituation. She was also able to replicate the findings that high arousal items resulted in poor immediate recall compared with low arousal items after 2 minutes, but relatively better recall than for low arousal items after two days. In addition, she conducted a second experiment with different materials. The stimuli for this experiment differed along the concreteness-imagery dimension; half being high and half being low in concreteness-imagery. The responses were, as in her first experiment, single-digit numbers. Low-concreteness nouns were high in arousal value as defined by GSR responses while high-concreteness nouns were associated with low GSRs. As Butter had predicted, associates of high-concreteness nouns showed high STR but poor LTR while low-concreteness nouns showed the reverse.

A problem which cannot be ignored in attempting to evaluate the concept of arousal is its relationship to the orienting reflex. Levonian (1966) has pointed out that the GSR is a common measure of both arousal and orienting. The orienting response precedes the stimulus and should facilitate both short- and long-term retention. However, an elevated GSR following the stimulus reflects arousal and should inhibit STR but facilitate LTR according to the predictions of the Michigan group. He used a film on traffic safety as his stimulus material and measured GSRs to the material presented. A questionnaire was administered immediately following the film and one week later. Based on these responses, Levonian identified items for which both better STR and LTR were found and items for which better long-term than STR was found (reminiscence). He then analyzed GSR occurring both prior to and following the relevant point of information asked about in the questionnaire. His hypothesis was supported; that is, items for which both STR and LTR were superior were items for which an elevated GSR had been found prior to presentation of the relevant point of information, while reminiscence was found for those for which elevated postinformational GSRs were observed. Kaplan, Kaplan, and Sampson (1968) have also reported larger GSRs for items showing poor short-term recall but better long-term recall. Lavach (1971) has patterned a study after Levonian using continuously presented oral information and found evidence for the predicted interaction of arousal and retention interval.

In a more direct test of the relationship of magnitude of GSR during acquisition and recall, Corteen (1969) has determined correlation coefficients between GSR magnitude during acquisition and free recall after 2 minutes, 20 minutes, and 2 weeks. Significant positive correlations for all retention intervals were found. However, as he has pointed out, this finding does not support the prediction of the Michigan group for STR since a negative correlation would be expected for large GSRs and immediate retention. One particularly interesting aspect of his study is that the GSR was always allowed to return to the baseline after presentation of an item. Very long times for this return were reported for 5 practice items and durations of 30 to 60 seconds per word were reported even for test items actually used in the analysis. Studies using shorter intervals may result in interference from GSRs to previously presented stimuli. That such interference may occur is corroborated in data obtained by Grings & Schell (1969) using successive presentation intervals of 2, 4, 5, 6, 8, and 10 seconds.

Many of the studies reported have used 12-second interitem intervals and have filled that interval with a color-naming task. From Corteen's data, it appears likely that a 12-second interval length is not sufficient to allow GSR dissipation from one item before another is presented. It is also likely that presentation of colors (a noninformational stimulus) may increase GSRs and may confuse differences attributed to arousal value of the verbal stimuli. Another problem in these studies is adequacy of procedures to control for rehearsal. Corteen (1969), using misleading instructions to prevent rehearsal, believes these instructions were successful in preventing rehearsal since Ss could easily have memorized the entire list in the long interitem intervals, but forgetting did occur.

Maltzman, Kantor, and Langdon (1966) have used auditory presentation of the eight high- and eight low-arousal items of the Walker and Tarte (1963) study presented at 10 second intervals for two trials. GSR and cephalic vasomotor activity were both measured and a free-recall test was employed. Their findings do not support the consolidation hypothesis prediction since more high- than low-arousal items were recalled after both 2 minutes and 30 minutes. They also report that a differential GSR to the two types of items did not occur initially but developed during the presentation of the list. They obtained no difference in cephalic vasodilation, a commonly used index of the orienting response (Lynn, 1966). Kaplan and Kaplan (1968) have commented that they have not replicated their original findings of an interaction of arousal with time of recall when a free-recall procedure is used.

A problem in the evaluation of any retention measure is that differences in original learning may have occurred even if the same criterion of learning is imposed (Underwood, 1964). However, in those studies showing relative superiority of LTR for high-arousal material, an interaction of arousal with time of recall has occurred, suggesting that facilitation of high-arousal items in LTR cannot be accounted for by greater initial learning.

In summarizing these studies using response-inferred definitions of arousal, the only two studies which do not support the consolidation hypothesis for STR are the Corteen study in which long inter-item intervals were used and the Maltzman et al study (1966) in which auditory presentation and free recall were used. These findings suggest the need for more data on the influence of intertrial interval, mode of presentation of items, and type of recall measure. The only study not supporting the finding that high arousal produces relatively greater LTR (the definition of long-term varying from 45 minutes to 2 weeks) than low arousal, is Maltzman et al; however, the effects of differential rehearsal for the two types of items indeed appears likely.

STIMULUS-MANIPULATED AROUSAL

Characteristics of the material.   Berlyne, Borsa, Craw, Gelman, and Mandell (1965) presented Ss with paired associates in which the stimuli were visual patterns varying in complexity and the responses, male disyllabic names. As predicted from arousal theory, pairs using stimulus items of low complexity were retained better than high complexity stimulus pairs for immediate retention, while no difference in retention occurred after 24 hours suggesting differential, i.e., less rapid, forgetting, with the more complex and high arousal condition producing better retention.

Geometrical shapes and words rated for interestingness were used as arousal variables by Jones and Farley (1970). Nine conditions of interestingness were investigated, in which three levels of interestingness of both stimuli and responses and all combinations were investigated in a paired-associate learning task. Stimuli were always geometrical figures, and the responses, were words. Predicted interactions between arousal level and retention interval were not found. Items in which both stimuli and responses were high in arousal did not result in the poorest STR, nor did those items with low stimulus and response arousal result in the best STR. Results were also not in the direction predicted for the 48-hour retention measure.

It is significant to note that, although complexity and interestingness of materials are similar as difined by Berlyne et al. and Jones and Farley, the results of the Berlyne study supported consolidation theory while the Farley study did not. Berlyne, however, used an anticipation method of recall, while Farley used free recall.

Threatening versus nonthreatening words can also be viewed as differing in arousal value. Bergquist, Lewinsohn, Sue, and Flippo (1968) measured retention of these two types of words at intervals of 0-, 7-, and 15-seconds minutes and 40 minutes. The predictions for STR did not fit consolidation theory in that no differences were found for the 0-, 7-, or 15-second group. However, threatening words were better recalled after 40 minutes than the nonthreatening.

A few studies have used the items of the Kleinsmith and Kaplan and Walker and Tarte studies without use of concomitant GSR measures. Yarmey (1966) employed these stimuli and found results negative to the consolidation hypothesis, that is, high-arousal items were recalled better than low arousal after a 2-minute retention interval. The study differed from earlier ones in presenting the paired-associates orally at 2 second intervals and by alternation of study and recall trials. In recall trials, the stimuli alone were presented at 5-second intervals.

Farley (1969), again using the arousal items of Walker and Tarte (1963), found no difference for high- and low-arousal items in immediate retention, but did find relatively greater retention of high- than low-arousal items when recall was measured 3 days later. Immediate recall was very high and a "ceiling" effect may have prevented differences between arousal conditions from being evidenced. Again, free recall was used in this study and an attempt made to control for rehearsal between items by having Ss perform a simple motor task of connecting numbers with a pencil. This task does not seem an appropriate one to fill the interitem interval since it may induce muscle tension, another input used to produce arousal.

Induced muscle tension.   Courts (1939; 1942) demonstrated several interesting relationships between induced muscle tension and performance in verbal learning. Using six values of induced muscle tension, strength of a grip of a hand dynamometer defined by grips of 0, 1/8, 1/4, 3/8, and 3/4 of the maximum grip of each S, he found an inverted U-shape function relating muscle tension to acquisition. He also found some evidence consistent with an interpretation that individuals who differ in their placement along this inverted U-shape function respond to increases in induced muscle tension differently. Ss who demonstrated little or no facilitation of acquisition with required dynamometer tension showed greater patellar reflex amplitude when hand gripping was added to the learning task than Ss whose memorization was greatly improved by the addition of induced muscle tension. The effect of tension over trials was of concern in the

1942 study. He concluded that the maximal facilitation from tension occurred early in learning but not during the first trials. He further postulated that a disruptive effect from fatigue and emotion begins to build up as learning progresses which makes the overall function relating performance under tension to trials, an M-shaped curve.

Bourne (1955) suggested that the effect of tension might be upon performance rather than learning, and that if enough time elapsed to allow muscle tension to dissipate following acquisition, no permanent effect would be found. He employed a single learning trial for a 10-item paired-associate task. Time before recall was 0, 30, 60, 120, or 240 sec. Induced muscle tension was employed using a hand dynamometer during learning, recall, both or neither. No effect of muscle tension on recall was found if sufficient time was allowed for the tension to dissipate before testing. However, tension at the time of recall did facilitate recall. Bourne concluded that tension did significantly facilitate *performance* but not *learning.*

Frankel (1969), using induced muscle tension, tested the hypothesis that increases in arousal beyond that strong enough to bring a dominant response to maximum probability of occurrence will strengthen competing responses, hence the relative probability of dominant responses occurring will decrease. He experimentally "built in" high, medium, and low response dominances by varying frequencies of contiguous presentations of items in a paired-associate paradigm. Arousal was varied by magnitude of grip of a hand dynamometer, and sufficient time was allowed for tension to dissipate. As predicted, as arousal increased, frequency of dominant responses decreased, while the frequency of competing responses increased. It is again unfortunate for developing a parsimonious model that while these findings are consistent with the postulated inverted-U shape function relating arousal to performance, only the negative portion of the function is demonstrated and that the post hoc explanation must be that low enough levels of arousal were not present in the study to demonstrate the positive slope.

Delayed auditory feedback. Another type of sensory input which can be treated as arousal is delayed auditory feedback. King and Wolf (1965), using .2 second delayed auditory feedback introduced in the middle portion of a story, found that poorer immediate memory resulted for the delayed auditory feedback group than for a control, but after 24 hours there was no difference in recall. The relative gain of the delayed feedback group is consistent with the consolidation hypothesis when delayed auditory feedback is viewed as arousing. Physiological indices of GSR and pulse rate were also observed in this study and supported the contention that delayed auditory feedback was arousing.

White noise. White noise (WN) has been a frequently-chosen arousal stimulus since it has been demonstrated to produce both the activated EEG pattern (Magoun, 1963) and changes in the GSR (Davis, 1948; Berlyne & Lewis,

1963). That WN can thus be tied to both central and peripheral identification of arousal makes its use a particularly convenient way of investigating effects of arousal on verbal learning and retention.

Studies which have used additional WN synchronous with presentation of an *auditory stimulus* will not be included in this review since the WN provides a background aganist which a signal must be detected and there is the complicating effect of WN masking the stimulus. The arousal value cannot be separated from a consideration of the signal/noise ratio, which is a different question from irrelevant arousal input.

Berlyne and his students have reported several studies manipulating WN as an arousal stimulus (1965, 1966, 1968). All of these have used paired-associates and employed a within-Ss design. All have obtained some findings which are consistent with a consolidation hypothesis interpretation. Berlyne, Borsa, Craw, Gelman, and Mandell (1965) found inferior recall of items paired with WN during acquisition, while recall 24 hours later was better for these items. The addition of WN at recall produced no significant differences. Five intensities of WN were used during acquisition, 35, 45, 55, 65, and 75 *db*. Intensity, however, was not a significant variable. Berlyne, Borsa, Hamacher, and Koenig (1966) varied time of occurrence of WN for four conditions: (1) during both the stimulus and response presentation, (2) during neither, (3) in the six-second interval following the response, or (4) during the stimulus, response, and interpair interval. No effect of WN was found for any of the conditions for immediate retention. However, when WN was presented in condition (1) both during stimulus and response presentation, and (2) during stimulus, response and interpair interval presentation, significant facilitation of recall after 24 hours was produced.

Berlyne and Carey (1968) have used Turkish words as stimuli and English equivalents as responses. WN was presented during both stimulus and response presentation, during the stimulus alone, during the interval following when both the stimulus and response item appeared, or not at all. No measure of immediate retention was reported, but WN during either the stimulus alone or during the stimulus-response together resulted in superior retention 24 hours later.

In none of these studies was an attempt made to control rehearsal, nor was any physiological index used to determine if arousal had occurred as defined by such a measure. McLean (1969) conducted a study in which three methodological improvements were made. First, an attempt to control rehearsal was made, with Ss asked to name colors on slides during interitem presentations. Second, GSR was measured and analyses of results made for high and low responses as well as for WN and no WN items. Third, serial position was conterbalanced so that each of the six paired-associates appeared once in each serial position. Two experiments were employed, one in which Ss were not instructed that they would be tested on recall, and one in which they were. Interference for immediate retention was found for WN items, but facilitated retention was found for WN items 24 hours later, except in the experiment in which Ss had been asked to learn the items for subsequent retention and in which GSR was used as the basis of arousal determination.

Sloboda and Smith (1968) noted that effects of WN had been obtained only when the noise was administered at the same time as the stimulus material. In a serial-learning task, using digits, WN came after each stimulus item for two seconds at varying temporal locations in a 12-second interval. No effects of WN were found for any temporal location. However, concurrent GSR measures indicated no difference between WN and non-WN items.

Whether WN effects during acquisition on immediate recall and 24-hour recall would differ with paired associate, serial, or free learning was a question of interest for Haveman and Farley (1969). Independent groups of Ss were used for noise and no-noise conditions as well as for the three types of learning. No effect of the noise on either immediate or 24-hour retention was found for the serial or paired-associate list. WN did produce a significant interaction for free learning, however, with better recall of WN items than control items after 24 hours. Free learning consisted of presenting items on cards at 2-second intervals for 2 trials and asking S to pronounce each item. Haveman and Farley interpreted the results to suggest that difficulty of the task is a relevant variable and that free learning is easier than either serial or paired-associate learning; hence easy tasks may be more sensitive to the influence of arousal while more difficult ones are not. Differences other than the type of learning were also present in the three procedures, however, such as time of item exposure and total time involved in the learning task and recall procedures. Anticipation recall was used for serial and paired-associate learning while free recall was used for the free learning situation.

Relevant to the suggestion of Haveman and Farley that arousal effects are related to task difficulty is a study by Houston (1969), who manipulated both task difficulty and type of task. Two tasks were used, one which required inhibition of a response, and one which required no inhibition. Results of the task difficulty variable were not consistent with Farley's suggestion that WN effects would be more evident in an easier task, since no difference was found as a function of task difficulty. WN effects did differ, however, for the two types of tasks. The inhibitory task was the Stroop-Color-Word-Interference test in which *names* of colors are printed in a different color and S is required to inhibit the word and respond to the color in which it is printed. Presence of continuous WN during this task significantly facilitated performance on it as measured by time taken to complete the task. The noninhibitory task was simple color naming of the ink in which nonreward stimuli such as asterisks, letters, and bars were printed. WN interfered with performance on this task. Houston's interpretation of his data is that S had to inhibit a response to the noise and that this inhibition facilitated making an inhibitory response to the conflicting stimulus in the Stroop test. Pulse rate was measured in this experiment but showed no differences between WN and non—WN conditions.

Young (1969) was interested in WN effects on learning and recall of paired-associates consisting of CVC trigrams as stimuli and adjective responses, in which both noise and no-noise items were given to the same S. WN was sounded both during presentation of the stimulus and the stimulus and response together. Significant interference was found for WN items when measured by trials to attain the criterion of 9 of 12 correct responses. Both free recall and anticipation recall were tested one week later. When initial learning differences were held constant by analysis of covariance, no differences between WN conditions resulted for either free or anticipation recall. This differential forgetting with relatively less loss for WN from STR to LTR is consistent with the consolidation hypothesis.

An additional question of interest concerns the effect of arousal introduced initially at the time of recall. Uehling and Sprinkle (1968) compared groups which had learned serial lists of neutral items to the criterion of one perfect anticipation trial after retention intervals of 2 minutes, 24 hours, and 1 week. Experimental groups were presented with bursts of WN for 3 minutes prior to the recall trial or were required to squeeze a hand dynamometer for a 3-minute period. Control groups were instructed to relax. Recall was significantly facilitated by WN for both the 24 hour and 1-week groups. That it did not do so for the 2-minute retention group is probably due to the "ceiling effect" of a high degree of retention. Induced muscle tension had no effect.

WN arousal has also been studied in intentional recall and forgetting (Archer & Margolin, 1970). The task involved auditory presentation of 16 2-digit numbers. For half of the numbers, a 1-second burst of WN either immediately preceded the number or preceded the instruction regarding the number given 3 seconds later. The instruction was either "remember it" or "don't remember it." For the remaining half of the numbers, no WN was presented. Retention of both "remember" and "don't remember it" items was tested by a recognition measure. WN had no effect on intentional forgetting, but did produce significant facilitation of recall of "remember" items.

In summarizing the effects of stimulus manipulations on learning and retention, considerable evidence can be found from data manipulating stimulus inputs such as arousal characteristics of the material (e. g., complexity, and threatening verus nonthreatening items), induced muscle tension, and delayed auditory feedback, to support the consolidation hypothesis. One study with negative findings employed free recall, and the other perhaps could not detect differences because of a ceiling effect on learning. As for the effects of WN on learning and retention, there is again considerable evidence to support the consolidation hypothesis. Two of the studies reported show no interference for WN on immediate retention (Berlyne et al. 1966; Haveman & Farley, 1969) while the remainder of the studies have resulted in interference with arousal on immediate retention. Studies in which WN has produced interference in STR have used both between- and within-groups designs, have employed a variety of stimulus materials, have measured short-term memory effects by measures during acquisition and immediately-given recall trials, have used a variety of intensities of WN, and have differed in attempting to control for rehearsal. The two studies with findings negative to the consolidation hypothesis for STR have both reported relatively poor learning of the materials. Thus, degree of learning rather than difficulty of the task may be a relevant variable.

Although concerned with arousal effects on intentional remembering and forgetting, Archer and Margolin (1970) obtained facilitation of WN items in a STR measure. There were three important methodological differences between this study and those finding no effect of arousal on STR or interference. One was the use of the recognition measure; another, timing of the WN presentation, and finally, the use of auditory rather than visual presentation.

In summarizing the findings in LTR it is important to consider the relative changes from STR to LTR. Almost all studies support the finding of differential forgetting of high- and low-arousal items for LTR. Sometimes the change is from interference in STR to facilitation in LTR for high arousal; sometimes from interference to no difference, sometimes from no difference to facilitation, but with the exception of one study, there is less of a relative loss for WN items. The one exception is Haveman and Farley (1969) for two of three conditions, and these were conditions with relatively poor learning.

Two studies support the conclusion that the effects of WN are limited to concurrent presentation of the noise with the stimulus and the response and that noise during the interitem interval is not effective (Berlyne et al. 1966; Sloboda & Smith, 1968). There is also evidence that WN presented before recall will facilitate LTR (Uehling & Sprinkle, 1968), although Berlyne et al. (1965) found no increase in 24-hour retention when WN was added at that time. There are two major differences between these two studies. One is the degree of first-list learning: a high degree of learning was used in Uehling and Sprinkle and a relatively low degree in Berlyne; the second, that Uehling and Sprinkle used 3-minute bursts of WN before recall began, thus inducing a generalized arousal prior to the session, while Berlyne used prompted recall in which WN was introduced synchronously with the stimulus.

PHYSIOLOGICAL MANIPULATIONS OF AROUSAL

Very little has been done to attempt the manipulation of central nervous system arousal directly and then study subsequent effects on verbal learning. The possibilities for direct central nervous system intervention are lesions, chemical or electrical stimulation, and drugs. Systematic investigation by the two former techniques is generally out of the question with humans, so the third technique, drugs, is generally the stimulus of choice, but this also provides difficulties. The first question when using a drug to manipulate arousal is the question of whether the drug can be specified to act on, and only on, those structures thought to underlie arousal. A second problem is to use a sufficient dosage range to get an adequate test of effectiveness. A third problem is a behavioral consideration of whether the behaviors chosen for study are those which do in fact reflect "arousal." Fourth, will a placebo or other drugs not acting on arousal structures produce the same effects?

Batten (1967) used Dexedrine and phenobarbital to manipulate arousal and investigate effects on verbal learning. The former drug is a stimulant of brainstem activity, and the latter, a depressant. Unfortunately, only one level of each drug was employed and in addition to the drug, instructions varied in their arousal properties.

AROUSAL IN PERSONALITY INDICES

Eysenck (1967) has postulated that introverts have higher states of internal arousal and therefore should demonstrate stronger consolidative processes immediately after learning than extroverts. It follows that relatively inferior performance should occur for introverts on immediate retention since the ongoing consolidative process interferes with immediate recovery, but relatively greater performance on long-term measures should occur as compared with extroverts. Howarth and Eysenck (1968), using a paired-associate learning task of CVC trigram pairs, have found evidence supporting this prediction. Extroverts showed superior performance on immediate and 1-minute recall, while performance was nearly equal after 5 minutes, then superior for introverts at 30 minutes and 24 hours. Berlyne and Carey (1968), on the other hand, have reported evidence of superior retention for extroverts after 24 hours.

McLaughlin and Eysenck (1967) have extended this prediction for immediate retention to neurotic and stable extroverts as well as neurotic and stable introverts. Two levels of difficulty of CVC trigram pairs were used. They predicted that extroversion should result in better STR than introversion, and, further, that neuroticism should facilitate performance on an easy task, but interfere on a difficult one. The rank orders obtained for the groups are not completely consistent with the hypothesis, but are interpreted as confirming the superiority of extroverts to introverts on immediate retention with both levels of difficulty and that moderate anxiety is superior for learning the easy list, while low anxiety is superior for the more difficult.

SUMMARY

The lack of either physiological or behavioral unidimensionality of arousal as a construct is evident from the review of studies presented in this paper. Centrally, arousal has been defined electorcortically and autonomically. Peripherally, it has been defined by peripheral measures, such as the GSR, heart rate, pulse rate, and vasoconstriction of blood vessels. Operationally, it has been defined by sensory inputs such as induced muscle tension, white noise, and delayed auditory feedback; by stimulus materials which are arousing according to a priori considerations; and by personality characteristics such as introversion and extroversion. Few studies have checked correspondence among these measures and, unfortunately, there has been little systematic attack on variables which influence arousal defined in any of these ways. Often the concept has merely been invoked as a post hoc explanatory notion.

The predictions cited at the beginning of the paper regarding arousal can be evaluated in the light of the evidence reviewed. Few studies have tested the first prediction that performance is related to arousal by an inverted-U shape function, and the evidence from these is conflicting. As discussed earlier, the problem with the predicted relationship is that, after the fact, a positive or negative function relating performance to arousal can always be explained as a failure to include a sufficient range of arousal values to obtain the entire function.

Much more research has been generated by the second discussed prediction, that high arousal leads to interference in STR but facilitation of LTR. Some considerable evidence resulting in high-arousal interference has been found in studies using GSR, delayed auditory feedback, and WN. Results not in agreement with this finding using GSR measures of arousal have been found in studies using auditory presentation, free recall, and in a study which employed the atypically long interitem intervals which permitted the GSR to return to baseline. The studies employing WN which have obtained results negative to the hypothesis of high-arousal interference for STR are ones in which auditory presentation has been used and somewhat lower degrees of learning attained. Further work on these variables needs to be done to determine the limits of the generalization regarding arousal and STR, particularly the mode of presentation, since all studies finding negative results used the auditory modality for the learning tasks.

It is apparent from the present review, however, that a great deal of evidence has been found consistent with the consolidation hypothesis that arousal interferes with STR. However, alternative explanations are possible. Arousal concurrent with, or inherent in, elements to be learned may provide a distraction or become a compound stimulus, thus decreasing the time available to process, encode, and store the stimulus as compared to low arousal items. The Corteen (1969) study in which a negative correlation was not found relating magnitude of GSR and immediate retention would tend to support this interpretation, since time intervals between items were sufficient to allow arousal as measured by the GSR to dissipate. Time available to process the stimulus was considerably greater. If arousal does act as a distractor, thus increasing processing time, manipulation of the iteritem interval should result in interference for high-arousal items for short intervals, but decrease as interitem time intervals increase until no difference or facilitation is obtained.

Another possible interpretation of these results is that high-arousal items, because of similar autonomic responses elicited by the stimuli, are more similar to each other than low-arousal items are to one another, hence high intralist similarity results in lower learning which measures of immediate retention reflect. Independent manipulation of high- and low-intralist similarity of high- and low-arousal items appears needed to test this hypothesis.

In attempting to generalize across studies for effects of high and low arousal items in LTR, changes from STR must be considered rather than a direct comparison of high- and low-arousal items in LTR. There is a great deal of evidence that high arousal in acquisition does produce differential forgetting in that LTR is relatively better for high arousal than low. Although these findings are again consistent with the consolidation hypothesis of the Michigan group, other alternatives are possible. It may be that the effect of high arousal is to produce more active rehearsal during extended retention intervals, particularly if *S* suspects that he will be tested again (vis., McLean, 1969 using GSR). This rehearsal does not appear to be what is meant by "consolidation." The distinction between rehearsal and consolidation, however, appears untestable. Whatever the theoretical interpretation, the empirical finding is an important one and warrants additional work to determine the effect of such variables as type of retention measure, time limits for which the finding holds, and effects of individual difference variables such as introversion-extroversion, anxiety, age, and sex.

Another finding regarding arousal has been that arousal introduced at the time of recall can influence retrieval even if arousal had not been deliberately introduced during learning. That this is not simply the effect of stimulus change in arousal conditions from learning to retention can be ruled out by the nature of the arousal manipulation since WN was administered in a 3-minute period prior to recall, not during actual stimulus presentation in testing recall.

The third hypothesis that *changes* in arousal level from low to intermediate levels or high to intermediate levels will increase learning has not been tested directly but again has been used primarily as an "after the fact" explanation. Certainly, many of the studies have involved arousal increments but initial and changed arousal levels have not been specified. And finally, the treatment of arousal as generalized drive in the Hull-Spence sense is provocative though again little systematic research has been done. The hypothesis that arousal will interact with task difficulty has received some attention but has not been sufficiently investigated to permit a conclusion.

In sum, it appears that arousal as an explanatory concept in verbal learning has not been as valuable as some might hope. That so many investigators have found some treatment of an activation continuum important in explaining behavior is not to be ignored. The considerable commonality of results found for changes from STR to LTR with arousal across a diversity of definitions of arousal is important. The concept needs the sharpening influence of analytic and systematic attention to variables influencing it in order to increase its heuristic value.

REFERENCES

Archer, B. U., & Margolin, R. Arousal effects in intentional recall and forgetting. *Journal of Experimental Psychology*, 1970, 86, 8–12.

Batten, D. E. Recall of paired-associates as a function of arousal and recall interval. *Perceptual and Motor Skills*, 1967, 24, 1055–1058.

Bergquist, W. N., Lewinshon, P. M., Sue, D. W., & Flippo, J. R. Short and long term memory for various types of stimuli as a function of repression-sensitization. *Journal of Experimental Research in Personality*, 1968, 3, 28–38.

Berkowitz, L., & Breck, R. W. Impulsive aggression: reactivity to aggressive cues under emotional arousal. *Journal of Personality*, 1967, 35, 415–424.

Berlyne, D. E. Arousal and reinforcement. In D. Levine (ed.) *Nebraska symposium on motivation*. Lincoln, Neb.: University of Nebraska Press, 1967.

Berlyne, D. E., Borsa, D. M., Craw, M. A., Gelman, R. S., & Mandell, E. E. Effects of stimulus complexity and induced arousal on paired-associate learning. *Journal of Verbal Learning and Verbal Behavior*, 1965, 4, 291–299.

Berlyne, D. E., Borsa, D. M., Hamacher, J. H., & Koenig, I. D. V. Paired-associate learning and the timing of arousal. *Journal of Experimental Psychology*, 1966, 72, 1–6.

Berlyne, D. E., & Carey, S. T. Incidental learning and the timing of arousal. *Psychonomic Science*, 1968, 13, 103–104.

Berlyne, D. E., & Lewis, J. L. Effects of heightened arousal on human exploratory behavior. *Canadian Journal of Psychology*, 1963, 17, 398–410.

Berry, R. N. Skin conductance levels and verbal recall. *Journal of Experimental Psychology*, 1962, 63, 275–277.

Bourne, L. E., Jr. An evaluation of the effect of induced tension on performance. *Journal of Experimental Psychology*, 1955, 49, 418–422.

Butter, M. J. Differential recall of paired associates as a function of arousal and concreteness-imagery levels. *Journal of Experimental Psychology*, 1970, 84, 252–256.

Corteen, R. S. Skin conductance changes and word recall. *British Journal of Psychology*, 1969, 60, 81–84.

Courts, F. A. Relations between experimentally induced muscular tension and memorization. *Journal of Experimental Psychology*, 1939, 25, 235–256.

Courts, F. A. Relations between muscular tension and performance. *Journal of Experimental Psychology*, 1942, 80, 504–511.

Davis, R. C. Motor effects of strong auditory stimulation. *Journal of Experimental Psychology*, 1963, 65, 257–275.

Duffy, E. The psychological significance of the concept of "arousal" or "activation." *Psychological Review*, 1957, 64, 265–275.

Eisdorfer, C. Arousal and performance: experiments in verbal learning and a tentative theory. In G. A. Talland (ed.) *Human ageing and behavior: Recent advances in research and theory.* New York: Academic Press, 1968, Pp. 189–216.

Eysenck, H. J. *The biological basis of personality.* Springfield, Ill.: Thomas, 1967.

Farley, F. Memory storage in free learning as a function of arousal and time with homogeneous and heterogeneous lists. Technical Report No. 87, June, 1969, Wisconsin Research and Development Center for Cognitive Learning, Contract OE 5–10–154, U.S. Office of Education, Department of Health, Education, and Welfare.

Feldman, S., & Waller, H. Dissociation of electrocortical activation and behavioral arousal. *Nature,* 1962, 196, 1320–1322.

Frankel, A. S. Effects of arousal on hierarchically organized responses. *Journal of Experimental Psychology,* 1969, 82, 385–389.

Grings, W. W., & Schell, A. Magnitude of electrodermal response to a standard stimulus as a function of intensity and proximity of a prior stimulus. *Journal of Comparative and Physiological Psychology,* 1969, 67, 77–82.

Haveman, J., & Farley, F. H. Arousal and retention in paired-associate, serial, and free learning. Technical Report No. 91, July, 1969, Wisconsin Research and Development Center for Cognitive Learning, Contract OE 5–10–154, U. S. Office of Education, Department of Health, Education, and Welfare.

Hebb, D. O. Drives and the C. N. S. (conceptual nervous system). *Psychological Review,* 1955, 62, 243–254.

Houston, B. K. Noise, task difficulty and Stroop color-word performance. *Journal of Experimental Psychology,* 1969, 82, 403–404.

Howarth, E., & Eysenck, H. J. Extraversion, arousal, and paired-associate recall. *Journal of Experimental Research in Personality,* 1968, 3, 114–116.

Jones, M. E., & Farley, F. Short- and long-term retention as a function of variations in stimulus and response interestingness. Technical Report No. 150, December, 1970, Wisconsin Research and Development Center for Cognitive Learning, Contract OE 5–10–154, U. S. Office of Education, Department of Health, Education, and Welfare.

Kaplan, S., & Kaplan, R. Arousal and memory: a comment. *Psychonomic Science,* 1968, 10, 291–292.

Kaplan, R., & Kaplan, S. The arousal-retention interval interaction revisited: the effects of some procedural changes. *Psychonomic Science,* 1969, 15, 84–85.

Kaplan, S., Kaplan, R., & Sampson, J. R. Encoding and arousal factors in free recall of verbal and nonverbal material. *Psychonomic Science,* 1968, 12, 73–74.

King, D. J., & Wolf, S. The influence of delayed auditory feedback on immediate and delayed memory. *Journal of Psychology,* 1965, 59, 131–139.

Kleinsmith, L. J., & Kaplan, S. The interaction of arousal and recall interval in nonsense syllable paired-associate learning. *Journal of Experimental Psychology,* 1964, 67, 124–126.

Kleinsmith, L. J., & Kaplan, S. Paired-associate learning as a function of arousal and interpolated interval. *Journal of Experimental Psychology,* 1963, 65, 190–193.

Kleinsmith, L., Kaplan, S., & Tarte, R. The relationship of arousal to short-term and long-term memory. *Canadian Journal of Psychology*, 1963, 17, 393–397.

Lacey, J. I. Somatic response patterning and stress: some revisions of activation theory. In Mortimer H. Appley and Richard Trumbull (eds.) *Psychological stress*. New York: Appleton-Century Crofts, 1967.

Lavach, J. F. The effects of emotional arousal on short versus long term retention of continuously presented information. Paper presented at the meeting of the Eastern Psychological Association, New York, April, 1971.

Levonian, E. Attention and consolidation as factors in retention. *Psychonomic Science*, 1966, 6, 275–276.

Lindsley, D. B. Emotion. In S. S. Stevens (ed.) *Handbook of experimental psychology*. New York: John Wiley & Sons, Inc., 1951, Pp. 473–516.

Loftus, G. R., & Wickens, T. D. Effect of incentive on storage and retrieval processes. *Journal of Experimental Psychology*, 1970, 85, 141–147.

Lynn, R. *Attention, arousal, and the orientation reaction*. Oxford: Pergamon Press, 1966.

Magoun, H. W. *The waking brain* (2nd ed.) Springfield, Ill.: Chas. C. Thomas, 1963.

Malmo, R. B. Activation: a neurophysiological dimension. *Psychological Review*, 1959, 66, 367–386.

Maltzman, I., Kantor, W., & Langdon, B. Immediate and delayed retention, arousal, and the orienting and defensive reflexes. *Psychonomic Science*, 1966, 6, 445–446.

McLaughlin, R. J., & Eysenck, H. J. Extraversion, neuroticism, and paired-associates learning. *Journal of Experimental Research in Personality*, 1967, 2, 128–132.

McLean, P. D. Induced arousal and time of recall as determinants of paired-associate recall. *British Journal of Psychology*, 1969, 60, 57–62.

Obrist, P. A. Some autonomic correlates of serial learning. *Journal of verbal Learning and Verbal Behavior*, 1962, 1, 100–104.

Schlosberg, H. Three dimensions of emotion. *Psychological Review*, 1954, 61, 81–88.

Sloboda, W., & Smith, E. E. Disruption effects in human short-term memory: some negative findings. *Perceptual and Motor Skills*, 1968, 27, 575–582.

Taylor, S. P., & Epstein, S. The measurement of autonomic arousal. *Psychosomatic Medicine*, 1967, 29, 514–525.

Uehling, B., & Sprinkle, R. Recall of a serial list as a function of arousal and retention interval. *Journal of Experimental Psychology*, 1968, 78, 103–106.

Underwood, B. J. Degree of learning and the measurement of forgetting. *Journal of Verbal Learning and Verbal Behavior*, 1964, 3, 112–129.

Walker, E. L. Action decrement and its relation to learning. *Psychological Review*, 1958, 65, 129–142.

Walker, E. L., & Tarte, R. D. Memory storage as a function of arousal and time with homogeneous and heterogeneous lists. *Journal of Verbal Learning and Verbal Behavior*, 1963, 2, 113–119.

Weiner, B. Motivational factors in short-term retention: II. Rehearsal or arousal? *Psychological Reports*, 1967, 20, 1203–1208.

Weiner, B., & Walker, E. L. Motivational factors in short-term retention. *Journal of Experimental Psychology*, 1966, 71, 190–193.

Yarmey, A. D. Word arousal in verbal mediation. *Psychonomic Science*, 1966, 6, 451–452.

Young, C. C. Arousal effects on paired-associate list learning and recall. Unpublished M. A. thesis, Emory University, 1969.

11 | Verbal Discrimination

WILLIAM P. WALLACE
University of Nevada, Reno

The present essay represents an attempt to review the empirical facts and thinking that have accompanied the use of verbal discrimination as an analytical research technique. The major purpose is to present a reassessment of the frequency theory of verbal-discrimination learning, formally proposed by Ekstrand, Wallace, and Underwood (1966). Data which have been presented as evidence favorable to the theory will be reviewed, as well as data interpreted as unfavorable to the theory. In the latter cases, an attempt will be made to specify the implications such "negative" evidence has for the theory. Finally, some minor adjustments in the frequency theory will be proposed.

The verbal-discrimination paradigm is one standard task for laboratory investigations of recognition memory. Although there may be variations, the basic task procedure involves the presentation of pairs of items. One member in each pair is designated the "correct" item, or the item the subjects must learn to choose as that pair appears. The task confronting subjects is quite simple. As each pair of items is presented, the subject indicates which member of the pair he wishes to choose. The experimenter immediately informs the subject which is the correct member of the pair, or he waits until the subject has made his selection for all pairs before revealing the correct item in each pair. Learning is demonstrated by a gain in the number of correct responses over trials, or performance after an initial trial that surpasses the level of performance that would be expected had no trial been given.

There are two key features in tests of recognition memory. Recognition-memory procedures generally involve the presentation of "target" items during an early stage in an experiment. These same items are presented later, and recognition memory refers to the subjects' recollection that these items were the target items. Thus, the first key feature is that reproduction of specific items is not required. The target item is presented, and the subject merely indicates whether or not that item is the earlier presented target item. The second feature is that distractor items are also presented during the test. Distractors are nontarget items, so the recognition test requires the acceptance of target items and the rejection of distractors. Following an initial period of inspection of target items, the recognition test may involve a long list of targets and distractors (e.g., Allen & Garton, 1968), or a series of multiple-choice tests, each with one target and one or more distractors (e.g., Kintsch, 1968). Another popular variation involves the presentation of a continuous series of items in which target items are repetitions of items that appeared earlier in the series, and distractors are items that appear a single time or the first appearance of targets (e.g., Underwood, 1965). The verbal-discrimination procedure represents yet another variation of the recognition-memory format. If we consider the correct member of each verbal-discrimination pair as the target item and the incorrect member as the distractor, then we may conceive of verbal discrimination as a recognition-memory paradigm in which a given target and distractor consistently appear together during both inspection (study) and test phases of the experiment. No attempt is made here to analyze similarities and differences in processes and task requirements among different recognition-memory paradigms since the present discussion is restricted to verbal-discrimination learning.

VERBAL-DISCRIMINATION LINEAGE

The verbal-discrimination procedure has been described, and one may inquire at this point why researchers have been interested in this task. A brief historical digression may best serve the purpose of answering this question. In this way the interests of early investigators which led to the development of verbal discrimination may be examined, as well as the interests which contribute to the continued use of the task.

The verbal-discrimination task is a relative newcomer. Perhaps its first appearance, as we know it today, was not until 1942. However, there were events that preceded this date that were important to the development of the task. Peterson (1920) introduced a modification of a serial maze task. He was interested in the backward elimination of errors in maze learning, but he was worried that the spatial mazes used in maze-learning studies with rats and humans resulted in unnecessary complications. Specifically, he believed complications were introduced after an error was made in a spatial maze. Retracing the paths to correct an error could produce confusion in spatial orientation and contribute to additional errors. Also, he noted the difficulty in scoring and interpreting "partial" entries and returns in a spatial maze. In an effort to eliminate these difficulties, Peterson used two letters to label each choice point in a maze, and then read these labels to his subjects. For example, he would read "A" and "B," and the subject would respond by selecting A or B. If the subject selected the correct alternative the experimenter would read the labels of the next choice point. If the subject erred, the experimenter would repeat the label of the correct choice and the correct label at the previous choice point. Selection of the latter was considered to be equivalent to "retracing" in this maze.

A second episode which was indirectly important in the development of verbal discrimination centered on an early interest in comparing the acquisition and retention of motor habits and ideational habits (e.g., McGeoch, 1932;

McGeoch & Melton, 1929). The motor habits were assessed by standard maze-learning tasks, and the ideational habits were assessed by serial learning of nonsense syllables. Although McGeoch was cautious in interpreting the data from such comparisons, it was suggested that "materials which are verbal and ideational in character are, when learned to a uniform criterion, uniformly retained, over both relatively short and relatively long intervals, better than are maze habits" (McGeoch, 1932, p. 679).

Van Tilborg (1936) was also interested in the comparison of acquisition and retention of motor habits with verbal habits. However, he was critical of the procedures which had been used to equate the structure of the two types of tasks. He modified Peterson's "mental maze" and used this modification for comparison with performance on a finger-maze task. Van Tilborg's mental maze consisted of 20 pairs of nonsense syllables which were used to designate correct paths and blind alleys of a hypothetical maze. Selection of the correct member of a pair "led" the subject to the next pair, and an error resulted in the experimenter rereading the pair until the subject made the correct choice.

The final alteration remaining for the mental maze to evolve into the verbal-discrimination task was the introduction of variation in the serial order of the choice points. Of course, interests in comparing acquisition and retention of finger mazes and mental mazes required a constant order of choice points. The final development did not come until another use for the mental-maze task was considered.

A phenomenon that received some attention in the early literature was reminiscence. Reminiscence refers to an increase in recall over time without practice, or the opposite of forgetting. An experiment by Hovland (1938) illustrates a typical procedure. His subjects learned a serial list of 12 nonsense syllables to either a criterion of one perfect recitation or seven out of 12 correct. The experimental groups then had a 2-minute rest period filled with a color-naming task prior to a recall test, and the control groups had their recall test immediately. Reminiscence, defined by higher recall for the experimental groups compared to the control groups, was observed in this study. A major interpretation of reminiscence was based on differential forgetting of strong and weak habits, i.e., weak habits are forgotten more rapidly than strong habits. It was assumed that in the course of acquiring a serial list, remote associations develop (e.g., an association between the first item in the serial list and the third item in the serial list), as well as the correct associations between items in adjacent serial positions. The remote associations were presumed to be weaker than the correct associations, and it was believed that they were a source of interference. Reminiscence was attributed to forgetting over the brief time interval, but since there was more forgetting of the weak interfering habits than the strong correct habits, the net result was improvement in recall.

McClelland (1942a 1942b) was interested in testing the differential forgetting hypothesis of reminiscence. He believed that the mental-maze task with varying serial order was well suited for this purpose because of an advantage in specifying the nature of the interfering response. McClelland reasoned that the interfering tendency in this task is saying the wrong item when a pair is exposed. Contrary to the serial-learning task, the interfering tendency in "verbal discrimination" is at maximum strength on the initial trial and declines as learning progresses. Thus, McClelland argued that verbal discrimination was a task with the influence of interfering habits at a minimum. Consequently, if the differential forgetting hypothesis of reminiscence were true, reminiscence should not be observed in verbal discrimination.

McClelland uncovered some interesting relations with the verbal-discrimination task; however his interest in reminiscence obscured these relations and their importance was not emphasized until some 20 to 30 years later (e.g., Anderson, 1969; Underwood & Freund, 1970b; Underwood, Jesse, & Ekstrand, 1964). Specifically, McClelland (1942b) noted the importance of "familiarity" in governing the selections made by subjects, and he suggested the possibility that familiarity "fades" during retention intervals. Further studies on reminiscence by McClelland (1943a; 1943b) introduced the additional procedural variation of single presentation of each item accompanied by the appropriate correct or incorrect designations. This variation moves away from the standard verbal-discrimination procedure and will not be considered further; however, it should be mentioned that with this procedure McClelland (1943b) included a manipulation which has received some recent attention. At some point in learning, all the "right" words were switched to "wrong" and all of the wrongs switched to rights (reversal). There was a slight performance decrement as a result of this manipulation, ease of reversal increased with a higher degree of learning prior to reversing item functions, and reversal learning was far superior to learning without any prior training.

There is, perhaps, some risk in attempting a classification of the scientific motives that lead to the adoption of specific experimental procedures. In the remainder of this section I have attempted to identify general patterns of interest that give rise to current use of verbal discrimination. The interests of current investigators who use the verbal-discrimination task appear to conform to at least one of three identifiable objectives. Although this classification may be incomplete, it is hoped that at least some major interests may be identified.

McClelland's original use for verbal discrimination was as a vehicle to investigate general learning phenomena. Similarly, other investigators have employed the task as a means to study specific principles of learning and retention (e.g., Postman, 1962b; Spear, Ekstrand, & Underwood, 1964). Most notably, investigators engaged with problems of reinforcement in human learning have turned to the verbal-discrimination task.

The Law of Effect has held a dominant position in the history of experimental psychology (see Postman, 1947; 1962a). There has been considerable interest in evaluating the reinforcing properties of saying "right" and "wrong" on the repetition of responses. Buss and Buss (1956) varied reinforcement in a concept-sorting task. Reinforcement combinations of "right" for a correct response and nothing for an incorrect response (R–N), "wrong" for an incorrect response and nothing for a correct response (W–N), and "right" for a correct response and "wrong" for an incorrect response (R–W) were compared. They found that W–N was as good as R–W and superior to R–N, which led to their claim that W was a stronger reinforcer than R. Spence and her associates (e.g., Spence, 1964; Spence, Armstrong, & Conrad, 1969; Spence, Lair, & Goodstein, 1963) explored various reinforcement combinations in verbal-discrimination paradigms. The verbal-discrimination paradigm has the advantage of controlling the informative feedback imparted by saying "right" and "wrong." That is, the correct word in each pair is completely identifiable based on the experimenter's response. The general finding from these investigations was that the R–N combination is inferior, but this appears to be due to ambiguity in the subject's interpretation of the meaning of N when combined with R. When subjects are fully informed concerning the meaning of N, the W–N superiority over R–N disappears (Kausler & Lair, 1968; Spence et al., 1969; Spence et al., 1963). In addition to current interest in reinforcing (information) properties of right, wrong, and nothing, the verbal-discrimination paradigm has been used to investigate effects of incentive magnitude in human learning (e.g., Estes, 1966; Lintz & Brackbill, 1966; Marston & Kanfer, 1963), reinforcement delay (e.g., Lintz & Brackbill, 1966; Markowitz & Renner, 1966) and self–produced reinforcement (e.g., Marston, 1964; Marston & Kanfer, 1963).

A second general application of verbal-discrimination procedures, often difficult to distinguish from the first, centers on an interest in determining the generality of principles of learning, and of phenomena that have been discovered with the more traditional verbal-learning tasks. For example, it has been demonstrated that, similar to paired-associate learning and serial learning, the recall method of verbal discrimination is superior to the anticipation method (Battig & Switalski, 1966; Fulkerson & Johnson, 1971; Ingison & Ekstrand, 1970). In the recall method all pairs are exposed in succession, and for each the subject must choose the correct item. After all the pairs have been shown, the correct items are presented alone and in succession, or the pairs are presented with the correct items designated. With the anticipation procedure each pair is shown and the subject is required to make his selection, and immediately following the exposure of each pair the correct item for that pair is indicated. Schulz and Hopkins (1968) indicated that, similar to serial learning, verbal discrimination with aural presentation was inferior to visual presentation with low meaningful material, but there was little difference between presentation modes with high meaningful material. Wike and Wike (1970c) reported an isolation effect with the anticipation procedure when the stimulus pair was isolated, but not when just the feedback item (the correct word shown subsequent to exposure of the pair) was isolated. Imagery value of words has been shown to facilitate paired-associate learning, serial learning, and free recall. Paivio and Rowe (1970) and Rowe and Paivio (1971) reported an advantage in verbal discrimination for high-imagery pairs, compared to low-imagery pairs. However, Ingison and Ekstrand (1970) reported no difference between abstract pairs and concrete pairs. Associations develop between corresponding pairs in a verbal-discrimination list, and these associations appear to conform to transfer laws derived from paired-associates studies (e.g., Kanak & Curtis, 1970; Kausler, Fulkerson, & Eschenbrenner, 1967). Finally, as has been reported in concept-learning studies, verbal-discrimination performance with reversal-shift paradigms is superior to performance with nonreversal shifts (e.g., Deichman, Minnigerode, & Kausler, 1970).

The final area of interest represented by verbal-discrimination research, and the area to which the remainder of this discussion will be devoted, concerns attempts to understand basic skills of memory that subjects call upon in mastering a verbal-discrimination list. While it is true that such an understanding demands a through analysis of the task requirements, it would be misleading to imply that research activities in this area are motivated solely by an interest in the task per se. Rather, the interest appears to be in the attributes of memory exposed with this task (see Underwood, 1969). The verbal-discrimination task owes much of its recent popularity to the fact that it has proven to be a very useful vehicle for investigating interesting features of the recognition-memory process.

VERBAL-DISCRIMINATION MECHANISMS

Frequency Theory

The major theoretical interpretation of verbal-discrimination performance emphasizes the discriminative cue properties of frequency (Ekstrand et al., 1966). According to this theory the subject has the power to discriminate differences in the frequency with which verbal-discrimination alternatives have been experienced, and the power is used to select the correct alternatives. The basic postulate of frequency theory is that the correct alternative in each pair acquires two frequency "units" on each exposure, whereas the incorrect alternatives acquire only one unit per exposure. This postulate was derived from considerations of verbal-discrimination procedures. Two critical aspects of these procedures form the basis of the counting postulate. First, the procedure involves the presentation of both members of each pair; thus we may conceive of this exposure as providing one frequency unit to each member of the exposed pair. Second, the correct member of each pair receives at least one additional frequency increment since the subject may be required to vocalize this item, and the experimenter indicates which member of each pair is correct (e.g., the correct word may be presented alone or underlined). The net result is that frequency accrues faster to correct alternatives than to incorrect alternatives. In summary, according to frequency theory, subjects have the power to discriminate differences in frequency, and since, in general, the frequency values of correct alternatives exceed the frequency values of corresponding incorrect alternatives, the subjects perform successfully in this task by selecting the members of pairs that "register" relatively higher frequency values.

The frequency theory has been tested in a variety of ways. The results of some of these tests have been favorable, while the results of others have pointed to difficulties with the theory. Despite these difficulties the theory currently presides as the major interpretation for acquisition of a verbal discrimination. Certainly one reason for this is that the theory draws support from some counterintuitive findings. Thus, alternative theories encounter an immediate difficulty of explaining a set of "unlikely" results. Since these counterintuitive results are of considerable importance, some illustrative experiments will be reported in detail.

Favorable evidence. Underwood et al. (1964) had subjects learn two verbal-discrimination lists in succession and varied the identity relations among items in the two lists. In one condition (R) the correct alternatives in the second list were the same words that were correct in the first list, and each was paired with a new incorrect word that had not appeared in the first list. A second condition (W) had the same words as incorrect alternatives on the two lists, with new correct items for the second list. A third group (C) learned a second list comprised of new words for both correct and incorrect alternatives. The subjects were completely informed concerning the nature of second-list construction. Performance for Group W was very good initially (relative to Group C), but subjects in this group showed very slow improvement. The subjects in Group C actually reached criterion (three successive errorless trials) sooner than subjects in Group W. According to frequency theory it is argued that during early trials on the second list there is a substantial frequency difference between the new correct and old incorrect alternatives for Group W (favoring the incorrect items). The subjects perform quite well on early trials by discriminating differences in frequency and selecting the alternatives which register relatively lower frequency values. The faster accrual of frequency to correct alternatives attenuated frequency differences across trials and increased the discrimination difficulty for Group W compared to Group C. Similar results have been reported by Kanak and Dean (1969) and by Kausler and Dean (1967). The R group advantage over the W group also appears when associative relations replace the identity relations between items in the two lists (e.g., Kanak & Dean, 1969; Kausler & Dean, 1967; Raskin, Boice, Rubel, & Clark, 1968). The final transfer manipulation considered here involves maintaining the same items in the two lists, but reversing the right and wrong designations. In general accordance with frequency theory, there is an advantage for reversed pairs relative to control pairs on initial trials, but performance is better for control pairs on later trials (Goulet & Sterns, 1970; Raskin et al., 1968).

Ekstrand et al. (1966) manipulated frequency within a single list in two ways. One procedure involved presenting specific items in two pairs and the other involved presenting a given word in one pair and a strong associate of that word in another pair. The rationale for the latter procedure was that the presentation of a specific word might increase the frequency value of its associate through the implicit occurrence of associative responses (see Bousfield, Whitmarsh, & Danick, 1958). In one set of conditions (R) the repeated words (or associated words) were always correct members in their respective pairs, and in another set of conditions (W) the repeated words (or associated words) were always incorrect. Application of the frequency counting postulate leads to the expectation that the R conditions will be superior in performance to the W conditions. Considering the repeated-item manipulation, the repetition of a correct item (Group R) results in a frequency value for that item of "4 units" after a single trial (since the correct item receives two units with each exposure). Incorrect items in the R conditions are presented a single time; thus the frequency difference between "rights" and "wrongs" is 4 to 1. However, the repetition of an incorrect item (Group W) results in a frequency value for that item of "2 units" (since an incorrect item receives only one frequency unit for each pair exposure). The single occurrence of a correct item results in two frequency units, thus after each trial for Group W the frequency increment for rights is two units and the frequency increment for wrongs is two units. Ekstrand et al. reported that the R groups were superior to the W groups, in accordance with expectations from frequency theory. It is also interesting to note that performance on a list with no repetitions and minimal associations was inferior to the R groups and slightly better than the performance of W groups.

The Ekstrand et al. results have been replicated and extended by Underwood and Freund (1969). They presented specific words in 1, 2, 3, or 6 different pairs of a 12-pair list. The repeated words were either always correct or always incorrect. As the number of pairs with the same correct word increased, verbal-discrimination performance improved. However, as the number of pairs with the same incorrect word increased, verbal-discrimination difficulty first increased and then decreased, in general agreement with expectations from frequency theory.

In summary, the major data supporting the frequency theory consist of the differential effects on performance resulting from manipulations of correct item frequency and incorrect item frequency. The counterintuitive aspect of these data is that the effects of frequency manipulations are not symmetrical. Increases in frequency value of correct items enhance verbal-discrimination performance. Similar enhancement is not observed following increases in frequency value of incorrect alternatives (in fact, such manipulations may have disruptive effects). These effects have been quite consistent with a variety of procedures, although on occasion they have not reached statistical significance (e.g., Crouse, 1967). Frequency has been manipulated by presenting the same item in two pairs (e.g., Ekstrand et al., 1966; Underwood et al., 1964), presenting associates or conceptually related words in the list (e.g., Crouse, 1967; Duncan, 1968; Ekstrand et al., 1966; Kausler, Erber, & Olson, 1970;

Mueller & Pickering, 1970; Raskin et al., 1968), forcing subjects to vocalize a special class of alternatives (e.g., Carmean & Weir, 1967; Goulet & Hoyer, 1969; Kausler & Sardello, 1967; Sardello & Kausler, 1967; Underwood & Freund, 1968), presenting only right words during the feedback interval, rather than both right and wrong alternatives (Ingison & Ekstrand, 1970), introducing new incorrect alternatives on successsive trials (Yelen, 1969), and prior exposures of items from the verbal-discrimination list (Lovelace, 1969; Smith & Jensen, 1971; Underwood & Freund, 1968; Wallace & Nappe, 1970; Wood, 1969). In addition, verbal discrimination-learning with a four-alternative list is superior to learning a two-alternative list (Radtke, McHewitt, & Jacoby, 1970). Although the results of such a comparison may pose some interpretative difficulties, the authors make a good case for the possibility that there is a greater difference in frequency between correct and incorrect alternatives in a four-choice task than in a two-choice task. Finally, with a recognition procedure similar to verbal discrimination that involved the presentation of target items in an inspection list followed by a test in which the target was paired with one distractor, it was reported that recognition performance was impaired when the same distractors appeared in more than one test pair (i.e., as the frequency of the distractors was increased) (Underwood & Freund, 1970c).

The general manipulation of frequency most disruptive to performance occurs when frequency value is increased for correct alternatives from some pairs and incorrect alternatives from other pairs. The "rule" to select the more frequent alternative will not lead uniformly to successful performance, rendering frequency alone as an ineffective cue. Within a list with such frequency manipulations, more errors are made on pairs for which the high-frequency alternative is incorrect, compared to pairs for which the high-frequency alternative is correct (e.g., Kausler & Farzanegan, 1969; Lovelace, 1966; Runquist & Freeman, 1960; Wallace & Nappe, 1970; Weir & Helgoe, 1968). If subjects attempt to discriminate on the basis of frequency in this situation, the "high-frequency-incorrect" pairs should be more difficult. The faster accrual of frequency to correct alternatives should attenuate frequency differences for these pairs, thus making frequency discrimination more difficult.

Indirect evidence. The literature also includes reports which have indirect relevance for frequency theory. For example, "tests" of frequency theory have been made by administering a recall or recognition test subsequent to verbal-discrimination learning. It should be emphasized that frequency theory is a theory concerning a specific type of recognition learning and not a theory about free or associative recall. "Memorizing" the right and wrong items or forming associations between corresponding rights and wrongs is not required in the verbal-discrimination task. An inability of subjects to reproduce any items from the list following verbal-discrimination acquisition would not be embar-rassing to frequency theory, since the theory does not demand that "incidental" learning occurs. Given that incidental learning does occur and assuming that frequency accrual in verbal discrimination has properties similar to exposure frequency in intentional free recall and paired-associate learning, then demonstrations of superior recall or recognition of right items, compared to wrong items, are consonant with the theory (Erlebacher, Hill, & Wallace, 1967; Kanak, 1968; Kausler & Sardello, 1967).

An indirect comparison that has produced mixed results concerns the application of Weber's Law to verbal-discrimination frequency. If this law applies, then it should be more difficult to develop a discrimination among items initially high in frequency value than among items initially low. The notion is that increments in frequency as a result of verbal-discrimination trials will be less discriminable if items are already high in frequency than if they are relatively low. When initial levels of frequency are estimated from prior laboratory exposures, results have been reported that agree with expectations from Weber's Law in showing better performance on low-frequency pairs than on high-frequency pairs (Berkowitz, 1968; Skeen, 1970; Wallace & Nappe, 1970), findings directly opposite of these (Lovelace, 1969), and findings of no difference (Runquist & Freeman, 1960). When frequency values (or meaningfulness) are estimated from preexperimental linguistic experiences, and the additional assumption that situational frequency (frequency values based upon laboratory experiences) combines with background frequency (frequency values based upon estimates of linguistic experiences) is made, the data have not produced much support for this application of Weber's Law (Ingison & Ekstrand, 1970; Keppel, 1966; Paivio & Rowe, 1970; Postman, 1962b; Putnam, Iscoe, & Young, 1962; Runquist & Freeman, 1960; Schulz & Hopkins, 1968).

Unfavorable evidence. While it is possible to marshall considerable evidence favorable to frequency theory, it must be acknowledged that difficulties exist, and some anomalous findings have been reported. One difficulty is that the counting postulate has not been verified in detail (e.g., Raskin et al., 1968; Underwood et al., 1964; Underwood & Freund, 1968; 1969; 1970b). The assumption that the correct item in each pair receives two frequency units per trial and the incorrect item receives only one has been useful in generating predictions that have received general confirmation. However, specification of the locus of maximum difficulty on lists with wrongs initially higher in frequency than rights poses some problems for the theory. At some point in learning such a list the rights must "catch-up" with the wrongs in frequency value. When this occurs the frequency cue will be ineffective and performance should deteriorate to a chance level. The "return-to-chance" level of performance has not been demonstrated. For example, the Underwood et al. (1964) group (W) that began second-list learning with an initial frequency advantage favoring the wrongs was eventually overtaken by a control group; however, Group W showed no indications of a return-to-change level of performance. Similarly, Raskin et al. (1968) failed to show a return-to-chance level of performance following a transfer procedure in which one group had their List-1 right items switched to

List-2 wrongs and List-1 wrongs switched to List-2 rights. Within a single 12-pair list Underwood and Freund (1969) varied the number of different words used as incorrect alternatives (2, 4, 6, or 12). Based on the counting postulate the point of maximum difficulty should occur when six different words (each presented in two pairs) were used as incorrect alternatives, since each correct word would gain two frequency units per trial and each incorrect word also would gain two frequency units per trial. Actually, the point of maximum difficulty occurred when four different words (each presented in three pairs) were used as incorrect items.

A related difficulty resides in the precision of frequency discrimination ability per se. Underwood and Freund (1970a) varied the number of times different words were presented prior to asking subjects to discriminate on the basis of frequency. That is, subjects were asked to choose the member of each pair that had been presented more often in the prior task. The absolute difference in frequencies between the two members of a pair was never greater than three exposures. When the less frequent member of a pair had been exposed four or more times in the prior task, subjects were very poor at making the discriminations. Similar results were reported by Hintzman (1969), although the decrement in discrimination ability as a function of increasing exposures of the "less frequent" member was not as striking. According to the counting postulate, the incorrect alternatives would reach the "critical" frequency value early in verbal-discrimination acquisition, perhaps calling into question frequency discrimination as a basic mechanism of performance on later trials.

The difficulties with frequency theory cited thus far revolve around the counting postulate. The seriousness of these difficulties depends upon how critical the details of the counting postulate are to frequency theory. It will be argued that the counting postulate provides a convenient source for general predictions, but that it is wrong in detail (cf., Underwood & Freund, 1970a). Thus the importance to frequency theory of this one aspect of the data cited above is difficult to evaluate at the present time.

In an earlier section evidence favorable to frequency theory was discussed. It should be noted that conflicting data have been reported concerning two of the procedures used for manipulating correct and incorrect item frequencies. The first procedure concerns manipulating frequency by including associatively related words in a single list. It was reported that performance was enhanced when both associates were right in their respective pairs, compared to when both were wrong (e.g., Ekstrand et al., 1966). Kanak, Cole, and Thornton (1970) failed to replicate this finding. In fact, they found that performance was superior when both associates were wrong in their respective pairs, compared to when both were right. The second procedure concerns manipulating frequency by forcing subjects to vocalize right and wrong alternatives. Contrary to previous findings, Goulet (1969) found that forcing nursery school children to name both the correct item and the incorrect item (line drawings) during the feedback interval facilitated verbal-discrimination acquisition.

The remainder of this section contains a review of several experiments which represent anomalies for frequency theory. The phenomena reported in these experiments may be embarrassing for frequency theory because the theory does not include provision for them. However, the anomalies may merely signal the incomplete nature of theory. That is, it may be possible to incorporate the "discrepant" phenomena within the theory by elaboration of theoretical constructs or the addition of auxiliary principles, or the phenomena may be excluded by setting boundary conditions to limit the range of applicability of the theory.

Frequency theory produced two rather unusual predictions and neither has been confirmed. First, the theory predicted there should be no forgetting (at least with regard to interference mechanisms). Although there is a high degree of retention in verbal discrimination, forgetting does occur (Postman, 1962b; Underwood & Freund, 1970b). Underwood and Freund presented evidence for a mechanism which could account for retention loss in verbal discrimination. They suggested that situational frequency "assimilates" to backgound frequency. Assimilation may be considered as an auxiliary principle to explain retention loss within a frequency-theory framework.

The second prediction was that performance would be impaired as a function of increasing the time a subject was allowed to make his response (anticipation interval). If it is assumed that the additional time prior to making a choice is evenly distributed between the correct and incorrect alternatives (equal increments in frequency value for both) and Weber's Law is applicable, then it follows that lengthening the anticipation interval may even have deleterious effects. Contrary to expectations concerning anticipation interval, performance has been shown to improve as a function of lengthening the anticipation interval (Radtke et al., 1970; Wike & Wike, 1970a). Wike and Wike suggested that the anticipation interval effects may be explained without violating the basic principles of frequency discrimination. They suggested that the frequency-theory prediction concerning anticipation interval is based on a faulty assumption, viz., that subjects limit their anticipation-interval activities to the currently presented pair. If subjects rehearse prior correct items during anticipation intervals, then longer anticipation intervals afford greater opportunity for such rehearsal. Their subjects, in fact, reported engaging in such rehearsal. If extra rehearsal of correct alternatives accounts for superior performance as a function of lengthening anticipation interval, then a similar relationship should obtain with study interval (the length of time separating the indication of the correct member in a pair and the presentation of the next pair). Wike and Wike demonstrated that performance improved as study interval increased from one to eight seconds, although the effect was significant in only one of two experiments they reported. Ingison and Ekstrand (1970) reported a reduction in trials to criterion as study interval increased from two to six seconds. Skeen (1970) failed to find a significant difference between study intervals of two and four seconds.

Two other puzzling results appear in the literature, and they have been interpreted as representing facts difficult to incorporate within frequency theory. These will be considered together because it will be argued later that they are *not* inconsistent with frequency theory and for similar reasons. The problem is that in order to derive these results from frequency theory it is necessary to expand on points included in the original statement of the theory. The experimental results will be reported here, but the "frequency-theory" interpretation of these results will be postponed until the final section of this review.

The first of these findings concerns the reported decrement in performance when correct items and incorrect items are re-paired (Kanak & Dean, 1969, Exp. II). The re-pairing manipulation involves "scrambling" the pairs after some point in acquisition. Each old correct word is paired with a different old incorrect word, and the pair members retain their original correct and incorrect functions. Kanak and Dean argued that frequency theory would not predict a decrement due to re-pairing, since right and wrong items retain their respective right and wrong designations. That is, the respective frequency values are unaltered by changing the pairings. Therefore, ease of frequency discrimination should not be altered by the re-pairing manipulation. The authors view the re-pairing decrement as an outcome that cannot be accounted for by frequency theory.

The second finding that will be reinterpreted later concerns the variable of similarity *between* correct and incorrect items. In general, high similarity interferes with verbal-discrimination learning with similarity of shape (Edwards, 1966), for similarity defined by number of letters shared by nonsense units (e.g., Putnam et al., 1962; Underwood & Archer, 1955; Underwood & Viterna, 1951; Yelen, 1969), acoustical properties of words (e.g., Kausler & Olson, 1969), and meaningful properties of words (e.g., Ekstrand et al., 1966; Palermo & Ullrich, 1968; Radtke & Foxman, 1969; Youniss, Feil, & Furth, 1965). However, the result of this manipulation of concern here is the contrast between the decremental effects of high similarity when it is between right and wrong items within the same pair (intrapair) and when it is between right and wrong items from different pairs (interpair). A consistent finding is that the disruptive effects of interpair similarity are far greater than the disruptive effects of intrapair similarity (Eberlein & Raskin, 1968; Fulkerson & Kausler, 1969; Kausler & Olson, 1969; Radtke & Foxman, 1969). The original statement of frequency theory provided for detrimental effects of high similarity, but the theory did not anticipate that interpair similarity would produce greater interference than intrapair similarity.

The final class of studies cited here as anomalies is grouped together because it is argued that it represents "special" cases that lie outside the range of applicability of frequency theory. It must be conceded that a list may be constructed which is impossible to learn based on frequency discriminations, or a procedure may be used which provides subjects with an "easy" code for correct and incorrect items. In these cases subjects may call upon skills other than frequency discrimination to perform the necessary discriminations. This statement represents an assertion that human subjects can invoke powers other than frequency discrimination in a verbal-discrimination task. The immediate difficulty is identifying the necessary conditions which lead to the initiation of these other memory skills. At a descriptive level, it may be stated that the presence of an "obvious" discriminative cue which makes the task very easy may preclude the development of frequency discriminations, or the subject may be forced to call upon some other attribute of memory if the task is such that frequency discriminations do not develop readily or do not differentiate right and wrong items.

Kausler and Boka (1968) presented a double function verbal-discrimination list for learning. A double-function list is one in which every correct item also appears in another pair as the incorrect alternative. Thus, for every pair the frequency values for rights and wrongs are equal, and such a list should be impossible to learn according to frequency theory. Although the double-function list is, indeed, difficult, learning does occur in this condition. It appears that the only possible conclusion must be that subjects have the capacity to invoke other skills to master a verbal-discrimination list in special cases when frequency discrimination cannot be used.

The availability of an easy coding device may eliminate the use of differential frequency as a cue. For example, if the correct alternatives always appear on the right-hand side of the memory drum when the pair is exposed, the subjects may discover that they will always be correct by saying the right-hand member of the exposed pair. The references to "Rule 1" (select the more frequent member of each pair) and "Rule 2" (select the less frequent member of each pair) by Ekstrand et al. (1966) are examples of what are referred to here as coding devices. Coding devices which do not make use of frequency discrimination (as in the illustration of invariant presentation positions) may be employed in special cases (cf., Paul, 1970; Wike & Wike, 1970b).

Supplemental Processes

The unfavorable evidence cited above is responsible for the proposal of alternative processes in verbal-discrimination learning. In this section two additional mechanisms of verbal discrimination are considered. The first is referred to as a multiple components analysis. According to this view, frequency theory is incomplete and must add an additional component or components in order to explain learning in the verbal-discrimination paradigm. To date, the component which has received major attention in this analysis is the role of incidental associations on intentional verbal-discrimination performance. The second mechanism which will be considered is referred to as a conceptual mediation process. Paul and his associates (e.g., Paul, 1970; Paul, Callahan, Mereness, & Wilhelm, 1968; Paul, Hoffman, & Dick, 1970; Paul & Paul, 1968) have provided the clearest exposition of this mechanism. According to this position items acquire equivalence from belonging to similar classes (e.g., all rights and all wrongs). The equivalence can then mediate various transfer behaviors. Thus, the conceptual mediation process, as it has been explicated to date, appears as an addition to frequency theory which is regarded as necessary in specified transfer situations.

Multiple component analysis. Multiple component analysis originated with studies which produced results difficult for frequency theory to explain. Specific difficulties involved the acquisition of a double-function list (Kausler & Boka, 1968), the decrement in performance following the re-pairing of rights and wrongs (Kanak & Dean, 1969), and the discrepancy of results between manipulations of interpair and intrapair similarity (e.g., Fulkerson & Kausler, 1969). It was proposed that a compensatory cue was activated in these cases to mediate the discriminations. The cue was the association between respective right and wrong members. Apparently, the associative cue aids in a "tagging" and "collapsing" process. For example, Fulkerson and Kausler (1969) proposed: "a process by which S [subject] 'tags' one member of a W–R pair as correct and then collapses the pair and tag together in memory storage. Intrapair associates are presumed to enhance S's ability to collapse the pairs into single chunks for storage" (pp. 307 and 308). It has been asserted that: "the tagging process is accomplished more readily when S is required to make simultaneous discriminations (the intrapair condition) between related words rather than successive discriminations (the interpair condition)" (Kausler & Olson, 1969, p. 141). Kanak and Dean (1969) concluded: "re-pairing conditions introduce a substantial amount of interference with the direct application of frequency cues through the influence of associative competition" (p. 306).

It is difficult to deny that the involvement of incidental associative processes in acquisition of a verbal discrimination has, at least, some descriptive appeal. It is difficult to describe the acquisition of a double-function list without alluding to pairwise associations, i.e., subjects learn word A is correct when paired with word B, B is correct when paired with C, C is correct when paired with A, etc. Further, there is substantial evidence that pairwise associations do develop. Subjects can recall the associations subsequent to verbal-discrimination acquisition (e.g., Kausler, Fulkerson, & Eschenbrenner, 1967), verbal-discrimination pairings provide a basis for grouping items together on subsequent tests of free recall (Delprato & Hudson, 1971; Fulkerson & Kausler, 1969), and transfer from verbal discrimination to paired-associates learning has been positive or negative depending upon whether verbal-discrimination pairs are maintained in the paired-associate list or re-paired, respectively (Battig & Brackett, 1963; Battig, Williams, & Williams, 1962; Keppel, 1966; Spear et al., 1964).

It has been argued that an incidental association process may be necessary to explain a wider range of verbal-discrimination phenomena than those for which it was originally intended (cf., Eschenbrenner, 1969). That is, rather than limiting the multiple component analysis to a very restricted range of phenomena, there has been some effort to describe more general verbal-discrimination learning in this way. The major justification for the claim that associative processes are important in general verbal discrimination is the evidence for *covariation* between the incidental associative component and the intentional discrimination component. The implication is that if covariation obtains, then the incidental associative component was involved in the acquisition of the intentional discrimination component.

The position that covariation implies that associative components contribute to verbal-discrimination performance is stated clearly by Kausler and Boka (1968, p. 563): "There is an apparent independence between intentional and incidental learning when the intentional component may be acquired by the utilization of cues that are apart from those provided by the incidental task. . . . There is an apparent dependence between intentional and incidental learning when the intentional component is unlikely to be acquired by the utilization of cues apart from those provided by the incidental component."

There have been several demonstrations of covariation. Pairwise associability is enhanced with intrapair associative relations in contrast to interpair relations, and overall verbal-discrimination performance is superior in the intrapair compared to the interpair case (e.g., Fulkerson & Kausler, 1969). Both Kausler and Boka (1968) and Fulkerson and Kausler (1969) have reported positive correlations between verbal-discrimination performance and measures of the associative component. Re-pairing rights and wrongs breaks up the established associations and also impairs verbal-discrimination performance (Kanak & Dean, 1969). Eschenbrenner (1969) reported similar temporal courses of retroactive inhibition (RI) in associative recall subsequent to verbal discrimination and performance on a delayed verbal-discrimination test trial.

The major criticisms of the multiple component analysis presented here are directed against those who argue that the mere demonstrations of covariation provide sufficient justification for the claim that incidental and intentional components interact. Among other things, the covariation argument suffers from general weaknesses that accompany attempts to infer causality from correlation. In addition, the conditions which result in covariation are not always specified a priori. Finally, there may be difficulties with this position arising from analyses of the temporal characteristics of associative acquisition and verbal-discrimination performance. Eschenbrenner (1969) had subjects learn two successive verbal-discrimination lists which conformed to an "old wrong-new right" paradigm. That is, the List-1 wrong items continued as wrong items in List 2, but each was paired with a new right word. Retroactive inhibition was demonstrated for both verbal discrimination and associative recall measures. But based on the evidence of covariation in RI, can it be, inferred that the List-1 associations were involved in acquisition of List-1 discriminations? The logic of such an inference is particularly interesting in view of an earlier study by Eschenbrenner and Kausler (1968). These authors employed a transfer paradigm in which List 2 consisted of List-1 right items paired with new wrong words. It should be noted that this paradigm and Eschenbrenner's earlier old wrong-new right paradigm are indistinguishable in terms of List-1 acquisition conditions. Thus, we should expect incidental associations to be involved in the acquisition of the List-1 verbal discriminations based on the evidence provided by Eschenbrenner (1969). Further, this "dependence" should be revealed by covariation in List-1 associative recall and List-1 verbal-discrimination recall. Eschenbrenner and Kausler (1968) did not include a List-1 verbal discrimination test subsequent to List-2 acquisition, but they did report RI in associative recall. Thus, RI must obtain for verbal discrimination, according to the covariation argument. In contrast, frequency theory would not lead to a prediction of covariation in the Eschenbrenner and Kausler experiment because during List-2 learning, the old List-1 rights are receiving additional frequency increments. While the contrast between the theoretical positions with regard to the old right-new wrong transfer paradigm must await empirical resolution, the many demonstrations of improved verbal-discrimination performance as a result of procedures which increase frequency of rights would seem to indicate that retroactive facilitation of verbal discrimination, rather than retroactive inhibition, would be observed in this paradigm. The RI in verbal discrimination demonstrated in the old wrong-new right transfer paradigm (Eschenbrenner, 1969) would be expected according to frequency theory since the continuation of old wrongs in List-2 should equalize or reverse frequency differences among List-1 rights and wrongs.

Zechmeister and Underwood (1969) varied the number of verbal-discrimination trials (5, 10, 20, or 35) prior to administering tests for incidental components. One interesting feature of the data they reported was that the incidental learning lagged behind the intentional learning. The mean trials to one perfect recitation in verbal discrimiation on a 12-pair list ranged from 6.64 to 8.78. This implies that the 35-trial groups averaged more than 25 overlearning trials on verbal discrimination. Yet free recall subsequent to verbal-discrimination did not vary as a function of number of prior verbal-discrimination trials and averaged about 50 percent correct, five of 14 subjects in the 35-trial group failed to obtain a perfect score on an associative matching test, and on the initial associative recall test trial (the subject is given one member of a pair and asked to produce the other member) the 35-trial group averaged about 8 out of 12 correct associations. Associative matching and associative recall were highest following 35 verbal-discrimination trials. The fact that successful performance on the incidental component lags behind successful performance on the intentional component seems to violate the antecedent-consequent logic of cause-effect relations. That is, if the incidental association is critical to performing a verbal discrimination, how is the subject able to discriminate successfully when the evidence indicates he has not mastered the associative component?

In summary, the multiple components analysis may be useful in describing a very limited class of verbal-discrimination phenomena. However, it is concluded here that attempts to characterize general verbal discrimination within this framework encounter serious difficulties.

Conceptual mediation. In a recent series of studies, Paul has argued that verbal-discrimination performance in specific transfer situations provides demonstrations of "rule-determined" behavior (Paul, 1966; 1968; 1970; Paul et al., 1968; Paul et al., 1970). This rule-determined behavior is accounted for within the system of *transfer-activated response sets* (Paul & Paul, 1968). Briefly, in the course of verbal-discrimination learning there is an acquired equivalence within the class of items that serves as correct alternatives and within the class of items that serves as incorrect alternatives. The acquired equivalence may mediate behavior in a transfer situation. The ease of reversal learning relative to learning new pairs, facilitation of reversal learning following overtraining on the original list, and the tendency to overgeneralize the rule to reverse or not reverse, depending upon the proportion of list items reversed, may be interpreted as consistent with the operation of "conceptual mediation."

If only a portion of the items in a list are reversed (partial reversal), performance is inferior to the case in which all items are reversed, and error patterns indicate the subjects overgeneralize the appropriate rule (e.g., Paul, 1967; 1968). When a small proportion of items are reversed, most of the errors result from subjects continuing to give the prereversal correct response to "reversed" pairs, and when a large proportion of items are reversed, most of the errors result from subjects starting to respond with the prereversal incorrect response to "nonreversed" pairs.

The conceptual-mediation position as stated by Paul does not deny frequency as a basis for intrapair discriminations, but he does insist that additional assumptions are necessary to explain transfer performance in some situations. He emphasizes acquired equivalence via correct and incorrect labels for items. In a recent experiment (Paul, 1970) a two category sorting test followed verbal-discrimination learning. One half of the verbal-discrimination items were assigned to one letter label, and the other one half were assigned to another letter label. Performance on the sorting test was enhanced when all the rights were assigned one response letter and all the wrongs were assigned a different response letter. Of course, the equivalences need not be restricted to right-wrong labels, as there are other discriminative attributes correlated with right and wrong (e.g., frequency value, vocalized versus nonvocalized, etc.), and other equivalence cues are capable of mediating the transfer performance (Paul et al., 1970).

Paul identifies a class of verbal-discrimination behavior for which he claims the frequency theory does not apply. He argues for the operation of a conceptual mediation process for these cases. Earlier it was acknowledged that verbal-discrimination procedures could be devised with an "easy" coding principle available, making it unnecessary to establish frequency discriminations in order to perform successfully on the task. Paul's data indicate that equivalence based on a conceptual-mediation factor may provide subjects with an "easy" code and simplify a subsequent reversal task.

There is one possible implication of Paul's "right-wrong" labeling notion which deserves further comment. Although Paul does not make this claim, it is possible that one could reject frequency theory completely and embrace a two-category labeling theory as the mechanism of general verbal-discrimination learning. That is, performance in a verbal-discrimination task may be viewed as two-category concept acquisition, which merely requires that subjects associate one half of the items with one category label (right) and the remaining half with the other category label (wrong). The differential effects of number of repetitions of right and wrong items (which presumably underlies frequency or associative strength) poses a serious difficulty for such a position. In addition, data difficult to reconcile with frequency theory would also be difficult to reconcile with an alternative right-wrong labeling theory (e.g., Kanak & Dean, 1969; Kausler & Boka, 1968).

In summary, two supplemental processes have been proposed to account for verbal-discrimination performance in special cases. Certainly, one can construct a task such that frequency discriminations are very difficult or impossible. A multiple components analysis may be fruitful in explaining behavior in these situations. Similarly, a verbal-discrimination task may be devised in which an easy conceptual principle can mediate successful performance. A conceptual mediation analysis may be fruitful in explaining behavior in these situations. Objections to these alternatives apply mainly to their general involvement in verbal-discrimination learning. Thus, it is claimed here that, in general, verbal discrimination is accomplished by frequency discrimination, and that other attributes of memory may be called upon in special cases. The two classes of special cases discussed were those in which an easy rule for performance was available and those in which frequency discrimination was made extremely difficult. Of course, and inherent weakness exists in imposing these boundary conditions on frequency theory in that a detailed specification of the class of procedures which produce "easy" or "difficult" conditions cannot be provided.

FREQUENCY THEORY "ADJUSTMENTS"

Two major points will be emphasized in this section. The first point involves a liberalization of the counting postulate of Ekstrand et al. (1966). It is emphasized here that there is variability in the accrual of frequency to individual items in a verbal-discrimination list (even after only a single presentation of the list). Correct alternatives will vary in frequency values, as will incorrect alternatives, although the assumption that, in general, frequency builds up faster to correct alternatives than to incorrect alternatives is still retained.

Many of the difficulties reported for frequency theory are eliminated when this assumption of a quantum relation between frequency value and item presentation is abandoned. Of course, an argument that variable, subjective frequency is critical circumvents some empirical difficulties, but unless more is specified concerning subjective frequency, there is the definite risk of the criticism that the notion is offered just to explain away a class of observations discrepant with the theory. Thus, it is important that a methodology develop which permits some assessment of frequency value. Recent techniques that involve recording rehearsal responses during acquisition in free recall have promise in this respect (e.g., Rundus & Atkinson, 1970). However, for present purposes we may assume the existence of a rough and less-than-perfect correlation between item presentations and frequency values (within the class of correct and incorrect alternatives separately).

One mechanism responsible for variability in frequency values is implicit rehearsal. It is the contention here that rehearsal activities are not equally divided among list items. One major factor responsible for this uneven distribution of rehearsal activity is the correct-incorrect item designations (cf., Ekstrand et al., 1966). Consistent with the original statement of the theory, it is assumed that correct items receive a greater proportion of the rehearsal time than incorrect items. In addition to item designations, there are two other important determinants governing the rehearsal distributions. One concerns factors specific to individual items, and the other concerns factors specific to points in time during which items are presented. That is, item-specific features may influence rehearsal activities, and temporal relations among list items and extraneous events which accompany the presentation of items may influence rehearsal activities. For example, a particularly salient word may have a relatively high-frequency value after a single presentation because it "commands" a greater proportion of the total study time than other less salient items; or the presentation of items in an ordinal position which favors extra rehearsal may enhance frequency value.

A very important corollary of these latter two assumptions about critical determinants of differential frequency values is that frequency values of specific list items may be *yoked* due to common item factors and common event factors. For example, if a specific word receives extra rehearsal when presented which enhances its frequency value, the frequency value of a related word in the list may also be enhanced (perhaps through the implicit occurrence of associative responses or through shared linguistic features that may be responsible for saliency); or if early study position enhances frequency value, it may be expected to do so for both correct and incorrect items which share the position.

Thus, one major point involves the assumption that frequency values of items vary, even though they may have similar input histories and the corollary assumption that specific items (particularly across right-wrong boundaries) may be yoked in frequency values.

The second major point emphasized in this section involves an assumption about general performance on a verbal-discrimination list. When all list pairs do not conform to a common frequency "rule" (e.g., the correct item is the more frequent member of each pair), overall verbal-discrimination performance is impaired. When a common rule to guide selection based upon frequency discriminations cannot be applied to all pairs in a list, frequency alone is an ineffective cue. It has been demonstrated that verbal-discrimination lists structured to approximate this condition are, indeed, very difficult (e.g., Ekstrand et al., 1966; Wallace & Nappe, 1970). The rationale for this performance assumption is that subjects are forced to call upon some other attribute of memory (in addition to or in lieu of frequency) to perform the required discriminations, and this complicates the task.

It was mentioned earlier that data from re-pairing rights and wrongs and comparisons of interpair and intrapair similarity were difficult to reconcile with frequency theory. The preceding adjustments may remove these difficulties.

The re-pairing decrement refers to the report by Kanak and Dean (1969) in which they found a marked increase in errors when they re-paired rights and wrongs, as compared to a condition which continued with the same right-wrong pairings. When the same pairs are kept intact, specific event yoking operates in such a way that correct items with relatively high-frequency values are paired with incorrect items with relatively high-frequency values (within their respective distributions of frequency values for right items and wrong items). For example, a favorable ordinal position may result in high frequency due to extra rehearsal, and since both right and wrong items in the same-pair condition share this favorable position, they both should be high in frequency values. Similarly, low-frequency rights will likely be paired with low-frequency wrongs. Re-pairing rights and wrongs will result in some cases in which a relatively high-frequency right is paired with a relatively low-frequency wrong, and some cases in which a relatively low-frequency right is paired with a relatively high-frequency wrong. In these latter cases the wrongs may actually exceed the rights in frequency value, producing a more difficult list according to the performance assumption (since all pairs are no longer uniform with regard to the appropriateness of a single frequency rule).

A recent experiment (Wallace & Nappe, 1971) provided data relevant to this analysis of the repairing effect. The performance of a control group, which was tested on the same pairs they viewed during study (S), and two re-pairing groups was compared. During the study trial on a list of 24 pairs of common words, eight pairs were exposed twice, eight pairs were exposed four times, and eight pairs were exposed six times. One re-pairing condition (R-SF) had rights and wrongs within the same frequency class re-paired (i.e., the right item from a pair exposed twice during the study trial was re-paired on the test trial with a wrong item that had been exposed twice, etc.). The other re-pairing condition (R-CF) maximized the likelihood that re-pairing would produce cases for which the frequency value of wrongs of some pairs would exceed the frequency value of the corresponding rights. Re-pairing was between frequency classes, so a correct item exposed two times was re-paired with an incorrect item exposed four or six times. Thus, Groups S and R-SF were tested on three sets of eight pairs each with right-wrong exposure frequencies of 2–2, 4–4, and 6–6. Group R-CF was tested on six sets of four pairs each with right-wrong exposure frequencies of 2–6, 2–4, 4–6, 4–2, 6–4, and 6–2. The results of this experiment (two-second study rate) are illustrated in Figure 1.

Since rights and wrongs differed in number of exposures for Group R–CF, a common baseline of frequency difference (derived from the 2:1 counting postulate) was used in Figure 1. These results reveal that the re-pairing decrement was not as large as in the Kanak and Dean experiment, but consistent with the present analysis, overall performance was poorest for the group with re-pairing between exposure-frequency classes.

The adjustments proposed in this section also permit a frequency-theory interpretation of the differential decrement produced by interpair and intrapair similarity in verbal-discrimination learning. Yoking according to specific item factors is emphasized in explaining why the decrement is greater with interpair similarity than it is with intrapair similarity. Consider the following illustration involving the words: *table, chair, hot,* and *cold*. Assume table is a correct word in its pair and that it is relatively high in the distribution of frequency values among the class of correct alternatives. The notion of specific item yoking implies that chair will be high in frequency value relative to the class of incorrect alternatives. Further, assume that hot is low in frequency value among the class of correct alternatives, and correspondingly, cold is low in frequency value among the class of incorrect alternatives. An intrapair manipulation is illustrated by pairing table with chair and hot with cold, or, if the yoking assumption is valid, one pair with both alternatives relatively high in frequency value (table-chair) and one pair with both alternatives relatively low (hot-cold). An interpair manipulation is illustrated by pairing table with cold (a high-frequency right with a low-frequency wrong) and hot with chair (a low-frequency right with a high-frequency wrong). The performance assumption leads to the expectation that interpair similarity will be more detrimental to verbal-discrimination performance than intrapair similarity, since it is more likely that the frequency value of some wrongs will exceed the value of their respective rights with interpair similarity.

An unpublished experiment[1] performed at the Nevada Laboratory tested the preceding interpretation of interpair-intrapair similarity decrements. A free-recall familiarization task preceded interpair and intrapair verbal-discrimina-

[1] This experiment was carried out with support from Grant MH 19323–01 from the U.S. Deparment of Health Education and Welfare.

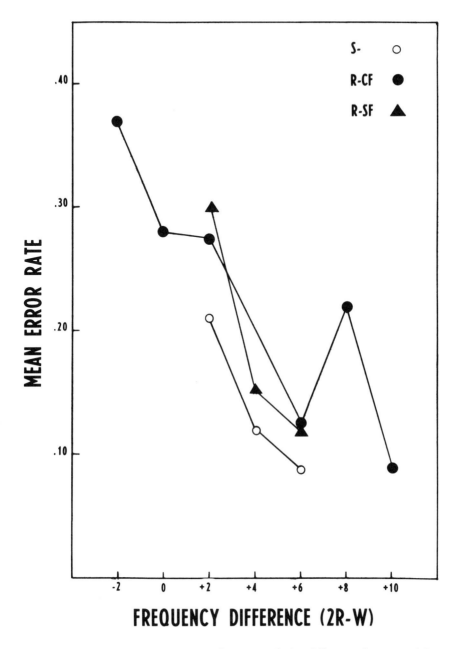

Figure 11—1. Mean error rates as a function of the difference between rights and wrongs in exposure frequencies Note: For Group S and Group R-SF the respective exposure frequencies for rights and wrongs which produce each of the indicated difference values are as follows: The difference value of $^+2$ derives from pairs with exposure frequencies of 2:2 (rights and wrongs, respectively); $^+4$=4:4; and $^+6$=6:6. For Group R-CF the frequency difference values and corresponding exposure frequencies are: -2=2:6; 0=2:4; $^+2$=4:6; $^+6$=4:2; $^+8$=6:4; and $^+10$=6:2.

tion learning. Half of the verbal-discrimination items appeared during the free-recall task. There were four basic conditions determined by the factorial combination of interpair or between pair (B) versus intrapair or within pair (W) similarity in verbal discrimination and prior free recall of a list of associated (A) versus unrelated (U) words. The logic of this experiment may be understood best by tracing the history of two pairs in the four experimental conditions. The verbal-discrimination list for the interpair conditions had the correct word *table* paired with the incorrect word *cold*, and the correct word *hot* paired with the incorrect word *chair*. The corresponding right-wrong pairs in the intrapair condition were: table-chair and hot-cold. The prior familiarization task involved only half of the verbal-discrimination items, with an equal number of correct and incorrect alternatives included. Thus, the familiarization list containing associated words included table and chair (but not hot and cold), whereas the list containing nonassociated words included table and cold (but not hot and chair). Now if it is assumed that familiarized words are high in frequency value at the outset of verbal discrimination and nonfamiliarized words are low, then the initial state of the verbal-discrimination pairs was as follows (the familiarized words appear in italics): Following familiarization with the associated list, the intrapair condition would have one pair in which both alternatives were high in frequency value (*table-chair*) and one pair in which both were low (hot-cold). The interpair condition would have one pair in which the correct word was high in frequency value and the incorrect word low (*table*-cold) and one pair in which the correct word was low and the incorrect word was high (hot-*chair*). It was expected that interpair similarity would be more disruptive than intrapair similarity since wrong-word frequency exceeded right-word frequency for some pairs. However, following the familiarization task with unrelated words, the intrapair condition should be more disruptive than the interpair condition, a prediction opposite of the general findings in the literature. The intrapair condition would have one pair in which the correct word was high in frequency value and the incorrect word low (*table*-chair) and one pair with the correct word low and the incorrect word high (hot-*cold*). Both pair members are either high (*table-cold*) or both low (hot-chair) in the interpair case.

The experiment consisted of free-recall training on a 16-item list to a criterion of 13 out of 16 correct, followed by verbal-discrimination learning to a criterion of two consecutive perfect trials. A minimum of five study-test trials (beginning with a study trial) was administered to each subject. Subgroups were included so that all verbal-discrimination items were equally represented on the free-recall list, and right and wrong functions for specific items were balanced. There were 16 subjects[2] in each of the four major conditions. Since similar results were produced by the trials-to-criterion measure and number correct over the first five trials, only the latter data will be reported. The verbal-discrimination acquisition data are presented in Figure 2. The predicted interaction was

---

[2] One subject in Group U-B made only 36 correct responses over the first five trials and was discontinued after failing to achieve a perfect score on any of the first 20 trials. This subject was replaced, and in order to minimize a subject-selection bias, the poorest performing subject in each of the three remaining groups was discarded and replaced.

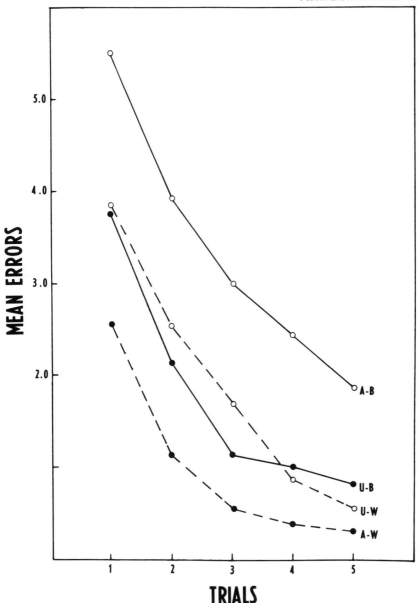

Figure 11—2. Mean errors across trials.

significant, $F(1, 60) = 14:76$, $p < .01$. The only other significant effects involved the main effects for trials, $F(4, 240) = 71.06$, and the main effect for similarity (B versus W), $F(1, 60) = 11.69$, $p < .01$. It is apparent from Figure 2 that W was superior to B following free recall of the A list, but B was only slightly superior to W following free recall of the U list. As expected in free recall, the associated list resulted in fewer trials to criterion ($\overline{X} = 2.12$) than the unrelated list ($\overline{X} = 3.28$), $F(1, 60) = 14.07$, $p < .01$.

In summary, the first major adjustment stressed in this section involved the counting postulate. Liberalizing the counting postulate appears to be an adjustment forced upon the theory. An attempt was made in this section to conceptualize the variable nature of frequency accrual in verbal discrimination. Three major components of the task were identified as critical determinants of frequency through their influence on the activation of an implicit rehearsal mechanism. These components were item designation (correct versus incorrect), specific item features, and specific event factors. In addition, it was emphasized that there are intralist relations among items such that given items are yoked in frequency value. The second major adjustment concerned the assumption that overall verbal-discrimination performance is impaired when all pairs do not conform to the same frequency rule. These adjustments in frequency theory enable the frequency theorist to account for the re-pairing decrement and the differential effects of interpair and intrapair similarity without alluding to supplemental processes. The results of two preliminary experiments provided support for the present conceptualizations.

SUMMARY

Current use of verbal discrimination as a research tool derives from its suitability for investigations of specific phenomena and principles of learning, interests in demonstrating generality of verbal-learning phenomena across laboratory tasks, and efforts to understand basic skills of recognition memory. The present discussion emphasized the third orientation.

The major interpretation of verbal-discrimination is provided by frequency theory (Ekstrand et al., 1966). According to frequency theory, frequency accrues faster to correct alternatives than to incorrect alternatives. Subjects have the power to discriminate differences in frequency, and, in general, they perform the verbal-discrimination task by selecting the more "frequent" response alternative in each pair. The major empirical support for frequency theory comes from studies which demonstrate differential effects of frequency manipulations among correct alternatives compared to frequency manipulated among incorrect alternatives. Specifically, performance is enhanced as a function of increasing the frequency values among the class of right items, but similar increases in frequency value among the class of wrong items do not result in improved performance.

Not all the data reviewed were favorable to frequency theory. The "negative" data seem to indicate that the counting postulate of frequency theory is wrong, and that some auxiliary principles may be necessary. Special cases exist which signal the necessity to establish boundary conditions for the theory. Supplemental or alternative processes may be necessary to explain performance in the special situations in which frequency does not differentiate correct and incorrect alternatives, and for cases in which the discriminations can be acquired readily by conforming to a "rule" that does not require frequency discriminations.

Adjustments to frequency theory were proposed in the final section of this essay. The development of these adjustments provided an interpretation of data for which frequency theory was previously silent. It was argued that the re-pairing decrement and the differential effects of interpair and intrapair similarity could be accomodated within frequency theory. Initial experiments relevant to these adjustments yielded favorable returns.

REFERENCES

Allen, L. R., & Garton, R. F. The influence of word-knowledge on the word-frequency effect in recognition memory. *Psychonomic Science*, 1968, 10, 401–402.

Anderson, N. H. Effects of choice and verbal feedback on preference values. *Journal of Experimental Psychology*, 1969, 79, 77–84.

Battig, W. F., & Brackett, H. R. Transfer from verbal-discrimination to paired-associate learning: II. Effects of intralist similarity, method, and percentage of occurrence of response members. *Journal of Experimental Psychology*, 1963, 65, 507–514.

Battig, W. F., & Switalski, R. W. Comparison of anticipation and recall procedures in verbal-discrimination learning. *Psychonomic Science* 1966, 6, 65–66.

Battig, W. F., Williams, J. M., & Williams, J. G. Transfer from verbal-discrimination to paired-associate learning. *Journal of Experimental Psychology*, 1962, 63, 258–268.

Berkowitz, J. Verbal discrimination learning as a function of experimental frequency. *Psychonomic Science*, 1968, 13, 97–98.

Bousfield, W. A., Whitmarsh, G. A., & Danick, J. J. Partial response identities in verbal generalization. *Psychological Reports*, 1958, 4, 703–713.

Buss, A. H., & Buss, E. H. The effect of verbal reinforcement combinations on conceptual learning. *Journal of Experimental Psychology*, 1956, 52, 283–287.

Carmean, S. L., & Weir, M. W. Effects of verbalizations on discrimination learning and retention. *Journal of Verbal Learning and Verbal Behavior*, 1967, 6, 545–550.

Crouse, J. H. Verbal discrimination transfer in two paradigms as a function of conceptual similarity and anticipation interval. *Journal of Verbal Learning and Verbal Behavior*, 1967, 6, 277–281.

Deichman, J. W., Minnegerode, F. A. III, & Kausler, D. H. Selection strategies and reversal-nonreversal shifts in verbal discrimination transfer. *Psychonomic Science*, 1970, 18, 209–210.

Delprato, D. J., & Hudson, R. L. Association by contiguity: clustering in free recall. *Psychonomic Science*, 1971, 22, 98–99.

Duncan, C. P. Mediation and interference in verbal concept learning. *Journal of Verbal Learning and Verbal Behavior*, 1968, 7, 767–770.

Eberlein, E., & Raskin, D. C. Intrapair and interpair associations in verbal discrimination learning. *Psychonomic Science*, 1968, 14, 145—146.

Edwards, D. C. Similarity in verbal discrimination. *Perceptual and Motor Skills*, 1966, 23, 815—820.

Ekstrand, B. R., Wallace, W. P., & Underwood, B. J. A frequency theory of verbal-discrimination learning. *Psychological Review*, 1966, 73, 566—578.

Erlebacher, A., Hill, W. F., & Wallace, W. P. Differential accrual of frequency in verbal-discrimination learning. *Journal of Verbal Learning and Verbal Behavior*, 1967, 6, 420—422.

Eschenbrenner, A. J. Jr. Retroactive and proactive inhibition in verbal discrimination learning. *Journal of Experimental Psychology*, 1969, 81, 576—583.

Eschenbrenner, A. J. Jr., & Kausler, D. H. Unlearning of List 1 wrong items in verbal discrimination transfer. *Journal of Experimental Psychology*, 1968, 78, 696—698.

Estes, W. K. Transfer of verbal discrimination based on differential reward magnitudes. *Journal of Experimental Psychology*, 1966, 72, 276—283.

Fulkerson, F. E., & Johnson, J. E. Methodological variables in verbal discrimination learning. *Psychonomic Science*, 1971, 22, 68—69.

Fulkerson, F. E., & Kasler, D. H. Effects of intrapair and interpair bidirectional associates on verbal-discrimination learning. *Journal of Verbal Learning and Verbal Behavior*, 1969, 8, 307—310.

Goulet, L. R. The effect of verbalization on discrimination learning and transfer in nursery school children. *Journal of Experimental Child Psychology*, 1969, 7, 479—484.

Goulet, L. R., & Hoyer, W. J. The effect of verbalization on verbal discrimination learning and associative recall in young children and adults. *Journal of Experimental Child Psychology*, 1969, 7, 434—439.

Goulet, L. R., & Sterns, H. L. Verbal-discrimination learning and transfer with verbal and pictorial materials. *Journal of Experimental Child Psychology*, 1970, 10, 257—263.

Hintzman, D. L. Apparent frequency as a function of frequency and the spacing of repetitions. *Journal of Experimental Psychology*, 1969, 80, 139—145.

Hovland, C. I. Experimental studies in rote learning theory: I. Reminiscence following learning by massed and by distributed practice. *Journal of Experimental Psychology*, 1938, 22, 201—224.

Ingison, L., & Ekstrand, B. R. Effect of study time, method of presentation, word frequency, and word abstractness on verbal discrimination learning. *Journal of Experimental Psychology*, 1970, 85, 249—254.

Kanak, N. J. The effects of rate of exposure upon simultaneous intentional and incidental verbal-discrimination learning. *Psychonomic Science*, 1968, 12, 141—142.

Kanak, N. J., Cole, L. E., & Thornton, J. W. Inter-item manipulations of implicit associative responses in verbal-discrimination learning. *Psychonomic Science*, 1970, 18, 359—361.

Kanak, N. J., & Curtis, C. D. Unlearning of context-item and specific associations in the W_1-R_1, W_2-R_2 paradigm. *American Journal of Psychology*, 1970, 83, 256—263.

Kanak, N. J., & Dean, M. F. Transfer mechanisms in verbal discrimination. *Journal of Experimental Psychology*, 1969, 79, 300–307.

Kausler, D. H., & Boka, J. A. Effects of double functioning on verbal discrimination learning. *Journal of Experimental Psychology*, 1968, 76, 558–567.

Kausler, D. H., & Dean, M. G. Direct and mediated transfer for right and wrong responses in verbal-discrimination learning. *Journal of Verbal Learning and Verbal Behavior*, 1967, 6, 672–674.

Kausler, D. H., Erber, J. T., & Olson, G. A. Taxonomic instances as right or wrong items and selection strategies in verbal-discrimination learning. *American Journal of Psychology*, 1970, 83, 428–435.

Kausler, D. H., & Farzanegan, F. Word frequency and selection strategies in verbal-discrimination learning. *Journal of Verbal Learning and Verbal Behavior*, 1969, 8, 196–201.

Kausler, D. H., Fulkerson, F. E., & Eschenbrenner, A. J. Jr. Unlearning of List 1 right items in verbal-discrimination transfer. *Journal of Experimental Psychology*, 1967, 75, 379–385.

Kausler, D. H., & Lair, C. V. Informative feedback conditions and verbal-discrimination learning in elderly subjects. *Psychonomic Science*, 1968, 10, 193–194.

Kausler, D. H., & Olson, R. D. Homonyms as items in verbal discrimination learning and transfer. *Journal of Experimental Psychology*, 1969, 82, 136–142.

Kausler, D. H., & Sardello, R. J. Item recall in verbal-discrimination learning as related to pronunciation and degree of practice. *Psychonomic Science*, 1967, 7, 285–286.

Keppel, G. Association by contiguity: role of response availability. *Journal of Experimental Psychology*, 1966, 71, 624–628.

Kintsch, W. An experimental analysis of single stimulus tests and multiple-choice tests of recognition memory. *Journal of Experimental Psychology*, 1968, 76, 1–6.

Lintz, L. M., & Brackbill, Y. Effects of reinforcement delay during learning on the retention of verbal material in adults. *Journal of Experimental Psychology*, 1966, 71, 194–199.

Lovelace, E. A. Knowledge of correct and incorrect items in verbal discrimination. *Psychonomic Science*, 1966, 6, 363–364.

Lovelace, E. A. Verbal-discrimination learning: varied familiarization on correct and incorrect items. *Canadian Journal of Psychology*, 1969, 23, 227–232.

Markowitz, N., & Renner, K. E. Feedback and the delay-retention effect. *Journal of Experimental Psychology*, 1966, 72, 452–455.

Marston, A. R. Response strength and self-reinforcement. *Journal of Experimental Psychology*, 1964, 68, 537–540.

Marston, A. R., & Kanfer, F. H. Human reinforcement: experimenter and subject controlled. *Journal of Experimental Psychology*, 1963, 66, 91–94.

McClelland, D. C. Studies in serial verbal discrimination learning: I. Reminiscence with two speeds of pair presentation. *Journal of Experimental Psychology*, 1942, 31, 44–56. (a)

McClelland, D. C. Studies in serial verbal discrimination learning: II. Retention of responses to right and wrong words in a transfer situation. *Journal of Experimental Psychology*, 1942, 31, 149–162. (b)

McClelland, D. C. Studies in serial verbal discrimination learning: III. The influence of difficulty on reminiscence in responses to right and wrong words. *Journal of Experimental Psychology*, 1943, 32, 235–246. (a)

McClelland, D. C. Studies in serial verbal discrimination learning: IV. Habit reversal after two degrees of learning. *Journal of Experimental Psychology*, 1943, 33, 457–470. (b)

McGeoch, J. A. The comparative retention values of a maze habit, of nonsense syllables, and of rational learning. *Journal of Experimental Psychology*, 1932, 15, 662–680.

McGeoch, J. A., & Melton, A. W. The comparative retention values of maze habits and of nonsense syllables. *Journal of Experimental Psychology*, 1929, 12, 392–414.

Mueller, J. H., & Pickering, J. P. Correction procedures in three-alternative verbal discrimination lists with intertriad associations. *American Journal of Psychology*, 1970, 83, 401–411.

Paivio, A., & Rowe, E. J. Noun imagery, frequency, and meaningfulness in verbal discrimination. *Journal of Experimental Psychology*, 1970, 85, 264–269.

Palermo, D. S., & Ullrich, J. R. Verbal discrimination learning as a function of associative strength between the word-pair members. *Journal of Verbal Learning and Verbal Behavior*, 1968, 7, 945–952.

Paul, C. Verbal discrimination reversal as a function of overlearning and percentage of items reversed. *Journal of Experimental Psychology*, 1966, 72, 271–275.

Paul, C. Verbal discrimination reversal as a function of overlearning and percentage of items reversed: an extension. *Journal of Verbal Learning and Verbal Behavior*, 1968, 7, 270–272.

Paul, C. Acquired equivalence of correct alternatives after verbal discrimination learning. *Journal of Experimental Psychology*, 1970, 86, 123–125.

Paul, C., Callahan, C., Mereness, M., & Wilhelm, K. Transfer-activated response sets: effect of overtraining and percentage of items shifted on a verbal discrimination shift. *Journal of Experimental Psychology*, 1968, 78, 488–493.

Paul, C., Hoffman, C., & Dick, S. Acquired (conditional) equivalence: a basis for response-set effects in verbal-discrimination reversal performance. *Journal of Experimental Psychology*, 1970, 85, 361–367.

Paul, C., & Paul, H. Transfer-activated response sets in verbal learning and transfer. *Psychological Review*, 1968, 75, 537–549.

Peterson, J. The backward elimination of errors in mental maze learning. *Journal of Experimental Psychology*, 1920, 3, 257–280.

Postman, L. The history and present status of the Law of Effect. *Psychological Bulletin*, 1947, 44, 489–563.

Postman, L. Rewards and punishment in human learning. In L. Postman (ed.), *Psychology in the Making*. New York: Knopf, 1962. (a)

Postman, L. The effects of language habits on the acquisition and retention of verbal associations. *Journal of Experimental Psychology*, 1962, 64, 7–19. (b)

Putnam, V., Iscoe, I., & Young, R. K. Verbal learning in the deaf. *Journal of Comparative and Physiological Psychology*, 1962, 55, 843–846.

Radtke, R. C., & Foxman, J. Number of alternatives and similarity in verbal-discrimination learning. *Journal of Verbal Learning and Verbal Behavior*, 1969, 8, 537–544.

Radtke, R. C., McHewitt, E., & Jacoby, L. Number of alternatives and rate of presentation in verbal discrimination learning. *Journal of Experimental Psychology*, 1970, 83, 179–181.

Raskin, D. C., Boice, C., Rubel, E. W., & Clark, D. Transfer tests of the frequency theory of verbal discrimination learning. *Journal of Experimental Psychology*, 1968, 76, 521–529.

Rowe, E. J., & Paivio, A. Discrimination learning of pictures and words. *Psychonomic Science*, 1971, 22, 87–88.

Rundus, D., & Atkinson, R. C. Rehearsal processes in free recall: a procedure for direct observation. *Journal of Verbal Learning and Verbal Behavior*, 1970, 9, 99–105.

Runquist, W. N., & Freeman, M. Roles of association value and syllable familiarization in verbal discrimination learning. *Journal of Experimental Psychology*, 1960, 59, 396–401.

Sardello, R. J., & Kausler, D. H. Associative recall in verbal-discrimination learning as related to pronunciation and degree of practice. *Psychonomic Science*, 1967, 8, 253–254.

Schulz, R. W., & Hopkins, R. H. Presentation mode and meaningfulness as variables in several verbal-learning tasks. *Journal of Verbal Learning and Verbal Behavior*, 1968, 7, 1–13.

Skeen, D. R. Study interval, manipulated frequency, and verbal discrimination learning. *Psychological Record*, 1970, 20, 111–117.

Smith, S., & Jensen, L. Test of the frequency theory of verbal discrimination learning. *Journal of Experimental Psychology*, 1971, 87, 46–51.

Spear, N. E., Ekstrand, B. R., & Underwood, B. J. Association by contiguity. *Journal of Experimental Psychology*, 1964, 67, 151–161.

Spence, J. T. Verbal discrimination performance under different verbal reinforcement combinations. *Journal of Experimental Psychology*, 1964, 67, 195–197.

Spence, J. T., Armstrong, J., & Conrad, R. Contribution of instructions to the effects of two types of symbolic reinforcers on the discrimination learning of children. *Psychonomic Science*, 1969, 17, 107–108.

Spence, J. T., Lair, C. V., & Goodstein, L. D. Effects of different feedback conditions on verbal discrimination learning in schizophrenic and normal nonpsychiatric subjects. *Journal of Verbal Learning and Verbal Behavior*, 1963, 2, 339–345.

Underwood, B. J. False recognition produced by implicit verbal responses. *Journal of Experimental Psychology*, 1965, 70, 122–129.

Underwood, B. J. Attributes of memory. *Psychological Review*, 1969, 76, 559–573.

Underwood, B. J., & Archer, E. J. Studies of distributed practice: XIV. Intralist similarity and presentation rate in verbal-discrimination learning of consonant syllables. *Journal of Experimental Psychology*, 1955, 50, 120–124.

Underwood, B. J., & Freund, J. S. Two tests of a theory of verbal-discrimination learning. *Canadian Journal of Psychology*, 1968, 22, 96–104.

Underwood, B. J., & Freund, J. S. Verbal-discrimination learning with varying numbers of right and wrong terms. *American Journal of Psychology*, 1969, 82, 198–202.

Underwood, B. J., & Freund, J. S. Relative frequency judgments and verbal discrimination learning. *Journal of Experimental Psychology*, 1970, 83, 279–285. (a)

Underwood, B. J., & Freund, J. S. Retention of a verbal discrimination. *Journal of Experimental Psychology*, 1970, 84, 1–14. (b)

Underwood, B. J., & Freund, J. S. Testing effects in the recognition of words. *Journal of Verbal Learning and Verbal Behavior*, 1970, 9, 117–125. (c)

Underwood, B. J., Jesse, F., & Ekstrand, B. R. Knowledge of rights and wrongs in verbal-discrimination learning. *Journal of Verbal Learning and Verbal Behavior*, 1964, 3, 183–186.

Underwood, B. J., & Viterna, R. O. Studies of distributed practice: IV. The effect of similarity and rate of presentation in verbal-discrimination learning. *Journal of Experimental Psychology*, 1951, 42, 296–299.

Van Tilborg, P. W. The retention of mental and finger maze habits. *Journal of Experimental Psychology*, 1936, 19, 334–341.

Wallace, W. P., & Nappe, G. W. Verbal-discrimination learning following a free-recall familiarization training procedure. *Canadian Journal of Psychology*, 1970, 24, 27–33.

Wallace, W. P., & Nappe, G. W. Re-pairing rights and wrongs in verbal discrimination. *Journal of Experimental Psychology*, 1971, 87, 355–360.

Weir, M. H., & Helgoe, R. S. Vocalization during discrimination: effects of a mixture of two types of verbalization patterns. *Journal of Verbal Learning and Verbal Behavior*, 1968, 7, 842–844.

Wike, S. S., & Wike, E. L. Presentation rates and verbal discrimination learning. *Psychonomic Science*, 1970, 19, 253–254.(a)

Wike, S. S., & Wike, E. L. The effect of a coding cue on verbal discrimination learning. *Psychonomic Science*, 1970, 20, 107–108. (b)

Wike, S. S., & Wike, E. L. The isolation effect and verbal discrimination learning. *Psychonomic Science*, 1970, 20, 217. (c)

Wood, G. Associations and recognition learning. *Psychonomic Science*, 1969, 17, 222–223.

Yelen, D. Verbal discrimination as a function of similarity and frequency of incorrect items. *Journal of Verbal Learning and Verbal Behavior*, 1969, 8, 552–553.

Youniss, J., Feil, R. N., & Furth, H. G. Discrimination of verbal material as a function of intrapair similarity in deaf and hearing subjects. *Journal of Educational Psychology*, 1965, 56, 184–190.

Zechmeister, E. B., & Underwood, B. J. Acquisition of items and associations in verbal discrimination learning as a function of level of practice. *Journal of Experimental Psychology*, 1969, 81, 355–359.

12 | Transfer in Serial Learning

ROBERT K. YOUNG
University of Texas at Austin

The five studies presented here were intended to clarify the status of a transfer task in which two successive serial lists are learned. In this situation each item of the second list is related to a comparable item in the first. In the paradigm of major interest, the related pairs of items hold the same ordinal positions in their respective lists. This transfer task is the Same-Order paradigm and the two lists can be symbolized A-B-C-D-E, etc., and A' -B' -C' -D' -E', etc. A second paradigm is developed when the related items do not hold common ordinal positions and instead are randomly ordered in their respective lists. This is the Random-Order paradigm and the two lists can be symbolized A-B-C-D-E, etc., C' -E' -A' -D' -B', etc.

Irion (1946), in a retroactive inhibition experiment, found evidence suggesting that both the Same-Order and the Random-Order conditions were paradigms of zero transfer. When the second list contained synonyms of the first-list items, second-list learning was at the same rate regardless of the arrangement of the second list. In contrast, Young and Saegert (1966), while investigating transfer from one language to another in a bilingual population, found about 50 percent positive transfer when items and their translations were arranged in the same order in two successive serial lists and found consistent, but nonsignificant, negative transfer when the items and their translations were arranged in different orders in the two lists. Unfortunately, both papers were only peripherally concerned with the Same-Order and Random-Order transfer paradigms themselves. In addition, procedural differences between the experiments presented in the two papers were great enough to prohibit direct comparisons.

The question of the direction of transfer between successive serial lists is of considerable theoretical importance. Both the chaining and the ordinal position hypotheses (cf. Young, 1968) would predict positive transfer in the Same-Order paradigm and yet Irion's data suggest there may be no transfer at all. Absence of positive transfer then, would appear to be critical of both major theoretical notions of the functional stimulus.

Thanks are due to Joel Saegert who supervised the collection and analysis of most of these data and to Erwin Janek, Ann Hatten, F. Steven Brenner, Elizabeth Neal, Dennis Awbry, Carol Caton, and Marshall Roberts who collected the data.

For the Same-Order paradigm, the chaining hypothesis would conceive of the task as an A-B, A'-B' paradigm of positive transfer (with A-B and A'-B' representing successive first-list pairs of items and their respective synonym pairs from the second list). For the ordinal-position hypothesis, the task would be an A-B, A-B' paradigm of positive transfer (with A representing the common ordinal position in both lists and B and B' representing the synonyms occupying that position). A similar analysis could be developed to show that both hypotheses also predict negative transfer in the Random-Order paradigm.

Thus, the Young and Saegert (1966) data are consistent with both the chaining and ordinal position hypotheses while the Irion (1946) data are consistent with neither. However, because of the nature of the design, the Irion experiment did not have a control group which would specifically allow evaluation of direction of transfer. The first experiment to be reported here was designed to replicate Irion's synonym conditions using a control which would allow evaluation of direction of transfer.

The chaining and ordinal position hypotheses disagree as to what constitutes an appropriate control (cf., Young, Hakes & Hicks, 1967). However, in the context of the present series of experiments a condition employing two unrelated serial lists would appear to be the most appropriate control despite the fact that such a control apparently yields slight negative transfer (Young & Evans, 1970).

A comparison of the procedures employed by Irion (1946) and by Young and Saegert (1966) reveals several large differences, any one of which may account for the divergent results of the two experiments. One possible reason for these divergent results is that translated items may be more closely associated with one another than would be the case with synonyms. Experiment 2 was designed to reduce these apparent differences by approximating in English the same degree of association that exists between items and their translations. Experiment 2 investigated the Same-Order paradigm using as related pairs of items, responses and their respective stimuli taken from free-association norms. For each pair, the stimulus was in the first list and its respective associate held the same ordinal position in the second list. In this case, during second list learning, if the functional stimulus elicited an item holding the appropriate position but from the first list, the second list response would be assumed to be more readily available than would be the case when synonyms are used.

Another explanation of the differences found between the Irion and Young and Saegert research is suggested by an experiment by Postman, Keppel, and Stark (1966). In their experiment amount of retroactive inhibition was found to be related to the discriminability of the successive responses classes employed. Spanish nouns and their English equivalents (as used by Young and Saegert) represent two easily discriminable classes of responses while adjectives and their synonyms (as used by Irion) or pairs of associates (as used in Experiment 2) may represent sets of response classes which are considerably less easy to discriminate. Thus, discriminability of response classes may be a variable of great importance in these experiments. Experiment 3 was designed to investigate the influence of this variable on the Same-Order transfer paradigm. Using the same set of verbal materials, the responses of successive lists were designed to be highly discriminable in one condition and much less discriminable in a second condition. From previous results it would be expected that with transfer paradigm held constant, greater positive transfer would be obtained as response discriminability increased.

Postman and Stark (1967), among others, have found results suggesting that instructions are of considerable importance in measuring transfer to serial lists. In their experiment, transfer was measured from serial to paired-associate learning. Instructions as to the relationship between successive lists increased amount of positive transfer when arrangement of items in the paired-associate lists was the same as that in the serial list. For this reason Experiment 4 was conducted using the Same-Order paradigms of Experiment 3 with the instruction variable added.

The serial anticipation procedure was employed in Experiments 1–4. Battig and Lawrence (1967) have shown that mode of presentation is of critical importance in studies investigating transfer in serial learning and for this reason Experiment 5 was conducted using a serial recall procedure. The Same-Order paradigm was again used.

EXPERIMENT 1

Method

Design. Each of 48 Ss learned two serial lists of adjectives. For the two experimental groups, the second list consisted of synonyms of the first-list items. The second-list items of the Same-Order condition were arranged in the same order as that held by their synonyms in the first list while the items of both lists in the Random-Order condition were arranged in different random orders. The two serial lists of the Control group were unrelated. Two samples of items were used, and within a sample all groups learned a common second list, different first lists defining the groups. Thus, the design can be summarized as a 2 X 3 factorial (N = 8 per cell).

Procedure. The synonym pairs for successive lists were taken from adjective lists prepared by Melton and Safier (Hilgard, 1951) and by Haagen (1949). The 19 Melton and Safier pairs had a mean similarity rating of 2.60 and the 5 Haagen pairs had a mean similarity rating of 1.69. The synonym pairs were as highly similar as possible, consistent with the requirement of low formal and meaningful intralist similarity. The 12-item serial lists were presented on a Lafayette memory drum at a 2-second rate with a 6-second intertrial interval. The initial item in each list served as a cue symbol. The criterion of learning for all groups was one errorless trial. Approximately one minute separated the learning of the two lists to allow time to change tapes and give additional instructions. The Ss were given standard serial anticipation learning instructions but were *not* told about the relationship between the two lists. The Ss were recruited from introductory psychology classes and had never previously served in a verbal learning experiment. Assignment of Ss to the six groups was on the basis of a predetermined random order. Two Ss were dropped because of failure to learn the first list; each was replaced by the next S to appear at the laboratory.

Results

As may be noted from Table 1, no significant differences were found in the analyses of trials to learn the first or second lists. Similarly, no significant differences were found in analyses of transfer early in second-list learning. These analyses were based on number correct per trial and on criteria of learning reached early in learning. It is apparent that transfer from one list to a second composed of synonyms of the first-list items yields zero transfer (other than learning to learn) whether the items are arranged in a manner consistent or inconsistent with their ordering in the first list. Thus, the results of the present study closely parallel Irion's (1946) transfer data and are not consistent with the results of Young and Saegert (1966).

Analysis of intrusions from the first list during the second-list learning also yielded negative results. Means of .06, .04, and .04 first-list intrusions per trial were obtained for the Same-Order, Random-Order and Control groups, respectively. In this analysis all Fs were less than 1.00.

The results of Experiment 1, while consistent with Irion's data and not consistent with the Young and Saegert data, support neither the ordinal position nor the chaining hypotheses of serial learning. This somewhat intriguing result suggested that an attempt should be made to find, if possible, those variables which led to positive transfer between two serial lists. One possible explanation for the lack of transfer in Irion's data and in Experiment 1 and for the transfer observed in the Young and Saegert experiment was that the item pairs in the two

Table 1. Trials to learn List 1 and List 2 in Experiment 1.

	Condition					
	Same Order		Random Order		Control	
List	M	SD	M	SD	M	SD
First	18.13	6.60	19.06	7.47	20.94	8.05
Second	13.13	3.77	12.69	4.00	12.33	4.97

lists, i.e., the items holding the same serial position in the experiment, were more closely related in the latter experiment. Experiment 2 was conducted with this in mind by using in successive lists either contrast-coordinate or functional pairs taken from free-association norms.

EXPERIMENT 2

Method

Design.   Each of 72 Ss learned two 12-item serial lists. For the experimental groups, the second list consisted of common associates of the first-list items, divided evenly into contrast-coordinate; e.g., *up-down, bitter-sweet,* etc., and functional associates, e.g., *tobacco-smoke, scissors-cut,* etc. The second-list associates were arranged in the same order as that held by their corresponding contrast-coordinate and functional stimuli in the first list. Thus, the experimental lists had the same relation to one another as did the lists of the Same-Order condition in Experiment 1. The items in both the experimental and control groups were taken from lists of free associates developed by Moran (1966). The items of the control lists were equated with the experimental items in terms of the number and strength of associates. The positions of the contrast and coordinate pairs were randomly distributed throughout the serial list and were counterbalanced across lists in such a way that contrast-coordinate and functional associates were both represented at each serial position. Two control lists were used. Within a given condition all Ss learned the same second list, the first list determining the condition of transfer. Finally, two Es were used, making the design a 2 X 2 X 2 mixed factorial, with 2-second lists, 2 transfer conditions, and 2 Es, (N = 9 per cell).

Procedure.   The lists were learned by the anticipation method at a 2-second rate with a 6-second intertrial interval to a one perfect recitation criterion. Approximately one minute separated the learning of the first and second lists. The lists were constructed so that each had low meaningful and formal intralist similarity. As in Experiment 1 the Ss were given standard instructions and not told about the relationship between the two lists. Other details of the procedure were the same as in Experiment 1. Four Ss were dropped because of failure to learn List 1 and each was replaced by the next S to appear in the laboratory.

Results

No significant differences were found in the analyses of trials to learn in the first or second list, nor were there any significant differences in the analyses of transfer early in second-list learning. It is apparent from Table 2 that transfer from one list to a second composed of strong associates of first-list items yields

322   Robert K. Young

Table 2.   Trials to learn List 1 and List 2 in Experiment 2.

List	Experimental		Control	
	M	SD	M	SD
First	15.53	6.10	15.33	8.51
Second	9.19	3.11	10.03	4.69

zero transfer attributable to the experimental manipulation. Again the data are consistent with those of Irion (1946).

Analyses of serial position curves, transfer as a function of antonymity and synonymity, and errors were completed. The results of these analyses were consistent with the previous results in that they yielded essentially negative results.

Both Experiments 1 and 2 have yielded transfer data which are not consistent with the positive transfer obtained by Young and Saegert (1966). One possible explanation, which is tested in Experiment 3, is that the absence of positive transfer in Experiment 2 and in the Same-Order paradigm in Experiment 1 was related to the difficulty of discriminating list membership. That is, the S may have known that either *icy* or *frozen* was correct in Experiment 1 or that *up* or *down* was correct in Experiment 2 but was unable to select the correct response often enough to facilitate learning. Some evidence for this is found in a free-recall experiment by Shuell (1968) who found greater recall when both previously learned lists were recalled than when either one was recalled by itself.

In the bilingual transfer situation, the S had both the concept and the language to facilitate selection of the correct response. Thus, knowing that the correct concept was table and that the language of the list was Spanish, produced the response *mesa*. Experiment 3 attempted to develop an analogue of this by using lists containing words which could be classified as either male or female. Thus if the lists were homogeneous with reference to sex, the S could use the concept and the sex of the concept to facilitate selection of the correct response. Thus, knowing that the concept was parent and that the sex was male, the correct response *father* could be produced and facilitation in learning should occur. On the other hand when the items in a list were heterogeneous with reference to sex, facilitation should not occur because the S should have difficulty in discriminating list membership.

EXPERIMENT 3

Method

Procedure. Each of 48 Ss learned two serial lists, each composed of 14 nouns plus a cue symbol. The 24 Ss of the Homogeneous (*Ho*) group were subdivided into Experimental (*Ex*) and Control (*C*) groups. The *S*s of the *Ho Ex* group first learned a list composed entirely of *male* nouns (e.g., *brother, father, son, man,* etc.) and then learned a second list composed of the female equivalents of the first-list nouns (e.g., *sister, mother, daughter, woman,* etc.). These female nouns were arranged in the same order as their respective male counterparts. Thus the *Ho Ex* group conforms to the Same-Order paradigm.

The *Ho C* group learned the same second list and a first list composed of common male, female, and neuter nouns which had no equivalents in the second list.

The 24 *S*s of the Heterogeneous (*He*) group were also subdivided into *Ex* and *C* groups. The first list of the *He Ex* group was constructed by randomly selecting half the first-list *Ho Ex* items and combining these with the female equivalents of the first-list *Ho Ex* items *not* selected (e.g., *brother, mother, daughter, man,* etc.). The second list was then constructed by taking the opposite sex equivalents of the *He Ex* first-list items, again retaining the same serial order (e.g., *sister, father, son, woman,* etc.). As in the *Ho Ex* group, the Same-Order paradigm was formed. The *He C* group learned the same first list as the *Ho C* group and the same second list as the *He Ex* group.

Thus, the design contains two levels of each of two variables: *Ho versus He* and *Ex versus C*. In addition, two *E*s were employed, adding an additional variable to the experiment and making it a 2 X 2 X 2 factorial design (N = 6 per cell). In all other particulars, such as selection of *S*s, rate of presentation, instructions, etc., Experiment 3 was identical to Experiment 1.

Results

First-list learning. The analysis of trials to learn the first-list failed to yield any significant differences. The largest effect found was $F(1,40) = 1.56$, which is far from significant. Thus, the hypothesis of equivalent groups and lists cannot be rejected.

Second-list learning. Trials to learn the second list were analyzed; the only significant difference obtained in this analysis was the *Ho-He* X *Ex-C* interaction which yielded $F(1,40) = 4.10, p < .05$.

It can be seen from Table 3 that, relative to their respective control groups, the *Ho Ex* group showed positive transfer while the *He Ex* group showed negative transfer. It can also be seen that the largest difference between any two groups was between the two control groups. This apparent difference, although not significant, with $F(1,20) = 4.05, p > .05$, may be related to the fact that lists composed entirely of words of the same sex, as were the lists of the *Ho* groups, may have somewhat higher intralist similarity than the lists of the He groups and hence may be of somewhat greater difficulty. An analysis of trials to three correct responses measured transfer early in second-list learning. In this analysis no differences were found in either the *He* versus *Ho* or *Ex* versus *C*

Table 3. Trials to learn List 1 and List 2 in Experiment 3.

		Ex		C	
	Group	M	SD	M	SD
List 1	Ho	20.33	7.14	18.17	5.54
	He	17.00	4.75	16.83	7.24
List 2	Ho	9.91	4.19	13.33	5.05
	He	11.58	4.83	9.58	3.58

comparisons. However, the interaction between these variables was significant, with $F(1,40) = 4.25$, $p < .05$. The transfer relationships were the same as those obtained in the trials to criterion analysis. Thus it is apparent that the transfer effects obtained in Experiment 3, while small, first appeared relatively early in second-list learning.

Intrusions from the first list occurred only in the *He Ex* group. The mean number of first-list intrusions per trial for each *S* in this group was .16 which is significantly different from .00 with $t(11) = 2.49$, $p < .05$. If such data may be used as evidence for interference, then interference occurred in the *He Ex* group for which negative transfer was found, but not in the *Ho Ex* group for which positive transfer occurred.

Serial position effects were also analyzed. As in Experiment 1 the differences between groups were negligible. Similarly, mean correct responses per trial were analyzed. No significant differences were found.

The results of Experiment 3 may be taken at best as only suggestive of transfer. The data do not strongly support the hypothesis of differential transfer as a function of the homogeneity or heterogeneity of item sets within a list. That is, the observed interaction may be in large part due to different rates of learning of the second list by the two control groups.

The results obtained in Experiment 3 and those obtained by Young and Saegert differ considerably. Perhaps the fact that all the items in the *Ho* condition were the same sex was not as salient a cue as was the fact that all the items in the bilingual transfer situation were homogeneous with respect to language. If such were the case it would be less likely that *S*s would recognize and subsequently use this as an aid to facilitate transfer from one *Ho* list to another. Because of this and because a replication of the interaction was desired, Experiment 3 was run again. In Experiment 4 additional groups were added so that some of the *S*s of the Experimental groups were specifically instructed as to the relations between lists. In this way it was felt that the effectiveness of the independent variables could be manipulated.

EXPERIMENT 4

Method

Design. Each of 96 Ss learned two serial lists, each composed of 14 nouns plus a cue symbol. The 48 Ss of the Homogeneous (Ho) group were subdivided into Control (C), Experimental-Uninstructed (EU) and Experimental-Instructed (EI) groups. The 48 Ss of the Heterogeneous (He) groups were similarly subdivided. Within the experimental subgroups, the first and second lists were counterbalanced; within each control subgroup, half the Ss learned a control serial list and then one of the two experimental lists. Thus, the design can be summarized as a 2 X 3 X 2 (N = 8 per cell) with Ho versus He, three subgroups, and counterbalancing of experimental lists being factorially combined.

Procedure. All Ss were given standard serial anticipation learning instructions. In addition, the Ss in the instructed experimental groups (EI) were given additional instructions after learning the first serial list which explicitly pointed out the relationship between the first and second lists. New lists were constructed for Experiment 4 which differed only slightly from those used in Experiment 3. Some items were changed and list orders different from Experiment 3 were employed. In all other particulars, such as selection of Ss, rate of presentation, etc., Experiment 4 was identical to the previous experiments.

Results

First-list learning. Trials to learn the first list were analyzed and no significant differences were observed. The largest F observed was between the Ho and He groups with $F(1,84) = 2.67$, $p > .05$. Thus, the hypothesis of equivalent groups cannot be rejected.

Second-list learning. Trials to learn the second list were analyzed, and several significant differences were obtained. It can be seen in Figure 1 that the Ho lists were easier to learn than the He lists, with $F(1,84) = 7.65, p < .01$; and that the Experimental and Control conditions differed from one another, with $F(2,84) = 3.88$, $p < .05$. Both of these differences are in large part due to the extremely discrepant He-EI condition, as shown by the interaction of degree of Homogeneity and Condition, with $F(2,84) = 4.14, p < .05$. Thus, although there is slight positive transfer in the Ho groups, considerable negative transfer was found in the He groups when the Ss were specifically instructed as to the relationship of the items in the two lists. The two experimental conditions in the

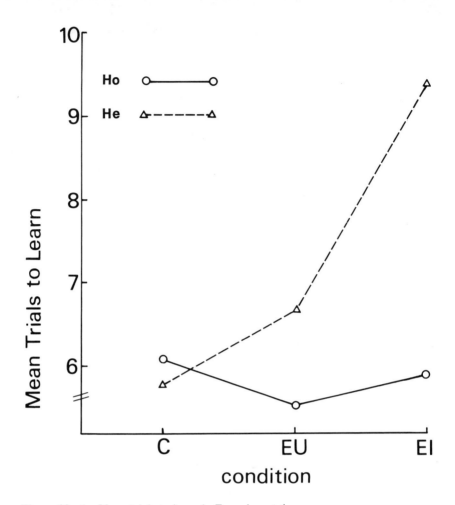

Figure 12–1. Mean trials to learn in Experiment 4.

He group show negative transfer, with $F(1,84) = 7.60, p < .01$; and the EI group shows greater negative transfer than the EU group with $F(1,84) = 7.80, p < .01$.

Mean correct responses per trial were also analyzed. These data are presented in Table 4. It can be seen from Table 4 that both positive and negative transfer effects were observed. Although neither of the main effects of interest was significant, the interaction between the degree of Homogeneity and Condition was significant, with $F(2,84) = 3.85$, $p < .05$. In contrast to the trials-to-learn data, the positive transfer observed in the *Ho* groups was significant, with F $(1,84) = 6.05$, $p < .05$ (when the EU and EI groups are combined) while the negative transfer observed in the He groups was not with $F(1,84) = 2.12, p < .20$.

Similar transfer effects were obtained in the analysis of learning early in the second list. In this analysis the response measure was the number correct during the first three trials of learning. These data are presented in Table 5. It can be

Table 4. Mean correct per trial on the second list in Experiment 4.

	Condition					
	C		EU		EI	
	M	SD	M	SD	M	SD
Ho	7.44	1.46	8.63	1.24	8.19	.82
He	8.06	1.48	7.88	.78	7.19	1.41

Table 5. Mean correct per trial on the second list during early learning in Experiment 4.

	Condition					
	C		EU		EI	
	M	SD	M	SD	M	SD
Ho	5.34	2.46	6.62	2.42	6.33	1.80
He	5.74	1.61	5.30	1.69	4.66	2.34

seen that *Ho* items were given correctly more often than were *He* items, with $F(1,72) = 4.91$, $p < .05$, while the interaction between degree of Homogeneity and Condition was not significant, with $F(2,84) = 2.06$, $p < .10$. None of the comparisons within groups indicates that significant positive or negative transfer was obtained. Even so, these data generally indicate that positive transfer was found in the *Ho* groups and negative transfer was found in the *He* groups early in the second-list learning. By the fifth trial these differences had disappeared.

When trials to learn was used as the response measure in Experiment 3, a significant interaction was obtained between condition of Homogeneity and experimental versus control, suggesting slight positive transfer in the *Ho* groups and slight negative transfer in the *He* groups. These results were replicated in Experiment 4, but even with instructions the amount of positive transfer obtained in the *Ho* groups was minimal. On the other hand, massive negative transfer occurred in the *He* conditions when instructions were given. Thus, the results of Experiments 3 and 4 are consistent in the finding of very slight positive transfer in the *Ho* conditions and large amounts of negative transfer in the Instructed *He* conditions.

On the other hand, the mean correct per trial data are not consistent from Experiment 3 to Experiment 4. No differences were found in Experiment 3 while a significant interaction was found in Experiment 4 indicating positive transfer in the *Ho* group and negative transfer in the *He* group. Since the greatest amount of positive transfer was found in an Uninstructed group, a similar difference should have been found in the comparable condition of Experiment 3 but was not. Thus, it would seem that replication of the relatively large amount of positive transfer found in the Ho-EI condition of Experiment 4 would be difficult.

The differences which have been found in the previous experiments tend to be inconsistent and to be of a smaller magnitude than might be expected in an experiment where positive transfer is predicted. It has been shown that a serial recall procedure tends to be able to find differences which either are obscured or do not exist when a serial anticipation procedure is employed (Battig & Lawrence, 1967). For this reason, the fifth experiment in this series employed a serial recall procedure while retaining the basic *Ho* paradigm used in Experiment 3 and 4.

EXPERIMENT 5

Method

Design. Each of 64 Ss learned two serial lists of 14 items each. In the experimental groups, half the Ss first learned a list containing all male words and then learned a second list containing the corresponding female words. The other half of the experimental Ss learned the lists in reverse order. Again the Same-Order paradigm was used. The Ss in the control conditions first learned a neutral control list and then learned either the male or female list. Finally, two Es were employed in the experiment. Thus, the experiment can be summarized as a 2 X 2 X 2 design, with two conditions (E versus C), two second lists (Male versus Female) and 2 Es being factorially combined (N = 8 per cell).

Procedure. The major procedural difference between the present experiment and previous experiments was that a serial recall procedure was employed. That is, the lists were presented at a 2-second rate and then, after a 6-second intertrial interval, an XXX appeared followed by 13 rows of 3 asterisks each. Responding was paced, that is, as each new row of asterisks appeared S was told to call out the appropriate response. The lists used in Experiment 5 were the same as those used in the *Ho* conditions of Experiment 4. Other specifics of the experiment were the same as in the previous experiments.

Results

No differences were observed in the analysis of either first-list or second-list learning. Both trials to learn and transfer early in second-list learning were analysed with negative results. Since these data tend to be in agreement with the major portion of the data taken from similar transfer conditions in Experiments 3 and 4, it must be concluded that the serial recall and serial anticipation procedures both give essentially the same results within the limits of the transfer conditions employed in these experiments.

DISCUSSION

A survey of the recent literature concerning transfer between serial lists reveals relatively few studies in which overall positive transfer was obtained. Slamecka (1964), using a derived-list paradigm, found positive transfer between two lists, the items of which consisted of single letters. Battig and Lawrence (1967) and Young and Saegert (1966) found positive transfer under conditions previously described.

Each of these studies found positive transfer under conditions which may be best described as unique. For example, although the derived-list paradigms have long been considered paradigms of positive transfer, they have been recently shown to be paradigms of negative transfer (Hakes, James, & Young, 1965). Moreover, the Slamecka (1964) study was specifically designed to allow the S to take advantage of the highly overlearned alphabetic sequence. Under such conditions positive transfer was obtained.

Considerable difficulty was encountered in demonstrating positive transfer in the present series of studies despite the fact that the Same-Order paradigm was employed in each experiment. This paradigm is one for which both the ordinal-position and chaining hypotheses would predict positive transfer.

The first experiment employed pairs of synonyms in the Same-Order and Random-Order paradigms in an initial attempt to differentiate between Irion's (1945) results and those of Young and Saegert (1966). Irion's data were replicated in that no evidence for transfer—either positive or negative—was found in the experiment. It should be noted that, compared to the other experiments presented here, Experiment 1 most closely resembles traditional paired-associate transfer experiments—at least in terms of the class of verbal materials employed. When this same class of material is used in paired-associate transfer studies, relatively little difficulty is found in producing the amount and direction of transfer desired. But no positive transfer was found in Experiment 1 although both major hypotheses predicted such would be the case.

The Same-Order paradigm was employed in Experiment 2, and again no measureable transfer was obtained. In this second experiment it was predicted that the stimulus conditions—conditions based either on the previous item in the list or on the position of the item in the list—which led to the elicitiation of the correct response in the first list would similarly elicit the second-list response with the first-list responses being used as mediators. Since each second-list response and its first-list mediator were strongly associated, positive transfer should have been obtained. Such expectations were not, of course, confirmed. This is of interest when compared to a paired-associate study (Barnes & Underwood, 1959) in which Ss report using first-list responses as mediators.

Next, two Same-Order paradigms were employed in Experiment 3. The only difference between the two was that in the Homogeneous conditions all the items in a list were nouns referring to the same sex while in the Heterogeneous conditions half the items were male items and the remaining half were female items. In both conditions the equivalent opposite-sex noun was employed in the same ordinal position in the second list. Hence, the same transfer paradigm (Same-Order) was used in both conditions, and the independent variable was assumed to be ease of discriminability of list membership. The results of Experiment 3 supported the hypothesis that positive and negative transfer would be obtained. However, the greatest difference found in the Experiment was between the two control groups. While such a difference could be explained on the basis of differential intralist similarity, i.e., the items of the Homogeneous lists were more similar than those of the Heterogeneous lists, it was felt that the magnitude of the transfer obtained was not large enough to explain the transfer obtained in the Young and Saegert (1966) experiment. For this reason, Experiment 4 was conducted.

The only major difference between Experiments 3 and 4 was that some of the experimental groups of Experiment 4 were specifically told about the relationship between the two lists used in the experiment. Such instructions did not influence the trials-to-learn response measure in the Homogeneous condition. However, in the Heterogeneous condition approximately 60 percent negative transfer was found in the Instructed condition despite the fact that the specific transfer relations were such as to expect positive transfer. Since this negative transfer was obtained only in the Instructed Heterogeneous conditions, it is apparent the instructions created a set that actually hindered acquisition of the second list. Thus, as in the Young, Hakes and Hicks (1967) study, instructions in an apparent positive transfer paradigm do not uniformly yield positive transfer. And as in the Young et al. study, sometimes instructions apparently give the subject the set to engage in a type of learning activity which is inappropriate to the task at hand. In Experiment 4 the Subject apparently attempted to use information about the structure of List 1 to facilitate the learning of List 2. Such information did not facilitate learning because of the S's inability to differentiate list membership when half the items of each list were male and the other half female. When S has no external basis for differentiating between alternative responses he may use a variety of cues such as the relative strength (Young & Jennings, 1964) or familiarity (Ekstrand, Wallace, & Underwood, 1966) of the item. The strategy may work for awhile but must fail if the strength or familiarity of the weaker (and correct) items become strong enough to provide S no basis for selection of the responses.

Uninstructed Ss often spontaneously remarked that they saw the relationship between the first and second lists in the Homogeneous conditions. However, neither the uninstructed nor the instructed Ss showed much positive transfer. In terms of trials to learn, no significant positive transfer was obtained, while positive transfer was found when mean correct per trial was used as the response measure. The greatest amount of positive transfer was found in the Uninstructed Ho condition. Since there was no similar significant difference for the same condition in Experiment 3, the evidence favoring positive transfer must be considered weak at best.

Battig and Lawrence (1967) found positive transfer between serial lists when they used the serial recall procedure. Experiment 5 was conducted to determine if mode of presentation were the crucial variable. But again, no significant positive transfer was obtained.

Thus, the results of this series of five experiments tend to agree that no positive transfer occurs between serial lists. Negative transfer can be obtained under specific conditions, but positive transfer which was searched for in the five experiments remains a will-o'-the-wisp and, as such, it eludes us yet.

On the other hand, there is a whole class of serial-learning paradigms which would yield positive transfer. The paradigm which apparently would yield maximum positive transfer is that employed in the continued learning of a single serial list. Here the paradigm is A-B-C-D, etc., to A-B-C-D, etc., from Trial N to Trial N + 1 and a great deal of positive transfer should occur here. Variations on this type of paradigm would include those experiments dealing with transfer between two serial lists such that the same items maintain the same sequence between the two lists. For example, if half the serial list were first learned and then the whole list with the first-list sequence being maintained in the second, positive transfer would be expected. Indeed, Postman and Goggin (1964) found that learning two halves of a serial list and then learning the whole list actually took less time than did learning the whole list by itself.

Thus the major problem in finding positive transfer between two serial lists occurs when either the sequence of items is changed from one list to another or when the items themselves are changed. Changing the items has not appeared to be a great problem in the study of transfer of training in paired-associate learning. For example, positive transfer occurs in the A-B, A-B' and the A-B, A'-B paradigms where similar responses are substituted in the second list in the former paradigm and similar stimuli employed in the second list in the latter paradigm.

There is some evidence, however, that stage of practice is related to direction and amount of transfer in the A-B, A-B' paradigm. Postman (1964) interpreted his results to indicate that Ss must learn appropriate use of mediators before measureable positive transfer can occur. A similar interpretation may be appropriate to the serial-learning paradigms under consideration. However, if stage of practice should prove to be a critical variable in the serial paradigms, the basis for the positive transfer obtained in the Young and Saegert study would remain unidentified and no closer to a satisfactory resolution.

It may be that previous research in serial learning provides a reason for our inability to find positive transfer between successive serial lists. The several studies testing various hypotheses about the functional stimulus in serial learning have provided evidence for, among others, the ordinal-position hypothesis, the chaining hypothesis, and a combination of the two (Young, 1968). The results of a variety of experiments have suggested, for example, that the subject learning a serial list forms associations between successive items (Postman & Stark, 1966) or can learn the list in the absence of the sequential situation which would be necessary to the formation of associations between successive items (Slamecka, 1968). It seems that if the task demands that S learn through the use of chaining, he will; if the task demands that he learn through the use of position cues, he will; and if the task demands that he learns in the absence of both chaining and sequential cues, he can do that also. Based on this observation and that of previous experimenters (e.g., Ebenholtz, 1963), it would seem that the S has a large number of alternative ways of learning a serial list—he might use chaining cues in one part of the list and ordinal position cues in another part of the list. Indeed, there is no general agreement as to where in the list the S may use chaining or position as a cue. Under such conditions, it may be that S uses whichever cue yields the correct response and that he varies the functional cue from place to place both within and between lists. Thus, if the stimulus for the fifth item in the first list is the immediately preceding item while the stimulus for the fifth item in the second list is the fifth position, no positive transfer would be expected. In terms of the paired-associate transfer analysis used previously, if the responses were related in some way, the transfer paradigm employed would be an A-B, C-B' paradigm of, perhaps, slight negative transfer. It is not our intent to insist that the items of one list are learned, say, by chaining and that the items of the second list are learned by ordinal position. Rather, we would assume that most subjects would, for a specific position, tend to use the same stimulus in both lists but that such a tendency would be easily modified by a subject if he found he could give a correct response by using the alternate stimulus. It would take only a few such stimulus changes to result in zero transfer.

This position is consistent with that of Battig, Brown, and Schild (1964) who found evidence, especially in the middle of the serial list, for the formation of complex associative units in which "each item is associated with a complex of cues including several preceding items." In the transfer paradigms employed in the present series of studies, all items change from·one list to the next and if only a single second-list item failed to serve the same function as its counterpart in the previous list, the stimulus complex would presumably be changed enough to result in zero transfer.

The negative transfer obtained in Experiment 4 suggests that Ss do follow instructions and try to use the relationships between the lists to their advantage. In the Heterogeneous conditions such instructions lead to negative transfer. The Ss try to use the relationships between the lists, but for the Homogeneous conditions instructions failed to produce positive transfer. The Ss of the Heterogeneous conditions were influenced by the instructions and, hence, apparently used them; thus, the Ss of the Homogeneous condition can also be assumed to have used the instructions. Such use should have resulted in positive transfer if our original analysis of bilingual transfer was correct; the subject would have the concept (e.g., parent) from the first list and the sex (e.g., male) from the second list and thus would be able to call out the appropriate response (e.g., father). This did not occur—the mean correct responses per trial for the instructed groups was only .05 per item more than the control condition. It is difficult to specify a possible source of interference which would both nullify the expected positive transfer and occur as a result of instructions. It may be that the Ss who tried to use the instructions got some items correct but that retrieval of the concept plus the additional requirement of using a rule to determine the sex of response took too long to be a very efficient method.

In any event, the present series of studies have shown considerable agreement over a wide range of procedures. Positive transfer from one serial list to another appears to be virtually nonexistent. Traditionally, it has been said that paired-associate learning is a better vehicle for investigating transfer from one task to another because stimulus and response function could be separated in paired-associate learning but not in serial learning.

The present series of studies while providing no evidence contrary to this point of view does suggest that investigation of transfer in serial learning is difficult not only because of the difficulty of specifying stimulus and response function but also because of the difficulty in identifying positive transfer paradigms. Just as in the serial to paired-associate transfer situation (cf., Horton & Turnage, 1970), the question is not whether positive transfer exists in serial learning, but rather the problem is to specify the conditions under which the transfer occurs. While we have not been overly successful in identifying such conditions in the present paper, we hope that we have made a start by showing a number of conditions under which positive transfer does not occur.

REFERENCES

Barnes, J. M., & Underwood, B. J. "Fate" of first-list associations in transfer theory. *Journal of Experimental Psychology*, 1959, 58, 97–105.

Battig, W. F., Brown, S. C., & Schild, M. E. Serial position and sequential associations in serial learning. *Journal of Experimental Psychology*, 1964, 67, 449–457.

Battig, W. F., & Lawrence, P. S. The greater sensitivity of the serial recall than anticipation procedure to variations in serial order. *Journal of Experimental Psychology*, 1967, 73, 172–178.

Ebenholtz, S. M. Position mediated transfer between serial learning and a spatial discrimination task. *Journal of Experimental Psychology*, 1963, 65, 603–608.

Ekstrand, B. R., Wallace, W. P., & Underwood, B. J. A frequency theory of verbal-discrimination learning. *Psychological Review*, 1966, 73, 540–549.

Haagen, C. H. Synonymity, vividness, familiarity and association value ratings of 400 pairs of common adjectives. *Journal of Psychology*, 1949, 27, 453–463.

Hakes, D. T., James, C. T., & Young, R. K. A re-examination of the Ebbinghaus derived list paradigm. *Journal of Experimental Psychology*, 1964, 68, 508–514.

Hilgard, E. R. Methods and procedures in the study of learning. In S. S. Stevens (ed.), *Handbook of Experimental Psychology*. New York: Wiley, 1951.

Horton, D. L., & Turnage, T. W. Serial to paired-associate learning: utilization of serial information. *Journal of Experimental Psychology*, 1970, 84, 88–95.

Iron, A. L. Retroactive inhibition as a function of the relative serial positions of the original and interpolated items. *Journal of Experimental Psychology*, 1946, 36, 262–270.

Moran, L. J. Generality of word-association response sets. *Psychological Monographs*, 1966, 80, #612.

Postman, L. Studies of learning to learn II. Changes in transfer as a function of practice. *Journal of Verbal Learning and Verbal Behavior*, 1964, 3, 437–447.

Postman, L., & Goggin, J. Whole versus part learning of serial lists as a function of meaningfulness and intralist similarity. *Journal of Experimental Psychology*, 1964, 68, 140–150.

Postman, L., Keppel, G., & Stark, K. Unlearning as a function of the relationship between successive response classes. *Journal of Experimental Psychology*, 1965, 2, 111–118.

Postman, L., & Stark, K. Studies of learning to learn IV. Transfer from serial to paired-associate learning. *Journal of Verbal Learning and Verbal Behavior*, 1967, 6, 339–353.

Shuell, T. J. Retroactive inhibition in free-recall learning of categorized lists. *Journal of Verbal Learning and Verbal Behavior*, 1968, 7, 797–805.

Slamecka, N. J. An inquiry into the doctrine of remote associations. *Psychological Review*, 1964, 71, 61–76.

Slamecka, N. J. Serial learning and order information. *Journal of Experimental Psychology*, 1967, 74, 62–66.

Young, R. K. Serial learning. In D. L. Horton & T. R. Dixon (eds.) *Verbal behavior theory and its relation to general S-R theory*. Englewood Cliffs, N.J.: Prentice-Hall, 1968.

Young, R. K., & Evans, P. Warm-up effects in serial learning. *Journal of Experimental Psychology*, 1970, 84, 183–184.

Young, R. K., Hakes, D. T., & Hicks, R. Y. Ordinal position number as a cue in serial learning. *Journal of Experimental Psychology*, 1967, 73, 427–438.

Young, R. K., & Jennings, P. C. Backward learning when the same items serve as stimuli and responses. *Journal of Experimental Psychology*, 1964, 66, 64–70.

Young, R.,K., & Saegert, J. Transfer with bilinguals. *Psychonomic Science*, 1966, 6, 161–162.

Bibliography of
Benton J. Underwood

JOURNAL ARTICLES

1942

_____. Three comparisons of retroactive and proactive inhibition. Iowa Academy of Science, 1942, 49, 425–429.

1943

McGeoch, J. A., & _____. Tests of the two-factor theory of retroactive inhibition. *Journal of Experimental Psychology*, 1943, 32, 1–16.

Thune, L. E., & _____. Retroactive inhibition as a function of degree of interpolated learning. *Journal of Experimental Psychology*, 1943, 32, 185–200.

1944

_____. Associative inhibition in the learning of successive paired-associate lists. *Journal of Experimental Psychology*, 1944, 34, 127–135.

1945

_____. The effect of successive interpolations on retroactive and proactive inhibition. *Psychological Monographs*, 1945, 59(3, Whole No. 273).

1948

_____. "Spontaneous recovery" of verbal associations. *Journal of Experimental Psychology*, 1948, 38, 429–439.

_____. Retroactive and proactive inhibition after five and forty-eight hours. *Journal of Experimental Psychology*, 1948, 38, 29–38.

Kendler, H. H., & _____. The role of reward in conditioning theory. *Psychological Review*, 1948, 55, 209–215.

1949

_____. Proactive inhibition as a function of time and degree of prior learning. *Journal of Experimental Psychology*, 1949, 39, 24–34.

1950

Morgan, R. L., & _____. Proactive inhibition as a function of response similarity. *Journal of Experimental Psychology*, 1950, 40, 592–603.

335

_____ . Proactive inhibition with increased recall-time. *The American Journal of Psychology*, 1950, 63, 594–599.

_____ . Retroactive inhibition with increased recall-time. *The American Journal of Psychology*. 1950, 63, 67–77.

Greenberg, R., & _____ . Retention as a function of stage of practice. *Journal of Experimental Psychology*, 1950, 40, 452–457.

_____ , & Hughes, R. H. Gradients of generalized verbal responses. *The American Journal of Psychology*, 1950, 63, 422–430.

Ribback, A., & _____ . An empirical explanation of the skewness of the bowed serial position curve. *Journal of Experimental Psychology*, 1950, 40, 329–335.

1951

_____ , & Goad, D. Studies of distributed practice: I. The influence of intra-list similarity in serial learning. *Journal of Experimental Psychology*, 1951, 42, 125–134.

_____ . Studies of distributed practice: II. Learning and retention of paired-adjective lists with two levels of intra-list similarity. *Journal of Experimental Psychology*, 1951, 42, 153–161.

_____ . Studies of distributed practice: III. The influence of stage of practice in serial learning. *Journal of Experimental Psychology*, 1951, 42, 291–295.

_____ , & Viterna, R. O. Studies of distributed practice: IV. The effect of similarity and rate of presentation in verbal-discrimination learning. *Journal of Experimental Psychology*, 1951, 42, 296–299.

_____ . Associative transfer in verbal learning as a function of response similarity and degree of first-list learning. *Journal of Experimental Psychology*, 1951, 42, 44–53.

Archer, E. J., & _____ . Retroactive inhibition of verbal associations as a multiple function of temporal point of interpolation and degree of interpolated learning. *Journal of Experimental Psychology*, 1951, 42, 283–290.

1952

Oseas, L., & _____ . Studies of distributed practice: V. Learning and retention of concepts. *Journal of Experimental Psychology*, 1952, 43, 143–148.

_____ . Studies of distributed practice: VI. The influence of rest-interval activity in serial learning. *Journal of Experimental Psychology*, 1952, 43, 329–340.

_____ . Studies of distributed practice: VII. Learning and retention of serial nonsense lists as a function of intralist similarity. *Journal of Experimental Psychology*, 1952, 44, 80–87.

Ellis, D. E., Montgomery, V., & _____ . Reminiscence in a manipulative task as a function of work-surface height, prerest practice, and interpolated rest. *Journal of Experimental Psychology*, 1952, 44, 420–427.

_____ . An orientation for research on thinking. *Psychological Review*, 1952, 59, 209–220.

1953

_____. Studies of distributed practice: VIII. Learning and retention of paired nonsense syllables as a function of intralist similarity. *Journal of Experimental Psychology*, 1953, 45, 133–142.

_____. Studies of distributed practice: IX. Learning and retention of paired adjectives as a function of intralist similarity. *Journal of Experimental Psychology*, 1953, 45, 143–149.

_____. Studies of distributed practice: X. The influence of intralist similarity on learning and retention of serial adjective lists. *Journal of Experimental Psychology*, 1953, 45, 253–259.

_____. Learning. *Annual Review of Psychology*, 1953, 4, 31–58.

_____. Studies of distributed practice: XI. An attempt to resolve conflicting facts on retention of serial nonsense lists. *Journal of Experimental Psychology*, 1953, 45, 355–359.

Duncan, C. P., & _____. Retention of transfer in motor learning after twenty-four hours and after fourteen months. *Journal of Experimental Psychology*, 1953, 46, 445–452.

1954

Young, R. K., & _____. Transfer in verbal materials with dissimilar stimuli and response similarity varied. *Journal of Experimental Psychology*, 1954, 47, 153–159.

_____. Speed of learning and amount retained: A consideration of methodology. *Psychological Bulletin*, 1954, 51, 276–282.

_____. Intralist similarity in verbal learning and retention. *Psychological Review*, 1954, 61, 160–166.

Scheible, H., & _____. The role of overt errors in serial rote learning. *Journal of Experimental Psychology*, 1954, 47, 160–162.

_____. Studies of distributed practice: XII. Retention following varying degrees of original learning. *Journal of Experimental Psychology*, 1954, 47, 294–300.

1955

_____, & Richardson, J. Studies of distributed practice: XIII. Interlist interference and the retention of serial nonsense lists. *Journal of Experimental Psychology*, 1955, 50, 39–46.

_____, & Archer, E. James. Studies of distributed practice: XIV. Intralist similarity and presentation rate in verbal-discrimination learning of consonant syllables. *Journal of Experimental Psychology*, 1955, 50, 120–124.

1956

_____, & Richardson, J. Verbal concept learning as a function of instructions and dominance level. *Journal of Experimental Psychology*, 1956, 51, 229–238.

————, & Richardson, J. Some verbal materials for the study of concept formation. *Psychological Bulletin*, 1956, 53, 84–95.

————, & Richardson, J. The influence of meaningfulness, intralist similarity, and serial position on retention. *Journal of Experimental Psychology*, 1956, 119–126.

1957

————. Studies of distributed practice: XV. Verbal concept learning as a function of intralist interference. *Journal of Experimental Psychology*, 1957, 54, 33–40.

————, & Richardson, J. Studies of distributed practice: XVII. Interlist interference and the retention of paired consonant syllables. *Journal of Experimental Psychology*, 1957, 54, 274–279.

Feldman, S. M., & ————. Stimulus recall following paired-associate learning. *Journal of Experimental Psychology*, 1957, 53, 11–15.

————. Studies of distributed practice: XVI. Some evidence on the nature of the inhibition involved in massed learning of verbal materials. *Journal of Experimental Psychology*, 1957, 54, 139–143.

Richardson, J., & ————. Comparing retention of verbal lists after different rates of acquisition. *The Journal of General Psychology*, 1957, 56, 187–192.

————. A graphical description of rote learning. *Psychological Review*, 1957, 64, 119–122.

————. Interference and forgetting. *Psychological Review*, 1957, 64, 49–60.

1958

————, & Richardson, J. Supplementary report: interlist interference and the retention of paired consonant syllables. *Journal of Experimental Psychology*, 1958, 55, 95–96.

————, & Richardson, J. Studies of distributed practice: XVIII. The influence of meaningfulness and intralist similarity of serial nonsense lists. *Journal of Experimental Psychology*, 1958, 56, 213–219.

Jantz, E. M., & ————. R-S learning as a function of meaningfulness and degree of S-R Learning. *Journal of Experimental Psychology*, 1958, 56, 174-179.

1959

————, & Schulz, R. W. Studies of distributed practice: XIX. The influence of intralist similarity with lists of low meaningfulness. *Journal of Experimental Psychology*, 1959, 58, 106–110.

————, Runquist, W. N., & Schulz, R. W. Response learning in paired-associate lists as a function of intralist similarity. *Journal of Experimental Psychology*, 1959, 58, 70–78.

Twedt, H. M., & ————. Mixed vs. unmixed lists in transfer studies. *Journal of Experimental Psychology*, 1959, 58, 111–116.

Barnes, J. M., & ————. "Fate" of first-list associations in transfer theory. *Journal of Experimental Psychology*, 1959, 58, 97–105.

————. Verbal learning in the educative processes. *Harvard Educational Review*, 1959, 29, 107–117.

1960

_____, & Postman, L. Extraexperimental sources of interference in forgetting. *Psychological Review*, 1960, 67, 73–95.

_____, & Schulz, R. W. Response dominance and rate of learning paired associates. *Journal of General Psychology*, 1960, 62, 153–158.

_____. Verbal learning. In *McGraw-Hill Encyclopedia of Science and Technology*, 1960, 301–305.

1961

_____, & Schulz, R. W. Studies of distributed practice: XX. Sources of interference associated with differences in learning and retention. *Journal of Experimental Psychology*, 1961, 61, 228–235.

_____, Ten years of massed practice on distributed practice. *Psychological Review*, 1961, 68, 229–247.

_____, & Schulz, R. W. Studies of distributed practice: XXI. Effect of interference from language habits. *Journal of Experimental Psychology*, 1961, 62, 571–575.

_____. Distributed practice on the Tsai-Partington numbers test. *Perceptual and Motor Skills*, 1961, 12, 325–326.

1962

_____, Keppel, G., & Schulz, R. W. Studies of distributed practice: XXII. Some conditions which enhance retention. *Journal of Experimental Psychology*, 1962, 64, 355–363.

_____, & Keppel, G. An evaluation of two problems of method in the study of retention. *American Journal of Psychology*, 1962, 75, 1–17.

_____, & Keppel, G. One-trial learning? *Journal of Verbal Learning and Verbal Behavior*, 1962, 1, 1–13.

_____, Rehula, R., & Keppel, G. Item-selection in paired-associate learning. *American Journal of Psychology*, 1962, 75, 353–371.

_____, Ham, M., & Ekstrand, B. Cue selection in paired-associate learning. *Journal of Experimental Psychology*, 1962, 64, 405–409.

Keppel, G., & _____. Retroactive inhibition of R-S associations. *Journal of Experimental Psychology*, 1962, 64, 400–404.

Keppel, G., & _____. Proactive inhibition in short-term retention of single items. *Journal of Verbal Learning and Verbal Behavior*, 1962, 1, 153–161.

1963

_____, & Keppel, G. Retention as a function of degree of learning and letter-sequence interference. *Psychological Monographs*, 1963, 77, 1–16.

_____, & Keppel, G. Coding processes in verbal learning. *Journal of Verbal Learning and Verbal Behavior*, 1963, 1, 250–257.

Ekstrand, B., & _____. Paced versus unpaced recall in free learning. *Journal of Verbal Learning and Verbal Behavior*, 1963, 2, 288–290.

_____, & Keppel, G. Bidirectional paired-associate learning. *American Journal of Psychology*, 1963, 76, 470–474.

1964

_____, & Ekstrand, B. R. Studies of distributed practice: XXIII. Variations in response-term interference. *Journal of Experimental Psychology*, 1964, 68, 201–212.

Spear, N. E., Ekstrand, & _____. Association by contiguity. *Journal of Experimental Psychology*, 1964, 67, 151–161.

_____. Articulation in verbal learning. *Journal of Verbal Learning and Verbal Behavior*, 1964, 3, 146–149.

_____. Degree of learning and the measurement of forgetting. *Journal of Verbal Learning and Verbal Behavior*, 1964, 3, 112–129.

_____. Forgetting. *Scientific American*, 1964, 210 (3), 91–99.

_____, Jesse, F., & Ekstrand, B. R. Knowledge of rights and wrongs in verbal-discrimination learning. *Journal of Verbal Learning and Verbal Behavior*, 1964, 3, 183–186.

_____, Schwenn, E., & Keppel, G. Verbal learning as related to point of time in the school term. *Journal of Verbal Learning and Verbal Behavior*, 1964, 3, 222–225.

Saufley, W. H., Jr., & _____. Cue-selection interference in paired-associate learning. *Journal of Verbal Learning and Verbal Behavior*, 1964, 3, 474–479.

Wallace, W. P., & _____. Implicit responses and the role of intralist similarity in verbal learning by normal and retarded subjects. *Journal of Educational Psychology*, 1964, 55, 362–370.

1965

_____. False recognition produced by implicit verbal responses. *Journal of Experimental Psychology*, 1965, 70, 122–129.

Ekstrand, B. R., & _____. Free learning and recall as a function of unit-sequence and letter-sequence interference. *Journal of Verbal Learning and Verbal Behavior*, 1965, 4, 390–396.

_____, & Erlebacher, A. H. Studies of coding in verbal learning. *Psychological Monographs*, 1965, 79(13, Whole No. 606).

Schwenn, E., & _____. Simulated similarity and mediation time in transfer. *Journal of Verbal Learning and Verbal Behavior*, 1965, 4, 476–483.

_____, Ekstrand, B. R., & Keppel, G. An analysis of intralist similarity in verbal learning with experiments on conceptual similarity. *Journal of Verbal Learning and Verbal Behavior*, 1965, 4, 447–462.

1966

_____, & Ekstrand, B. R. An analysis of some shortcomings in the interference theory of forgetting. *Psychological Review*, 1966, 73, 540–549.

_____. Individual and group predictions of item difficulty for free learning. *Journal of Experimental Psychology*, 1966, 71, 673–679.

Ekstrand, B. R., Wallace, W. P., & _____. A frequency theory of verbal-discrimination learning. *Psychological Review*, 1966, 73, 566–578.

1967

_____, & Ekstrand, B. R. Studies of distributed practice: XXIV. Differentiation and proactive inhibition. *Journal of Experimental Psychology*, 1967, 574–580.

_____. Effect of distributed practice on paired-associate learning. *Journal of Experimental Psychology*, 1967, 73 (Monogr. Suppl. 1).

Wood, G., & _____. Implicit responses and conceptual similarity. *Journal of Verbal Learning and Verbal Behavior*, 1967, 6, 1–10.

_____, & Ekstrand, B. R. Response-term integration. *Journal of Verbal Learning and Verbal Behavior*, 1967, 6, 432–438.

Keppel, G., & _____. Reminiscence in the short-term retention of paired-associate lists. *Journal of Verbal Learning and Verbal Behavior*, 1967, 6, 375–382.

_____, & Ekstrand, B. R. Word frequency and accumulative proactive inhibition. *Journal of Experimental Psychology*, 1967, 74, 193–198.

1968

_____, & Freund, J. S. Effect of temporal separation of two tasks on proactive inhibition. *Journal of Experimental Psychology*, 1968, 78, 50–54.

_____, & Freund, J. S. Errors in recognition learning and retention. *Journal of Experimental Psychology*, 1968, 78, 55–63.

_____, & Freund, J. S. Two tests of a theory of verbal-discrimination learning. *Canadian Journal of Psychology*, 1968, 22, 96–104.

_____, & Freund, J. S. Transfer of stimulus discrimination: can response terms be used to differentiate stimulus terms? *Journal of Verbal Learning and Verbal Behavior*, 1968, 7, 825–830.

Schwenn, E. A., & _____. The effect of formal and associative similarity on paired-associate and free-recall learning. *Journal of Verbal Learning and Verbal Behavior*, 1968, 7, 817–824.

_____, & Freund, J. S. Effect of temporal separation of two tasks on proactive inhibition. *Journal of Experimental Psychology*, 1968, 78, 50–54.

_____, & Ekstrand, B. R. Differentiation among stimuli as a factor in transfer performance. *Journal of Verbal Learning and Verbal Behavior*, 1968, 7, 172–175.

_____, & Ekstrand, B. R. Linguistic associations and retention. *Journal of Verbal Learning and Verbal Behavior*, 1968, 7, 162–171.

Zimmerman, J., & _____. Ordinal position knowledge within and across lists as a function of instructions in free-recall learning. *Journal of General Psychology*, 1968, 79, 301–307.

1969

_____. Attributes of memory. *Psychological Review*, 1969, 76, 559–573.

Zechmeister, E. B., & _____. Acquisition of items and associations in verbal discrimination learning as a function of level of practice. *Journal of Experimental Psychology*, 1969, 81, 355–359.

_____. Some correlates of item repetition in free-recall learning. *Journal of Verbal Learning and Verbal Behavior*, 1969, 8, 83–94.

Zechmeister, E. B., Biers, D. W., & _____. Bidirectional unlearning. *Journal of Verbal Learning and Verbal Behavior*, 1969, 8, 54–58.

_____, & Freund, J. S. Further studies on conceptual similarity in free-recall learning. *Journal of Verbal Learning and Verbal Behavior*, 1969, 8, 30–35.

_____, Freund, J. S., & Jurca, N. H. The influence of number of response terms on paired-associate learning, transfer, and proactive inhibition. *Journal of Verbal Learning and Verbal Behavior*, 1969, 8, 369–377.

_____, & Freund, J. S. Verbal-discrimination learning with varying numbers of right and wrong terms. *American Journal of Psychology*, 1969, 82, 198–202.

Freund, J. S., & _____. Storage and retrieval cues in free recall learning. *Journal of Experimental Psychology*, 1969, 81, 49–53.

1970

_____, & Freund, J. S. Word frequency and short-term recognition memory. *American Journal of Psychology*, 1970, 83, 343–351.

Bach, M. J., & _____. Developmental changes in memory attributes. *Journal of Educational Psychology*, 1970, 61, 292–206.

_____, & Freund, J. S. Retention of a verbal discrimination. *Journal of Experimental Psychology*, 1970, 84, 1–14.

Freund, J. S., & _____. Restricted associates as cues in free recall. *Journal of Verbal Learning and Verbal Behavior*, 1970, 9, 136–141.

_____, & Freund, J. S. Testing effects in the recognition of words. *Journal of Verbal Learning and Verbal Behavior*, 1970, 9, 117–125.

_____, & Freund, J. S. Relative frequency judgments and verbal discrimination learning. *Journal of Experimental Psychology*, 1970, 83, 279–285.

_____. A breakdown of the total-time law in free-recall learning. *Journal of Verbal Learning and Verbal Behavior*, 1970, 9, 573–580.

Williams, R. F., & _____. Encoding variability: tests of the Martin hypothesis. *Journal of Experimental Psychology*, 1970, 86, 317–324.

1971

_____, Zimmerman, J., & Freund, J. S. Retention of frequency information with observations on recognition and recall. *Journal of Experimental Psychology*, 1971, 87, 149–162.

_____, Patterson, M., & Freund, J. S. Recognition and number of incorrect alternatives presented during learning. *Journal of Educational Psychology*, 1971, 63, 1–7.

1972

_____, Shaughnessy, J. J., & Zimmerman, J. S. Learning-to-learn verbal-discrimination lists. *Journal of Verbal Learning and Verbal Behavior*, 1972, 11, 96–104.

_____, Shaughnessy, J. J., & Zimmerman, J. List length and method of presentation in verbal-discrimination learning with further evidence on retroaction. *Journal of Experimental Psychology*, 1972, 93, 181–187.

Zimmerman, J., Shaughnessy, J. J., & _____ . The role of associations in verbal-discrimination learning. *American Journal of Psychology*, 1972, in press.

Shaughnessy, J. J., Zimmerman, J., & _____ . Further evidence on the MP-DP effect in free recall learning. *Journal of Verbal Learning and Verbal Behavior*, 1972, 11, 1–12.

CHAPTERS IN BOOKS

An evaluation of the Gibson theory of verbal learning. In C. N. Cofer (ed.) *Verbal learning and verbal behavior*. New York: McGraw-Hill, 1961.

Stimulus selection in verbal learning. In C. N. Cofer and B. S. Musgrave (eds.), *Verbal behavior and learning: problems and processes*. New York: McGraw-Hill, 1963.

The representativeness of rote verbal learning. In A. W. Melton (ed.), *Categories of human learning*. New York: Academic Press, 1964.

Laboratory studies of verbal learning. In E. R. Hilgard (ed.) *Theories of learning and instruction*. Chicago: University of Chicago Press, 1964.

Some relationships between concept learning and verbal learning. In H. J. Klausmeier and C. W. Harris (eds.), *Analyses of concept learning*. New York: Academic Press, 1966.

The language repertoire and some problems in verbal learning. In S. Rosenberg (ed.), *Directions in psycholinguistics*. New York: Macmillan, 1965.

Motor-skills learning and verbal learning: Some observations. In E. A. Bilodeau (ed.), *Acquisition of skill*. New York: Academic Press, 1966.

Recognition memory. In H. H. Kendler and J. T. Spence (eds.), *Essays in Neobehaviorism: a memorial volume to Kenneth W. Spence*. New York: Appleton-Century-Crofts, 1971.

BOOKS

Experimental psychology. New York: Appleton-Century-Crofts, 1949.

Elementary statistics. New York: Appleton-Century-Crofts, 1954. (with C. P. Duncan, J. A. Taylor, and J. W. Cotton).

Psychological research. New York: Appleton-Century-Crofts, 1957.

Meaningfulness and verbal learning. Philadelphia: Lippincott, 1960. (with R. W. Schulz)

Experimental psychology (second edition). New York: Appleton-Century-Crofts, 1966.

Elementary statistics (second edition). New York: Appleton-Century-Crofts, 1968. (with C. P. Duncan, J. A. Taylor, and J. W. Cotton).

Name Index

Smith, S., 291, 313
Solso, R. L., 155, 187
Spear, N. E., 5, 22, 286, 297, 313, 340
Spence, J. T., 129, 201, 287, 313, 342
Spence, K. W., 120, 121, 124, 129, 130, 201
Sprinkle, R., 274, 275, 281
Stanton, S. K., 155
Stark, K., 28, 36, 48, 51, 55, 69, 76 82, 95, 104, 108, 223, 228, 238, 260, 318, 319, 331, 334
Sterns, H. L., 289, 310
Stevens, S. S., 281, 334
Strand, B. Z., 40, 55, 89, 100, 108
Suci, G. J., 190, 202
Sue, D. W., 270, 279
Sullivan, M. J., 65, 68, 72, 81, 82
Switalski, R. W., 287, 309

Talland, G. A., 280
Tannenbaum, P. H., 190, 202
Tarte, R. D., 50, 56, 264, 265, 266, 267, 268, 270, 281,
Taylor, J. A., 124, 343
Taylor, J. D., 260
Taylor, R. L., 191, 192, 202
Taylor, S. P., 263, 281
Thomson, D. M., 149, 153
Thorndike, E. L., 44, 55, 89, 91, 108
Thornton, J. W., 293, 310
Thune, L. E., 29, 55, 335
Thurstone, L. L., 117, 130
Tolman, E. C., 113, 130
Trafimow, E. S., 155, 187
Trager, A., 155
Trapold, M. A., 121, 131
Trumbull, R., 281
Tucker, L. R., 118, 126, 127, 128, 131
Tulving, E., 15, 22, 100, 103, 108, 112, 131, 149, 153
Turnage, T. W., 88, 89, 108, 333, 334
Twedt, H. M., 13, 22, 219, 223, 260, 338

Uehling, B. S., 263, 274, 275, 281
Ullrich, J. R., 295, 312
Underwood, B. J., 4, 5, 6, 8, 9, 10, 11, 12, 13, 14, 15, 16, 17, 18, 19, 20, 21, 22, 23, 28, 29, 30, 31, 32, 33, 35, 37, 38, 39, 40, 41, 42, 43, 44, 46, 47, 48, 49, 50, 51, 52, 53, 55, 56, 60, 61, 62, 63, 81, 82, 83, 84, 85, 86, 87, 88, 89, 91, 92, 94, 95, 98, 100, 104, 105, 106, 107, 108, 109, 111, 112, 118, 119, 120, 121, 122, 123 129, 131, 134, 135, 144, 147, 148, 149, 150, 152, 153, 155, 185, 186, 187, 189, 190, 191, 196 200, 203, 209, 219, 223, 228, 239, 245, 255, 256, 258, 260, 261, 269, 281, 283, 284, 286, 288, 289, 290, 291,

292, 293, 294, 295, 296, 299, 301, 302, 303, 308, 310, 313, 314, 315, 329, 330, 333, 335, 336, 337, 338, 339, 340, 241, 342, 343

Van Ormer, E. B., 60, 82
Van Tilborg, P. W., 285, 314
Viterna, R. O., 295, 314, 336

Walen, S. R., 88, 109
Walker, E. L., 50, 56, 264, 265
Wallace, W. P., 10, 21, 30, 42, 53, 122, 131, 185, 186, 283, 289, 290, 291, 293, 295, 296, 301, 302, 303, 308, 310, 314, 330, 333, 340
Wallach, M. A., 259
Waller, H., 263, 280
Walls, R. T., 239, 258
Wapner, S., 40, 55, 101, 108
Ward, S., W., 136, 153
Waters, R. M., 43, 53
Waugh, N. C., 81
Weaver, G. E., 155, 187, 205, 207, 209, 210, 216, 217, 219, 238, 239, 242, 245, 255, 256, 260, 261,
Webb, W. B., 64, 81
Weiner, B., 265, 281, 282
Weir, M. W., 291, 309, 314
Weiss, E., 47, 56
Weiss, W., 4, 23
West, J. N., 68, 71, 81
Whitmarsh, G. A., 190, 201, 290, 309
Wheeler, J., 155, 186
Wichawut, C., 184, 187
Wickens, D. D., 35, 54, 76, 81, 122, 131, 155, 187, 194, 238, 261
Wickens, T. D., 265, 281
Wike, E. L., 287, 294, 296, 314
Wike, S. S., 287, 294, 296, 314
Wilcox, S. G., 40, 41, 52
Wiley, R. E., 210, 224, 225, 255, 257, 259
Wilhelm, K., 296, 312
Williams, J. G., 297, 309
Williams, J. M., 297, 309
Williams, R. F., 4, 23, 342
Williams, R. L., 64, 81
Winograd, E., 28, 30, 32, 33, 34, 35, 42, 43, 44, 47, 50, 53, 57
Winokur, S., 121, 131
Wolf, S., 271, 280
Wolfgang, A. K., 155
Wollen, K. A., 133, 140, 150, 153
Wood, G., 8, 23, 291, 314, 341,
Woodrow, H. A., 117, 131
Woodworth, R. S., 62, 82

Yarmey, A. D., 270, 282
Yaroush, R., 72, 74, 82

Subject Index